A Paradise of Reason

Recent titles in
RELIGION IN AMERICA SERIES
Harry S. Stout, General Editor

TENACIOUS OF THEIR LIBERTIES
The Congregationalists in Colonial
Massachusetts
James F. Cooper, Jr.

IN DISCORDANCE WITH
THE SCRIPTURES
American Protestant Battles over
Translating the Bible
Peter J. Thuesen

THE GOSPEL WORKING UP
Progress and the Pulpit in Nineteenth-
Century Virginia
Beth Barton Schweiger

BLACK ZION
African American Religious Encounters
with Judaism
*Edited by Yvonne Chireau and
Nathaniel Deutsch*

GOD FORBID
Religion and Sex in American Public Life
Edited by Kathleen M. Sands

AMERICAN METHODIST WORSHIP
Karen B. Westerfield Tucker

TRANSGRESSING THE BOUNDS
Subversive Enterprises among the
Seventeenth-Century Puritan Elite in
Massachusetts, 1630–1692
Louise A. Breen

THE CHURCH ON THE WORLD'S TURF
An Evangelical Christian Group at a
Secular University
Paul A. Bramadat

THE UNIVERSALIST MOVEMENT IN
AMERICA, 1770–1880
Ann Lee Bressler

A REPUBLIC OF RIGHTEOUSNESS
The Public Christianity of the Post-
Revolutionary New England Clergy
Jonathan D. Sassi

NOAH'S CURSE
The Biblical Justification of American
Slavery
Stephen R. Haynes

A CONTROVERSIAL SPIRIT
Evangelical Awakenings in the South
Philip N. Mulder

IDENTIFYING THE IMAGE OF GOD
Radical Christians and Nonviolent
Power in the Antebellum United States
Dan McKanan

SOME WILD VISIONS
Autobiographies by Female Itinerant
Evangelists in 19th-Century America
Elizabeth Elkin Grammer

NATHANIEL TAYLOR, NEW HAVEN
THEOLOGY, AND THE LEGACY OF
JONATHAN EDWARDS
Douglas A. Sweeney

BLACK PURITAN, BLACK REPUBLICAN
The Life and Thought of Lemuel Haynes,
1753–1833
John Saillant

WITHOUT BENEFIT OF CLERGY
Women and the Pastoral Relationship
in Nineteenth-Century American Culture
Karin E. Gedge

A. J. TOMLINSON
Plainfolk Modernist
R. G. Robins

FAITH IN READING
Religious Publishing and the Birth of Mass
Media in America
David Paul Nord

FUNDAMENTALISTS IN THE CITY
Conflict and Division in
Boston's Churches, 1885–1950
Margaret Lamberts Bendroth

A Paradise of Reason

William Bentley and Enlightenment
Christianity in the Early Republic

J. RIXEY RUFFIN

OXFORD
UNIVERSITY PRESS

2008

OXFORD
UNIVERSITY PRESS

Oxford University Press, Inc., publishes works that further
Oxford University's objective of excellence
in research, scholarship, and education.

Oxford   New York
Auckland   Cape Town   Dar es Salaam   Hong Kong   Karachi
Kuala Lumpur   Madrid   Melbourne   Mexico City   Nairobi
New Delhi   Shanghai   Taipei   Toronto

With offices in
Argentina   Austria   Brazil   Chile   Czech Republic   France   Greece
Guatemala   Hungary   Italy   Japan   Poland   Portugal   Singapore
South Korea   Switzerland   Thailand   Turkey   Ukraine   Vietnam

Copyright © 2008 by Oxford University Press, Inc.

Published by Oxford University Press, Inc.
198 Madison Avenue, New York, New York 10016

www.oup.com

Oxford is a registered trademark of Oxford University Press

Library of Congress Cataloging-in-Publication Data
Ruffin, J. Rixey (James Rixey)
A paradise of reason : William Bentley and Enlightenment
Christianity in the early republic / J. Rixey Ruffin.
    p. cm—(Religion in America series)
Includes bibliographical references.
ISBN 978-0-19-532651-2
1. Bentley, William, 1759–1819.   2. Christianity and politics—United States—
History—18th century.   3. Republicanism—United States—History—18th
century.   4. Christianity and politics—United States—History—19th century.
5. Republicanism—United States—History—19th century.   I. Title.
BR520.R84 2007
285.8092—dc22 [B]   2007000076

9 8 7 6 5 4 3 2 1

Printed in the United States of America
on acid-free paper

To the memory of my brother Kirk

Acknowledgments

This work was assisted by fellowships and grants from the University of Delaware, the American Antiquarian Society, and the University of Wisconsin–Stevens Point.

I would like to thank Don Meyer, Christine Heyrman, Anne Boylan, and Leo Lemay for helping get this project under way; a student could not ask for a more knowledgeable or kinder dissertation committee. At the American Antiquarian Society, thanks to Nancy Burkett, Joanne Chaison, John Hench, Caroline Sloat, and especially Tom Knoles, who helped introduce me to Bentley and who shared his own knowledge and enthusiasm for the man.

Thanks also to the Reverend Jeffrey Barz-Snell of the First Church in Salem for making available the church archives and creating a congenial atmosphere in which to study them; to Kay Piemonte at the Tabernacle Church, Salem, for providing access to the records of that congregation; to Emily McDermott of the University of Massachusetts, Boston, Department of Classics, for translating the Latin passages in Bentley's diary; to Alisa M. Kahler for the map; to Gregory Colati, Sheri Kelley, and Anne Sauer in the Digital Collections and Archives of Tufts University; and to the generous, patient, and expert staff members at the James Duncan Phillips Library at the Peabody Essex Museum, the Harvard University Archives, Houghton Library, Andover-Harvard Theological Library, and Tufts University.

And warm thanks to those who have provided ideas, inspiration, and friendship along the way: John Bernstein, Dan Breen, John

Brooke, Charles Clark, Helen Deese, John Dempsey, Jay Fliegelman, Brian Hale, Carol Hirschi, Theresa Kaminski, Sarah Moldenhauer, Michael Sugrue, Greg Summers, Jan Swinford, and David Williams.

My appreciation also to Cynthia Read, Daniel Gonzalez, and Linda Donnelly at Oxford University Press, to Oxford's anonymous reader, and to Norma McLemore, copyeditor. Ron Numbers and Jonathan Sassi read early versions and greatly improved what came later. Thanks most of all to Chris Grasso, who twice read drafts of the complete manuscript and each time made what followed immeasurably better. I am deeply in his debt.

My gratitude and my love to Anna, who has come to mean so much.

Thanks, finally, to my mother, father, and brother Jack. Dedicating this book to the memory of my other brother, Kirk, is an all-too-small way of letting his family know how much he and they are in my thoughts.

Contents

Introduction, 3

Prologue, 19

Part I: 1783–1791

  1. The Revolution on the Corner
     of Main and Hardy, 31

  2. Classical Liberalism, 45

  3. Christian Naturalism, 61

  4. Spiritual Libertarianism, 79

  5. Republicanism Emergent, 91

Part II: 1791–1805

  6. Economic Republicanism, 107

  7. The Liberal Symbiosis, 119

  8. Republicanism Victorious, 133

  9. Vox Populi, Vox Dei, 153

  10. William Bentley and the Limits
      of Revolutionary Ideology, 161

Epilogue, 181

Notes, 189

Bibliography, 231

Index, 261

A Paradise of Reason

William Bentley, 1759–1819. Oil on canvas by James Frothingham. Photo by Mark Sexton. Courtesy of the Peabody Essex Museum.

Introduction

The meetinghouse of the East Church of Salem, Massachusetts, was a small rectangular building with a tunnel-shaped roof running to a steeple on one end from whose top perched a rooster wind vane, still broken from a storm. Inside and beneath, a center aisle bisected a grid of box pews that otherwise covered the floor. Visitors and servants worshiped from the gallery that hung along one wall above diamond-shaped windows that let in what little sunlight brightened the room.[1] The focus of all this attention, of course, was the pulpit, reached by a short series of steps, to which William Bentley rose twice each Sabbath during the summer of 1783 to explain to the parishioners that nearly everything they had heard preached from that spot during the previous half century was wrong.

The man who had been preaching those things for that fifty years was there too, listening as the young candidate for the position of assistant pastor systematically tore down nearly all that he had built up. The Reverend James Diman had been a Calvinist. William Bentley was not. Bentley was offering to Salem's East a new version of Christianity, one of a benevolent deity and salvation through moral living, one that contrasted sharply with Diman's arbitrary God and salvation through conversions. The congregation liked what it heard, went on to offer Bentley the position, and in 1785 forced the senior pastor into retirement. And so two years after the end of the Revolutionary War, the East Church won its own independence.

Bentley's idea—called Arminianism—was new to this particular congregation, but it was hardly new to Christianity. Bentley was in fact operating within a tradition that reached back at least to the Italian humanism of the Renaissance and then forward through the Dutch Remonstrants (of whom Jacobus Arminius was one), English latitudinarians, Scottish moralists, and a generation of Arminians preceding Bentley in New England, together constituting a religious liberalism for centuries winding contrapuntally to Augustinian, Calvinist, and Edwardsian piety. Indeed, a Christianity such as his had become, by the late eighteenth century, the preferred brand of Christianity for numerous cosmopolitan churches in eastern Massachusetts.[2] But at the same time, Bentley was not like the others. Though he was an Arminian on questions of salvation, he was a rationalist on what were then the more provocative and divisive questions facing eighteenth-century Christians, namely questions about the attributes of God and the limits of God's power to act in the world. Unlike deists, Bentley believed in the God of the Bible, the Judeo-Christian God who has a will and a personality and a hope for humanity, and, further unlike deists, he believed in the essential Christian narrative of creation, declension, and redemption. But more important, unlike the other Arminians, he also believed that God has chosen, since the resurrection of Jesus, to stand back from the natural realm and watch, without interference, the unfolding of the Christian message and the slow march to the promised paradise. Bentley's God may have interfered in biblical times, but no longer. This theology—one that may be called "Christian naturalism"—promised to offer to New Englanders an opportunity for them to keep their faiths in both Christianity and in reason. At least so thought its one American practitioner.

His adoption of Christian naturalism set his career, indeed his life, on a course unusual for a New England Congregationalist pastor. Arminianism set him at odds with his church's senior pastor, but Christian naturalism set him at odds with other Arminians. He was soon linked by print with the circle of English Rational Dissenters that spun around Joseph Priestley, and from this association moved gradually during the 1790s into the political opposition. When in 1800, his townspeople were also ready to embrace Jeffersonian Republicanism, it was Bentley who guided them to it, working in print as well as from the pulpit to raise to power those men in whose hands he thought liberty most secure, those who would best ensure the freedom of conscience and expression so essential to a moral republic.

Hardly five feet tall and weighing in at two hundred pounds, he cut an unusual and dynamic figure, driven by what one friend called "that mercurial stimulant which seems to move you." Bentley "marched well," he said, "tho' stately."[3] Headstrong, snobbish, and imperious, Bentley does indeed march stately through these pages, but though anchored in the experiences of one man, this is less biography than a study of ideas and of their context and their consequences.[4]

Of ideas he had plenty, and he was a meticulous keeper of them, leaving account books, commonplace books, correspondence, and a diary of some twenty-three hundred published pages. Most important, though, are his sermons. Written out, numbered, and dated, there are twelve hundred sermons collected from 1783 to 1799—he typically preached two different sermons each Sunday, one in the morning and another at an afternoon service—at which point he began preaching from rough outlines, most of which do not survive. His is one of the largest extant collections of manuscript sermons of one minister from that period, all the more remarkable considering their unique message—and messenger. Placed in the context of his town—a picture of which emerges from close analysis of a variety of documents—the records of his life demonstrate how theology, with its epistemological, ontological, and scriptural underpinnings, interacted with social realities to form new ideological imperatives about political power and economic station in commercial New England.

To write about eighteenth-century New England religion, to write even about only late-century eastern Massachusetts Congregationalism, is to work within a tremendous body of literature. Historians have written broadly, extensively, and insightfully on a broad range of subtopics, as even a truncated list of works will attest. Some historians, for starters, have approached the field through biography.[5] Others have looked more broadly at the Arminian and the evangelical strands at midcentury, unpacking as they went their myriad social consequences.[6] Some historians have worked to uncover the tensions within and between establishment and dissent, showing in the process the complex ideological implications of sectarianism and those who resisted it.[7] Some have drawn out the meaning of deism for New Englanders.[8] Some have tried to connect religious thought with political and social ideologies such as republicanism and classical economic liberalism.[9] Some have found new manifestations of the dynamics of power in pulpit rhetoric and the politics of language.[10] Some have looked more explicitly at religious debate as part of the new public sphere of the eighteenth century.[11] Some have tried to examine New England's religiosity, especially its liberal Christianity, against the backdrop of the broader Enlightenment.[12] Some historians have narrowed in on the social consequences of liberal Christianity's relationship with mercantile congregants.[13] And still others yet have woven the meaning of Bentley's place and time into their larger overviews of the American religious experience.[14]

The work in hand is indebted to all of these lines of inquiry; it borrows from each and, I hope, contributes to each in turn. That it can occupy a niche of its own is ascribable largely to the singularity of its subject. William Bentley was a Christian liberal who was also a rationalist; a man who was called to an established Congregationalist church but then eagerly disestablished it; a man who was a supernaturalist in his interpretation of the biblical past but a naturalist in his views of the present; a man who began as a member of what historian Henry May called the "moderate" Enlightenment but who ended as a member of its "revolutionary" strand. Studying William Bentley forces us to see New England not as a continuum or even a cross-cutting of several continuums, but rather as a kaleidoscope of factors all coming together to create an array of options for a new free people.

Given all these options, it must be added, Salemites did not choose his. Christian naturalism all but died when Bentley did, and although he did help create a successful new political party in Salem, it cannot fairly be said that the party would end up as what he had hoped to create. But his ideas and his experiences—and those of his congregation and townspeople, too—are important anyway, for several reasons. For one, his takeover of the East Church is a singular and vivid example of Americans' growing religious autonomy in the wake of the Revolution. His factionalized self in the 1780s, for another, helps us understand that factionalized decade and to see how liberalism and republicanism could coexist within a citizenry and indeed within one person. Moreover, his move to Jeffersonian Republicanism in the 1790s, initiated by his participation in an imagined community of transatlantic Christian rationalism and hastened by growing social and personal hostilities, can serve as a microhistory for the larger forces polarizing Americans in the beginning of the first party system. Then, his uncomfortable union with sectarians after 1800 animates the religious framework of New England Jeffersonianism and oppositional politics in general. William Bentley was not the region and time's only religious radical. New England in the early Republic was a time and place of great religious experimentation, even boldness, with the experimenters bringing to republicanism their attendant ideologies of denominational discontent, populist neo-antinomianism, and evangelical agrarianism, but Bentley's radicalism, a rational libertarian radicalism, was unique in intention and outcome even among these.

Bentley did not "mix" religion with politics. His religion was *infused* with politics, and his politics with religion. In the 1780s, those politics were of the economic and social kind and were, in a word, liberal; in the 1790s, they were of the partisan kind and were republican. But he worked at both religion and politics because, by the mid-1790s, he saw that both, when rightly understood, had the potential to liberate the human condition. Others would share with him one half or the other of his conclusions but not the two in combination. Christian naturalism, it seems, was too intellectually elitist for the poor and too socially radical for the rich. He had religious allies who were political opponents and political allies who were religious opponents, and in the end he was odd man out, embraced by neither as both came together in the idea that an intervening God rewards wealth and smiles on America.

Finally, he is important because he alone confronted the epistemological and ontological demands of the later Enlightenment while still defining himself as a Christian. Seemingly picayune doctrines and obtuse inquiries mattered. Philosophical questions of ontology (naturalism versus supernaturalism) and epistemology (rationalism versus empiricism), and religious questions of providence (special versus general), soteriology (salvation through conversion versus salvation through morality), and Christology (Arianism versus Socinianism) all made a difference. Questions of biblical interpretation mattered, too: literal understandings of a text redounded to consequences different from those of allegorical understandings, and individuals who thought a text entirely false felt one way if it was a falsehood born of mistranslation and another if it was a falsehood born of an outright lie. Distinctions like these mattered to Bentley and to the people around him. They mattered not least because they lay at the heart of what was perhaps the most fundamental religious question of all in the eighteenth century: namely, what had to be retained in the faith to call it Christianity at all. Bentley's very cross-cuttings, in the issues listed here and in others, present a singular opportunity to explore that question.

This study takes those distinctions and connects them to the real lives of believers, to their griefs and joys, their resentments and charities, their rebellions and communions, their economic choices and political visions. It triangulates among the liberals, the evangelicals, and the one Christian naturalist in an effort to unravel the ideological consequences of religious faith in the early Republic, to understand the implications of theology for party politics and, more important, for politics writ large: the struggles for power between governors and the governed, the ministry and the laity, men and women, slaves and masters, and, perhaps most fundamental, the mind and the heart.

This book is about reason as much as it is about revelation, but not about the core figures of the American Enlightenment, the pantheon that was Thomas Jefferson, Benjamin Franklin, David Rittenhouse, Benjamin Rush, and others. William Bentley was on the periphery of their clique, but not in it. (Franklin once found himself unable to decipher a Russian book on comets he had been given, so he passed it along to Salem's Andrew Oliver, who, equally at a loss, gave it to Bentley. Oliver had heard that Bentley had "made no small proficiency in acquiring the knowledge of the Russian tongue.")[15] But it is his peripherality which is instructive. Only an individual such as Bentley who demanded both empirical reliability *and* some form of Christianity can show us how, in short, the Enlightenment's will to rationalism interacted with inherited orthodoxies. Deists, after all, were not ministers. As much and as deeply as men such as Franklin, Jefferson, and Paine thought about reason and faith, they were not obligated by profession to confront and then reconcile the contradictory imperatives therein or to accept the full personal and social implications of their decisions. They never had to explain Scripture, lead souls to heaven, console the grief-stricken, or foster a community of believers. Bentley *was* so obligated, and thus it is his conclusions rather than theirs which shed so much light on the exchanges between the Enlightenment and the Christian tradition.

What this study provides is the mechanism whereby those exchanges were spread by print and by voice, and in circles beyond those of the Founding Fathers and their scientific friends. At heart, it is a study of the Enlightenment as a dynamic presence, as a force moving geographically, in books and in speeches, across the Atlantic and out to the common people of America; as a force moving chronologically, from the moderate to the revolutionary stages; and as a force moving conceptually, barging its way into the domain of inherited faith. It is a uniquely close look at how conflicting ontological and epistemological demands were negotiated in the late eighteenth century, at how Christianity and rational thought were combined and compromised, used and manipulated, disseminated and politicized; at how the merchants and artisans, sailors and goodwives of Salem's East Church heard, sang, recited, embraced, and rejected the Enlightenment. This is, in short, a book about how the Enlightenment—the later Enlightenment, in its critical painful stage—was understood and lived.

Bentley's time—his motives, his expectations—was one that would not come again. William Channing and the rest of the early-nineteenth-century liberals would try to balance faith and reason, too, but only as part of what historian Henry May called the "didactic" Enlightenment. They had little interest in the critical, bold, public, dangerous spirit of the Enlightenment. Indeed, Bentley possessed more of such spirit than many liberal Christians who followed him even a century later. Not until Darwin would the outlines of the ontological debates set during Bentley's generation be altered. Bentley's era was not the last of the systematic attempts to have both reason and faith, but it was the last to be convinced that the solution would make both stronger. It was a time, indeed the final one, when it still seemed possible to have it all.

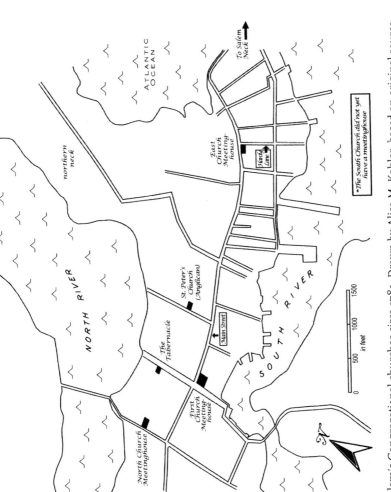

ATLANTIC OCEAN

northern neck

NORTH RIVER

SOUTH RIVER

North Church Meetinghouse

The Tabernacle

St. Peter's Church (Anglican)

First Church Meetinghouse

Main Street

East Church Meeting-house

Hardy Lane

To Salem Neck

*The South Church did not yet have a meetinghouse

0   500   1000   1500
in feet

Salem's Congregational churches circa 1783. Drawn by Alisa M. Kahler, based on original source material used by permission of the Phillips Library at the Peabody Essex Museum.

Ideas become ideologies only in a social context. For reasons secular as well as sacred, Salem provides a remarkable laboratory for seeing exactly that transformation. Salem was a port, a commercial community twelve miles northeast of Boston. It filled a small peninsula that jutted eastward into a harbor tucked under Cape Ann, bounded north and south by small rivers flowing into that harbor. The peninsula was roughly rectangular, stretching for a mile and a half east to west but only a half-mile north to south. At its eastern end, the shore pinched and then widened into a large oval patch, and a second, smaller pasture bulged into the North River. But most of the homes and shops were on the main peninsula, through which Main Street ran like a backbone along the town's east-west axis with alleys branching off both north and south like so many ribs. It was in 1783 the sixth-largest town in the new nation, with a population (a year or two later) of nearly seven thousand.[16] It was also one of the nation's busiest. "This place," one visitor had recently noted, "has a rich and animated appearance," and with peace came expectations of trade unhindered by navigation acts, blockades, or privateering—expectations, that is, of new markets, new goods, and new levels of prosperity. Longboat oarsmen ferried crews to and from shore, tall masts swayed with the waves, and sloops wended their way among anchored vessels, tacking this way and that to the harbor islands and beyond. The kinetic energy was everywhere visible and pleasing to the eye for those who saw in such bustle the promise of the new republic. "The ships and edifices which appear intermingled," marveled the visitor, the Marquis de Chastellux, "form a very beautiful picture."[17]

Salem was one of the more important ports in New England, and its mariners and captains among the best and most successful in America. In fact, in the spring of 1783, the season of Bentley's arrival, it was Salem's John Derby who brought to New England the news of the preliminary cease-fire between the British and the Americans. Derby had been in Nantes when the delegates signed the peace preliminaries and had soon thereafter made his way westward across the Atlantic. Upon his landing, local printer Samuel Hall set the type and ran the broadsides, and from Salem the news spread that the Revolutionary War was over.[18] Commerce, politics, war, and news: these were the forces that infused secular life in Salem and lent to the town the vibrancy and importance it would enjoy in the first three decades after independence.

But if these were men and women attuned to the lures of commerce and the machinations of power, they were also full participants in New England's rich religious traditions. A Massachusetts town second in size only to Boston, Salem had fewer but a wider array of congregations than did its larger neighbor, and it was one of only two towns outside Boston in 1783 to have abolished any of its parish lines, giving Salemites an unusual mix of churches and the freedom to attend them. Bentley's East Church was located, as the name suggests, in the eastern half of the Salem peninsula, and it was the only Congregational church there. But the western half was home to *four* Congregational churches, two holding to Arminian views of salvation and two with evangelical views.

The First Church, one of the Arminian ones, was ministered to by John Prince, son of a Boston hatter and holder of a freshly minted master's degree from Harvard. Prince had always shown a bent for tinkering, and his early apprenticeships to a pewterer and tinsmith must have been pleasant ones for a man who would acquire modest renown in England and America for his scientific instruments and inventions. He spent much of his time either in his workshop surrounded by gears and lenses or in his parlor demonstrating, like the central figure in Joseph Wright of Derby's famous painting, the mysteries of the air pump, but on Sundays he took to the pulpit to thank the Creator for a world in which gears meshed, lenses focused, and pumps pumped just so.[19] His pulpit was the most prestigious in town, for the First was the parent of the others as well as the earliest gathered and covenanted church in New England.[20] Roger Williams had preached there before being driven from the colony, as had Hugh Peter before he left for England, where his Cromwellian sympathies led to his body being quartered and his head perched like a gargoyle atop London Bridge. Then came John Higginson, who guided his church through the years of the witch trials (in which he did not directly participate, the accusations taking place in the separate parish of Salem Village); his passing, when it came at the turn of the eighteenth century when he was ninety-two, was among the last of those who had arrived in the heady days before 1630, the last of those very few who had witnessed the entirety of the Puritan experiment.

The eighteenth century brought to the First both increased wealth to its members and increased Christian liberalism to its pulpit. By the century's second decade, the town's merchants, most of whom attended First Church, owned about five times as much shipping as did their peers in the next-largest New England town, Newbury.[21] Two more generations followed, each enjoying the silk clothes, liveried coaches, and Georgian mansions that to John Adams were "the most elegant and grand that I have seen in any of the maritime towns."[22] They had less affluent neighbors, to be sure—Appleton the cabinetmaker, Chase the shoemaker, Gale the barber, men who lived with their families above the shops or in back rooms—but there was no mistaking the tenor of the neighborhood. It reeked of money—old, connected, Anglo money. And it reeked of fish. For what had brought them such wealth was the codfish, dried, salted, and sent to Iberia and the West Indies in return for olives, oils, cloth, sugar, and molasses, and in a gesture part whimsy, part reverence,

Benjamin Pickman had directed carpenters to attach a gilded carving of a cod to each riser of his mansion's staircase.

Down the century the First had engaged a series of prominent and ever more Arminian ministers, and John Prince would step fully into the role. (His predecessor, Asa Dunbar, had served for only three years before resigning, later dying too soon to see the wedding of his daughter Cynthia to John Thoreau or the birth of their son—his grandson—Henry David Thoreau.)[23] Prince had received his call in 1779, was there when William Bentley arrived in town in 1783, and would continue to serve that congregation through and beyond Bentley's tenure at the East.

In theology and social temperament, the North Church was exactly like the First, only more so. Its founding members had amicably left the First in 1772 over the choice of who should succeed their ailing minister Thomas Barnard Sr. The majority had liked Dunbar, but others had preferred Barnard's son Thomas Barnard Jr. and so formed their own church so that they could extend a call. Thomas Barnard Jr. was still at the North in 1783 and well suited for his placement. He was, for one, literally at home in Salem, having moved there as a boy when his father accepted the ministry of the First. In fact, his uncle, grandfather, and great-grandfather had all been ministers in Essex County, and his social rank as an incoming freshman at Harvard, sixteenth out of forty-three, had reflected the school's respect for his family and its expectations for his future.[24] Four of his parishioners had been classmates in Cambridge, and because his church, the North, had been founded specifically to accommodate him, he continued to enjoy what a jealous colleague called the "uncommon attachment and affection" of his parishioners.[25] He appeared to one visitor "a man acquainted with letters," but his writings reflect neither incisiveness nor profundity, absences that garnered little condemnation because such men were expected to converse in breadth more than depth on the ideas of the day.[26] He, like John Prince at the First, was competent and intelligent, but neither seemed inclined to controversy. At thirty-five and thirty-one years of age, respectively, Barnard and Prince were young enough to look forward to long ministries and old enough to be suspicious of the latest innovations. Neither would be joining Bentley in his theological or political explorations.

The western half of town also hosted two evangelical churches as well as the two Arminian ones. The ideas that came from these pulpits were very different from those expressed at Prince's and Barnard's. What had been paradoxical and problematic for the seventeenth-century predestinarian—namely, the conversion moment—became for the evangelical of the eighteenth the central goal of existence. Only a soul convinced of its need for grace would in fact receive that grace, only a being whose natural pride had been sufficiently broken to admit its own alienation from God would be so reconciled and thus born anew, cleansed by Christ's love. The conversion moment was the sine qua non of evangelicalism, the core and essence of evangelical religiosity, for it and only it made a Christian out of a sinner. Only the converted were real Christians, and only they would join Christ in the hereafter. Evangelicals considered themselves the true saints, the "invisible" but real and eternal church, and with them alone was God well pleased. Thus when the Awakening washed over New England in the 1740s, the awakened abandoned their parish churches and established new ones where only converted ministers might preach and only converted congregants might worship, while those who stayed behind renewed their commitment to the parish system and condemned the arrogance of the evangelicals, who by God were not going to get *any* of the communion silver, much less half. But the evangelicals hardly cared. They had new demands upon them now, and to effect conversion experiences among those still slumbering became their new calling.

In 1783, the larger of the two evangelical congregations was the Tabernacle, a group that had grown from its formation in 1736 to become the largest congregation in Salem.[27] The First Church had divided that year over accusations that Reverend Samuel Fiske had forged an entry into the church record book. Fiske was driven out, but he took his supporters with him.[28] There was nothing apparently theological about the schism, but George Whitefield's visit a few years later gave the rivalry a theological component. Whitefield, the century's greatest evangelical, had come through Salem on his first tour of the colonies. A crowd several thousand strong crammed Salem's common that day in 1740. Some showed up, no doubt, from mere curiosity, but plenty more had come off the ships and in from the countryside to join the revival about which they had heard so much, to receive that infusion of the Holy Spirit that graced the worthy and prepared followers of the young evangelist. Whitefield was pleased. "The Lord manifested forth his glory," he wrote about his day in Salem, and "in every part of the congregation might be seen persons under great concern."[29] But that would be the high point of Whitefield's experiences in Salem. Five days later, on his way back to Boston, he preached from the pulpit of the anti-Fiske group, but his auditors there were less receptive than their neighbors had been on the common. These listeners considered alleged moments of conversion only so much derangement and delusion, and besides, the flailing and shouting was decidedly not the stuff of genteel worship. Whitefield no doubt expended himself as much there as elsewhere but, as he recalled, "saw no such power all the day as when I preached here a few days ago."[30]

The social influence wielded by the anti-evangelical elites made Salem a daunting place for the evangelicals who followed Whitefield's lead. Gilbert

Tennent preached there but left little impression on church members, and there is no evidence that James Davenport even bothered going to Salem.[31] And subsequent sowers of seeds would find Salem's soil rocky indeed. Fully thirty-three Salemites subscribed in 1743 to Charles Chauncy's anti-revivalist treatise; the town was noticeably absent from a 1744 collection of reports about evangelical successes; and in 1745, when Whitefield went on his second tour through Essex County, he avoided Salem altogether, keeping instead to the friendlier towns and parishes that surrounded it.[32] Only at Fiske's church did the seeds begin to take root until, in 1746, the evangelical interest was large enough to call an itinerant preacher, even against the wishes of Fiske himself. When Fiske directed the constable to pull Daniel Leavitt from the pulpit, the evangelicals marched to an apple orchard and ordained him there, a scene described by a member of Salem's gentility as "a perfect Rabble Rout" but more accurately was a bit of guerrilla theater quite in line with the evangelical critique of a complacent ministry and corrosive parish system.[33] The unconverted members of the original Fiske faction then resumed their memberships at the church they had left a decade earlier while the converted members, now a majority, forced Fiske out. Salem's evangelicals—originally a faction of a faction—finally had a church of their own.

The Tabernacle's minister in 1783 was Nathaniel Whitaker, a graduate of the College of New Jersey, a friend of Eleazar Wheelock's and a traveling companion to Sampson Occum. On both sides of the Atlantic, that is, Whitaker had preached up that rush of the Spirit into a heart sufficiently aware of its need for regeneration in Christ. With Whitaker in Salem, Whitefield could finally return to the town he had avoided for thirty years, in fact preaching one of his very last sermons from the pulpit of the Tabernacle, his death in 1770 coming not long thereafter in nearby Newburyport.[34] Whatever Whitefield saw in Whitaker, others saw as well, to judge from the fact that twenty-eight new members joined the church during his first full year alone, more than in any one year of the church's history up to then, and an additional seventy-two joined before 1783, which was more than double the number of new members at the First in that period.[35]

The other evangelical congregation was the South Church, formed in 1774 from a schism within the Tabernacle. For if he had established friendships in the highest ranks of transatlantic evangelicalism, Whitaker had also earned a reputation for vanity, hostility, and pettiness, characteristics that were surely not unknown among New England's clergy but that he demonstrated with particularly little provocation. And worse, much worse, Whitaker was a Presbyterian. Most New England churches used a congregational polity, one that gave to each congregation the right to choose its pastor, draw up its covenant, set its rules for membership, and discipline its members, all free from the interference of such ecclesiastical overseers as presbyteries and dioceses. But as a native of the middle colonies, Whitaker had none of the qualms of New Englanders about such bodies. Rather, he thought that the punitive power of the session and synod was just the thing to beat back the Arminian heresies with which he was newly surrounded and for which he blamed Congregationalism itself. The congregation had agreed to create them, surely thinking that this was the end of his Presbyterian hopes. But when Whitaker did not relent and when, after the meetinghouse burned down in 1774, he modeled and named its replacement after Whitefield's Tabernacle in London, a boxy and steeple-less tent pinnacled in the center—a protest in wood against the classic meetinghouse shape of the Congregationalists—a dozen members left to form the South Church, the fourth of the four Congregational churches in the western half of Salem and the second of the evangelical ones.

The South Church congregants then called one Daniel Hopkins to their pulpit. While at Yale, Daniel had adopted wholesale the subtle and sophisticated arguments that his brother, theologian Samuel Hopkins, had molded from the teachings of Jonathan Edwards. God's sovereignty, Samuel Hopkins argued, is not just absolute, but so absolute that sin exists only because God wills it; regeneration, therefore, is not just unconditional, but so unconditional that trying to please God may in itself be sinful; the glorification of God, finally, is not just righteous, but so righteous that believers should happily accept damnation to further that end. Arminians may have thought the Hopkinsian scheme nonsense, but twenty-one Salemites had seen fit to join the South since its origins.[36] Daniel Hopkins was still there in 1783, and he would continue to serve its members into the second decade of the nineteenth century. The Tabernacle, for its part, would rid themselves of Whitaker in 1784.

This then was a stew of theological differences crammed into the western half of town, one with which William Bentley would have to contend from his post over in the east. And contend he would, for each of these factions naturally claimed that theirs was the correct interpretation of Scripture, of the Puritan legacy, and of the requirements for salvation. Although the disputations and pamphlet wars had waned during the imperial crisis and war years, the return of peace in 1783 would bring their return as well. Indeed, there are few better times to analyze the social consequences of faiths than those very years after 1783. Newly freed from monarchy, the men and women of postwar Salem were poised to embrace the spirit of autonomy in ways spiritual as well as temporal. The language of revolution had been truly heard, and the people of Salem were about to exercise their hard-gained rights to happiness and security and the destiny of their choosing.

Salem had impressed the traveling marquis by its wealth and energy, and rightly so. But a quick glance such as his could hardly reveal what Salem meant to the people who lived and worked there. Salem was a launching point for farm boys who had tramped east and an entrepôt for people, things, and ideas migrating west; it was a trading floor for merchants and a shop floor for artisans; it was the first touch of land for grateful young seamen and the last port of call for weary old ones. Above all, it offered a place—and in 1783, a time—for a new beginning. Perched both on the edge of a continent largely unexplored and on the edge of a world order even more mysterious, the people of Salem now looked to the future with as much excitement and anxiety as they had for generations looked out to sea.

In 1783, a new social order was beckoning. *Everyone* wanted something from the Revolution. Merchants expected to return to commerce, since access to fishing grounds in Canadian waters had been part of the treaty, and they as yet did not know that Parliament would block Americans from the British West Indies. Workers and artisans expected access into the more fluid social structure, since privateering had suggested that mobility was more possible than ever, and if money still imposed its own hierarchy, it was not one as relentlessly exclusionist as were the prewar systems of patronage and heredi-tary privilege. Slaves and freedmen looked to reap the benefits of the ubiqui-tous rhetoric of liberty and were prepared to take matters into their own hands were they denied. Salem's women, who had contributed to the resistance be-fore 1775 and had suffered along with the men afterward, were hoping for tangible benefits of liberty as well. And the people, the *demos*, wanted the political rights inherent in the republican government just gained.

The Revolution had opened the way for self-actualization in the religious arena as much as in the political. Not that formal theology was less significant than in previous generations. Quite the contrary. Christian thought in all forms remained as important and as divisive in the early Republic as it had been in the colonial period. The fact that church membership in Salem hovered around 15–20 percent is less indicative of irreligiosity or indifference than it might appear, since the members of any one church, those who had in some way experienced a conversion, were far fewer than the pew proprietors, who were likewise a subset of the weekly congregants. Far more than a fifth of the town's adults, that is, sat in the pews each Sunday.[37] And their commitments to the importance of what they heard there remained strong as well. First Church member John Gardner, for one, believed in the importance of attending meet-ing. Gardner was captain of a militia unit, son-in-law of Richard Derby Sr., and a merchant in his own right, a man whose many obligations might well try his commitment to his church, but in fact he kept a sermon diary in which he recorded on each Sabbath between 1771 and 1779 the two verses from which Asa Dunbar had preached that day. Dunbar impressed Gardner greatly, once giving a sermon Gardner could "with great propriety say was one of the best I ever heard in my life (without prejuditch I hope)," and on another presenting "a verry noble discourse worthey the purrusall of every rational creature." Weekly sermons, he knew, remained powerful and effective vehicles for moral instruction, and he was not speaking loosely when he wrote that one of Dunbar's might well serve to "regulate future life and conversation."[38] Not everyone held sermons as highly as did Gardner, but he was not the only Salemite to take seriously the messages that came from the pulpits of the town. The two church schisms in the 1770s themselves suggest that Salemites had hardly become less concerned over polity and their spiritual health. In fact, many people in 1783 believed that religion had never been *more* important, since faith and the behavior it shapes would help ensure, or not, the success of the political experiment they were beginning. Behavior depended on morality, morality on theology, and theology on a combination of ontology, epistemology, and scriptural interpretation. At the end of the war and the beginning of peace, that is, Christianity in all its component parts remained as integral and as necessary to public life as it had at any time in New England's past. As New Englanders set off on their second great errand, this time in self-governance, they, like their ancestors before them, turned first and foremost to the churches for guidance, and a young minister like William Bentley, rising to the pulpit in Salem for the first time that Sunday in early May, the very first month of the nation's uncontested existence, had to know that his congregants no less than their ancestors were counting on him to lead them down the right path.

What, finally, makes Bentley such an important object of study is that his solo journeys along the frontier of faith—and the political lessons he picked up on the way—allow a new look at just how theology was used in the early Republic by all believers of all strands of Protestantism. Bentley provides a deeper understanding of religious discourse in this period, an opportunity to probe for the real implications of diverging theologies, for a detailed analysis of how power was wielded and received and of how freedom was granted and withheld by those who claimed prerogative over determining public morality. Bentley arrived at his new home in the middle of two great struggles. One was to make meaning of the American Revolution, to codify in law and entrench in practice the potential for freedom inherent in the military victory just obtained. The other was to make meaning of Scripture, to find fruitful and believable truths somewhere among the conflicting views of God, Christ, heaven, and hell. Following Bentley in Salem for two decades after 1783 lays bare the processes by which those struggles were played out in the later Enlightenment and illuminates the unease with which faith and reason coexisted in public discourse and private lives.

Prologue

Only later would the year of William Bentley's birth be celebrated as the *annus mirabilis*. There was nothing evidently miraculous about 1759 to those living in it, at least not to those colonists in Boston that summer preparing to go to Quebec. They had done this before. Every time the British engaged the French on the plains of Europe and in the shallows of the West Indies, Bostonians raised the men and the money to fight in the woods of North America. Thrice the English Protestants had fought the French Catholics, and after each, negotiators had signed a treaty leaving matters much as before. And now Bostonians were fighting again, a war that had only recently turned in their favor. Victories at Louisbourg, Fort Frontenac, and Fort Duquesne in 1758 had emboldened the colonists to again attack the fortress on the St. Lawrence.

The Bentley family, like most in eighteenth-century Boston, knew well of war. The paterfamilias had left England in 1711 to come to America to fight the French in the second of the colonial wars. He had placed his twelve-year-old son, Thomas, with a North End shipwright before leaving on *that* war's assault on Quebec and arranged to retrieve him upon return. The attack was a disaster, and Thomas, orphaned, served out his apprenticeship in Boston. The North End, where Thomas grew up and learned to build ships, stuck out from the Shawmut peninsula like a lopsided bubble blown through a short straw, its once-smooth edges by then stubbled with piers. The North End was Boston's maritime district, packed with narrow houses and taverns and the artisans and sailors who peopled them.[1] For sixty years, Thomas Bentley lived there, building the ships that tied up to those wharves with the goods that connected Boston to the rest of the Atlantic world. In February of 1725 he married Susannah Townsend, a shoemaker's daughter, soon pregnant with twin sons. But both Thomas Jr. and James died at four months, so it was Joshua, arriving two years later, who grew up as his father's eldest son and who took up his father's trade. Thomas and Susannah went on to have nine more children, losing four during infancy, another to smallpox, and another at sea. Only three siblings, all sisters, remained alive in 1757 to witness Joshua's marriage to Elizabeth Paine.[2] Joshua was then thirty, and Elizabeth was eighteen.

The life on which the newlyweds embarked together would be a difficult one. For ship carpenters and the caulkers and finishers who worked beside them in the yards of the North End, the prospects of a living wage were threatened as much by international diplomacy and the transatlantic economy as by illness and weather. Worse, much of the shipbuilding work had relocated to Newbury, up on the Merrimac River, where timber was more readily available and the harbor more easily defended. Some of the shipbuilders who remained were all but indigent, and some acquired a substantial level of comfort. But most, like Joshua, settled with the economic security that a competency brought, though even that was often out of reach.[3] He supplemented his days with a small but growing role in civic affairs, serving variously as town assessor, surveyor of boards and shingles, and captain of the North End fire company.[4] These and others like it were the more humble town offices, filled usually by tradesmen because the gentry often opted to pay the fine for refusing to serve rather than have to bother with the irritants of weighing flour and rounding up hogs. They were positions that Joshua Bentley enjoyed, though, and he sought them out year after year. And during the war, the responsibility to fight fires in the North End excused him from the responsibility to fight the French in Canada, no small benefit given that almost a third of the eligible males in Massachusetts did serve, and more than three hundred Bostonians died in that service.[5] Thus he was there in the North End in June of 1759 when, as officers drilled militia on the common and quartermasters inventoried ordnance and townspeople listened to fast day sermons in churches across town, Elizabeth gave birth to their son William.[6]

Those who went to Quebec helped win the war. The fight on the Plains of Abraham was a terrific scene, full of the pomp and color of European battles, and the English emerged triumphant. They took Montreal the next year, and in 1763 the Seven Years' War was over. The French were deposed from the North American continent, and the colonists could look forward to what they expected to be a return to normalcy. But the fighting left behind more widows and orphans just as the end of hostilities terminated the military contracts of the artisans whose taxes supported the indigent.[7] Boston was in the grip of a downward spiral, and no group was squeezed harder than the maritime artisans and laborers for whom employment was irregular and unreliable as a matter of course. To make matters worse, the British began to enforce old trade laws and enact new ones to help subsidize the increased costs of running the colonial empire, all of which further threatened shipbuilders because their income depended directly on the success of merchants. Joshua emerged from the war years alive but barely making a living; perhaps that is why he and Elizabeth sent young William to live with her parents.

William Paine, Bentley's maternal grandfather, lived just several blocks away from his daughter and son-in-law. Paine was a miller, ostensibly another artisan, but his life was altogether different from Joshua Bentley's. The bubble of the North End bulged out on its west side, curving back in to form a cove between the North End and the rest of Boston. The water side of the cove had a gated dam that trapped the high tides for powering rudimentary grist mills, which in the 1760s were owned by William Paine. He had inherited the business from his father, and with it an income relatively unaffected by the contingencies of war, navigation acts, and overseas markets.[8] In fact, he did well for himself. Indeed, when William Bentley was still a boy living in his grandfather's large home facing the mill pond, Paine's real estate holdings were the most valuable in the North End. In 1771, for example, there were eight warehouses owned by North Enders; Paine owned three of them, while no one else owned more than one. There were seven slaves in his tax ward; Paine owned two, while no one else owned more than one. There were six mills, of which Paine owned four, and only one man in the North End owned as much wharfage as he did. In addition, he had a pew at the New Brick Church, which he had attended at least since his wife, Mary, had owned the covenant in 1735 and then likely with greater conviction after he and Mary were admitted as full members in 1750.[9] He was far from the wealthiest man in Boston—he owned neither vessel nor stock-in-trade and had no money out on loan—but he was better off than most artisans. No one knew this better, or resented it more, than his son-in-law Joshua, whose real estate holdings—consisting of only a home, and that perhaps a rental—were assessed at less than one-eighth those of William Paine.[10]

In the autumn of 1765, six-year-old William Bentley, still living with his grandfather, began his formal education at the North Writing School, where he practiced his letters under the careful eye of John Tileston. For many of Tileston's students, his was all the formal instruction they would ever receive.

Others, about 13 percent, went on to the North Grammar School, where they would begin a seven-year curriculum in Latin and Greek. With his knack for languages, Bentley was one of the lucky few and began in the following year a course of studies which—if similar to the one at the South Grammar School— led him through Aesop, Eutropius, Ovid, Virgil, Caesar, and Cicero in Latin before the New Testament and the *Iliad* in their original Greek.[11] It was a world in which he felt at home, one to which he could escape and mend the splitting of his soul between the worlds of his father and grandfather every day worsened by the events outside his window.

Paine's revolutionary sympathies are not completely clear, since he had no formal role in town politics and being a miller saved him from taking a public stand during the non-importation crises. And at sixty years old in 1770, he was an unlikely participant in the kind of street action about which family stories are told. But at least some level of Loyalism is suggested in the fact that he and Elizabeth continued to attend the New Brick even when Ebenezer Pemberton, a transplanted New York Presbyterian, began preaching a Toryism strong enough to attract Thomas Hutchinson himself. Joshua Bentley, by contrast, left no doubt about where he stood. Indeed, William Bentley's father fits quite neatly the pattern of poor, orthodox, and politicized artisans who served as the shock troops of colonial resistance, ransacking Hutchinson's home in 1765, intimidating importers in 1767, protesting the seizure of John Hancock's sloop *Liberty* in 1768, pelting British soldiers with snow in 1770, and emptying ships of tea in 1773.[12] Joshua had joined neither the Loyal Nine nor the North End Caucus, which met just a block from his home, the tradesmen members of which, like Paul Revere, were skilled in crafts that placed them higher than he in the artisanal hierarchy. But Joshua was there in the movement nonetheless, doing his part in ways that elude the historical record, and it surely was not his first contribution to the coming revolution when he sneaked out on the night of April 18, 1775, and with muffled oars rowed Revere across the Charles River to begin his famous ride.[13]

William Bentley was already at Harvard by then, having entered in 1773 with his grandfather's backing. But he took his isolation with him. He left no records of breaking windows, playing cards, or any of the violations common to students protected by family status and suggestive of fraternal merrymaking. Neither did he form more than one or two lasting friendships with classmates or forge meaningful relationships with either John Winthrop, the Hollis Professor of Mathematics and Natural Philosophy, or Edward Wigglesworth, the Hollis Professor of Divinity.[14] What he *did* like was languages, particularly those of the Old Testament, and he was good at them, so he worked with Stephen Sewall, the Hancock Professor of Hebrew and Other Oriental Languages and the third of Harvard's three professors. Sewall had established a reputation as one of the most accomplished linguists in the colonies, and Bentley followed him into the arcane world of the Samaritan, Chaldee, and other ancient tongues, spending at least one winter vacation copying Sewall's extensive handwritten notes.[15] He was talented indeed, but these talents hardly helped form a community of intellectual peers or friends; in fact, they just resulted in more time spent alone.

His grandfather had retired by the time war came in 1775, but his father took a position in the Continental Army as clerk at the "Laboratory," a munitions warehouse on Boston Common.[16] Perhaps his appointment was a favor from a neighborhood friend, since he served under artilleryman William Burbeck, a member of Revere's Freemason lodge. It was a position that suited Joshua Bentley well, and he was even able to get work there for William's fourteen-year-old brother, John. Another brother, Joshua Jr., eighteen, was captured by the British and died that same year in a ship prison in Halifax.[17] William Bentley, however, sat out the war. He was in Cambridge when fighting broke out several miles away, but like many of his classmates he took no part. When the half-dozen brick buildings around Harvard Yard were commandeered by American troops in April of 1775 and the school was forced to reconvene in Concord, Bentley went there, too. Though his peers may have "delighted the Concord maidens" who found in the influx of young men a crop of "student lovers," as Samuel Morison imagined, Bentley took the opportunity to perform his first religious service, substituting with "good success" for an ailing pastor in nearby Acton.[18] The British evacuated Boston in March of 1776, the students and faculty returned to Cambridge, and Bentley was able to resume the relatively stable life of the collegian and budding clergyman well out of range of musket balls and grapeshot. Although the war forced Harvard to cancel public commencements, "Gulielmus Bentley" took his place with the rest of the class of 1777.[19]

It was standard practice for graduates bound for the ministry to teach school for a few years while they dug deeper into their own theological studies. Bentley's old schoolmaster had taken up at the South Grammar School, and the Boston selectmen chose Bentley to assist him.[20] So right out of Harvard, he began to instill the fine points of Latin translation in seventy young students who were likely more enamored by Washington's campaigns in New York than Caesar's in Gaul. Assistant master at the South Grammar School was a position of some regard in town, not least to the merchant elite whose sons were Bentley's charge. The school educated many of Boston's most promising young men—Bentley's classes between 1777 and 1779 included Harrison Gray Otis and other future notables—and as their instructor, Bentley edged closer to acceptance into a social circle that had included neither his father nor his grandfather.

After two years at the South Grammar, he was named master of his boyhood Latin grammar school, and a year later, in 1780, with a master's degree in hand, he accepted a three-year appointment at Harvard as tutor of Latin, later of Greek.[21] So with copies of Sophocles, Xenophon, Demosthenes, and Homer taken from libraries of exiled Tories, he returned to Cambridge.[22] But his time there provided little of the friendship and mentoring that it might have to another tutor in another time. He never warmed to his fellow tutors, and the three professors had problems of their own: Wigglesworth, a declining interest in divinity among students; Samuel Williams (Winthrop's successor), a pattern of debt that would end in a forgery scandal; and Sewall, the alcoholism that would force his resignation in 1785. Of his students, Bentley admired Tobias Lear, enough to grieve at news of his suicide in 1816, but few others.[23] John Pynchon, the fragile and histrionic son of Salem's most distinguished lawyer, was likely a source of tension for the young tutor, as was Harrison Gray Otis, again under Bentley's care, who resented "the sophisticated jargon of a superstitious synod of pension'd bigots," an indictment that no doubt included his instructor in Greek.[24] And Bentley, it seems, resented them in return. "Do not fancy therefore that the tutor's life is pleasant and happy," he copied from one of his readings. "So far from it, it is rather a state of captivity."[25] The continued exposure to the spoiled sons of Boston's wealth was reaffirming his sense of social inferiority. The Revolution had challenged the traditional hierarchical social structure along with the claims about nature and God that had propped them up and the social customs that had affirmed them, but change was slow, and Bentley had been born too early to forget, or be allowed to forget, his humble origins. His father had been a ship carpenter, after all, and, though still at the Laboratory in 1780, Joshua ranked near the bottom of those Bostonians with assessable property and was even forced that year to petition the General Court for an increase in salary.[26] He was granted the raise, but Joshua's fortunes would never again turn: in 1783, with the end of the war, he would find himself unemployed and without savings, and at fifty-five he would be too old to get much work doing the only thing he knew how to do. Joshua Bentley, it turns out, would live for thirty-six more years, and not for one day was he more than a hair's breadth from abject poverty.

John Pynchon and Harrison Gray Otis thought themselves Bentley's superiors, and no doubt many of his other students thought the same. Bentley already knew the rules of social hierarchy when he entered into his commonplace book a lesson that lay at the core of earlier European novels about the proper places of men: "Let a man in a low station be ever so much injured by a person of quality," Bentley copied from an old Spanish romance, "he is obliged to put up [with] the affront, and speak away as if he himself was the aggressor."²⁷ But if he was not at the top of the strata, neither was he at the bottom. Instead he was trapped in some ill-defined middle zone, accepted by no group as its own, disdainful of the working life of his father and forced to bear with grace the condescension of those who might admire his ability to read Virgil but did not embrace him as their equal. An alienated intellectual, he hid in his books and cultivated self-worth in pedantry, making friends only with Albert Gallatin, the temporary French instructor, and James Winthrop, the college librarian and eccentric son of the mathematics professor who was denied his father's chair in favor of the debt-plagued Williams, and though it is not quite right to say that the three of them constituted some sort of proto-Republican clique at Harvard, it is not coincidental and not unimportant that Bentley's only friendships were with men who were as much on the periphery of society as he was and who later, with Bentley, would be among the few notable Jeffersonians from or with connections to New England.²⁸

In addition to serving as schoolteachers or Harvard tutors, aspiring ministers also usually spent an apprenticeship disputing theology, drafting sermons, fine-tuning pastoral skills, and, not least important, assimilating into the existing network of ministers. Not Bentley. At least there is no record of his doing so, and it fits his personality to not do so. But he was still able to supply local pulpits in a minister's absence. Not yet ordained, Bentley could neither baptize nor offer Communion, but he could deliver sermons and provide prayers for the congregation. This he had been doing here and there since his undergraduate days, and by 1778 he was preaching in the block house that Charlestown's First Church had been using since its meetinghouse burned during the Battle of Bunker Hill. From 1780 to 1783, he taught Greek to undergraduates on weekdays and filled pulpits throughout the Boston area on Sabbaths: a few months at the church in Cambridge, most of 1781 at "Little Cambridge" (now Brighton), a few Sundays in Marlborough, the winter of 1782 in Deerfield, three months in Woburn, one month at the New South Church in Boston, one month at the Third Church of Roxbury while William Gordon was traveling south to gather material for a history of the Revolution, and six months at the First Church in Beverly, supplying the pulpit left vacant when Joseph Willard resigned to become president of Harvard.²⁹ Still, no call had come from a church by April of 1783 when the Harvard Corporation voted to extend Bentley's tutorship for another three years. So he accepted the offer and even took another part-time job working on the library's catalog.³⁰ He had been there less than a month when the letter arrived inviting him to come to Salem as a candidate for the assistant pastorate of the East Church.

The church had been created in 1717 when the Massachusetts legislature halved the Salem peninsula to provide easterners a closer place of worship.[31] The venture had gotten off to a promising start when Cotton Mather delivered the sermon at the ordination of its first minister, but Robert Stanton died nine years later and was succeeded by William Jennison, whose eccentricity and health problems led to a dismissal after another nine years, whereupon he left his wife and three children in Salem and spent his remaining years drifting through eastern Massachusetts.[32] The church's record was not, then, an enviable one in 1736 when the congregation found itself in need of a third pastor, but neither was that of the man called. James Diman had graduated from Harvard, but he was neither scholarly nor gentlemanly enough to suit the Harvard overseers, who overruled his appointment to a tutorship, or to satisfy Salem's more elite First Church, who had rejected his candidacy. But he had been acceptable to members of the East and was called to its pulpit. There he had remained.

The forty-seven years of his ministry brought profound changes to the religious landscape of New England, apparent not least in the dissolution of the parish in the western half of town. But Diman's church had remained intact and still served the shipyards, warehouses, and workshops of the waterfront. Whatever popularity Diman had enjoyed earlier had by the 1770s worn thin. The tensions had become apparent when he "absented himself on prudence" from Asa Dunbar's ordination as assistant to the First in 1773, or so surmised Ezra Stiles, who knew about the dissension from down in Rhode Island.[33] Diman did agree to participate in the younger Thomas Barnard's ordination over the North Church later that year, but what he delivered to the packed assembly was a thinly disguised swipe at his own congregation, and nobody would have missed the point when Diman told Barnard, in front of the assembled crowd, how fortunate he was that "all his hearers are his friends," for such "is a favour that but few enjoy."[34] Matters continued to worsen: parishioners refused to pay parish taxes between 1775 and 1778, and in 1779 they refused his request for a raise to compensate for the inflated currency. When John Prince was called to the First Church in 1779, and Diman again found himself assisting an ordination, he took full advantage of the opportunity to restate his case. This time, he made no effort to hide his animosity. In his public remarks, he informed Prince that parishioners as a body are not to be trusted, cautioning him specifically against "depending too much on the long continuance of their esteem and affection" and warning him that although he might now feel beloved and secure, "many have had the same hopeful prospect that you now have, and have been disappointed." Ministers all too often complained about salaries, but when Diman lamented the poor clergy who were being "denied that support which was promised them" and spoke of parish-ioners who gave "hard speeches" against their ministers and "prejudice[d] their children" against them, it was no secret who he had in mind. And when he let loose on lax churchgoers who resent their ministers' warnings about sin, it was no secret just whose calls for repentance were going unheeded. Diman closed by trying to rally Prince and the other ministers, "however ill we may be treated," to bring sinners to salvation "at this time of great degeneracy and wickedness," but he was alone in his crusade. Barnard was getting along swimmingly with his church, Prince's prospects looked bright, and neither considered the time to be one of degeneracy or wickedness. Such talk was too gloomy for the cosmopolitans, and no doubt Diman was dismayed when, immediately after he finished, Barnard stood up to give the right hand of fellowship and opened with a jolly pun about the "PRINCE of peace."[35] But Diman's ministry was no joking matter either to him or to the members of the East Church. He refused their formal request that he step down but did agree, in April of 1783, to audit possible assistants.

Bentley was their first choice. He would preach for a few months on a trial basis, and if members liked what they heard, they would extend a call for him to join the church, undergo ordination, and assume the duties of assistant pastor. If not, Bentley would continue teaching at Harvard and preaching around town while the East Church sent another letter to another candidate. It would be an interesting summer for Bentley and his auditors. How would he, born into an artisan's family, raised by middling-sort grandparents, and educated at an elite institution, be accepted in a town committed to social distinctions in the midst of a revolution that eroded their very assumptions? And how would he fit into the town's ministerial community, one already wracked by dissent and suspi-cion? Back in 1778, another ministerial candidate had tried his luck in Salem and come away noting that "the whole town seems to be divided into separate parties and assemblies; as no two clergymen out of the five will exchange with each other."[36] In 1778, it was just the sort of situation for a young man to avoid, but now, five years later, William Bentley needed a pulpit, and he could hardly afford to be so choosy. He accepted.

The invitation, much less the call, was in many respects an unlikely one, given that Bentley's ideas were so obviously at odds with those of the senior pastor. Perhaps congregants saw in Bentley an antidote to Diman, since he had in spades the energy and commitment to pastoral duties that Diman lacked. Perhaps it was Bentley's tutorship; the East had long been stuck with Diman while the liberal churches called one prestigious pastor after another, and now, in 1783, easterners flush with privateering success wanted a minister who reflected their new sophistication. Indeed, Bentley's stint as a Harvard tutor was a fact significant enough for John Lathrop to mention in his ordination sermon, for William Pynchon to enter into his diary, and for the editors of the Salem *Gazette* to include in their brief notice.[37] But easterners knew, too, that Bentley was no Thomas Barnard born into and for the elites, and perhaps there in that knowledge lay his true appeal. For though Bentley was a tutor, he was *their* kind of tutor, raised in a mariners' neighborhood and sympathetic to the needs of seafaring parishioners. Perhaps, that is, they saw a little of themselves in Bentley, a man of his own making still at arm's length from polite society, a man whose story was theirs as well.

PART I

1783–1791

I

The Revolution on the Corner of Main and Hardy

William Bentley first preached at the East Church on the fourth day of May 1783. Apparently listeners liked what they heard, for they invited him back for the following week and then for the next one and then for each Sunday thereafter. Week after week he traveled to Salem for the Sunday services, during which he rose each time to dismantle another piece of the orthodoxy to which Diman had devoted his life, and by mid-July, twenty-five sermons in, the congregation knew it had found its man. The parishioners at large resolved their desire that he settle among them, but the actual decision was made by the male members in full communion, who voted, with one exception, unanimously.[1] The ordination and installation ceremony was in September. Most of the attending clergymen were Bentley's friends or local clerics of similar views: Salem's Thomas Barnard offered the introductory prayer, John Prince the right hand, Boston's Samuel Cooper the consecrating prayer, and John Lathrop the sermon.[2] Polite and pro forma greetings all. Then there was Diman, whose job was to give the Charge. Everyone knew that Bentley and Diman had different views, but one wonders how many people knew that the lone vote against Bentley had in fact been Diman's. But the old man—he was seventy-six—would not be cowed. He knew exactly what he thought his twenty-four-year-old new colleague ought to do, even if nobody else in the room agreed. "Let the threatenings as well as promises of the Gospel be often the subjects of your preaching," he told Bentley that day. "Fear not the faces of men;

but fear God, to whom you must give account. Let it be your constant care and endeavour to convince and convert sinners, and to stir up saints to the greatest zeal and diligence in the divine service. . . . Great will be the opposition you will meet with, from Satan and his instruments, and many will be your discouragements."[3] Whatever Diman thought about this advice, it meant nothing to Bentley: he did not fear God, he had no interest in stirring anybody to zeal, and he did not believe in Satan. In fact, the opposition he would meet with would come not from the devil but from Diman himself.

James Diman was a Calvinist. The fine points of his Calvinism are elusive, since no manuscript sermons or listeners' pew notes have come to light. But he did publish a sermon, one delivered just before an execution of a condemned rapist, and he also wrote a theologically infused letter to the *Gazette,* so it is possible to get a fair approximation of how he conceived the human condition and the Christian duty. The cornerstone of Calvinism was belief in humanity's alienation from God as remnant from the Fall. The imputation of Original Sin has left everyone as much in need of redemption as were the first pair after their expulsion from Eden. Christ's sacrificial death made that redemption possible, but only those individuals ever since who sufficiently recognize their need for it will receive it. Only those who repent, that is, will receive saving grace and reconcile themselves to God. Those who do will, upon the death of the body, go on to heaven; such souls, Diman said, are "plucked as brands out of the burning, and made happy forever." Those who do not will be sent to hell for a punishment infinite in both duration and intensity, an afterlife that Diman described to the execution audience as an "exquisite and everlasting misery."[4]

Though Diman eschewed the typical behaviors of those evangelicals who revivified the Calvinist narrative during and after the 1740s—at least, there is no evidence that he invited George Whitefield to preach at the East Church during any of Whitefield's tours through Essex County or that he became part of the network of evangelical exchanges and courtesies that included Salem's Nathaniel Whitaker and Ipswich's John Cleaveland—he was clearly sympathetic to their *ideas.* He signed the revivalists' testimonial in 1743, volunteered that he supported it in "substance, scope, and end," and tended, an observer once noted, to give lectures "upon the necessity of the new birth."[5]

And what Diman agreed with above all else was the conviction that humanity can do nothing to earn the grace that may come. For Calvinists, the totality of depravity has left humanity completely unable to move toward God in even the slightest way. People have "nothing more in them that capacitates them to love God than the trees or the beasts," Diman wrote in his letter to the newspaper. Corruption of the soul is an inescapable attribute of post-Edenic humanity, an inherent part of being a descendant of Adam and Eve. Paul had said so himself in Romans 5:12 ("Wherefore, as by one man sin entered into the world, and death by sin; and so death passed upon all men, for that all have sinned"), a verse Diman cited even in his execution sermon. Redemption, if it comes, is a "free gift" given by God through the cross, utterly unconnected to human efforts to bring it about.

Bentley offered a different theory about the means to salvation. The central idea of his Arminianism is that grace *can* be earned, that humans *are* capable of acts that please God and thus reconcile the actors of them to God. The sinfulness humans suffer from is not an immutable state of depravity but instead a tendency toward immorality, one that can be overcome by following the morality that Christ preached. Humans, in short, are flawed but well-meaning creatures of free will and goodness fully able, should they choose, to satisfy and reconcile themselves to God through the type of behavior enjoined by Christ. They need to do so, but the power is theirs.[6]

Bentley began preaching Arminianism as soon as he arrived. What Paul really was referring to in that passage to the Romans, he told his new congregants, was merely the *inclination* of humanity to make wrong choices.[7] The change derived from a new understanding of sin as finite rather than infinite and also pointed toward a new understanding of conversions as gradual rather than instant. Sin was true indeed, he explained, but "culpable error" only, not "malice or rebellion" against God.[8] The necessary conversion was therefore manifest not in a single cleansing experience but in a life spent turning away from the temptations of the passions to follow instead the previously muted voice of conscience. "Except a man be born again, he cannot see the kingdom of God," Jesus had said. Bentley agreed, but his version of being "born again" was the state of having made the decision to act conscientiously and then living one's life according to it.[9] Those who do so can count themselves converted and look forward to an afterlife in heaven, for God, he told them, will "accept certain habits of mind . . . and admit the possessors into glory."[10] And although those who do not can expect to go to hell, the suffering there would be in duration and intensity proportionate to the errors committed in life. The punishment, that is, would reflect the limited nature of human action rather than the infinite alienation from God. "Every man," Bentley said soon after being ordained, "should come out of punishment as soon as he was fit" and proceed on to heaven.[11] He had placed a limit on hell's time and terror that, whatever adults thought, allowed the children of the church, who while catechized by Diman had forecast for themselves "an everlasting fire in hell," to relax in the new knowledge from Bentley's catechism that they were headed to a place merely "miserable."[12]

These two men, James Diman and William Bentley, were presenting the East Church with two very different teachings about what one might call the Christian narrative of an individual life—a person's passage, or not, from sinfulness through conversion to the salvation that awaits after death. But it is important to underscore that Arminianism redefined but did not reject the basic elements of that narrative. Sin was still real, albeit now limited and redeemable; God was still alienated, albeit now hopeful; conversions were still necessary, albeit now manifest in a lifetime of right behavior. The debate was not over the existence of that narrative or even the existence of its elemental parts, for neither side doubted the reality of sin or the need for forgiveness or the power of grace. The debate, rather, was over differing *definitions* of those elements: of the attributes of that sin, of the means by which to receive that forgiveness, and of the mechanism by which that grace is granted. Moreover, beneath their different versions of the narrative lay differing versions of the attributes of God. Both sides claimed to articulate the necessary benevolence of God, Arminians locating it in God's willingness to allow persons to save themselves, and Calvinists finding it in God's willingness to sacrifice his son. And both sides claimed to understand and express the justice of God, Calvinists thinking it perfectly manifest in the infinite punishment due sinners against infinite goodness, and Arminians imagining it possible only if finite sins bring finite punishments. Whatever the accusations of one side against the other, in fact neither rejected the basic components of Christian theology.

But those differing definitions meant a great deal. They did to the two men involved, of course, since getting parishioners into heaven is the very essence of the calling. But they meant a lot to listeners, too, who were plenty interested in what was required for them to go to heaven. The choice mattered to the ten individuals who left the East Church because of Bentley, most going to Nathaniel Whitaker's Tabernacle or Daniel Hopkins's South Church, both evangelical congregations.[13] And it mattered to another person who had been a member for all of Diman's fifty years at the church and was now profoundly disturbed by the young associate's message. He called himself "A Distressed Old Man" in an open letter he wrote in Salem's newspaper asking for assistance with the spiritual crisis that Bentley's preaching had caused. "I am one of those unhappy persons," he began, "who have been brought up under a minister that has spent fifty years teaching his people that they cannot love God." His minister, "whom I have constantly taken to be an understanding and good man, for fifty years upon the stretch has been sounding this my inability in my ears." And so he had not, by his reckoning, loved God. He had never felt a moment of blame for this, though he had felt "ten thousand [such moments] respecting the conduct of Adam, and ten thousand times more respecting the conduct of God." But now, having heard Bentley's assertion that he did indeed have the ability to love God and thus all along had been *choosing* not to, "language cannot describe the consternation, the surprise, and indignation of heart" which he was thrown into. He had had it backward for all those years; now he saw that he was supposed to love rather than to blame God and that what he thought was an inability to do so was in fact a sinful choice.

The identity of the writer is unknown. Abraham Watson had been a member for fifty years; perhaps it was him.[14] Or perhaps it was someone else, or even Bentley himself. But real or not, the persona of the Distressed Old Man reflected exactly what was at stake between Calvinism and Arminianism, at least from the perspective of Arminians like Bentley, namely that Calvinism's false claims about an inability to love God imperiled not God but the believer. The Old Man had come to believe that his soul was quite in danger. "Oh! What distress did all these things throw me into!"

> Blackness of darkness forever and ever seemed to be my just portion from the Lord—I have had no comfort in hearing my old minister go on with his cannots, and I dare not tell him that he is preaching souls to hell—I dare not tell anybody what I feel, what horrours upon horrours harass and torture my mind—sin now appears to me an evil infinitely greater than ever it did before—I see it in all my imaginations, feelings, and actions—I feel myself an accursed creature—I cannot eat, nor drink, nor sleep, nor labour, nor converse as I used to do—I choose no more to be seen among men of the world—the well-cultivated farms and the well-fraught stores, the coffers of gold and silver have lost all their charms. I am now in the most retired place I can get—I am ashamed to show my face to my children and children's children, to my neighbours and familiar acquaintance, and therefore keep out of their view as much as I can—but alas! I cannot get out of the view of the omniscient God. These things have worn down my constitution, and the king of terrours is making fast strides towards me. I read, I pray, I weep, I tremble—but it is all with a voluntary enmity of heart against God, whom I am now convinced is just. I feel nothing in my way of repenting, believing, and loving God, but the free choice of my heart—and this is like ten thousand daggers plunged into my soul.[15]

He was writing, he concluded, to see whether a reader might be able to help him. As it was, he could tell nobody of his new fears, least of all Diman. "My minister will think hard of me," he added, "if I tax him with preaching errours." Surely not everyone who was offered these two options entered into such a crisis as did the Distressed Old Man, but the letter does suggest that at least to some listeners the choice between Calvinist and Arminian arguments about the necessary preconditions to salvation could be a wrenching one.

But when the listeners at Salem's East Church came to choose between the two men, they did so not over their respective soteriologies—beliefs about salvation—but instead over their sacramental policies. Under Diman's long tenure, Communion had been offered only to those individuals who had experienced what the observer had called the New Birth, that instant infusion of grace that erases sin and confers membership in a universal, invisible church. Only individuals who had done so were worthy of the reaffirmation of godliness conferred by Communion. But Bentley, as an Arminian, understood a conversion to be a decision to live one's life rightly, or what he called a person's new "disposition to do, or get, good."[16] It was manifest not in an instant but instead in recurrent choices to act according to Christ's instructions. So he proposed opening Communion to anyone who asked for it on the grounds that the act of asking was itself a sufficient indicator of that desire. "Everyone who wished to open his mind with a love to God and man" would be welcome. This was not to be understood as removing all standards, and he meant it when he said he did not want the "hoaring monster...drunkard...cruel extortioner...better would it be that you stay away than that you disgrace the cause," but it was to be understood as making morality the only standard, one that when met opened the table to all comers.[17]

Baptism was more problematic and, as it turned out, more important. Early in the seventeenth century, New England churches had offered baptism to the children only of the converted. Though it had no saving power per se, they figured, baptism was not without *some* linkage to Christ, a cleansing perhaps or a preparation for the cleansing that conversion brings and so rightfully due only to those infants whose parents were already converted and who were thus most likely to be so themselves. But a rising generation of unconverted parents had necessitated a modification called the Half-Way Covenant, by which baptism was extended to the child of any baptized parents who were willing to make a profession of faith whether they had had a conversion experience or not. The Half-Way Covenant had been adopted by Salem's First Church late in the seventeenth century, carried on to the East Church in 1717, and had remained there ever since. But Bentley thought that even it was too restrictive. He believed that the desire to have a child baptized was itself reflective of the necessary moral conscientiousness, and so he advocated baptism to the children of any parent who asked, even without a profession of faith. "If a parent applies for Christian baptism to his children," he hypothesized to his audience, "the application supposes him to be a Christian."[18]

Diman's response to all this was not only to ignore the suggestions but also to refuse to allow Bentley to administer the sacraments even under the existing terms. For eighteen months after his ordination, Bentley was allowed to give the sermons while Diman continued to baptize children and offer Communion, all under the old rules. A situation as awkward as this could hardly last for long, and in the spring of 1785 events began moving toward a resolution. The communicants convened a meeting at which they voted unanimously (excepting only Diman himself) that, after propounding and answering some simple questions, "all baptized persons shall obtain baptism for their children."[19] Diman again refused to accept this, the decision of his own church, and from there things fell apart rapidly. Accusations and recriminations flew back and forth, some issues about religion and some not, some predating Bentley and some very much about him. Diman accused the church of intentionally underpaying him, and they responded with charges of mismanagement of charity funds; Diman said the parish had encouraged "new doctrines and fatal innovations," while they said he had been obstructing their obvious desires by refusing to accept the young assistant they selected. On it went for six months until finally, in October, Diman was forced to resign.[20]

This at least is how Bentley recorded the affair in his diary, and to read that account, one would think that he had nothing to do with it. In fact, he thought as much: "Thus ended a most perplexing dispute," he wrote once it was over, "carried on with a total want of candor by the Parish Minister [Diman] and great violence by the people."[21] In terms of ecclesiastical authority, Bentley's self-exculpation was accurate, since only the actual members of the church could act to force out their minister. But a reading of his sermons that fall suggests that Bentley was hardly neutral or shy. They are in fact riddled with references to and condemnations of religious hypocrites and critics, and he got more confident as the weeks progressed, warning first about generic "Pharisees," then more precisely about wrongheaded ministers who cover the gospel with the "false glosses of their own confused minds," and then more precisely yet about ministers with "fifty years' experience" who ought to know better.[22] "Why dost thou judge thy brother?" Paul had asked in Romans 24:10. Bentley built one of these sermons on that single verse, and it is impossible to imagine listeners not knowing just who was being asked this question. But Bentley was not afraid of using verses with even greater import. In July, he used I Corinthians 13:13 ("Now abideth faith, hope, charity, these three; but the greatest of these is charity") to argue that Paul meant charity not in an economic sense but in the sense of tolerating different views, a lesson, Bentley went on to say, that ought to be heeded by those who focus on the "little niceties" of faith rather than on the essential truths of morality.[23] Soon he preached a sermon on no less than the early verses of the seventh chapter of Matthew, one articulation of Jesus' speech on motes and beams and measures for measures. "Judge not, that ye be not judged," it begins. It was Jesus' strongest injunction against falsely pious critics and a lesson Bentley apparently thought appropriate to the day.[24] Not long after that came the sermon on the ministers with fifty years of experience, and with it all pretense of objective sermonizing was gone. He could no longer even pretend that he was not talking about the man who was still sitting right there listening week after week. So in a rare turn to the first person, he concluded that sermon with an apology and a promise not again to speak of the topic. "From this day I shall renounce it," he said, "and proceed in that pure and peaceable manner which becomes a minister."[25] It was a promise he did not need to keep for long: ten days later Diman was out.

Whatever he convinced himself about his lack of responsibility, Bentley was in fact very much responsible, for even putting aside the pulpit prodding, it was only with his arrival that the church took action to remove a man with whom they had long been at odds. Understanding the reason they did so—and how and why they did it when they did—requires a close look at who made up the congregation.

In terms of secular class distinctions, the men in the church occupied the full range of social places in a seaport town. A number were ship captains or petty merchants, men not of great wealth but with some security and a modicum of comfort. Beneath them were the artisans, the men who made things rather than imported them, with their incomes generally reflective of the difficulty of the making. Some were doing well, but a greater number probably would have identified with the anonymous carpenter who wrote to Bentley, "I would inform you that I have been absent from the congregation these fore sabbaths past the reason is that I have not a hat nor shoes that is fit to ware and I am not abel to get them at preasant and there is a number of gentelmen in the parish that will be there."[26] Whatever a carpenter's concerns, he was likely better off than the fishermen and sailors who joined him in the pews on Sundays and who represented, vagrants and servants aside, the bottom of the range. Security for these men was particularly hard to come by, even without the vagaries of injury and economy. Few fishermen owned their own boats, and most mariners who were not promoted to mate, master, or captain by their mid-thirties quit the sea and turned to a shore-bound life for which they had no preparation. If married, their wives worked, too, bringing in what money they could from spinning, weaving, and light household production, but the children needed tending, especially when ill. Most of these families lived at the subsistence level, trying to save what they could for the difficult winter months when storms and ice prevented construction and locked in the ships, halting income just when prices for food and firewood were on the rise. It was a hardscrabble life, and they received little for it: these men, making up 30–40 percent of the town's taxpayers, owned less than one percent of its wealth.[27]

But in addition to economic divisions, the congregation had ecclesiastical ones, too. Individuals who had had conversion experiences were the actual members of the church, those who were granted Communion. But any parish included within its boundaries persons who had *not* undergone a conversion experience but who also attended. In fact, they were required to. When Bentley arrived, the East Church was an established parish church, and all residents of the East Parish were obligated by state law to attend and subsidize the services. The unconverted nonmember parishioners could, if themselves baptized, have their children baptized under the Half-Way Covenant but were not in any event given Communion.

This two-tier system of members and parishioners was typical for established parishes in New England, and although these distinctions played important roles in the schisms of other churches elsewhere, the story of Diman's expulsion centers instead on a third subset of church participants, one with no formal ecclesiastical definition but with a great deal of power nonetheless. This was the group of pew owners, or, more properly, the pew proprietors, individuals who had purchased pews for the use of their families. They were the ones who were the driving force behind Diman's removal. It is true that only members could vote in church affairs, but Diman was not in fact voted out. He resigned. And he did so after pressure was brought to bear not from the handful of members but from the larger, more prestigious, and wealthier group of pew proprietors. To be certain, the members did not like Diman either, and whenever they did vote, they voted against him. But they did not take the lead in the whole affair; the proprietors did.

To understand the interplay of formal ecclesiastical power and informal social power, a grasp of the church's demographics is again crucial.[28] In line with other churches, the East Church had many more female members than male ones—the membership was around 90 percent female—but also in line with the policies of other churches, these women could not vote. Meanwhile, the proprietorship was around 80 percent male, and the great majority of those 20 percent who were female were widows who owned the pews only by virtue of being heirs to their late husbands' ownership. Women were as important in Bentley's church as they were in other churches of the time, and here too they no doubt exerted pressures that elude the historical record. Even so, the final decisions about Diman were made, it seems, largely by men.

The group of proprietors is best seen against the backdrop of the group of male church members. In economic terms, the eight men who voted at Bentley's ordination presented something of a mixed bag, but none was near the top of the social ladder or particularly wealthy.[29] To be sure, a few, including William Browne, who had expanded his earlier tailoring trade into tanning and real estate, were doing fine; perhaps his relative prosperity is why he was made deacon and one of the church's two wardens.[30] Others, among them Benjamin Ward, once a captain in the Continental Army but now a glazier, and Abraham Watson, the carpenter who may have been the Distressed Old Man, were securely among the middling sort, neither poor nor rich. Ward was the other warden, and Watson was church treasurer, but they were not men of great consequence in the secular or economic affairs of the town.[31] But the rest were struggling. Ebenezer Phippen, another carpenter, had fared poorly since the war and was on his way to what Bentley would later call "a very hard death," leaving behind a deaf wife and seven children with no support.[32] Thomas Diman (no relation to the minister) was a fisherman, but he probably worked as a laborer and sailor, too, hauling in sheets and fishing lines when he could and knocking about the sail lofts and rope-walks when on shore. Men of his class had a rough go of things, and him particularly so: not long after he would fall into a fire while drunk, hastening, as Bentley wrote, "that death which was before fast approaching"[33] None of the eight men members, it ought be added, was destitute. The 1785 tax list indicates that all of them owned a house or a portion of a house plus some personal estate. Even Thomas Diman had something to assess in 1785—though only £20 worth—and most had more, real and personal estate ranging in the hundreds of pounds. But as a whole, the male East Church members occupied places that were average to low on Salem's social scale.[34]

Compare that to the group of male proprietors. At Diman's exit, there were fifty-two proprietors, thirty-nine of whom were male.[35] Unlike the membership, which required a conversion experience, there was no spiritual requirement to be a proprietor. One did not need to be a member to be a proprietor, and indeed, most—thirty-four—were not. That is, 87 percent of the male proprietors had not yet met Diman's experiential requirements for actual membership but were nonetheless committed enough to their church to purchase pews. Of these, a few were fishermen and a dozen or so were artisans, but, most important, twenty-one, or nearly two-thirds, were captains. These were men like Edward Allen, George Crowninshield, George Dodge, John Fiske, Edward Gibaut, Robert Stone, Nathaniel Silsbee, and Joseph White, men who were not only captains but who had served as captains of privateers during the Revolution. Privateering was the defining characteristic of the proprietorship at the time of Bentley's arrival. It was no easy matter to stop an enemy vessel on the high seas, imprison her men in the hold, and assign a prize crew to sail her back into port for auctioning, but the rewards were high for those who were successful. And if captains did not earn as much from a sale as did the actual owners of the ships they commanded, they earned much more than they would have in peacetime commerce. Here was a chance for relatively fast money, and many of the men of the East Church had taken advantage of it.[36] As a group, the proprietors were much wealthier than the members. The assessed wealth of individual proprietors in 1785 typically ranged not in the hundreds but in the thousands of pounds, including assets like shipping stock, warehouses, wharves, distilleries, and even "continental certificates" in the case of George Crowninshield and "plate money at interest" in the case of George Dodge.[37] Though members had the vote, it was the proprietors who wielded the real power at the East Church.

With that power they allied with the new minister to drive out the old one. It was not his opening of Communion that was so appealing, to judge by the later lack of participation even under his new rules. It was, however, very much his opening of baptism or, more precisely, his making baptism available even without a profession of faith. To get a child baptized without having to make a profession of faith: this is what these men wanted. The full phrasing of the baptism resolution in May of 1785 makes this clear. It read that baptized parents could apply to have their child baptized "without owning a covenant or making any profession, beside that which they virtually make by regular application for such baptism, and by answering such rational questions as the minister may propose."[38] One suspects that by "rational questions" the resolution meant what Bentley meant: questions about the applicant's conviction of the importance of Christian education and conscientiousness. But no other obligations or tests would they require, certainly not on doctrine. The profession of faith, decided the church, would be real but only "virtual," implicit in the applicant's commitment to a moral life.[39] Just as Bentley had done in the pulpit, the church had redefined, not rejected, the inherited traditions. There is no reason to conclude that the proprietors were trying to weaken the Christianity in their church, much less remove it, any more than Bentley was. But they were seeking to free themselves from a *form* of Christianity they no longer could accept.

The Revolution allowed them to take what was a drastic and unusual step. After all, lots of ministers in New England churches wore out their welcome but were not removed, since Congregationalist ministers expected—and *were*

expected—to serve for life, barring irreconcilable differences or gross mis-
conduct, and it occasioned much sorrow and acrimony whenever an ecclesiastical council was convened to expedite a dismissal. Though the Awakening of
the 1740s and the depreciated salaries of the 1770s had, for quite different
reasons, led some shepherds to leave their flocks and vice versa, neither condition applied here, and Diman would have had no reason to expect that he
would not die a minister of the East Church. That he did not was a result, it
seems, of the specific arrival of a newcomer during a much broader time of
redefining the relationships between the empowered and the powerless. At the
very least, it is clear that only with privateering had the men of the East Church
become wealthy enough to afford a second minister through whom they could
force out the existing one. Not only were they willing to pay a second salary;
they also were willing to do so by themselves. Diman's salary was paid by taxes
levied on all parishioners, but Bentley's, the church agreed, would be paid by
new taxes levied on the pew proprietors.[40] The plan was that this would continue until Diman's death, at which time the parish taxes would be abolished
entirely, and the sole remaining salary, Bentley's, would continue to be paid by
the pew proprietors. Far from wishing to alleviate their responsibilities for
maintaining a clergyman, the proprietors, were in fact happy to pay for their
new minister and even to let the other parishioners off the hook altogether.
Only the new wealth from privateering allowed them to do so, and in this
mundane way if no other, the fight for political freedom had brought to the
East Parish some spiritual freedom as well.

This rivalry at the East Church between Arminianism and Calvinism illuminates one aspect of the liberating power of the American Revolution. But it
is also instructive in understanding some small facet of the Enlightenment's
interaction with Christianity. However sudden it appeared to listeners at
Salem's East Church after 1783, the debate between grace or faith on the one
hand and morality or works on the other had been ongoing nearly as long as
Christianity itself, manifest not only in the struggle between Calvin and Arminius but also in those between Luther and the Catholic Church, between
Augustine and Pelagius, and indeed between Paul and James, at least in how
each interpreted the sacrifice of Isaac.[41] But at the same time, there *was*
something different about this particular iteration. More than any other was
this phase a debate over just how it is that God acts and must always act in a
reasonable manner. The very insistence from both sides that God does act
reasonably was new, or at least newly important, in the late seventeenth and
eighteenth centuries, a reflection of the allure and power of reason and reasonableness in an age of Enlightenment. None of the earlier representatives on

the side of works had argued their point explicitly, if at all, from the premise of divine reasonableness. And none of the earlier representatives of the faith side had taken so much time to explain how their version was reasonable, too. By the time William Bentley assumed the pulpit, both sides were operating fully under the assumptions that they were part of the Enlightened age. And both were right. But to say that both sides insisted on a reasonable God is not to say that both insisted on similar *kinds* of reason or a similar relationship of God to it. They did not. And therein is the point: their insistence on a reasoning God made both sides modern, but their differing versions of that reasoning set them down separate and hostile tracks into and through that modernity. For Calvinists, God's actions are always reasonable by virtue of the fact that they are God's. They can be, a priori, nothing else but reasonable. In this way even the imputation of depravity and the infinitude of hell are made reasonable: the very fact that God does them makes them reasonable things to do. Diman said as much: everlasting punishment "is what God has ordered," he preached before the rapist's execution, "and therefore must be just and right."[42] It was simply part of the definition of God. For Arminians, however, God's actions are always reasonable because God always chooses to do that which is already established (by God) as the reasonable choice. And because God has surely implanted that same sense of reasonableness in human beings, that which God does is also that which seems to people to be the reasonable thing to do. To continue the example, God thus surely determines an individual's afterlife based on behavior and surely, in the case of damnation, limits it in accordance with the finite capacities of humanity.

The discourse on reasonability informed and energized debates over divine benevolence and divine justice, issues that combined to create in New England two very different versions of God and of the necessary faith. Arminians claimed that the Calvinist version rendered God irrational and whimsical, a deity always capricious and at times verging on nasty. Calvinists claimed that the Arminian version restrained God, and worse, restrained him to how *Arminians* thought he should act. Each side thought the other was factually wrong and thus harmful to listeners, but the tension ran deeper than that. Each side also thought that the other was committing the sins against which Christ warned. The errors of their opponents were part of the problem that each side had dedicated itself to fix. Arminians thought that Calvinists were censorious and vindictive, hardly the spirit of forbearance and love preached in the Sermon on the Mount. Calvinists, meanwhile, thought that Arminians, in claiming to know God's will, were manifesting the very pride that lay at the core of alienation from God. As Salem's midcentury evangelical John Huntington put it, the Arminians had abandoned belief in depravity because they were not "fully able to comprehend them with their boasted, tho' darkened reason; and because [those doctrines] do not constitute such a scheme of religion as *they* should have chalked it out, by the dim light of nature. And one principal reason, perhaps, is, because these doctrines are mortifying to their corruptions and humbling to their pride."[43]

Both sides were wrong. Contra the Calvinists, Arminians were not unchristian; they just defined Christianity differently. And contra the Arminians, Calvinists were not unreasonable; they just defined reason differently. But it was too late for subtlety. Meaning had already become implication, implication perception, and perception accusation. And so the supposedly ignorant irrationalists would remain at odds with the supposedly prideful humanists in a war of words as well as ideas that continued through Bentley's life and well beyond. The conflict was not unique to the East Church even in Bentley's day, but rarely elsewhere did two opponents clash from the same pulpit and for the favor of the same congregation. It was a conflict as geographically broad as the Anglo-American world, but the church on the corner of Main and Hardy in Salem provides a glimpse of what one small part actually looked like from the perspective of the people who were living it.

Diman continued to live in the parsonage after 1785, but Bentley had little to do with him. Bentley declined to serve as a pallbearer at the funeral of Diman's wife, and when Diman himself passed away in 1788, Bentley neither preached the sermon nor contributed to the subscription to help defray the costs of the funeral. Most ministers who had served a church for half a century could take comfort that they might receive at least a few kind words after their demise, but Bentley was apparently unable to muster even that: the following Sunday, when he stood to address the congregation on the passing of their ex-minister, the best he could say about the deceased was that Diman had been a man "who, tho' he could reason little about temperance, could ever practice it, who tho' he could not give a theory of moral sentiment, always felt it." Later, Diman's son initiated a long and ultimately successful legal campaign for his father's back wages, the Diman family pew was sold, and in 1790 Diman's youngest daughter chose John Prince rather than Bentley to officiate at her wedding. With her subsequent move to Malden, the last of the family was gone, and the parsonage was put up for sale.[44]

2

Classical Liberalism

In replacing Calvinism with Arminianism, Bentley had changed
one theological idea for another. But his Arminianism was also attached to a different set of ideas about social, economic, and political
relationships, one called classical liberalism. As a social ideology,
classical liberalism was concerned less with humanity's proper relationship to God than with each human's proper relationship to every
other, but the lines between theology and ideology were thin indeed. Bentley was as much an ideological liberal as he was a theological Arminian, and in introducing to the East Church the one, he
also brought the other.

Eighteenth-century Arminianism was not equally popular among all
social classes. Historians have long debated the extent of affinities
between Arminian Christianity and mercantile success on one hand
and between evangelical Christianity and what H. Richard Niebuhr
described as "social dispossession" on the other, but in Salem there
was no question: the Arminian congregations were *much* wealthier
than their evangelical opposites.[1] The First Church, in 1783 under
the very Arminian Reverend John Prince, was the traditional church
of Salem's merchant families. The congregation included lesser
members, but its character was shaped by the handful of wealthy
and powerful families who dominated it. Before the war, the Orne,
Pickman, Lynde, Gardner, Cabot, Bowditch, Oliver, and Holyoke
families—men and women linked by enormous incomes, elective

and appointed positions of leadership in town and provincial politics, and a catacomb of intermarriages—had all worshiped there. Almost every aspect of public life in Salem had been firmly in their hands—a group small enough to sit at a single table, which on many occasions they did, in a seemingly end-less circuit of dinners, balls, and sea-turtle picnics on the Neck.[2] The amicable 1772 schism over the choice of pastor simply meant that two churches in Salem rather than one would be wealthy Arminian ones thereafter. In fact, the North Church under Thomas Barnard Jr. was even wealthier than the First they had just left: of the six First Church men who in 1771 owned merchandise assessed at £3,000, four would join the North Church later that year, as would the only two men who had that much out on loan and the men who together owned about two-thirds of the wharfage in Salem.[3] As a congregation, the North was wealthy enough to build for Barnard and themselves the largest meetinghouse in Salem, one hundred and one square box pews parsed by four broad aisles door to pulpit, and their prominence was burnished further by the joining to them of E. A. Holyoke, first president of the Massachusetts Medical Society and later president of the American Academy of Arts and Sciences.[4] Barnard's mentor could not hide his envy when in his ordination sermon he noted the "comfortable support" the new minister would enjoy, nor could he have failed to notice the luxuriousness of the ordination ceremony itself.[5] It was, as the Essex *Gazette* reported, "carried on with propriety, elegance, and solem-nity."[6] Many of the assembled revelers had come in from Boston, and the North Church hosts spared no expense in providing the best "genteel enter-tainments," including more than two hundred pounds of beef, four legs of bacon, two turkeys, thirty-two chickens, six legs of mutton, and a pair of ducks, all washed down with a barrel of cider and an unknown number of bottles of wine and topped off by nine dozen gift pipes and tobacco.[7] The opulence marked this day as the debut of the North Church into polite society, and members would have it no other way, even if, as they found out, the party set them back £60, or about half of their new minister's annual salary. But even if the North was particularly prosperous, the First was doing just fine, and with no bad blood and much in common the two congregations would thenceforth continue on quite in lockstep as the spiritual homes of commercial wealth and gentility in Salem.

The point can be made more sharply by comparing the First and the North with the two evangelical congregations that shared their neighborhood. In 1745, the year of Daniel Leavitt's ordination in an apple orchard over the church that would become the Tabernacle, the highest tax paid by any of his twenty-two covenanters was less than the tenth-highest tax paid by members of the First. In the 1771 tax assessment of Salem, at a time when twelve proprietors of the First had merchandise assessed at more than £1,000 and thirty-one had real estate valued at more than £20, only one member of the evangelical congregation (the sole one at that time) had as much merchandise, and only a few owned as much real estate.[8] When in 1774 their meetinghouse burned down, church members had to plead for outside help to finance construction of a new one, and when Bentley arrived a decade later, the building was still unfinished.[9] The other evangelical church in 1783—Daniel Hopkins's South Church—was just as bad off. It did not exist in 1771, so the tax assessment of that year is of little use, but in stark contrast to the opulence of Barnard's installment, for example, "little attention" was paid by discerning Salemites to Hopkins's 1778 ordination, and members were still without a meetinghouse in 1783 and held services in the town's old assembly hall.[10]

The East Church—Bentley's new home—is not quite so easily characterized. Because the East Parish was still unified in 1783, the congregation included laborers and merchants alike. But it had also, since its founding, tilted more toward poverty than prosperity, and certainly so compared to the Arminian congregations. In the tax list of 1718, the year after the East Church split from the First Church, only two men from the East were assessed more than a pound, whereas twenty men from the First were assessed that much. Little had changed over the next two generations, and in the general assessment of 1771, only three members of the East Church (compared to twelve at the First) had merchandise worth £1,000 or more, and only three (compared to thirty-one) had real estate worth £20 or more[11] When Bentley arrived in 1783, the church had had no money to subsidize charitable donations or to refurbish the Communion silver. It could not even afford to repair its own wind vane. The rooster's tail had snapped off in a storm before Bentley's arrival, and the rest had since spun uselessly, surely a pitiful symbol for a waterfront church whose spire was visible from the harbor.[12] Some individual members during the colonial period had done well for themselves at one time or another, but those who did, like the Derby family, usually moved to the western half of town, transferring their memberships to one of those congregations. The eastern parish and the East Church had been for the comers, not the arrived, and it had been a mark of a man's success that he could buy a home in the western part of town and remove his family from the salty chaos of the waterfront. But the latest wave of up-and-comers, the privateering proprietors who led the way in calling Bentley to the pulpit and, later, in forcing out James Diman, had different ideas. They were not planning to leave for the western Arminian congregations. Instead, they had brought an Arminian minister to them. And though they liked above all else his sacramental policy, they just as surely appreciated what an Arminian would tell them about order and purpose in the social world.

Bentley did not disappoint. He was more than equipped to validate the place of the wealthy on top of the local social order. For Arminians, the first of even first principles was the reality and the rectitude of hierarchy. The whole universe was one big hierarchy, Bentley believed, ranging up and down along what was called the Great Chain of Being, starting with God at the top and then moving down through the angels and then humans and then farther down through the rest of creation in an ill-defined order of decreasing complexity. "The whole circle of being seems complete," Bentley preached one Sunday, improving on Ecclesiastes 1:9 ("Nothing new under the sun"). "The forms of nature are fixed at the original births."[13] Or as his congregants would sing from his hymnal about humanity's slot in the divine order of nature:

> His place, thy forming hand assign'd,
> But just below th' angelick kind;
> With noblest favours circled round,
> And with distinguish'd honours crown'd.[14]

The Chain of Being describes humanity as a whole in relation to other kinds of beings and so was of limited use in discussions of hierarchies within humanity itself, but Bentley believed in them, too, and as the clear will of God manifest by naturally differing attributes of individuals apparent even at birth. Some people are simply more capable of success than others, and to them the rest must defer. "Absolute claims of superiority must exist in civil society," Bentley told his church. "Indeed there may be real claims whenever there may be a real difference in the moral and natural capacities of men."[15] It followed, therefore, that individuals ought to accept their place in that hierarchy as what God wants. "Be ashamed then, O Christian," he once told listeners, "who despises to view the place which thy Creator chose for thy birth."[16] With stratification sanctified and envy made a sin, what was, as much for Bentley as for Alexander Pope, was right.

Belief in the righteousness of hierarchies of one kind or another was hardly unique with Bentley or with New England's Arminians.[17] But Arminianism added its own reason that people ought to submit to them—namely, that doing so was one of the virtues that has the power to effect salvation. Everything that changing the existing order requires—envy and resentment at one's own station and indecorous public agitation for modifying it—was, to Arminians, simply a remnant of Original Sin. To act for change was to act on the worst side of human nature, whereas to be moderate, disciplined, restrained, and gracious signified ongoing victory over sin. All this was good news to the merchants and the successful captains who aspired to become merchants, men who already imagined themselves possessing exactly those virtues, men such as those who brought Bentley to the East Church.

But the ideology of submission and moderation meant something different to the non-captains and the non-merchants. Whatever Arminian morality offered to wealthy white males, it served only to rein in the aspirations of women, African Americans, and the impoverished.

The list of qualities that William Bentley thought necessary for women was quite short: amiability, temperance, and industry. "Without these qualities," he wondered from the pulpit one Sunday, "what is the female sex?" The "purposes for which they were created" were to "bestow their amiable benefits on society, and to soften human life," and if they do not do so, "they live a perversion of the works of God, a disgrace to themselves and the dishonor and misery of man."[18] All this from the first sermon he delivered on the roles of women in society. He would go on to give many more sermons on how women ought to see and carry and envision themselves, but not for a long time would he diverge from the ideas laid out here in the beginning.

Eighteenth-century Arminians were no less convinced of the need for female domesticity than were their Puritan forebears. The rules of commercial exchange had actually encouraged domesticity by forcing out the barter system in which women had played a predominant role, and if Arminians were not the only ones who valued Solomon's advice in Proverbs 31:27 to "looketh well to the ways of her household, and eateth not the bread of idleness," they were nonetheless particularly fond of it. Boston minister Simeon Howard was sufficiently fond of the verse to use it as the foundation of the eulogy of the woman who had been the widow of his predecessor in the West Church pulpit, Jonathan Mayhew, before becoming his own wife.[19] Bentley, too, thought domesticity a fine idea and did not hesitate to remind the females of his church, in language echoing Proverbs, that "the principal care of a good woman is to look well, or carefully inspect the ways of her house."[20]

Views such as his were hardly unique to Arminians like him, but they do seem more acute in the context of the views of the Arminians' theological opposition. Evangelicalism by itself did not necessarily lead to an advocacy of women's equality, but New England's antinomian and evangelical tradition before 1800 did offer to women a public role unavailable by Arminian standards. The fact that the most notable and most public anti-Arminian of the seventeenth century was a woman was not forgotten even a century later. To Arminians of the eighteenth, Anne Hutchinson remained representative of all that was dangerous and subversive about experiential Christianity. Charles Chauncy had thought it necessary to preface his criticism of the Awakening with an account of how Hutchinson had "diffus'd the Venom of these Opinions into the very Veins, and Vitals of the People in the Country."[21] And William Bentley, a century and a half after her banishment from New England, was still upset. "That gentlewoman of a bold and masculine spirit," he described her, who "upon a pretense of exalting the free grace of God, destroyed the practical part of religion and opened a door to all sorts of licentiousness."[22] By the destruction of religion he meant what Arminians supposed to be the tendency in experiential theologies to elevate the conversion moment over ongoing moral behavior; what exactly he meant by the sorts of licentiousness he did not say, but it is safe to guess that he meant Hutchinson's willingness to violate the assumptions about the proper roles of women, in her case by lecturing to groups of both sexes at once. This is what Hutchinson had been charged with, after all, and the memory of her criminality still lingered, at least in the minds of Arminians.

And when, in the late eighteenth century, the Newburyport Presbyterian John Murray gave a funeral encomium for the grown daughter of his predecessor, Proverbs was nowhere in sight. He celebrated her agency, not her submissiveness. Phoebe Parsons Lane was a good Christian, he said, because of her willingness to "stand forth . . . an avowed advocate for religion." She had "greatly dared to be singular in this respect," he went on, "subjected to the public eye every Lord's day, while she publicly led in the praises of her God."[23] Newburyport was much like Salem, a mercantile community with the same strict attention to female propriety, but for Murray, it was cause to celebrate that Lane had defied those expectations for the sake of the faith.

The question of the proper limits for women's public behavior was newly important after the American Revolution. Women's participation in spinning bees and boycotts had helped keep the Revolution going, but the question of continuing public roles in a time of peace was a different matter.[24] In fact, the Arminians had not been particularly supportive of their activity in war: of the ten spinning bees in Essex County, not one had been hosted by an Arminian.[25] And Bentley was no more eager than his older Arminian peers for women to remain in the public eye. The bees had been an unfortunate expediency of war, he told his church, and one that was best forgotten, since the proper Christian woman "can have no concern with the world as far as it relates to business, but as she may cooperate with her husband, and the principal care will lay upon him, so that in common business she can have little to do."[26] Women had long been revered for their Christian virtues of patience and meekness, but by demonstrating a commitment to imperial resistance, they had shown that they possessed the potential for *civic* virtue as well. Bentley and other Arminians, however, would have them simply return to their homes.

In the case of women, the advocacy of moderation and restraint was meant to apply to them, the subjects of the advice. On the issue of race, however, it was meant to apply not only to blacks—slaves in particular—but also to those who would help them. William Bentley opposed slavery. He knew firsthand about it, having been raised in a house with two slaves.[27] So it was a considered opinion when from the pulpit he came out clearly against what he called "the cruel practice of making slaves of innocent and defenseless men, or any slavery which gives no hopes of freedom," which, he added, "from my soul I abhor."[28] But mere opposition was no longer the acid test; by the end of the Revolution, northern ministers of nearly every stripe opposed it. The question was who would actually *do* something about it.

Arminians had a poor track record of doing something about it. No doubt they perceived that slavery was incompatible with both moral accountability and a benevolent God, and none could have missed the similarity between an inheritable, inescapable slavery and the imputed depravity against which they railed, but still they said little. Chauncy, for example, had expressed some opposition but only as a small part of an unrelated project, one paragraph buried a hundred pages into an anti-episcopacy treatise. Other Arminians did even less, and Samuel Cooper, the most politically radical of the prewar Arminian ministers, seemed not at all troubled by it.[29] To be sure, evangelical Christianity was no guarantee of antislavery sentiments, as southern evangelicals were already demonstrating, but as for New England in the late eighteenth century, some meaningful contrasts can be drawn between the willingness of Arminians and the willingness of evangelicals to act on their shared convictions. Some, like Timothy Pickering Sr., deacon of the Tabernacle, had been acting on his convictions for decades, in 1755 petitioning for a law that would tax blacks as persons rather than as property and inquiring, to no avail, about the "mind of the town" respecting the slave trade.[30] Others, like Samuel Hopkins, had since taken the lead, publicly indicting not just the trade itself but the whole commercial system on which it was built.[31] Little wonder, then, that both Phillis Wheatley and Samson Occum—"America's two most famous non-whites" at the time of the Revolution—were connected not to the liberals but to the transatlantic network of evangelicals, which included among others Hopkins's brother Daniel and Nathaniel Whitaker, ministers of Salem's South and Tabernacle churches, respectively.[32]

Perhaps the Arminians' reticence was simply prudence. In their pews, after all, sat more than a few of the men and women who were slave owners. Such was indeed the case in Salem, where most of the slave owners had attended the First Church rather than the East or the Tabernacle.[33] To be sure, all three of Salem's Congregational churches in 1771—neither the North nor the South had yet split from its respective parent—included slave owners, and evidence suggests that Bentley's predecessor, James Diman, may have owned one through marriage, but the greatest number in absolute and relative terms was at the Arminian First.[34] Even those merchants that did not own slaves were invested in the system. The First Church men who imported molasses for their distilleries[35]—molasses made by West Indian slaves—were surely not making the rum solely for local consumption. And even those who were in no way involved in the slave trade still benefited from the institution where it existed: it was not free men, after all, who grew the sugar, rice, and tobacco that was so essential to Salem's coastal commerce.

But prudent or not, their silence was also part of a general reluctance to agitate or disrupt the social harmony. Chauncy's opposition was less outraged than embarrassed. He considered slavery an "abomination," yes, but his descriptors, "horribly shameful" and a "dishonor to Englishmen," suggest that he was more anguished by its indelicacy than its wrongness. As for actually confronting it, he suggested something through legal channels, an act of Parliament preferably, and he was even willing to settle for one that would merely "restrain the cruelty of the planters."[36]

The war had brought freedom to many of Salem's slaves. Most of the town's seventy-five "servants for life" in 1771—such was the awkward euphemism used by the Massachusetts Tax Valuation that year—were, by war's end, no longer in bondage.[37] Slaveholder William Hunt, for example, owned two slaves in 1771, but none was mentioned in the inventory of his estate taken in 1780; Fred Coombs had a slave in 1771, but there was nothing in his inventory a decade later; Elizabeth Cabot owned two slaves in 1771 but none in 1782.[38] But this was hardly ascribable to the benevolence of the largely Arminian slave-owning class. Some may have manumitted their slaves, but evidence suggests that many slaves had seized upon the rhetoric of the Revolution to declare their own independence. Jacob Crowninshield's probate record is one such piece of evidence. The inventory taken at Crowninshield's death in 1775 included a black male worth £60 and a woman and child worth £35, but when a second inventory was taken in 1780 after all the notes were in, the executors subtracted the £95 because the "negroes appraised in inventory have since claim'd and taken their freedom."[39] Sometime between 1775 and 1780, that is, Crowninshield's slaves had simply declared themselves free. Meanwhile, Elizabeth Cabot's slave Titus had refused her offer of £40 and freedom at her death if he would stay on because, as one observer noted, he was already making plenty of money on his own as an agent for privateers and had even taken to wearing silk clothes and dancing minuets at Harvard's commencement.[40] And as Benjamin Lynde flatly put it in 1778, "my man Primus left us."[41]

But if slavery in Salem was nearly over when Bentley arrived, it was not yet entirely over. The month after Bentley's ordination, the will of Richard Derby Sr., the wealthiest man in Bentley's new congregation, bequeathed Cate and Caesar to Derby's daughters.[42] And runaways who had taken refuge in Salem still faced the threat of recapture, if the men who forced their way into the home of Cato Devereaux and dragged out "a Negro Woman named Violet King" were bounty hunters, as seems likely. Salem's selectmen offered a reward to "whosoever will take up said villains and bring them to justice, and rescue said Negro woman," but King's fate remains unknown.[43] And the slave *trade* continued to operate out of Salem. In May of 1783, the month that Bentley arrived, the *Gazette* announced that the *Porus*, a Salem privateer, had arrived in Martinique with a prize vessel from Africa "with upwards of 200 slaves on board, taken previous to the cessation of hostilities."[44] At the end of that month, newspaper advertisements promoted the planned auctions of just-retired privateering vessels and their armaments, two of which, including the *Porus*, were "well calculated for the African trade."[45] So even if slavery was practically over in Salem, there was plenty for a pastor who opposed the institution to say. What such a minister did say would have mattered because ministers, more than any other group, shaped public opinion on moral issues, and it was public opinion that legitimated the liberation of slaves when a hesitant legislature, confined judiciary, and impotent board of selectmen could not.

But here was an opportunity untaken. Bentley's claim that he abhorred slavery from his soul, while no doubt sincere, came a full three years into his ministry, and although he did speak up when he learned that a member of his church was sending out a slaving ship, in violation of its prohibition by the Massachusetts legislature no less, Bentley backed down when he was confronted. The latter episode was a dreary one. Trading in persons showed "the greatest moral depravity," he wrote privately in the fall of 1788 when a slaving vessel owned and captained by his parishioners had cleared Salem.[46] But he was about to discover the price of taking those thoughts public. The owner, who had remained in Salem, blamed the ministry for its role in enacting the state law which he had just broken. So on the following Sabbath—the five-year anniversary of his ordination—Bentley gave a sermon defending ministers' rights to comment on perceived immoralities. Only a small segment of the sermon was about those who "traffic in the souls of men and bid defiance to heaven by these horrid transactions," but it was enough to bring the owner of the vessel to Bentley's room that night where he "demanded satisfaction whether it was a personal affair and without waiting for an answer, threatened his resentment."[47] The argument subsided, but Bentley decided not to broach the topic again. His "existence as a parish minister" depended on his new discretion, he concluded.[48] Perhaps it was consolation when word arrived that the captain on that voyage had been killed during a slave insurrection, and though Bentley included the captain in his public prayers that Sunday, in private he approved of the slaves' "generous attempt to recover their liberty."[49] But even so, he abided by his resolution and did not again from the pulpit condemn the illegal slave trade.

He certainly had the chance. In 1792, Stephen Cleveland, a Salem resident, brought suit on behalf of the commonwealth against John Waters and Joseph Sinclair, the owner and captain of a schooner recently cleared for Africa. The 1788 law had imposed a fine of £50 for every slave transported by a state resident and an additional £200 fine per vessel, so when word returned that Sinclair had ninety slaves en route to Havana, Cleveland sued for £4,700. Waters's other vessels were subsequently attached, but Sinclair, still at sea, had insufficient assets, so the prosecutors stayed the proceedings and waited for his return. When Sinclair arrived from the islands, the sheriff went to arrest him, and although Sinclair grabbed a gun, ran to an upstairs room, barricaded himself in, and then jumped out the window, he was captured, and the suit could proceed. The dramatics petered out, however, when in court the case became entangled in the defense's argument that the state law of 1788 had been nullified by the Constitution's moratorium on interfering with the trade and that federal courts had jurisdiction in maritime cases anyway, and the final outcome of Cleveland's efforts is unclear. Sinclair, we know, was soon preparing for another run, although he had at least for the moment to go to New York to gather a crew. Through all this, Bentley remained quiet. He preached nothing either to criticize the captain or to defend the arrest. In fact, he gave instead a sermon he called "Peace of the City" in which he pleaded with listeners simply to be content with things as they are. "In being a friend to peace," Bentley told them, "he is necessarily a friend to it as the world stands, not as his giddy imagination would frame it," thus effectively dismissing the idealism and courage that had prompted and sustained the prosecutors. Cleveland could have used Bentley's help. By 1792 public opinion was clearly against the trade, and no doubt most readers agreed with Wilberforce's arguments that filled the front pages of the Gazette, but Cleveland nonetheless was facing a "considerable number" of enemies whose insults and threats Bentley might with good effect have countered. In private, Bentley was dismayed at the "certain class of people" who supported the defendants, but in the pulpit he said nothing. And Cleveland, a shopkeeper, needed more tangible aid as well. Bentley might well have taken up a collection, for example, but he did not, and there is no evidence that Salem's liberal merchants offered either their substantial wealth or their considerable legal talents to help their townsman. Cleveland finally got the help he needed, but only from Samuel Hopkins and the Quaker Moses Brown, both in Rhode Island. The illegal slave trade continued out of Salem into the nineteenth century, and Bentley through it all stayed silent.[50]

In the meantime, Bentley failed to assist Salem's freed blacks as well. The process called warning out was used by colonial New England towns to protect themselves from the costs of maintaining their poor, and it was usually directed at the transient population. Seaports like Salem had a constant influx of sailors and laborers who in hard times needed tax-supported charity funds or admission to the poorhouse. The warning-out system was intended to free residents from the financial and moral responsibility of that support. Sometimes the decree meant nothing more than that the town indemnified itself of those on the list, while at other times it mandated their physical removal from the community. In 1785, for example, the selectmen voted that the constables round up the "beggars and vagrants" and "carry them to their respective places of abode."[51] Warning out was a powerful weapon of social control, and in December of 1790, Salem wielded it again. This time, the town's voters warned out its blacks, 158 of them, including 60 married couples.[52] The federal census earlier that year had counted 260 African Americans in Salem, a number that suggests that 62 percent of Salem's blacks were warned out.[53] But the census figure included children, while the warning-out listed only adults, so a new computation is needed. If we figure—conservatively—one child per couple, then 60 children should be added to the 158 adults, in which case about 220 blacks, 85 percent of the number in the census, were in fact warned out. And if we subtract from the remaining 15 percent those who lived in elite homes as caretakers and those who were so elderly or sick that even Salemites could not send them on their way, then the number of blacks who were allowed to stay on their own virtues was a small one indeed. It seems then that white Salem was trying nothing less than to rid itself of as much of its black population as it could get away with.

Nor is that all. The warning-out system was ostensibly an economic rather than racial policy, and it is true that just the next year Salem voted again to warn out its poor, this time two hundred adults and an unknown number of children, all of whom were white. But there was a difference. The whites who were warned out were transients; the town record even lists the geographic origins of each individual on the list.[54] But the blacks warned out in 1790 were not. No towns are listed by their names, and, what is more, their surnames strongly suggest that they were the ex-slaves of Salem's slave owners. Rose Hodges, Titus Cabot, Caesar Endicott, Scipio Daland, Primus Manning, Primus Gardner, Pluto Browne, Nero Paine, and others: these were former slaves, not transients, freed men and women who perhaps had lived their entire lives in Salem but were now cast out. One looks in vain for Bentley's comments. Adding to the omission was the fact that most of Salem's blacks lived in his half of town, many in a "group of Negro cabins" near his home which he would later describe as "invariably an injury to the neighborhood, depreciating property, dispersing all the good tenants, and subjecting the persons near to every interruption." He made this comment after a neighbor erected another hut on the spot from where the previous ones had been cleared after the warning-out. The parishioner erected the shack for his former slave London, but Salem's freedmen, "seeing this building destitute of every accommodation, sent to take place of their former incumbrances, they remained long in disquiet, till repairs were begun, and then in the night they ruined the building. A prosecution is on foot, and very great threats are against the supposed offenders."[55] And so, that very week, Bentley delivered a strongly worded sermon on the need for deference among servants. Good servants, he began, "should never impose their own will and judgment in concerns not under their own authority, but in the business of the master let his will be sole and absolute." And so it went before he closed by reminding servants to "remember the danger and punishment of disobedience is great. [When] you ruin your temper, your habit, and your reputation . . . you act against religion."[56]

Against religion, that is, as Arminians had defined it. William Bentley's religion had no place for public activism, for the Arminian sacralization of decorum and moderation precluded the passions that protest requires. When it came time to deliver his five hundredth sermon, he chose as his text Paul's instruction to the Corinthians to "let every man abide in the same calling, wherein he was called" (I Cor. 7:20). Much of the sermon was on submission to station, but it included a discussion of slaves as well as of lower-sort laborers, and in it was a distillation of his whole position. The passage was prone to being used as a defense of bondage, for example by petitioning proslavery Virginians in 1785, the signers of which might not have been displeased by Bentley's interpretation.[57] Of Paul's real intent, Bentley said, "Liberty to slavery he bids them prefer, when it was their choice, but cautiously he exhorts them to abstain from any interruption to the order of civil society."[58] Preference for freedom was acceptable, even understandable, but action to make it happen was not.

Though the problems of sexual and racial inequalities could be addressed simply by urging submission on those who were already subordinate, economic inequalities required a more nuanced solution. The difficulty was one of fluidity: unlike women and African-Americans, poor white males could leave their dispossession. The need was to explain the poverty of those who remained mired in what they might have escaped.

If poverty was not inherent, what was its cause? For Arminians, the very attributes of God precluded his being responsible. Chauncy had made plain that he was writing *Benevolence of the Deity* to counter those who "find fault with their Maker and vent themselves in reflections on his goodness as though it were greatly defective."[59] Bentley agreed. As far as he was concerned, he preached during his probation, "we shall not have solace in our misfortunes, that they were not the consequences of our personal guilt and dealt out by an unequal hand." (One hopes that he tempered his response to the Newburyport woman who wrote to him begging charity on the grounds that "the Almighty has seen fit in his Infinite Wisdom to reduce me to poverty.")[60] The possibility of systemic or circumstantial causes never got much traction either. Marblehead, a Cape Ann fishing town whose residents were as tough and hardworking as any in New England, was hit particularly hard by the depression that followed the British closure of West Indian ports and the reduction of the fisheries, but Bentley was unmoved. "Nothing but a characteristic want of economy, even in the worst state of the fishery," he concluded, "can be the cause of suffering."[61]

Which is to say, Arminians were left to conclude that an individual's impoverishment was attributable solely to imprudent choices made under the sway of weak morals. "The guilt," Bentley summed up for auditors, is "justly chargeable on ourselves."[62] Poverty was the fault of the pauper, and Bentley would shed no tears for those "destitute of laudable ambition, [who] are but sailors still, while others, who were of the same rank, have risen into distinction, acquired a respectable interest, and can live at home and employ others." Some people have simply acted virtuously and prospered, he sermonized, while others "are dragging on a miserable life which their vices have brought upon them."[63] Toward the poor who happened to wander into Salem, he was merciless. "It is highly scandalous," he thundered, "that our public street should be infested with vagabonds . . . the disgrace even to a Popish country," and he advocated the public stocks as a way to "suppress an evil which . . . must in a short time fill our streets with thievery, robbery, and every disgraceful iniquity."[64] As we have seen, Bentley applauded the warning out of the transient poor, and he anonymously defended the selectmen in a newspaper piece when they hauled three particularly suspicious vagrants out of town in a cage.[65] Bentley could see no excuse for a healthy man's poverty, and so the East Church's charity funds, when it finally acquired some, went almost exclusively to widows.[66]

Arminians were hardly alone in condemning what they considered the unworthy poor, but their tendency to sanctify morality did prepare them particularly well to do so.[67] For one, they were convinced that conversion was itself a cause of immorality, at least insofar as it, so they imagined, freed the converted from fretting over the daily morals so necessary for success in a mercantile world. So it was fully in character when Bentley, responding to the death of an impoverished woman who was "addicted to intemperance and very zealous in religion," pointed the finger at her enthusiastic piety. The loss of yet another misguided evangelical who had been led to vice by a faith that en- courages an easy conversion over the discipline of daily rectitude was, he wrote, just another of the "unhappy examples of these associations."[68] He was hardly surprised at the later poverty of those who fled the East for the Tabernacle upon his arrival, and when, twenty years later, one such woman died at the poor- house, it was to him merely "another proof that strong passions in religion never subdue strong passions in the world."[69]

Another, and ultimately more important, factor in the Arminian views on wealth and poverty was that, simply put, the morals they thought necessary for salvation were also the ones they thought necessary for commercial success. The Arminian virtues—moderation, self-discipline, education, temperance, and others of like sort—seemed also, to Arminians, to contribute to the pros- perity of the holder. In short, what made a good Christian was also what made a good capitalist.

Two streams of eighteenth-century thought thus came together, each drawing power from the other. Both were expressions of that century's con- ception of liberalism. Arminianism was the soteriological part of what was considered "liberal" Christianity, which here means the desire to liberate the individual from the bondage of imputed depravity. Meanwhile, liberalism in the secular sphere, perhaps best called "classical" liberalism to distinguish it from both the sacred kind and the many versions of liberalism that have since followed it, sought to liberate the individual from kingly and aristocratic whim through guarantees of private property and the means of its increase. Con- ceived in the seventeenth-century context of English monarchy, landed aris- tocracy, and mercantilist Parliamentary laws, classical liberalism retained its allure and power well beyond the place and time of its birth. Indeed, the idea that property and its manipulation under the rules of capitalism were the surest defenders of an individual's freedom was already well established in America by the time of the Revolution, and in few places more so than among the mer- chants of New England.[70]

There, in New England, these two liberalisms merged most completely. The synthesis was an old one, to be sure. After all, the foundational documents of both liberalisms had come from the same man, John Locke, whose pen had brought forth *The Reasonableness of Christianity* as well as *The Second Treatise on Government*. The alliance had matured under Hugo Grotius—whose contri- butions included both the liberal alternative to the Anselmic atonement and the liberal insistence on property rights in a natural jurisprudence—and subsequently under Francis Hutcheson and Adam Smith, Scottish moral theorists who effectively wound the two strands together, tying Christian virtue to market success.[71] By the time Bentley was in the pulpit, Christian liberalism and economic liberalism had become inseparable. What was a release from the arbitrary moral codes of Calvinism became in the economic sphere a justification for acquisition, for that possessive individualism so often linked to liberal thought. To subscribers, it was self-evident that merchants were rich because they had worked hard and taken risks with their lives and their capital, outlasting hurricanes and northeasters or outrunning pirates and privateers, and if in the course of all this they had made a little profit along the way, it was no more than what a reasonable and benevolent God expected of them. The argument that material success proved a moral superiority that further justified increasing wealth was a feedback loop of enormous power, and no wonder Boston merchant John Rowe went to hear Thomas Barnard Sr.'s 1768 Dudleian Lecture and came away pleased at what he called "a most sensible Discourse."[72] The synthesis had become in fact a symbiosis.

Wealth that was unearned—rent payments received from cottagers on one's land—implied nothing about the virtuousness of the holder, but wealth that was earned, when gained in a system that requires morality for success, suggested a great deal about the virtues of the holder. With such a conviction in place, it was easy to conclude, as Arminian merchants did, that God approved of their wealth. Whatever difficulties other Christians might have had reconciling the accumulation of money to the teachings of Jesus, America's merchant elites saw no problem at all. Thus, finally, was the merchants' place on top of their local social order truly validated. The symbiosis of economic and Christian liberalisms allowed them their wealth and their consciences both, exactly what the rising merchants of Salem's East Church wanted most of all.

Beneath even the symbiosis of Christian and economic liberalisms lay another meaning, or intention, of liberalism in the eighteenth century. What liberalism of both kinds truly wanted was to liberate the individual from arbitrariness and whim, not into anarchy but rather into law. For liberals, the only true freedom is freedom within and under law itself. This of course applied to the realm of civil law, so although liberals were revolutionaries against England in 1776 because the law they wished to elevate needed to be generated by themselves rather than imposed from without, once independence was gained and the question became one of balancing the imperatives of social order and individual liberty, they sided always with order. There is no better example than the liberals' response to the rebellion of debtor farmers in central Massachusetts against what they considered unfair state laws. In November of 1786, on the first Sunday after Shays's Rebellion in Worcester, Bentley gave a sermon entitled "Going Down to Sodom" about those who "commence a war against society"; not long afterward he told the East Church that "rebellion is the highest crime against God and man"; in January of 1787 he improved on Jesus' admonition to "render unto Caesar"; and in March he based a sermon on I Samuel 15:23 ("For rebellion is as the sin of witchcraft"), a verse explicitly equating lawlessness and sinfulness.[73] "The end of society is security," he told listeners early in his ministry, and "our social happiness will ever be commensurate with our submission to the established authority."[74] But it applied in the spiritual realm equally as well. For Arminians, the moral law is itself liberating, insofar as acknowledging and then following that law liberates a person from his or her own worse impulses. If evangelicals wanted to free the soul from the bondage of total depravity through conversions, Arminian liberals wanted to free the soul from the passions and vices through education. Awareness of the moral obligations was to them the first step of liberation from the bonds of envy, ignorance, intemperance, and, finally, misery. In freeing individuals to be better, they would, supposedly, free them to be happier as well.

3

Christian Naturalism

Replacing Calvinism with Arminianism was not the end of William Bentley's theological revisions at the East Church, for questions of salvation were not the entirety of reason's problematic interaction with Christianity. There were other problems that ran even more deeply within the fiber of Christianity. These were the problems of reconciling reason to the very attributes and power of God.

It is important to add that the groups of Christians discussed here did not embody the whole of Christianity's encounter with the Enlightenment. Calling James Diman a member of the Enlightenment expands the term a bit too much, but few colonists better understood Locke than did Jonathan Edwards, and few Americans were as well-versed in European letters as was Timothy Dwight, neither of whom would be counted in the categories of Enlightenment Christians put forth in this chapter. The groups discussed here were indeed not the only ones participating in the new discourses of reason, but unlike Edwards and Dwight, they followed their reason away from, not toward, orthodoxy.

Bentley's solutions to the problems of the attributes and power of God were in many ways more important than was his Arminianism, for several reasons. For one, they put him in a category of Christians that was his alone, isolating him even from his Arminian peers, much more his Calvinist and evangelical antagonists. For another, these were problems that emerged from tenets shared by practically all Christians, not just by Calvinists; his struggles, then, speak to those of Christians well beyond New England and well beyond the eighteenth century. Finally, the "reason" that drove them was a more rigorous and ultimately more threatening kind of reason than was the "reason" that fueled Arminianism. The reason that had insisted on making salvation contingent on behavior was reason in only the casual sense of the word, more a perception of reasonableness rather than a conclusion derived by reasoning. But the reason that threw into doubt God's attributes and power was reason in that latter, philosophical sense, and so it presented a more systemic set of challenges to the faith than did the Arminians' assumptions about a reasonable deity's behavior.

Traditional epistemology—the study of trustworthy sources of knowledge—allows for two means by which reasoned knowledge may be derived. The first, rationalism, works by using the laws of logic to derive conclusions—more properly, to deduce them—from known axioms. If the axioms are true and the laws are rightly followed, the resulting deduction will necessarily also be true. The second, empiricism, works by deriving conclusions—inducing them—from systematic observation of the physical. To be certain, empiricism employs logic to refine its conclusions, but confidence in the truth of its conclusions comes not from their logical necessity but from the success of their predictive power.

The problem facing Bentley and others so inclined was that Christianity included elements that violated both kinds of reason: the doctrine of the Trinity seemed contradictory to rationality and logic, and claims of divine interpositions seemed inconsistent with the inductions from empirical observation. Together the Trinity and interpositions were the two arenas in which, at least for Bentley and his contemporaries, faith and reason were negotiated in the eighteenth century. They are not merely different questions; they are different kinds of questions, and Bentley's solutions to them—solutions that were new to New Englanders—illuminate not only the man but also the era in which he lived.

The most problematic part of Christian orthodoxy insofar as the formal sense of rationalism was concerned was the doctrine of the Trinity. According to this idea, the Godhead is composed of three parts, namely the Father (God), the Son (Jesus Christ), and the Holy Spirit, each of which is discrete and distinct from the others yet also coexistent, meaning of the same substance, and co-eternal, meaning extant since before Creation, with the others as well. And while all three are equal, the Father is nonetheless superior over the other two. To critics, such claims seemed to violate the very laws of logic.

The problem was hardly new in the eighteenth century, for rationalism itself was hardly new. Being pressed on the point in the fourth century was what forced the Catholic Church to issue its most important defense of the idea, the Athanasian Creed, the central tenet of which was that although neither Jesus nor the Spirit had been created per se, Jesus had been "begotten" of God, and the Spirit had "proceeded" from God. These scenarios, carefully and ingeniously wrought to maintain God's supremacy within a Godhead of equals, were successful enough to remain Catholic orthodoxy for more than a thousand years and then, after the sixteenth century, to be adopted wholesale by the Reformers and their spiritual descendants.

But the problem remained nonetheless, and by the late eighteenth century the Trinity had emerged as a particularly contentious point in New England as elsewhere. Those Christians who accepted the Trinity, a group that included the great majority of New Englanders, employed a variety of supporting evidences to make their case. Generally their first recourse was to point to relevant passages from the Bible. "For there are three that bear record in heaven," reads I John 5:7, a particular favorite. "The Father, the Word, and the Holy Ghost: and these three are one." A more elaborate proof text was provided by the opening verses of the Gospel of John, which make explicit the preexistence of Jesus as the Logos or Word. On the opening verses of John more than any other rested Trinitarian claims for the coeternality and coexistence of Christ, and New Englanders were as attuned as was John himself to their importance. Singers using the Watts collection, for example, which had included those in the East Church under Diman, needed go no further than the first page of their hymnal to find a Trinitarian lyric based on them:

> Ere the blue heav'ns were stretch'd abroad,
> From everlasting was the word:
> With God he was; the word was God,
> And must divinely be ador'd.

In the fourth verse, singers continued the story they read in John of the Incarnation into this world of an entity already extant in the other:

> But lo, he leaves those heav'nly forms,
> The Word descends and dwells in clay,
> That he may hold converse with worms,
> Dress'd in such feeble flesh as they.[1]

For members of the East Church under Diman, as for most Trinitarians elsewhere, the Bible put Christ's attributes beyond question: coexistent and coeternal, Christ was one with the Father, the Word made flesh. (The identity of the Holy Spirit is in these passages less important than the identity of Jesus, and so too was it less important in most eighteenth-century debates about the

Trinity. The Spirit, like God, was supposed to be immaterial and thus beyond the reach of reasoned discourse, but Jesus, being fully human as well as fully divine, came very much into the material plane, and so although the Spirit's equivalence with God was logically no less problematic than was Jesus', it was the attributes of Jesus rather than of the Spirit that were most often the center of controversy.)

But Trinitarians, at least those holding to a Calvinist view of salvation, could also point beyond biblical proof texts to the theological argument that Jesus must have been fully divine for his death to atone for human alienation *of* a divinity. This had a syllogistic sort of reasonableness to it, but its reliance on Paul's view of the Fall as outlined in Romans (and then expanded on by Augustine and Anselm) made it no more rationally satisfying than were the proof texts.

Just as often, Trinitarians conceded the field of formal reason altogether and defended the Trinity's possibility on the grounds that God can do whatever he wants, logical or not. As the Newburyport Presbyterian Jonathan Parsons put it, the Trinity is simply a truth "which reason could never comprehend."[2] The debate necessarily ended there, and for those New Englanders who counted themselves Trinitarians, it ended well.

But not all New Englanders were convinced by these arguments. Those who were not generally adopted one of two alternative understandings of the attributes of Jesus, and thus also of the Godhead. Arianism was the belief, roughly put, that Jesus was semidivine. The Arian Jesus was not quite coeternal, predating time but also created, and he was not quite coexistent, a being of some divine essence but not of the same stuff as God himself. The idea was an old one—the term is from the fourth-century heretic Arius, whose teachings had in fact necessitated the Athanasian Creed—but it had gathered new life in the seventeenth century by being adopted by England's Arminians and then in the eighteenth by New England's.

Arianism was an ungainly solution, and it had no passages as supportive of it as I John 5:7 was of Trinitarianism, but what it lacked in elegance and proof texts it made up for in utility. After all, whatever the theological, biblical, or aesthetic defects of a half-divine savior, it was *logically* acceptable. Moreover, Arianism fit Arminian soteriology just as nicely as Trinitarianism fit Calvinist soteriology, since the Arminians' denial of infinite depravity eliminated the need for an entirely divine redeemer. As Grotius taught them, the Crucifixion atoned for the rottenness of sins, not for humanity's alienation of an infinite being; or as Thomas Barnard Sr. put it, the Crucifixion saved humanity "not from God's anger, but from the misery our sins have brought us."[3] And finally, Arianism also accorded with the temperament of its believers, all of whom appreciated a compromising and conciliatory solution when they saw one. For a variety of reasons, then, most of New England's Arminians had, by the end of the Revolutionary War if not earlier, become Arians as well.[4]

The second option available to those New Englanders troubled by the Trinity was Socinianism, so-called after the sixteenth-century Italian Fausto Sozzini, Latinized as Faustus Socinus. This was the idea that Jesus was entirely human and nothing more. The Socinian Jesus was neither coexistent nor coeternal; he was not God nor part of the Godhead in even a halfway measure. God, before and at Creation, was alone, unified and singular. There was no Christ already begotten, as Trinitarians believed, and no subordinate Christ somewhere milling about, as Arians suggested. There was just God. The human being called Jesus would come later, created around the year zero by the one single unified God.[5]

This was the solution that William Bentley chose. Spurred on by factors and individuals discussed in a later chapter, Bentley adopted and began preaching a Socinian interpretation of Jesus as the one plausible way out of the dilemma posed by the Trinity. (He denied the divinity of the Trinity's third component too. His "Holy Spirit" referred only to the power of God manifest in natural law, not to a discrete supernatural being. When the New Testament was written, he explained, the phrase referred to God's bestowal of miraculous powers: both the dove that descended upon Jesus at his baptism and whatever it was that descended upon the apostles at the Pentecost signified their new ability to violate natural law, in both cases real and true but as a power rather than an entity.[6])

Bentley not only preached Socinianism but also transformed the church's other theological forums as well. Before his arrival, the church had been using the Westminster Shorter catechism, with its hundred-plus questions and answers on nearly every facet of Calvinist doctrine, including Trinitarianism.[7] It enjoyed widespread use and was a stock piece in the *New England Primer*, but Bentley thought it "not only utterly unintelligible to children but to most who teach it."[8] So he found a version he liked better, edited it, had copies made, and presented them to the children of his church. Now his catechists faced only forty-six questions, and the answers they gave were brief, simple, and Socinian. When asked what makes Christ superior to the earlier prophets, for example, they answered, "The perfection of his example, the purity of his precepts, and the importance of the motives by which he enforced them."[9] They said nothing, that is, about his divinity. Bentley, meanwhile, had not liked Diman's hymnal any more than he'd liked his catechism, so he borrowed 163 hymns from another collection, added (and edited) forty Tate and Brady psalms, took the compilation to the printer, bound the three hundred copies he received back, and distributed them to his congregants.[10] Needless to say, the Trinitarian hymn that opened the Watts version was not part of this new one.

Bentley thought that Socinianism was the only rational choice, and he saw little that ought stand in the way of the choosing. The Bible was no obstacle, because he dismissed supposed Trinitarian passages as mistranslations or misinterpretations: I John 5:7, for example, was "satisfactorily proved by Sir Newton to be a forgery," and as for the opening passages of the fourth gospel, if John had meant that Jesus was the preexistent Logos, why did he not say so elsewhere, too?[11] Nor was he concerned that Socinianism would diminish the sovereignty of God. In fact, Bentley argued, it was the Trinity itself which insults God by positing beings whom he did not create and by extending to two other entities the glory that he alone was due.[12] Nor did Socinianism preclude the New Testament miracles, for Bentley's Jesus was merely the human instrument through which they were performed actually by God. Even the Resurrection was not proof of Jesus' divinity, for although Jesus was, Bentley thought, indeed resurrected, it was God, not Jesus, who actually did the resurrecting. In short, the miracles were divine, but the miracle worker was not.

But to say that Christ was human is not to say that he was like every other human. On the contrary, the Socinian Christ was unlike *any* other human, before or since. He was on a singular mission, specially chosen by God at birth to spread God's desire for human behavior and given miraculous powers with which to support his claims. From Bentley's perspective, the Socinian version of Christ was just like that of the Arians and Trinitarians in every real and essential way. His Christ, like theirs, was sent by God to guide humanity back to its original goodness. His Christ, like theirs, led a perfectly moral life backed by God's wisdom and direction. His Christ, like theirs, demanded of humanity an ethical system that was God's will for creation and God's criteria for salvation. His Christ, like theirs, was resurrected as a sign of God's love and proof of an afterlife and was brought to heaven where he still sits at the right hand of God. In fact, the Socinian Christ did *all* the things that the other versions of Christ did. The Socinian Christ could even be the Son of God, if in the allegorical sense of being specially chosen; so too was he Lord, if in the sense that he taught the true path to righteousness. Though he was a human, that is, Jesus was also much more than *merely* a human.

As with his turn from Calvinism to Arminianism, Bentley was here redefining, not rejecting, the inherited tenets of Christianity; and here too was he acting to improve that faith, not to undermine it. But although Bentley could see many reasons to redefine Christ as human and no good reason not to, few others in the Congregationalist ministry agreed. In fact, none of them did.[13]

And no cleric had come to this conclusion before Bentley, either. A smattering of skeptics in the seventeenth century had raised questions about the mechanisms of the Atonement but with little effect. In the mid-eighteenth century, a writer had accused the Arminian minister Lemuel Briant of Socinianism, but with little cause. And Jonathan Mayhew had made some oblique references to the Trinity in 1755—perhaps it was he the next year who pushed for the reprinting in Boston of an English anti-Trinitarian pamphlet—but they were sporadic and isolated pokes at the Trinity, not positive sustained avowals of Socinianism like those that Bentley was making.[14]

Nor did any Congregationalist join Bentley after 1783. Calvinists certainly did not, and the other Arminians remained Arian, clearly and explicitly so. According to Charles Chauncy in 1784, God sent Christ "into our world to become incarnate." Harvard president Joseph Willard preached in 1785 that Christ had "assumed the nature" of humanity, and Cambridge pastor Timothy Hilliard described Christ in 1787 as God's "only begotten Son."[15] In 1789, John Eliot, a Boston minister in a position to know, wrote that "the boldest Socinian is Bentley."[16] But Bentley was not only the boldest Socinian among New England's Congregationalist ministers; he was also the only one.

While the rules of rational deductions were running afoul of God's attributes, the lessons gained from empirical inductions were running afoul of his power. The great legacy of Newtonianism, beyond the actual laws Newton discovered, was the general conviction that *all* natural phenomena follow physical law. The problem was that traditional Christianity includes a variety of assertions of violations of such laws. In short, how was an Enlightenment Christian to reconcile a Newtonian universe with miracles and providential interpositions?

Because this debate built on important philosophical assumptions, it may be useful first to outline in bare bones just what those assumptions were. A word or two is necessary, that is, about ontology, or the inquiry into the attributes of existence. The fundamental premise of Anglo-American ontology was that the universe contains two realms of existence. One is this realm, the natural realm (or, in other terms, the physical or material realm) of those things that extend into space and time and are subject to natural law (or what is commonly called physics). The other is the supernatural realm (or metaphysical or immaterial realm), a realm without matter or extension located somehow near or next to the natural one—in the Christian context the place of heaven and hell but in any context a realm beyond the reach of natural law. Nobody argued that natural law ought to be able to explain what happens in the supernatural realm, but interpositions occur in the natural one and yet do not follow natural law. Put differently, they are breaches of the ontological barrier, originating in the supernatural plane but ending up in the natural one. How ought these moments be understood?

A quick way to sort out the array of eighteenth-century responses to this problem is to divide them into the two camps known as deism and latitudinarianism.

Deism was not new with Newton, nor for that matter was it solely English, but Newton's work did lend it a new currency, particularly in England, at the turn of the eighteenth century. Inspired by empiricism's success in understanding nature, deists applied empirical criteria to religion as well, resulting in their removal of every claim about the supernatural realm save three. The first of the three was the existence of God, induced by what was called the argument from design, the argument that a manifestly intelligent creation seemingly required a Creator, a singular generative force behind and beyond the natural plane. The second was the existence of moral laws incumbent upon humanity, induced from the seeming universality of conscience. The third was the existence of a place of punishment in the supernatural plane, induced from the need which a just God has for a place to send sinners who seemingly escaped retribution in this life. Only these three were knowable independently of tradition or revelation, so only these three would deists believe.

These inductions constituted "natural religion," and beyond them deists would not go. Though the commands of conscience *may* be the same as what Christ preached and though the arena of punishment *may* be the same as what others called hell, empirical reasoning does not allow a person to say so, and so deists would not. Not even the identity of the Creator could be known. The argument from design pointed to *a* god, but not necessarily to *the* God, that being who was Jehovah to the Jews and Father to the Christians. Deists preferred such terms as "Author" or "Architect" for those words' ability to reflect the creative power that was the sole attribute they were willing to ascribe to their deity.

Even if empiricism could allow these three inductions about the internal qualities of the supernatural realm, it could say nothing to verify the interpositions that originated there but ended up here. Deists particularly rejected scriptural stories that portrayed a nasty and vicious deity—stories like the command to sacrifice Isaac—but they rejected interventions on ontological principle before theological implication.[17] Nothing supernatural—beyond the three points which they induced from reason—would they allow into their faith. They began with reason, empirical reason to be exact, rather than Scripture and they ended exactly where that reason could no longer reach.

Latitudinarianism, meanwhile, constituted a more compromising stance. The name comes from its broad embrace of religious tolerance—orthodox critics complained that subscribers gave too wide a latitude to differing versions of the faith—but its core ideational characteristic was its effort to adopt the new lessons of empiricism while also maintaining the ontological claims of traditional (Protestant) Christianity. Most of Bentley's liberal peers were latitudinarians. That is, while they were Arminians on questions of soteriology and Arians on questions of Christology they were latitudinarians on questions of ontology.[18] It is important to draw a clear and firm distinction between latitudinarianism and deism. Although latitudinarians sympathized with the deists' desire to make Christianity as reasonable as possible—if nothing else, empirical deism was preferable to Cartesian *rational* deism[19]—they adopted none of the deists' restraints on God. Latitudinarians agreed with the three points of natural religion but saw them primarily as confirmation of what Scripture had already told them. For latitudinarians, the deists' Creator was in fact the biblical God, their commands of conscience were also Christ's, and their arena for punishment was the traditional hell.

In fact, New England's latitudinarians spent a great amount of energy expounding on the inadequacy of natural religion. Harvard established a lecture series just for this purpose, one sample as good as any other being the lecture given in 1768 by Salem's Thomas Barnard Sr., then minister of the First Church.[20] Each of these Dudleian Lectures struck roughly the same notes, the particular theme of Barnard's being an elaboration on Paul's directive to the Corinthians "that your faith should not stand in the wisdom of men, but in the power of God" (I Cor. 2:5). What Paul meant when he criticized the "wisdom of men," argued Barnard, was exactly the kind of reasoning so admired by deists, one that was a manifestly inadequate foundation for right religion. Latitudinarians began with Scripture rather than reason, and though they reveled in moments when both pointed in the same direction, in times of conflict latitudinarians would surrender the lessons of empiricism to the lessons of the text.

But if latitudinarians accepted biblical supernaturalism and the larger question of the possibility of supernatural interposition, they did so only after much maneuvering. Latitudinarians, who assumed that the laws in question were written by God in the first place, preferred therefore to frame the whole question as whether God would violate the laws of his own making. They saw it not as a question of whether God *could* violate his own laws—of this they had no doubt—but whether he chooses to. Their answer was that for the great majority of the time, God is happy to remain beyond the natural realm, to allow his creation to proceed along according to the laws he legislated for it, but when necessary, God does not hesitate to intervene, even if it means violating his own laws. Natural law, they believed, was accurate only insofar as it described the *normal* workings of the natural plane and did not deny God the power to violate that law at whatever time, in whatever form, and to whatever end he wishes. Latitudinarians, however, were never comfortable with law-breaking of any kind, and so usually tried to de-emphasize the violation of law and argue instead that interpositions still follow a law of some unknown kind, one perhaps not even natural. This was what they meant when they argued that God authored both natural and biblical revelation and surely would not contradict himself. And it was what they meant when they put forth their most sweeping defense, the imagined category of phenomena "above" reason. Latitudinarians claimed that some phenomena, such as miracles, can rightly be placed into an epistemological category that exists above, but not in conflict with, reason. Events in this category might seem to violate natural law but were actually following some other divine law unknown to humanity. This way, phenomena could be "above" human reason but not in conflict with all reason. By this simple move, latitudinarians had given themselves an out to all kinds of dilemmas, including, it should be added, the semidivinity of Jesus, too. *Anything* that seemed to run counter to law could be explained this way. Latitudinarians had no evidence beyond the scriptural texts they were justifying, but the utility of phenomena "above" reason was too great to abandon. Nor were latitudinarians ever clear whether the laws "above" reason were laws of nature that humans had not yet discovered (in which case the phenomena that follow them were not interpositions) or were laws of supernature that apply usually only in heaven (in which case their relationship to human reason was irrelevant). But if phenomena "above" reason was no more empirical than any other explanation of the mysterious, it *sounded* more empirical, and it provided latitudinarians with the confidence to pride themselves on being both empiricists and Biblicists, avid men of reason and yet also devout Christians.[21]

In his interpretation of Scripture, Bentley was a latitudinarian. Like other latitudinarians, he believed in the truth of the biblical stories of supernaturalism. In two early sermons for example, he spoke on the two most important Old Testament interpositions—sending the Deluge and commanding Abraham to sacrifice Isaac—and in each concluded that indeed God had intervened in violation of natural law.[22] And he accepted the supernaturalism of New Testament interpositions as well. Feeding thousands with some bread and fish, turning water into wine, walking on water, raising the dead to life, *being* raised from the dead—all these and more were to Bentley direct and unmediated interventions of divinity into the natural plane.

And they needed to remain that way for they—and only they—prove that the Christian message has supernatural significance. Whereas the deists' natural religion may have *implied* a causal link between behavior and afterlife consequence, only Scripture—its supernatural components, to be exact—made that link explicit. Even deists agreed that Jesus' commands were worthy and wise, but that those commands were more than worthy or wise, that they in fact came from God as criteria for heaven, was proved only by the miracles, the most important of which was the Resurrection. (Internal prophecies, or Old Testament prefigurings of the New Testament Savior, also served as proof, but they carried less weight with latitudinarians than did the New Testament miracles.) For the latitudinarians, only the miracles proved that Jesus was in some way carrying a revelation from God for humanity. Without them, Jesus was no different from Socrates or Confucius—no mean comparison, said the deists—but with them he was offering lessons that were not just prudent but were also the infinitely more important will of God. As Bentley himself preached early on, "If we induce a belief that there are not general supernatural truths in the Bible . . . we must remove the evidence of the truth of Christianity itself."[23] That Jesus urged admirable ethics nobody doubted, but for latitudinarians like Bentley, only the miracles suggested that acting ethically also lifted a person to heaven. So necessary was it that Jesus convince the masses of the divine source of his mission and the divine consequences of his message that God was willing to violate his own natural law for it.

But interpreting *scriptural* supernaturalism was not the whole of Christianity's conflicts with empirical lessons about nature. Christianity also makes claims about supernatural moments in the ongoing present. Deists, not surprisingly, thought these claims to be just as unfounded as the biblical ones, whereas latitudinarians accepted them, at times hesitating over the reliability of the claimant but never doubting the ontological possibility of the claim.

On this score, however, William Bentley was not among them. Just as he diverged from his peers on Christology, so too he diverged from them on ontology, and exactly on this point of postbiblical interpositions. Put succinctly, Bentley believed that although God did intervene in biblical times, he has not done so since. God simply acts differently in the post-apostolic world than he did during the time described in Scripture. It was not logically necessary, after all, that God still interfere simply because he did so in the past, and meanwhile Bentley had what he thought were compelling theological reasons to suspect that God has indeed decided not to. Bentley's God, for one, was above all else a reasonable God and so surely would not demand that humans comprehend phenomena beyond what his own gifts to them allowed. Bentley was not saying that God has not preserved mysteries up in heaven—on the contrary, the glass through which we darkly see is exactly the ontological barrier it-self[24]—but only that God has rightly limited his expectations of human knowledge to the domain of what humanity can reasonably know. "Our obligation ceases," Bentley told the East Church in a probationary sermon about their duties to Christian knowledge, "when just inquiry will not enable us to perceive it."[25] More important, however, Bentley saw Christ's mission— though the mission of a human being—as the ultimate interposition and thus the last. Supernaturalism was necessary in the time of the Bible because people back then needed proof that the message they were hearing was from God, but through Jesus the final iteration of that message was delivered. Sending Jesus and then performing miracles through him *was* God's last interposition. Bentley's God created the universe with certain laws to guide it, intervened during its early phases—including through Jesus—and then retreated back to the supernatural plane to watch subsequent events unfold in nature according to his natural laws. In Jesus, God said all he could say. It has been up to humanity ever since. And as far as Bentley was concerned, what Christians ought to mean by the Holy Spirit in their own time was not the biblical sense of the power to violate natural law but instead the benevolence that inheres to those laws. And so it was that Bentley, and Bentley alone among New England's ministry, banished God and anything that anyone else considered godlike from interfering in the natural realm of the postbiblical ongoing present.

He was offering up a radically new version of Christianity. Bentley was not a deist but neither was he like the other liberal latitudinarians. That he accepted biblical interpositions put him beyond deism, but that he rejected postbiblical ones put him beyond latitudinarianism, He had created a new interpretation, a new faction of Christian ontology of which he was the only representative.

Prohibiting God from intervening in the natural plane was no small alteration to eighteenth-century New England Christianity. Bentley's contemporaries interpreted a great variety of phenomena as interpositions, and to remove that interpretation was to remove much that they thought they knew about God's interactions with humanity.

Divine interpositions fell into two broad causal categories: those moments intended to hasten the salvation of an individual soul and those intended to chastise or reward behavior in the natural realm.

The first category includes the interpositions that Bentley's contemporaries assumed occurred at the sacraments. At the East Church, however,

Communion became only a public gesture of Christian togetherness, an event purely of this realm, and baptism became only a public statement of the parents' willingness to raise the child in Christian morals; nothing metaphysical actually happened to the child.[26] Even the conversion moment itself Bentley considered without supernatural consequences. To the orthodox, such moments were explicitly supernatural events, the result of the Holy Spirit's entry into a human soul sufficiently humbled. But latitudinarians, too, thought that conversions were supernatural. Even though as Arminians they had redefined conversions as gradual adoptions of saving morality rather than instant infusions of saving grace, they nonetheless believed that the Spirit slips in and hastens the process. Charles Chauncy wrote that the Spirit assists conversions by "superintending directly," while Cambridge's pastor Timothy Hilliard extolled "the special inspiration of the Holy Ghost."[27] Both the adverb "directly" and the adjective "special" were code words, serving to insist that the intervention of the Spirit is an immediate breach of the physical plane. But not Bentley. As an Arminian, he agreed that conversions were turns to lifetimes of moral behavior, but unlike the rest of them, he did not think that divinity played any direct role in that change. Bentley considered a conversion to be an individual's natural decision to listen to and follow the dictates of conscience, what he called "forsaking bad habits, not changing bad natures," an event that was real and good and necessary for the Christian life but one that was entirely of this realm.[28] Under his ministry, the converted Christian was one who simply decided to do what Jesus instructed. God was pleased by the decision but had done nothing to effect it, not even secondarily.

Only in one context did Bentley allow for anything approaching a supernatural moment, namely at the end of an individual's life when the soul moves to the supernatural realm. But then again, that migration is not in and of itself an ontological breach, because a soul is already supernatural. It does indeed exist within the natural plane, moving within a medium not its own like a drop of oil suspended in water, but nonetheless it is not itself natural, and so its move to the immaterial plane upon the death of the physical body that encapsulated it is therefore not a crossing from one plane to the other but rather an absorption of one small part of supernature back into the infinite pool of supernature. This movement of a soul to the supernatural plane was essential to Bentley's theological convictions; fortunately it was allowable under his philosophical ones as well.

But if interpositions on the soul were not technically inconsistent with empiricism because the thing being manipulated, the soul, was not itself physical, the second kind of interposition enjoyed no such wiggle room. This kind resulted in physical, sometimes public, often large-scale phenomena that by definition required violating natural law. So Bentley's negotiation of these claims points us more directly than does his naturalization of conversion or the sacraments to the problems inherent in maintaining a supernatural faith in an empirical age.

By the late eighteenth century, English Christianity had come to think of three modes by which God intervened in the physical world in these large-scale ways. The first, miracles, were moments of direct intervention, sudden changes of nature in immediate violation of the laws that normally govern it. It would be miraculous, for example, if lightning were to come from a clear sky. The second mode, what was called special, or particular, providence, was God's use of a natural secondary cause, or instrument, to nudge natural law toward a specific end. It would be specially providential if the lightning came naturally from a storm that God supernaturally sent. The third mode, general providence, was the natural outcomes of the set of natural laws legislated by God at creation and presumably expressive of God's desire for that creation. It was general providence that lightning is a part, and a good and necessary part, of the naturally occurring storms that form entirely according to the laws of nature created by God. More commonly, though, the concept of general providence referred to nonspecific phenomena, the regular and universal results of natural law such as the migration of fish or the changing of seasons or the summer storms that bring much-needed rain.

All three modes come from God and manifest God's will, but the ontological and epistemological characteristics differ in crucial ways. Consider another example, Poor Richard's well-known maxim "God helps those who help themselves." This little piece of advice could be interpreted as predicting a miracle, that is, as suggesting that God actually intervenes in this world to assist those individuals who labor to improve their own condition. Or it could be interpreted as special providence, which is to say that God tweaks natural law to "naturally" boost the fortunes of the hardworking. Or it could be interpreted as general providence, which is to say that although God does not intervene on behalf of any one diligent and disciplined individual, he *did* set up a system of natural laws that benefit the diligent and disciplined everywhere. The creator of the maxim, Benjamin Franklin, was a deist and so had no doubt about which interpretation he thought correct, but the phrasing cleverly allowed a variety of interpretations by his readers.

By the late eighteenth century, the debate among latitudinarians had come to hinge on the issue of special providence. Postbiblical miracles were for the most part rejected, whereas general providence was universally accepted (even by deists, for whom it was another expression for the argument from design). But special providence occupied a contested ground. At least it did once Bentley began contesting it. For their part, the other latitudinarians accepted it. They could accept even a destructive special providence, since well may a benevolent deity send chastisements for the greater good,[29] but the issue was not the theological one of divine goodness but the philosophical one of divine power, and on this point latitudinarians had no doubt. Special providence was just another one of those things "above" reason.

Again Bentley stood alone. To be sure, he accepted general providence and would happily affirm that the laws that govern nature were legislated by God the Creator, and, to be equally sure, he joined the latitudinarians in denying postbiblical miracles. But unlike the others, he denied special providence, too. His God did not interfere in even the smallest way. Bentley did not have to wait long for an occasion to say so. In late 1783, when Bentley was only a few months into his ministry, Governor John Hancock announced that the eleventh of December of that year would be a fasting day in the commonwealth, a time to acknowledge God's hand in the defeat of the British and to call to mind the continuing need for such grace. Across the commonwealth, Massachusetts's citizens went to their meetinghouses to hear their ministers explain God's role in the victory just won. In Newburyport the Presbyterian John Murray insisted that God "is not beholden to any instrument" of mediation, and in Billerica the Arminian Henry Cumings explained that "the veil of second causes and instruments" only masks what was really "the disposing hand of God in all events." Even Harvard's president, Joseph Willard, celebrated in a sermon in Cambridge the "proofs, innumerable proofs of a superintendency over the affairs of men." Meanwhile, Bentley in Salem was telling his listeners that "it is not the will of heaven continually to interpose in national events for injured virtue. He has left his system to general laws."[30] God was responsible to the extent that his universe tends to reward the virtuous, in this case the Americans, but only to that extent. Other than that, God had nothing to do with it. Among all Christians of all kinds in the early Republic, only those at Salem's East Church were told that God does not and will not interfere in their lives in any way beyond the natural laws written for their universe at the Creation.

Bentley really had no choice but to reject special providence. For all the talk of special providence's manipulation of natural law rather than its violation of it, special providence required *some* violation, *some* direct intervention to prompt the natural consequences that follow. Though God may not have violated natural law in causing the phenomenon in question (a fire, say, that was caused by the lightning), and may not have violated it in causing the cause (the lightning was part of a storm), and may not have violated it in causing even that cause (the storm spun off a larger weather pattern), at some time in the process he *must* have violated it. He must have performed some small miracle somewhere to bring about the end result, for if that result were to reflect God's will and thus have any moral meaning (as special providence was assumed to have), the chain of events had to be initiated after, not before, the human action that prompted it, because behavior, to these free-will-believing Arminians, could not have been foretold at the Creation. In other words, the phenomenon could not have been entirely the result of a long sequence of natural cause-and-effect laws established at Creation because God did not then know he would need to make it happen. God's response to contingent human behavior logically requires a miraculous intervention at some, perhaps minuscule, level. Which is why Bentley rejected that possibility altogether. To know God's thoughts, he preached, one ought look at the laws that govern nature; indeed, one can look *only* at those laws.

If, before 1783, the ontological conflicts between faith and reason resulted in the two broad solutions of deism and latitudinarianism, after 1783 there was a third solution: William Bentley's. He was a one-man faction of reasonable Christianity. He was not a deist. His starting point was the Bible, not reason; his god was the God of the Bible, not the god induced from Creation; he did accept biblical miracles, and he did interpret Christ's commands as being God's will. But at the same time, he broke from the latitudinarians, rejecting a semidivine Christ for a human one and denying supernaturalism in the ongoing, postbiblical present. In the important questions facing Christians who counted themselves obliged to reconcile their faith to empiricism, Bentley's answers were essentially his alone. He was the only person who believed what he did about the attributes and powers of God.

He was what one might call a Christian naturalist—a naturalist because he rejected ongoing supernaturalism, and a Christian because he defined himself as one. In his mind, the combination was not only sensible but also righteous. In fact, he considered claims to ongoing interpositions to be *anti*-Christian. In his view, such claims confused well-meaning people with wrong ideas about God; they let people think themselves free from the Christian virtue of self-responsibility; they led to very un-Christian persecution and intolerance; and, when tied to Trinitarianism, they blocked the spreading of the gospel by wrapping up Jesus' message in dubious assertions about the messenger. "I profess myself a Christian," Bentley said one Sunday in 1788. "And if I do not deceive myself I am one. I believe Christianity has done great good in the world, whenever it has been understood and adopted. I believe it will still do greater good in the world. I therefore wish it success, for I believe it to be the power of God unto salvation, unto all who believe. It has my heart, my labors, my property, and my life, and I firmly believe that my reward is with God."[31] He had never actually rejected any part of the inherited Christianity, only redefined each one. And he had done so in order to save, not destroy, the faith he held, preached, and loved. It is not possible to understand the agenda of the Christian naturalist without accepting that he was an ordained minister of Christ, a man who devoted his life's energies to spreading the gospel of Jesus as he saw it. He was driven to deny claims of ongoing supernaturalism in the full belief that Christianity does not need them and is better off without them. He was entirely convinced of the truth and value of Christ's teachings, and he wished to spread that good word. Bentley's desire was never to reduce or stain Christianity but to elevate it, cleanse it, and raise it up to the world in a form more accurate, more reverent, and more hopeful. Even with his Arminian modifications of Calvinism, his Socinian modifications of Arianism, and his naturalist modifications of latitudinarianism, Bentley never doubted that he was a Christian. In fact, as he saw matters, not only was he a Christian, he was the *best* Christian.

4

Spiritual Libertarianism

The banishment of God from the natural realm was a radical theological idea indeed, but it was also a radical political one. And whatever its theological consequences, its political ones—here referring to social and ecclesiastical politics—were clear: to deny that God intervenes in this plane was to challenge ecclesiastics whose power rested on claims of an ability to interpret such interventions. From those authorities and their claims, Bentley would seek to liberate the faithful.

Bentley's spiritual libertarianism was evident most obviously in his unique advocacy of the rights of Christians who professed other forms of the faith. In Bentley's Massachusetts, some sets of dissenters were tolerated, and some were not. Anglicans and Quakers and Anabaptists were in the former group, each granted that tolerance by the Massachusetts General Court long before Bentley's arrival in Salem. A variety of sects were in the latter group, most notably the post-Awakening "Baptists," who insisted on worshiping only with likeminded individuals who had been baptized after their "new birth" rather than the natural one, and by immersion rather than by sprinkling, and who in Bentley's time were demanding the same rights as those given the earlier Anabaptists.

The Baptists were part of that larger group of Congregationalist churches known as Separates, congregations that had left their parish churches during and after the Great Awakening to form churches open only to the converted, with some going on to become Baptists and some not but practically all agitating for relief from parish laws. Many of the towns in Massachusetts, that is, had some sort of dissenting element within them, and the lines were clear, rhetorically if not geographically, between the establishment and its opponents.

Defenders of that establishment included the liberal Congregationalists as well as the orthodox (but not Separate) ones. Even those liberals in Boston, where there had never been parishes, favored the parish system elsewhere. They did so on the grounds that the spiritual education provided by sermons was important enough to social harmony to warrant coerced attendance and support, and they pointed out that what they thought necessary was only *some* form of Christianity—Protestant Christianity, that is—rather than any *particular* form. Christianity was what was important; the denomination or doctrine was up to the believer. Thus Article III of the 1780 Massachusetts Constitution's Declaration of Rights required that individuals support *a* church, not necessarily the Congregationalist church of the parish in which they lived. Separates disagreed with the principle, of course, and Baptists with the practice as well, since they were in many cases still too few in any one area to support a minister on their own and thus were still required to attend and support their (often unconverted) parish church until sufficient numbers allowed them their own worship.[1]

But William Bentley once again charted a path entirely his own. In a region of liberal defenders of establishment and evangelical opponents, Bentley cut diagonally; he was a liberal opponent.

Cutting diagonally gave him a unique opportunity, and he took it: he was the first Congregationalist minister to eliminate the legal obligations of parishioners to attend and subsidize the church. No other cleric in New England history had arrived at an established, tax-supported parish and then set out to dissolve it.

Moreover, Bentley advocated when others would not for religious freedom beyond his parish. He had nothing for which to agitate in the rest of Salem, since the western parish, the First Parish, had been dissolved much earlier (for reasons of practicality, it ought to be added, not reasons of principle).[2] Once Bentley was through effectively disestablishing the eastern half of town, residents there were free to go where they wished as well. After 1785, that is, Salem had no parish system from which to dissent.

But he did have the chance in the 1780s to speak out in favor of dissenting groups in the southern part of the county outside of Salem. It was not the Baptists whom he had occasion to support since there were practically no Baptists in Salem in the 1780s; a Baptist itinerant had appeared in Salem in 1784, leading Ipswich's John Cleaveland, neither for the first nor last time, to take up his pen in protest, but Baptists remained few in number until the turn of the nineteenth century.[3] It was, rather, another set of dissenters, a group of Universalists up in nearby Gloucester. A Cape Ann town not far from Salem, Gloucester had become home to a small congregation under one John Murray (not the Newburyport Presbyterian by the same name) whose most singular claim was that everyone goes to heaven. This idea was the universalism from which the sect drew its name, and it was also exactly the problem. The issue with the Gloucester group was not one of insufficient numbers. Believers they had. The issue was whether what they believed was actually Christianity or not. Article III required that the public support a Christian church, but did a theology that had no hell count as Christianity? John Cleaveland was certain that it did not and so again he wrote to the public, this time to warn of the dangers posed by a theology without the fear of hell.[4] But forebodings about universalism were hardly just Cleaveland's; for a month preceding Murray's ordination in 1788, the Salem *Mercury* had been full of letters and essays about the Cape Ann Babylon.[5] Even the Baptists disapproved, since tolerating deniers of hell was not what *they* meant by tolerance either.

Bentley did not like Murray's theology any more than he liked the theologies of the Separates or the Baptists. Murray's form of universalism, after all, was not like Bentley and Chauncy's universalism: Arminian universalism removed only the infinitude of hell, not hell itself, but Murray's removed hell, or so everyone thought, and did so based on a supposed extension of satisfaction through the spiritual melding of humanity and Christ. And Bentley surely disapproved of Murray's reasoning about salvation, scoffing at what he called these "new vampt mysticisms." He also did not like the fact that Murray had simply set himself up as a minister rather than going through the proper channels of call and ordination, describing him as "an illiterate foreigner without credentials" and declining to officiate at the ceremony when Murray finally did become ordained. But even so, even with all of these objections, it was Bentley who defended their right to worship. When in 1790 Cleaveland went to the press, it was Bentley who replied. For all of his mockery of their ideas, Bentley also believed that Universalists had a right to them. "I do not approve of forming creeds," he began his newspaper essay, "but I admire the honest representation of their opinions: they have not my hearty assent to them; but by uniting together, they give consistency to their plan, vouch for their sober conduct, and become peaceful citizens at once. While they are regular, they will be as harmless as all other sects."[6] Bentley dismissed their theologies as superstitious nonsense, but it was he who would advocate for their rights to hold those ideas, and it was in fact he who helped a visitor try to set up a Catholic congregation in Salem that same year.[7] Bentley had nothing but disdain for Universalism and Catholicism, but he defended the rights of their adherents to worship when no one else in the area—not the evangelical Congregationalists, not the liberal Congregationalists, and not even the dissenting Baptists—would.

His Christian naturalism allowed him to do so, for several overlapping reasons. First, Universalists and Catholics *were*, by his lights, sufficiently Christian. In believing that Christ's instructions were not just wise but were also divine, Universalists and Catholics met his theological criteria for Christianity, and in acting morally they met his behavioral ones. For Bentley, any sect that encouraged morality was acceptable because morality was what Jesus commanded in the first place. Being moral *was* being a Christian, regardless of the theological beliefs tacked on. This was by no means theological relativism. He thought these sects wrong, and wildly and sadly so. He was entirely convinced that his was the correct interpretation of Scripture, the correct reading of nature, and the correct agenda for humanity, and he did not suffer gladly those who thought differently. But *any* faith that encouraged morality was acceptable, and so too even was being moral in the absence of faith altogether. True, only Jesus demonstrated that the conscience's commands of morality were not just prudent advice but were God's own will; but even so, it was the commands that were important, not the fact that it was Jesus giving them. Christian virtue, that is, was possible even without Christianity. Christianity, as Bentley put it, "ennobles" virtue but does not create it. The majority of individuals, he was sure, do *not* act virtuously or morally without the prodding of revelation and a minister, but those who do are already doing what God told Christ to tell humanity to do. They are Christians even if they do not identify themselves as such, even if they actively deny that they are Christians, and even if they have never heard of Christianity.

Second, sectarianism by itself does no harm because the sects differ exactly where their beliefs become irrelevant, namely at the ontological barrier. Their differences are exactly their superfluities, each being based on a false assumption of supernaturalism: the Separates' instant, saving new birth, the Baptists' soul-cleansing immersions, and the Universalists' mystic melding all required the postbiblical supernaturalism that Bentley had denied. What the sectarians had in common—namely, the belief that Christ's miracles proved his divine mission—was what was necessary because it alone was true, and as long as they continued to believe in that and act accordingly, Bentley would welcome them to stay, even if they also preached unfortunate but otherwise innocuous schismatic irrelevancies as well. To be certain, Bentley was also convinced that sometimes these differences *do* serve as prods to immoralities, a tendency to persecution chief among them, and in such cases ought to be condemned, but by themselves immaterial beliefs in immaterial ideas, true or false, neither anger God nor harm the believer. Finally, he thought, the sectarian tendencies of independent inquiry were an inevitable and even desirable part of humanity's progress toward what he thought the one right truth. He saw humanity as just then, in the eighteenth century, entering into a phase of intellectual development in which it could for the first time understand true Christianity. The Reformation of Catholicism had been a step in the right direction, as had the Arminian redefinition of Calvinism, but there was more that needed to be done before humanity would see that the sum of Christianity is the command to follow the ethical code preached by a divinely commissioned but human Christ. And the fact that inquirers might veer off the path as they struggle toward the light was to be expected. "The fact is," he wrote in defending the Universalists, "the Reformation was so partial, that new sects must arise, if Christianity is ever [to be] well understood." Bentley tolerated these errors in large measure because he thought that they were temporary. And his God was willing to wait. His God knew that natural means of persuasion—and there was no longer any other kind, interventions being literally a thing of the past—take time. Educating humanity toward reasoned comprehension of the benefits of Christian ethics is slow work, Bentley knew and assumed God knew as well. But it would happen, he was sure; the inherent reasonableness of Socinian Christian naturalism, he thought, would win people over, given enough time and enough education. In the meantime, it was better to allow the erroneous to carry on even though in error, to allow individuals the opportunity to explore wrong paths in order more surely to recognize the right one.

William Bentley was indeed tolerant in the sense of tolerating groups beyond his congregation and beyond Congregationalism, but his tolerance extended to matters within his own church, too. He had already dissolved the parish, so there was nothing left to do in that particular sense of toleration. But given that Congregationalist churches set their own terms of admission to the sacraments, it is no surprise that Bentley also tried on these grounds to assault what he considered the forces of intolerance and suspicion. Because such changes were effected by a vote of the adult male members, Bentley could only influence the voting membership rather than impose the changes himself. But influence them he did. As chapter 1 demonstrated, he had, while still assistant pastor, urged removing the requirement of the parents' profession of faith, and he continued on in the same spirit after Diman left in 1785, allowing baptism to children even of parents who were themselves unbaptized. His naturalization of the procedure allowed him to. His interpretation of baptism was solely as a public avowal of the parents' sincere desire to raise a child with an eye toward Christian morality, but this was itself a sufficient sign of redemption and a passport to Bentley's kind of church membership. In 1792, the church agreed to his request that Bentley could "act [his] own judgment about propounding or Christening any persons whatever." It was, he wrote, "a liberty which affords me great pleasure." Baptism into the East Church had become, as he wished, "free to all men."[8]

With the supernaturalism removed from the ceremony, Bentley could offer other expansions as well. He was willing to perform baptisms at the recipient's home, something that Diman never did and that even other liberals opposed.[9] The First Church's John Prince thought home baptism was "against all religious institutions," but to Bentley it was those exact institutions that all too often deterred the very individuals—in this case, the elderly or sick—who stood to gain the most from it.[10] Bentley's baptisms were events entirely of the natural plane and so were in no way made less effective by secular, and usually modest, locations. He was also willing to baptize on a day other than Sunday. Ebenezer Phippen was the first to ask. Phippen was one of the eight men who were members of the church at the time of Bentley's arrival, the struggling carpenter with a deaf wife and seven children. In 1790, he asked Bentley to baptize his newest children, numbers eight and nine, as soon as possible, not waiting until Sunday. Bentley did so. His diary explains why. Phippen, Bentley wrote several days later, "buried two children in one procession."[11] Other ministers would not have provided a baptism except on Sunday, but for Bentley baptism was an event of the natural realm, a sign of the parents' commitment to raise the child according to Christian morals and was every bit as efficacious on a Saturday as on a Sunday.

Most radically of all, he was willing to baptize children born or conceived out of wedlock without requiring a confession of sin by the parents. Other churches were not so forgiving. The Tabernacle required in such cases that the applying parents confess to the congregation their "breach of the seventh commandment" before being admitted to Communion and putting up the children for baptism. In some years a startlingly high percentage of its applicants had to admit as much. In 1751, for example, five of the eight female applicants did so; in 1756, eight of the twenty-seven women and two of the five men did. It was surely the most anticipated part of the ceremony, and one imagines that the Tabernacle congregation was particularly gratified in 1755 by one woman's confession to her "repetition" of the act.[12] Nor were the evangelical churches the only ones in Salem imposing such obligations on prospective members: even the liberal First continued to require public confessions of fornication until 1792.[13]

But for Bentley, the circumstances of the conception had no bearing on the sincerity of the parent to raise the child in the right atmosphere, and so he did away with the public confession.[14] And parents took him up on the offer. One Andover man, for example, brought his four children down to Salem exactly because his own church required a confession of sins, one he was reluctant to make because his first child had been born seven months into his marriage. They "appeared to be a loving family," Bentley thought, and he happily performed the service.[15] Another time Bentley christened children "begotten by several fathers, but born of one mother, whose continence," he added, "is surprising, excepting in this single respect."[16] On yet another occasion, in the middle of an October night, a young Salem couple in trouble knew just where to go. Bentley entered the episode into his diary in Latin, which in translation reads:

> In the evening a sailor comes to me, begging me to go in the middle of the night to join him [to his wife] in matrimony. In accordance with the laws, the notary refused to give him the papers before the time appointed by law. I remained with the family until the eleventh hour at that point in time I crossed to the house of his betrothed. There all things were prepared. The parents show grief mixed with joy. Now they converse about hope, now about grief, at times standing, sitting, walking, going to their daughter, begging her to be quiet through ten, through five, a few moments. Quickly, most quickly, says the father. Patience, darling, says the mother. The friends enter and they stand silent at the hearth. The betrothed comes in. He runs to apply dressings; the mother persuades him not to, 'It is already done.' The fiancée sitting, the fiancé standing, joining hands. They agree with neither prayers nor exhortations—the sacrament only—and she gives birth.[17]

Although Bentley was initially called to perform the wedding, the word "sacrament" in the last sentence can refer only to baptism, since Protestants do not consider marriage a sacrament, and there was no reason just then for Communion. Bentley, it seems, had agreed to baptize the illegitimate child about to be born. Then there was Anna Wyatt. She had been Bentley's favorite member of the East Church choir but was "betrayed by a young fellow and left to suffer for her confidence." Friends and neighbors had hounded her into quitting the choir, and she was soon taken in by another man who abused and abandoned her. After a subsequent stay in the Salem workhouse, she had moved to Andover from whence, in 1793, as she lay dying, she called for Bentley. Anna Wyatt died several hours before Bentley arrived, but when he returned to Salem that night, he had her two young children with him and two new homes waiting for them in town.[18] It was to William Bentley down in the other end of the county that she had entrusted the lives, and souls, of her children. And then there was this entry in his diary, from 1798. The editor of the diary's published version opted to omit it, but it is in the manuscript. It speaks for itself.

> This afternoon I was called to see the last of my amiable young friend, Lydia Gerry. She was resigned to death; she asked it. She was over-whelmed by her reflections, and she was tortured with her dying agonies. From a life of spotless innocence, by yielding to the seduction of the man she loved, and whose heart is not corrupt, she became exposed to the world. The thought sunk into the heart, and she per-ished. She asked baptism for her child. God had not forgotten, she had forgotten herself. She gave her child to him.[19]

Bentley alone was sympathetic to those well-meaning but imperfect individ-uals whose mistakes left them vulnerable to social derision and abandonment. Only he would baptize Lydia Gerry's child, or Anna Wyatt's, or the children by several fathers, or the child of the midnight couple, or the Andover children, without condemnation. The naturalization of the ongoing present meant that there was no invisible church to pollute with unworthies. His church was not an extension of God nor a part of the body of Christ in anything like a meta-physical sense. It was only and entirely the collection of people who try to treat others how Christ preached people ought. Anybody—*anybody*—who seeks to act virtuously is a member of that church and thus deserves baptism for his or her children.

This was no more an advocacy of moral relativism than it was of theological relativism. He was entirely convinced that his was the right understanding of moral behavior, and he did not suffer gladly those who acted differently, but he also understood that even good people make mistakes, errors that are impru-dent but not metaphysical, natural flaws which evoke in God more tenderness than spite. Bentley indeed thought Anna Wyatt guilty of "high passions," but high passions, while troublesome, did not pollute the supernatural realm.[20] Human frailty, though lamentable, should not prevent basically good people from joining his, and God's, family.

Statistics bear out the lure of Bentley's changes. Diman had baptized thirty infants per year, but Bentley averaged thirty-nine in his first few years as sole pastor, forty-nine annually between 1790 and 1794, and fifty-six annually be-tween 1795 and 1799.[21] In fact, he was baptizing more children in Salem than was any other minister, nearly two-thirds again as many as Barnard, five times as many as Prince, and three times as many as the minister at the Tabernacle, a factor not of size but rather of what Bentley knew to be the "difference of religious rules" among the churches.[22]

His new "religious rules" offered to parents who were unbaptized, to those who themselves sought baptism but were too ill to come to church, and to parents whose children were born out of wedlock a chance at the salvation available nowhere else. But one suspects an interesting disconnect in all this activity. It is doubtful that the parents who came to Bentley actually shared his naturalist view of baptism; likely the great majority *did* believe in a supernatural effect on their child. That Bentley did not believe in a supernatural consequence was of little importance. *They* believed it. They believed that something would happen to their child, and they knew that Bentley was willing to make it happen, even if he did not think it was in fact happening, when other ministers would not even try. The many men and women in Salem who met neither the spiritual requirements of the evangelicals nor the genteel expectations of the liberals knew to whom to turn. They knew whose was the door to knock on in the middle of that night when they most needed to feel the grace of God.

Whether it involved questions within his congregation or without, Christian naturalism was, as the 1780s progressed, coming to look, in the social sphere, more and more like libertarianism. This was not a willingness to look the other way at misbehavior; on the contrary, misbehavior as Bentley defined it remained the one available symbol of alienation from one's potential goodness. It was, rather, a willingness to refuse, beyond that examination of behavior, to sit in judgment of the quality of the soul.

In philosophical terms, Bentley had no other choice, since empiricism cannot allow a glimpse into the immaterial realm in which the soul rests. But he also did not want to judge for theological reasons. For his God does no judging either. His God is willing to let the laws that govern the moral universe play out in this life and then use the arenas of heaven and hell for the final accounting but otherwise takes no action to express his approval or disapproval in this realm. Nor, Bentley believed, should humans assume that role. Christian naturalism was an essential ingredient to Bentley's deep aversion to religious persecution. For supernaturalists who feel the need to please a God who might otherwise interfere in anger, there can be no room for mistakes, ideational or otherwise; acceptance of error is itself intolerable. If God wants something a certain way, then that is the right way and all other ways are the wrong way. And a God with the ability to act in this world will indeed do so in accordance with whether he is getting his way. So believers in ongoing supernaturalism were necessarily left trying to figure out just what God wants and who God likes, and then, once convinced they were right, had no choice but to abjure the guess of others.

Supernaturalists' simultaneous assumption that other, demonic, beings also enter this realm to detract and tempt only sharpened their obligations to act as God's lookout. Bentley would know, for he had moved to the town still best known for persecution of supposed supernaturalism, and the legacy of the witch trials even a century later lay heavily upon him.[23] Bentley had a general disdain for New England's early clerics—the Pilgrims, he once preached, were "injured in their minds," and of the Puritans in Massachusetts Bay, he said, "There was nothing in their religion itself to recommend it, unless to murder the innocent and distress weak consciences are recommendations"[24]—but he saved his harshest words for their roles in the witch trials. In one particular Thanksgiving day sermon, he rose to lofty, almost eloquent heights of criticism: "Rather let me boast to have been a follower of the immortal Penn in an attempt to improve human happiness," he sounded,

> than an ungovernable subject of as worthy a Winthrop, to abound in
> religious austerities and proclaim war with every innocent opinion
> and even the invisible world of imaginary beings. Sleep in eternal
> silence ye sons of that golden age, and let your fortitude only remain
> in the memory of your posterity. We have reason to glorify God that
> age is over and gone![25]

As he saw it, the Puritans' wars with "innocent opinion" and their wars against "imaginary beings" came from the same rotten source of imagined supernaturalism.

But Christian naturalism would sweep all this away. God's punishments—through natural law in this realm and the afterlife elsewhere—are real, Bentley was sure, but they are also God's alone to wield. What underlay moral condemnation of all kinds was the condemners' conviction that they knew what God wants and were acting to help him get it, but Bentley's God does not "want" in that sense and does not threaten vengeance anyway. His God does not welcome human cruelty in his name. In following through on the ideological implications of Christian naturalism, William Bentley was trying to liberate his people not only from the judgment of God but also from the judgment of other Christians.

On this score as in nearly every other, Bentley had placed himself into a category occupied by nobody else. His libertarianism was, and uniquely so, a theological rationalist libertarianism. Each adjective draws an essential distinction. His libertarianism was theological, not deistical: it was not like that of men such as Thomas Jefferson, who was just then in Virginia arguing for religious freedom but on the grounds of the abstract rights of citizens rather than Bentley's necessary steps in an unfolding history of Christocentric redemption. And his libertarianism was rationalist, not experiential: it was not like that of the Baptists, whose understanding of faith required ongoing supernaturalism in the life of every individual and made them quick to exclude those who had not yet felt it. Nobody else believed exactly as he did or acted on those thoughts in as public and radical a manner.

Meanwhile, he was, in the 1780s, also the classical liberal described in chapter 2, as committed to the need for physical freedom in property as to the need for spiritual freedom of worship described here. The decade of the 1780s allowed that kind of split personality, even when—indeed, particularly when—the two sides remained in real but unstated tension. The 1780s was the decade of factions, even factions within one person's own soul. But the luxury of faction would not last much longer, and the 1790s will pull all cross-cuttings into two mutually exclusive parties. Most of his classically liberal peers will slide easily into the emerging Federalist Party, the party busily adopting Burkean traditionalism and Hamiltonian finance in equal measure. Meanwhile, other spiritual libertarians were on their way toward the Jeffersonian opposition. Bentley, being both liberal and libertarian, had a more difficult road ahead. In the 1780s he could be both; in the next decade, he could not. The coming partisanship would not allow straddlers of lines.

5

Republicanism Emergent

Through the 1780s, William Bentley balanced two different ideologies, classical liberalism and libertarianism, that pointed in two different directions and asked of him and his listeners two different
things but were not yet actually in conflict. The former applied to the
realm of social and economic life and the latter to spiritual concerns, and in the 1780s these arenas did not much overlap. But in the
1790s they would, and he would end up challenging and then rejecting his own classical liberalism and in so doing turn his libertarianism into republican oppositionalism.

The story of his turn away from classical liberalism begins,
however, in 1785, with the arrival in Salem of William Hazlitt. Father
of the more famous literary critic of the same name, Hazlitt was an
ordained Irish Presbyterian traveling through America in search of
a pastorate. But he was not like most Presbyterians. In England, he
had been part of the circle of rationalist Christians who revolved
around the figure of Joseph Priestley. Best known for his discovery of
oxygen, Priestley was a minister as well as a natural philosopher, and
one who had deduced that the materialism of the soul rendered impossible the preexistence of Christ. So he had declared the Trinity
a Platonic corruption and announced his belief in the humanity of
Christ, or what he called "Unitarianism." The term meant the same
thing as Socinianism, but its prefix, particularly when set against
the "Trini-" of "Trinitarianism," made it a clearer expression of the
singularity of God. In 1774, his friend Theophilus Lindsey began

presiding over Unitarian services in London, and in 1778, Lindsey's Essex Street Chapel—the first Unitarian church in England—opened its doors. The movement had its internal varieties, to be sure. Some of the participants, such as Priestley, Joshua Toulmin, and Hazlitt, were already-dissenting Presbyterians, and some, including Lindsey, John Jebb, and John Disney, were Anglicans who resigned their preferments. A few, among them Richard Price, were Arians rather than Socinians. And not everyone shared Priestley's metaphysics. But all were committed to candor, freedom of conscience, and the truth and necessity of a rational—and for the most part Unitarian—Christianity.[1]

Hazlitt had been only a marginal member of the circle—he contributed an article or two to Priestley's *Theological Repository* under the name "Rationalis" and authored two modest works of his own—but it was he who became its apostle.[2] With the war over, confident that America would embrace him and hopeful that its professed religious liberty would protect him, he took it upon himself to convert the new nation.

He in fact converted practically no one. The orthodox clergy not only did not abandon their Trinitarianism but actively resisted him. At least two did in memorable episodes that suggest the kind of dynamics that followed Hazlitt on his travels. Up in Newburyport, John Murray in the Presbyterian church informed someone that Hazlitt was a deist. Word got back, and Hazlitt responded with a ferocious letter harping on rumors that Murray had forged his ministerial credentials and ending with this advice:

> Those who have forfeited all pretentions to character should learn a
> little modesty. I have nothing to do with your stupid Calvinism, or
> with your anti-scriptural Scotch Church. Attend more to yourself, and
> leave the friends of truth to their own enquiries. I can say more if
> you chuse to provoke me. At present I have only time to say that I
> despise all self-important malicious intermeddlers.[3]

That little exchange had occurred during Hazlitt's journey up to Maine, where he was going to try out for a pulpit in Hallowell and where he ran into a second antagonist, of all people Nathaniel Whitaker, the combative ex-minister of Salem's evangelical Tabernacle Church, who was at that time occupying a pulpit in nearby Canaan. Whitaker had been dismissed from the Tabernacle only the year before, and though the causes were not made public, rumors had spread, and Hazlitt apparently had heard them. So when Whitaker tried to block Hazlitt's call to the Hallowell church, Hazlitt opened fire. "I caution you," he began his note,

in future to meddle less than you have done with the characters of
those who are wiser and better than yourself. You have called
Dr. Priestley an infamous fellow and have classed him with the Devil
as his compeer. Upon what foundation have you done this? Had
Dr. Priestley ever been known to be a frequenter of stews? Has he
been known to have debauched the young women of his congregation under the pretence of converting them? Was he ever chargeable
with a single fraud, or a single lie? Can you insinuate a single circumstance against him, unless that he has more learning and real
religion than ten thousand Whitakers?[4]

It was perhaps inevitable that arguably the two most abrasive men in New
England would cross paths like this, but the nastiness of their crossing was
nonetheless remarkable. Then again, insofar as the accusations of debauchery
are concerned, Hazlitt may have been on to something.[5]

But the Arian liberals were hardly more approving of Hazlitt than were
the Trinitarian evangelicals. His tactlessness could not have helped, and surely
it was at least part of the reason for his being turned down for the presidency of
Dickinson College, being ignored by potential lecture audiences in Philadelphia, and being rejected by Boston's Brattle Street congregation, which was
then looking for someone to succeed Samuel Cooper.[6] He would never get a
call, explained Mary Cranch to her sister Abigail Adams in France, "unless he
will be more prudent (I call it) he says tis cunning."[7] He was "the most con-
ceited and most impudent" man John Eliot knew, and Jeremy Belknap had
never met anyone "whose company was so disgusting."[8] Even among a contentious and feuding ministry, "Paddy Whack"—as Eliot took to calling him
in private—outdid them all. But at least one of his Philadelphia contemporaries was more concerned about Hazlitt's preaching than his personality and
took "no pleasure in the company of a man who wishes to deprive me of
my only foundation of hope for eternity." This acquaintance, writing to Jeremy
Belknap, fairly gushed with the scandalous news. "I have been informed,
and that by his friends, that he is a *Socinian*."[9] Salem's liberals were likewise
keeping themselves at a distance. Both Barnard and Prince had allowed
Hazlitt to preach in their pulpits, but in neither had things gone well: at
the North, he tried out his Socinianism "much to the surprise of his hearers,"
and at the First he was received just as coolly.[10] He was not invited back to
either one.

One can get a sense of the widespread resistance to the new Socinianism
by the sudden appearance around 1785 of discussions about Christology. When

John Cleaveland Jr. was ordained that year, for example, he made a confession of faith that included believing that

> in God there are three personal subsistences, the Father, the Son and the Holy Ghost; that the Father is God, the Son is God, and the Holy Ghost is God; that there is one God in three person, and three persons in one God; and that the three persons are distinguished by their personal properties, and the part each one performs in the affair of redemption.[11]

This arch-Trinitarianism would have been rhetorical overkill had there not been Christians in the area who were claiming otherwise. Arians were even more insistent to elucidate just how they and Hazlitt differed, and it was not coincidental that it was in 1785 that Harvard's president and Cambridge's pastor went into print with the clear declarations of Christ being God's "only begotten son" and having "assumed the nature" of humans. Their normal preference for vague references to Christ's "commission" would not suffice when there was a new reasoned option afoot.

But Bentley had liked Hazlitt. By the summer of 1785 Hazlitt was trying his luck in Boston and also making occasional jaunts up to Salem, where Bentley welcomed him to the East Church pulpit over and again and even shared meals and stagecoach rides to Newbury.[12] Though Hazlitt would, not long after, return to England without ever having been offered a job, in William Bentley he had found a convert.

All of Bentley's Socinianism discussed in chapter 3 emerged full-blown only with Hazlitt's arrival in 1785. For the first fifteen months or so of his ministry, Bentley had actually been an Arian. He told his auditors during his probationary period that Christ had "left the mansions of peace to complete a work," a phrase intended to convey preexistence, if not coeternality, and then again, in the sermon preceding Christmas that year, reminded them that the birth they were about to celebrate was one of an individual "constituted between God and man," a figure "of man and of the Spirit."[13] He moved away from Arianism in 1784, arguing in the summer that "our enquiry extends no further than the proof that he was sent of God," meaning that empiricism did not allow any knowledge about Jesus other than what the miracles and Resurrection proved, which is that he was on a divine commission. And in the fall, in a sermon he called "Unity of God," he argued that the worship of Jesus was in fact idolatrous because God alone deserves the praise.[14] But even so, he seemed uncertain, hesitant, wishing to bring Christology to the same bar of reason that he had brought the rest of his theology but not yet sure whether or how to do so. It was Hazlitt who gave him that confidence, and in abundance, and Bentley began without reservation to strip away the divine trappings of the Trinitarian Jesus, denying first internal typologies, then the Trinity, the miraculous conception, and finally the possibility of an ontologically real present-day Christ.[15]

Hazlitt gave Bentley not only the confidence to develop his nascent Socinianism but also the intellectual community he had sought his whole life. Here was the chance for virtual camaraderie with a group of respectable English scientists and philosophers who thought much as he did; that Bentley had never met them and might never do so and that he was a part of their club only through their least liked and most peripheral figure meant little. Here was an intellectual home, his first. Bentley's identification with them was quick and complete.

And so he joined them in their efforts to spread the word, complete with its rational epistemology, its naturalist ontology, and, most explicitly, its Socinian Jesus. While Hazlitt was still in America, Bentley distributed works simply handed to him by his new friend, including a half-dozen copies of some of Priestley's Unitarian tracts that Hazlitt had edited and reprinted while in Philadelphia and a dozen of one of Hazlitt's own American sermons.[16] And once back in England, Hazlitt sent pamphlets across the ocean for Bentley to distribute. Unitarianism in printed form left England, entered America at Boston and then continued up to Salem and beyond.

The Boston connection was a crucial one. If Hazlitt converted anyone in addition to Bentley, it was James Freeman. Freeman was a classmate of Bentley's at Harvard who in 1782 had been chosen reader of Boston's King's Chapel when it reopened for services after the war. Encouraged by Hazlitt, Freeman persuaded members to allow him to modify the Book of Prayer along anti-Trinitarian lines.[17] The American Episcopal Church was not yet organized, so Freeman without ecclesiastical interference could omit from the liturgy all references to the Trinity, and in June of 1785, when the revision was adopted, King's Chapel became the first church in America with an officially Unitarian doctrine. When local bishops refused to officiate over his ordination in 1787, the laity ordained Freeman themselves. (As a Congregationalist, Bentley had no liturgy to revise, but he was preaching Unitarianism before or at the same time that Freeman was modifying his liturgy, and so arguably the East Church ought to share with King's Chapel the distinction of being considered the first Unitarian church in America.)[18]

Together Bentley and Freeman maintained a system of disseminating Unitarianism by print. Multiple copies of Unitarian tracts and sermons were sent by Theophilus Lindsey from Joseph Johnson's printing office in London to Freeman in Boston, then forwarded to Bentley in Salem where they were lent out or given away, sometimes to recipients who would pass them on yet again.[19] By 1787, Freeman could report to Hazlitt that they had circulated "great numbers" of tracts, particularly Priestley's *Appeal to the Serious and Candid Professors of Christianity* and *General View of the Arguments for the Unity of God*, and they could, Bentley wrote, "find room for many more."[20] So they kept at it, spreading copies of these and other works arriving from England. It was an efficient system, and in some cases the tracts were in Salem a month or two after publication. A 1788 reprint of Nathaniel Lardner's *A Letter written in the year 1730, concerning the question, whether the Logos supplied the place of an human soul in the person of Jesus Christ*—the work that had converted Priestley in his youth—was soon in Salem, as were 1790 editions of *The Vindication of Speaking Openly* and *Scripture Idea of Heresy*.[21]

Bentley's catechism and hymnal need to be seen as part of this print network, too. The hymnal was modified from a rationalist English one, and although Bentley had once seemed willing to settle for a Watts catechism, or "even John Cotton's," when he finally produced one of his own, it was based on one by Priestley.[22] He published it in 1785, soon after Hazlitt's visit, presumably shaped from a copy of Priestley's brought by the new arrival. The fact that the catechism was soon into its third printing and the hymnal into its fifth suggests that Bentley was distributing copies of both well beyond his own congregation.[23]

They were as eager to spread their version of Christianity as evangelicals were to spread theirs. "Whatever exertions the Orthodox may make," Freeman wrote to Hazlitt, "I am resolved not to be behind them in zeal. The ample supply of books with which Mr. Lindsey furnishes me, enables me to propagate Unitarian as rapidly as they can Trinitarian sentiments. I endeavour to diffuse these pieces as widely as possible, and I communicate them in particular to our young ministers."[24] In fact, this *was* a form of evangelizing. They, like others who proselytized a different version of Christianity, felt called to spread their understanding of the faith. The time had come, they believed, for only in their eighteenth century was humanity prepared to listen. Only now were people ready to see the inherent natural wisdom of Jesus' message without requiring the divinity of Jesus himself. The gift of the Enlightenment, as far as Bentley was concerned, was that it had readied humanity to reason themselves to knowing God's will, as God had preferred they do all along. The desire to proselytize shaped the very materiality of the works. Liberal books were generally lengthy ones—Charles Chauncy's *Benevolence of the Deity*, for example, coming in at 293 pages, his *Five Dissertations on the Scripture Account of the Fall and its Consequences* at 310, and his *Salvation of all Men* at 406—but Hazlitt's Philadelphia edition of Priestley's *Appeal to the Serious and Candid Professors of*

Christianity, even with the addenda, was all of 57 pages long. Bentley's cate-chism, meanwhile, was shorter than the already-short one by Priestley—an "Extract," of Priestley's, Bentley called it, intentionally so for the sake of dis-persal.[25] These were works meant to be easily and inexpensively reprinted, transported, and distributed, all en masse. As Bentley told his congregants on the day he circulated Hazlitt's American sermon, the new reformation would work only "by making information cheap and easy to the common people."[26]

Moderate liberal Christians were hardly opposed to the idea of printed works arguing a point. On the contrary, moderate liberal Christianity was articulated in a battery of published treatises and exegeses published throughout the cen-tury. Creating that corpus was largely an English endeavor, Chauncy's three aforementioned works aside, but American liberals were no less apprecia-tive than were their peers in England, and those in Salem created a library in large measure just for these works. The Social Library, begun in the early 1760s, was ostensibly public, but the fees were set high enough that mem-bership was restricted to only the wealthiest residents. The town's ministers were allowed in by default, but most of its few score members were the mer-cantile and professional elites of the liberal First and, later, North Churches.[27] The catalog was practically a syllabus of their moderate liberal Christianity. The major latitudinarians, John Tillotson and Samuel Clarke in particular, were available, although the minor figures—William Chillingworth, Edward Stil-lingfleet, Arthur Ashley Sykes, and Robert South—were not. The deists were absent, except for William Wollaston's *Religion of Nature Delineated*, which no one seems to have checked out very often; more popular were the scientific apologetics such as William Whiston's *New Theory of the Earth*. The liberals writing from the 1720s forward were well represented and much appreciated: Benjamin Hoadly on the sacraments was checked out often, as were William Sherlock on prophecy and William Warburton on grace. John Leland's *View of the Deistical Writers* was available, as was Jeremy Taylor's popular *Scripture Doctrine of Original Sin* and *Paraphrase with Notes on the Epistle to the Romans*. Salem's elites, it seems, took their reading seriously. Maybe this is what Boston minister John Eliot, who knew a member or two of the gentility himself, meant when he wrote of the First Church that "more literary characters were mem-bers of this church than of any in the province."[28] To be certain, not all of their selections were religious—they enjoyed their Alexander Pope and Jonathan Swift and Samuel Richardson, too—but few works were as popular as the defenses of liberal Christianity, and many members returned again and again to check out Jeremy Taylor's *Scripture-Doctrine* or Joseph Butler's *Analogy* or Clarke's sermons volume by volume.[29]

But the writings that Bentley was distributing were different from those writings in practically every regard. The central theological ideas were of course different, Socinianism rather than Arianism, but they were *ideologically* different as well. The new writings had an explicit agenda that the older works did not. They called readers to be bold in their quest for religious knowledge—"Inquire further," Priestley urged "Dare to avow the truth"—and to leave their old congregations once they found it.[30] John Disney had written both *Friendly Dialogue Between a Common Unitarian Christian and a Athanasian*, which Hazlitt gave to Bentley to distribute, and *Exhortation to Christian People to Refrain from Trinitarian Worship*, which Bentley would later receive from England, to persuade Anglicans to abandon their churches for Unitarian chapels, and if Bentley's recipients were New England Congregationalists rather than English Anglicans, the objective was the same.[31] None of the liberal writings that filled the Social Library had agitated for separation. None of those writings had agitated for anything. They were anti-Calvinist, to be sure, but not antiauthoritarian. Their authors thought reason ought to be used to solidify, not undermine, the establishment. The American readers agreed: neither Chauncy nor Cooper nor Mayhew nor any of the irenic Dudleian lecturers had ever directed readers—as Hazlitt did in his introduction to the Philadelphia reprint—to "publickly protest" against doctrinal corruptions, much less to separate themselves from their congregations. But the Rational Dissenters in England were doing so, and Bentley now was as well. He told his congregation as much on the day he handed out copies of Hazlitt's first American publication. He needed them, he said, to come together "with Christian boldness" in the fight against superstition in all its forms, including the lingering beliefs among other liberals in a semidivine Jesus. "Our zeal," he explained, "must be steady and unabated."[32] Social activism was still anathema, but intellectual activism was the order of the day.

But when Priestley urged readers to "inquire further," he was speaking less to the orthodox than to those liberals who, he thought, had already begun to use their reason but had stopped too soon. And in spreading such works, Bentley too was challenging—and for him the first time—the Christian liberal clergy of which he was in so many ways a part. To question the intellectual authority of Christian liberals was to strike at the very foundation of their self-styled superiority. For all of the liberals' talk of the universality of reason, they by no means considered everyone equally capable of having it. What is most striking about the liberal ministers' private correspondence over Charles Chauncy's universalist manuscript, for example, was their concerns about how poorly Chauncy's arguments would be understood by the masses. Chauncy's colleague John Eliot insisted that the public was not ready for the work, regardless of— no, because of—its brilliance. "It will not do to publish it at once," he wrote to

Jeremy Belknap, "if proper to expose it at all. It is too sublime for the soaring of vulgar imaginations, and would dazzle, if not blind, the eyes of the populace." Most people's minds, Eliot wrote, "are not ripe enough" for a study which "requires too much erudition to understand."[33]

So while liberal ministers wanted and expected intellectual deference by the people around them, here was Bentley, a liberal himself, advocating nothing less than a complete rejection of *any* authority not founded on reason. This was an insistence on the necessity—the duty, even—of each individual to judge for himself or herself what was true among competing claims, utterly without regard to the station—be it economic, social, political, ecclesiastical, or educational—of the claimant. The desire for individual interpretations of Scripture was as old as the Reformation, but here in Bentley's preaching and Hazlitt's writing was a palpable new level of defiance. They had a new motif, too, or proof text of sorts, in the biblical verse "search the scriptures." The phrase appears in the Bible most notably in the context of the Bereans, a New Testament community that had listened to Paul's message, considered what they themselves knew to be in the Scriptures, and then drawn their own conclusions. They were free and autonomous reasoners bound neither by creeds nor by councils, which for Bentley and Hazlitt made them the model congregation. In fact, Hazlitt so admired the Bereans that he worked their name into the pseudonym he used for his second American discourse. The topic, not surprisingly, was the attributes of Christ, and Hazlitt wrote it as "Bereanus Theosebes." "Theosebes" is a transliteration of the Greek word θεοσεβής, which in John 9:31 meant pious or God-worshiping, and "Bereanus" linked the discourse's inquiring spirit to the virtues of his favorite biblical people.[34] Bentley shared Hazlitt's appreciation and soon made it a frequent theme in his sermons, improving, for example, on Paul and Silas's visit to Berea in Acts 17:11 and on John 5:39 ("Search the scriptures for in them ye think ye have eternal life, and they are they, which testify of me").[35]

Distributing such pamphlets was no light matter, and there was an unmistakable element of subversion attached to the effort. When Bentley wrote to Freeman in 1788 thanking him for sending along more of Priestley's writings, he added that he was particularly grateful because in Salem, "books of a certain description, no person either purchases or circulates."[36] And indeed no person did. There were as yet no American imprints of these books; in fact, Bentley and Freeman's editions of Priestley's catechism were the only American printings of *any* of Priestley's religious writings in the decade after 1784.[37] Nor were these works made part of Salem's Social Library, for although members time and again checked out sermons by Clarke, Sherlock, Tillotson, and other latitudinarians, nobody donated—and the library did not purchase—any of the publications that Bentley was offering.[38] Nor were they likely to be found in the dry-good stores, since although merchants brought back an occasional work at Bentley's request—Russian dictionaries from St. Petersburg and Swedish dictionaries from Gothenburg—in general, Salem merchants did not deal in the wholesale book trade.[39] No bookstore existed in Salem until 1789, when John Dabney opened a small shop, and although he advertised "Priestley on Electricity" among his 160 titles, he had none of the books that Bentley had been distributing. It was not until 1794 that Dabney offered any of Priestley's religious works, and even then he offered nothing by Toulmin, Disney, Lardner, or the other English Unitarians whose works passed through Bentley's hands.[40]

Apparently, nobody else in a position to give or sell printed materials wanted to be associated with these particular ones. For this was a world in which the providers of print could be blamed for the ideas therein, as Bentley himself had come to learn. Though not a deist, he did own copies of deist books, and he was willing to lend them out to friends. He did so twice in 1787, and each time it came to a bad end. On one occasion he lent a copy of Matthew Tindal's *Christianity as Old as the Creation* to Captain Joseph White "under the solemn promise of a private examination," as his diary has it. White put it "under a pillow" where it was discovered by a woman, "lent to an aunt, read before her husband, and by him reported to Col. Carlton." The book finally made its way back to Bentley, where it was "hidden." The second episode, which involved a copy of Ethan Allen's *Reason the Only Oracle of Man*, was even more dramatic. Bentley lent it to Carlton "under solemn promise of secrecy," but Carlton then lent it to Joshua Grafton, who also hid it but died before it could be returned. Sometime after his death, the book was found in his room and "examined with horror by his female relations." They then passed it along to a Mr. Williams "whose shop is remarkable for news," and it was there viewed "as an awful curiosity by hundreds." The awfulness stemmed from the fact that Grafton had died a "confirmed infidel," and now the crowd had found the cause. And they knew who to blame, for there, in the book, were inscribed the initials "W. B." All of this was made worse by the fact that Grafton, just before dying several weeks earlier, had requested that Bentley visit to say last prayers and to be witness to the soundness of his mind. Bentley had gone to his house with a committee of other witnesses and, after being slowed on the ground floor by five women giving off a "most horrible wailing," had proceeded with the others up to Grafton's room. The interview was chaotic—the soundness of Grafton's mind being not at all certain—and soon everyone left "in the greatest confusion [and] insulted by the women." These women—the ones who had wailed at the door and insulted the committee and who would examine the book and then take it to the shop for public display—apparently also spread the word that Bentley's prayers had "encouraged infidelity" in Grafton's "dying hour," so that the up-shot of the entire episode was, as Bentley himself wrote, "a terrible opposition to me fixed in the minds of the devout and ignorant multitude."[41] No wonder that nobody else openly circulated "books of a certain description," but Bentley continued to do so even with the ongoing threats of social hostilities.

Bentley had good reason to be circumspect, historically speaking. The long history of anti-Trinitarianism is matched by an equally long history of reactionary persecution. Fifth-century councils, after all, declared anti-Trinitarianism to be heretical, and it is not accidental that the Spanish In-quisition was pointed most directly at Jews and Muslims, who differed from Christians precisely over the attributes of Christ. Protestants had been no more accepting of the idea. In the middle of the sixteenth century, the anti-Trinitarian Michael Servetus was tried and executed in Calvin's Geneva, and in the seventeenth century in England, Unitarians had been specifically excluded from the Act of Toleration. If prosecutions in the eighteenth century were rare, they were not unknown. Thomas Emlyn, for example, had been convicted of blasphemy in 1703, and Edward Elwall, whose trial in 1726 was the subject of the pamphlet Hazlitt attached to Priestley's, had been acquitted only be-cause of a neighbor's testimony to his general moral character.

Bentley was never particularly vulnerable to formal persecution, but that is not to say that he did not receive *unofficial* condemnation. Barnard and Prince certainly disapproved. They were "alarmed" at Bentley's criticisms of the Trinity, Freeman reported back to Hazlitt, and wished him "to desist."[42] Hints of criticisms from other quarters appear from time to time in Bentley's sermons. In 1786, for example, he discoursed on Paul's heresy trial before the Roman governor, and Bentley's defense of Paul—that he had preached suffi-cient Christianity when he preached that Christ's message was of eternal life, proven by the Resurrection—was clearly a defense of himself as well.[43] "I have found the force of prejudices in many instances," he confessed frankly the next year without elaboration, "and [am] every day seeing it more and more."[44] He surely was finding it from his own landlady, whose derision forced him finally to rent a room in another boarding house, and from his own evangelically in-clined father, who called Bentley's new hymnal a collection of "mutilations."[45] And he felt it from Newburyport's printer who refused to print his first effort at publication—a doctrinal sermon given at Freeman's King's Chapel—on the grounds that it was, Bentley reported, "not to be Gospel."[46]

Such resistance from the orthodox masses was hardly unexpected. But re-sistance from Barnard and Prince pointed toward something new. Bentley now had arrayed himself against the liberals as well as against the orthodox. He had created a third faction, his own, within late-eighteenth-century Congregationalist theology. And as the 1780s turned into the 1790s, it was the hostility he faced from other liberals, not the hostility he faced from Calvinists, that shaped the contours of his thought.

Between 1785 and 1791, the disagreement between Bentley and the other liberals was one restricted to the domain of theology. But after 1791, it entered the domain of politics as well. By the summer of 1791, the French Revolution was two years along, and its radicalizing course was dividing the Anglo-American world no less surely than it had France. The Rational Dissenters' support for natural rights, for government only by consent, and for resistance to authority in the absence of that consent—views expounded most clearly in Priestley's *Essay on the First Principles of Government* and demonstrated by their sympathy for the American colonies abroad and for repeal of discriminatory legislation at home—made them enthusiastic backers of what was going on across the Channel, but conservatives were less supportive. Richard Price, second only to Priestley among the Rational Dissenters, had spoken for the rest in his famous *Discourse on the Love of Our Country*, an oration delivered in November of 1789. That oration, among other things, led Edmund Burke to write *Reflections on the Revolution in France*, published in 1790, which in turn prompted Thomas Paine to write the *Rights of Man*, the first part of which came out in 1791. By 1791, that is, English Unitarianism, long associated with heresy, had become, in the eyes of conservatives, politically dangerous as well. And they were able to convince others of this as well, enough in Birmingham alone to constitute a mob which, in August of that year, destroyed Joseph Priestley's home, library, and laboratory.

Bentley was anguished by the news. He committed his eighth-anniversary sermon to the subject. Hearing about what had happened was the turning point in his ministry; indeed, it changed his very understanding of what a minister is supposed to do. Not because he feared a similar fate, though he certainly knew resistance and suspicion, but because of the unique quality of what had happened. Bentley's problem with Birmingham was not so much that a mob had destroyed Priestley's property as that the liberal elites had encouraged it to do so.

The key to understanding the sudden power of Bentley's turn was his feeling that the other liberal ministers had betrayed reason, their commitments to truth, and, not least, him. Going into 1791, he had thought that liberals were intellectually superior to the masses. After all, he *had* been a liberal. Bentley possessed in spades the intellectual snobbery of the liberals, comments reflecting which he was forced on more than one occasion to defend.[47] His sermons were more akin to an essay than to the "plain preaching" that at least one listener wanted. Diman's sermons had included numbered headings and subheadings to mark the shifts between text, doctrine, and application, but Bentley's style was more fluid, keeping the three elements but within a smooth prose format without markers, and when asked to switch to Diman's style, he refused.[48] The good minister, he told his listeners, "should prefer to go above the capacity of his hearers rather than below them. Nothing brings more contempt upon him than to be mean and groveling."[49] Diman was still senior minister and still sitting up there with Bentley, and no doubt this was aimed at him, if Diman was continuing to repeat what he had told Bentley in his Charge, that "a minister should take care not to soar above the capacity of his hearers; but should condescend to men of low degree."[50] Bentley, though, would have the men of low degree come up to his level. He did not care that his sermons did not reach down to the uneducated, that he could not say with Samson Occum that the "common people . . . can't help understanding my talk. It is common, plain, everyday talk. Little children may understand me. And poor Negroes may plainly and fully understand my meaning."[51] Other ministers intended their sermons to enrich listeners' piety, not their vocabulary, but for Bentley, plain preaching "attracted the vulgar" and "disgusted more civil people."[52]

But all of this was to say that he also expected liberals—including himself—to take seriously the responsibility that comes with intellectual superiority. He did not think that the "devout and ignorant multitude" who had blamed him for Grafton's deistical death could enlighten themselves; they needed to be *led* to enlightenment, and liberals, he always thought, had an obligation to do the leading. "As all little sects begin with the lowest and weakest minds," he told his church when handing out Hazlitt's pamphlet, "it obliges the attention of the more wise of men to the condition and depravity of the weak. . . They who are entrusted with the means of promoting truth should pay a great regard to the most indigent of mankind."[53] Proper stewardship of the souls of the masses was at stake. Insofar as the other liberals had made the leap from Calvinism to Arminianism, from supernaturalism to latitudinarianism, and from Trinitarianism to Arianism, and were willing to articulate and defend each in public, they were being good stewards. But the leap from Arianism to Socinianism was the final step, and one they were refusing to make. And now, as of 1791, they were proving themselves willing to try to stop those who had. Most egregious of all, liberals were letting the orthodox do their dirty work for them. Whereas liberals should have been enlightening the demos, they were using them instead. It began to dawn on Bentley that human happiness will more likely be blocked not by the superstitious masses themselves but by the liberal ministers who kept them bound in their superstition. His dream—spreading the wisdom of natural Christian morality—had not changed, but after 1791 he was convinced that it was the liberal elites on top, not the impassioned people below, who were the most formidable obstacle to its fulfillment.

PART II

1791–1805

6

Economic Republicanism

The news of the Birmingham riots had been the first time that Bentley had reason to suspect the ideological agenda of liberal Christianity. The liberal clergy of Massachusetts had had nothing to do with Birmingham, of course, but they had proved no more willing than their liberal peers in England to take what Bentley saw as the next, final, and necessary step toward rational liberation. Indeed their attempts to block even Bentley's efforts to help others take that step had convinced the Christian naturalist and Socinian that the hope he had placed in the cosmopolitan enlightened liberals around him—the men he had been emulating in so many ways—was hope misplaced. The next few years after 1791 would shake his faith in the wisdom of *secular* liberals as well.

Though Salem's mercantile elites had celebrated the French Revolution in the first few years after 1789, they began to fall away even before other Americans.[1] Most Americans who would end up retracting their support for France did so in the spring of 1793 when news arrived of the execution of Louis XVI and the republic's declaration of war against England, but Salem's merchants had beaten them to it by nearly a year. Their doubts had begun to emerge as early as the summer of 1792 with the news of France's war with Austria. "The first military efforts of the French Revolutionists appear to have fallen infinitely below their civic declamations," the *Gazette* editorialized in what was likely a reference to the death of General Theobald

Dillon at the hands of his own troops after the debacle at Pas de Baisieux. "Their insubordination, and hacking their officers to pieces, will not do, will not do, will not do—whatever they may chant to the contrary in their famous revolutionary song."[2] Nor was that the end of the drift. In October the newspaper warned voters that the goal of the "seditious, undermining faction" behind Jefferson's presidential campaign was "probably like that of his much admired French Revolution—to level all distinctions of order and authority, and even of property and life." By January of 1793, while civic celebrations marking the founding of France's constitutional republic continued across the country, not least a few miles away in Boston, the *Gazette* was tilting toward reaction at an ever-quickening pace.[3] The editor was willing to congratulate the French people on the "deadly blows which despotism has received" but was really more concerned about the "ebullitions of anarchy and party rage" that seemed more and more to characterize events. And when the spirit of *egalité* apparently brought disorder close to home, the paper's very fonts made clear their derision. "Last week," the paper reported, "*Citizen* Robert Flynn and *Citizen* Anthony Hart, devoted disciples of the fashionable doctrine of UNIVERSAL EQUALITY, were committed to the jail at Middlesex, for breaking open a store in Medford."[4] Louis's fate would only confirm what Salem's classical liberals had already come to see. The liberal conception that true happiness and freedom can come only through civil laws protecting property and through moral laws enjoining moderation and restraint was more persuasive than any single bit of news. And as the liberals went, so went their town. Salem never did have a civic celebration. It celebrated George Washington's birthday instead.

Bentley, however, continued to support the revolution in spite of the shifting sentiments around him. He still thought after 1793, as others did before then, that it was a necessary step toward greater human freedom. Looking back, it was an odd choice that the organizers of the Washington birthday celebration picked Bentley to give the keynote address. And surely they expected to hear a discourse on the manifest greatness of Washington and the principles of order and tradition which he embodied. And while Bentley's views in the 1780s, certainly his response to Shays's Rebellion, suggested he would provide just that, his private transformation since then pointed him in a different direction. Had the organizers known that he had recently begun to study the French language, thinking it would be "of great use or at least a great gratification on many occasions," or that just several months earlier, over at the East Church, Bentley had used his Thanksgiving sermon to defend the increasing violence of the French Revolution, they might well have withdrawn the invitation.[5] But apparently they did not know that, and no doubt it came as a most unwelcome surprise when in front of the gathered folk of Salem he lauded rather than admonished the French revolutionaries, even taking a moment of comparative history to justify the 1649 execution of England's Charles I as "opposite to the spirit of the government, but not to the Rights of Man."[6] Had Salem's leaders then known about the other regicide, of France's Louis XVI, they would have been even less pleased. But that news was still on its way across the Atlantic.

When the news did arrive, it confirmed the reactionary move of most classical liberals. The execution and the Reign of Terror that followed proved to their satisfaction that they, and other Burkean conservatives like them, were right: immoderation, especially an immoderation of liberty improperly understood, leads only to anarchy and chaos. William Bentley also was sorry that Louis had been executed. He wrote in his diary that it was "regretted most sincerely by all thinking people," and surely he counted himself one of them, for to favor the revolution was not necessarily to want to kill the king; even Paine, sitting in the National Assembly, had argued to spare his life. But its occurrence, Bentley also thought, was not sufficient reason to stop the revolution or to question its aims. The violence, though cause for regret, was justified. In fact, he said exactly that in the most remarkable passage from the manuscript of his diary that was omitted from the published version. "As Americans we regret the loss" of Louis's life, he wrote, but then added that "we remember that the liberties of mankind are dearer than any life whatever. Reprobate it, the measure, but admire the men."[7]

Bentley had broken another tie to classical liberalism. If liberals were content to continue to see liberty within law, after 1793 Bentley would see liberty as the separate and higher end. As he had told his whole congregation on the previous Thanksgiving, the "purchase of liberty is the most valuable, and it is better to deluge the earth with blood than to renounce it."[8]

Though real, Bentley's oppositionalism was as of yet drawing strength only from vague and theoretical notions about the rights of man, but events in 1794 would ground his new convictions in tangible and local experience. When the French revolutionaries declared war on England, neutral Americans—and Salemites foremost among them—were swept in anyway since American vessels, far from being immune to capture, were in fact vulnerable to capture by *both* sides, each trying to stop the nonbelligerent nations from trading with the other. In response, Congress, in the spring of 1794, passed a monthlong general embargo. Officially nonpartisan, it was in effect retaliatory against the more aggressive British rather than the French, and so in Salem, the public reaction fell out accordingly, with merchants opposing the measure and William Bentley giving it his full support.

The embargo was, as Birmingham had been three years earlier, a crucible of Bentley's ideological change, because opposing the embargo was the first time that merchants had acted in a way with which Bentley disagreed. Their decision awakened in Bentley a new sense of republicanism. Narrowly understood, republicanism was the conviction of the superiority of a republic over a monarchy, but, more broadly understood, it was the insistence that a republic requires above all else that its citizenry be willing to put aside their self-interest, usually understood to be economic, for the good of the commonwealth. This willingness, a trait often referred to as "civic virtue," was considered essential to the health of the republic, for its absence leads only to faction, strife, and, ultimately, the dissolution of the republic altogether. Thus it was with a new vocabulary that he described the responses to the embargo as a choice exactly between "honor or interest."[9] To accept the sacrifice of lost commerce was the choice of honor, in the strict sense of honoring the Franco-American Alliance of 1778 and in the more general sense of honoring the spirit of expanding human liberty. But to want to maintain the lucrative trade routes with England—to wish, that is, to profit at the expense of the French Republic even as that republic was fighting a war to expand human freedom—this was the latter choice, the choice of interest.

And it was a shock to discover that Salem's merchants picked self-interest. That he chose on one Sunday during the embargo to improve on Timothy 6:7 ("Charge them that are rich in this world, that they be not high-minded, nor trust in uncertain riches, but in the living God, who giveth us richly all things to enjoy") reflects the sharp turn in his attitude, for the willingness of merchants to seek profit over human happiness came as a rude awakening to this man who had bought so fully into the liberal conviction that wealth is a sign of superior morality. Riches, he preached during that sermon as if he had just discovered something new, "beget an interest easily separated by the possessor from the public good."[10] Classical liberalism, Bentley was learning, may well harden, rather than awaken, the heart to the promises of conscience.

To be clear, Bentley had never given merchants *full* reign to act on their acquisitiveness. Even in the 1780s he would, when the occasion called for it, remind them of obligations beyond profit, of laws beyond supply and demand. In 1787, for example, an Indian named Isaac Coombs was put to death in Salem for killing his wife. Bentley did not deliver the actual execution sermon, but he did address the event in his own church. He blamed the crime on vice, though in this case vice "wrought up into high habit." But murder was no ordinary crime, and even "high habit" would not explain what instead called for a searching analysis of root causes. Bentley found those causes in Coombs's anger, itself caused by his resentment at others' luxuries, which was itself caused by "politicians" who, in an effort to "humor vices," had "taught men that private vices were public benefits."[11] The reference was unmistakable. Bernard de Mandeville's well-known dictum "private vices, public benefits" was an extreme distillation of his argument that individual moral weaknesses are acceptable, desirable even, to the degree that they prompt employment and production to satisfy them. It was the great expression of a new subordination of morality to economics, and its appeal was broad among the merchant class, not least in Salem, where *Fable of the Bees*, Mandeville's articulation of the idea, was one of the most popular works available at the Social Library.[12] Bentley, though, would have none of it. To tolerate weaknesses among the lower sort was one thing, but to encourage it for monetary gain was something else; Mandeville had gone too far. But other classical liberals had not gone that far, and so outside such moments as when murder needed explanation, Bentley had been happy to see only the virtue inherent within and guaranteed by the rights to commerce. And that was what changed in 1794 when he saw for the first time that profit and what he considered virtue do not always go hand in hand.

Of course, Bentley's was only one side of the story. For their part, liberals did not think that they, in preferring trade over embargo, were choosing interest over commonwealth. Many were in the first place dubious of the supposed benefits to the American commonwealth of freezing commerce with England for the sake of what they considered to be a misguided nation and its dangerous delusions, especially given that the Alliance of 1778 had been signed with a government, namely Louis XVI's, that was no longer in place, indeed that was undone by the very revolution the embargo was aiding. But more generally, liberals argued as they had for decades that self-interest is itself good for the commonwealth. Merchants saw no contradiction between virtue and profit. Rather, the long liberal tradition saw virtue *in* profit, inasmuch as profit was the legitimate result of talents rightly applied. From the perspective of liberalism, liberalism itself—with its attendant convictions of the need for secure property and the moral rectitude of self-interested economics—was the best guarantee of the security of a republic. It alone ensured that citizens would be rightly held to the bar of proper morality; it alone had a built-in governor of human behavior. It was a powerful argument, and it had persuaded the William Bentley of the 1780s and early 1790s. But no longer. Not after 1794.

The embargo ran its course. Salem's merchants had abided by it, but they waited no longer than absolutely necessary before getting their cargo moving again. Ships were clearing the harbor the next morning. A changed man watched them sail. "How little integrity is to be seen," Bentley reported to himself. "Among them all not the best signs of public virtue." Even one of the hurriedly built privateers was quickly refitted and sent as a merchantman to the British islands. Bentley had learned the lessons, and the vocabulary, of republicanism. "Never," he fumed, "did interest discover its influence more forcibly."[13]

His new republicanism was not inherently and immediately sympathetic toward the impoverished, and certainly not toward what he continued to consider the undeserving poor, but his move to republicanism did make him conscious, and for the first time, of some of the problems facing the poor. True, even in the 1780s he had been aware of the insecurities of his lower-sort parishioners, and it was at least partially out of sympathy for these men and women that he allowed home baptism, since the carpenter who explained to Bentley that he had been skipping services because he owned neither hat nor shoes appropriate for it was not the only congregant in Salem to feel that way. For Bentley, who knew something about the nervousness of appearing in social settings with one's betters, it was exactly because "poverty may prevent the usual preparations" for baptizing that its mode should be, as he put it, "discretionary."[14] But such moments were episodic rather than systemic and were geared toward spiritual rather than economic ends. The sympathy was there, but the ideological foundation was not. Only in 1794 would he begin to see and care about the more tangible sufferings of the poor around him.

After all, it was the mariners, not the land-bound merchants, who were being plucked up at sea, imprisoned, or forced into the Royal Navy. Seamen had always faced the various risks of nautical work, but when the dangers came neither from nature nor from the usual course of things but instead from a political circumstance against which the merchants could protest but did not, the sailors and mates and captains had new grounds for discontent. For the first time, Bentley was awakened to suffering caused not by the vice of the sufferer but by choices—self-interested choices—made by others in positions of power. Just how startling his new republican populism must have been is made clear by one of the most astounding tidbits in his whole diary. Bentley noted on February 3, 1790, that he had walked that day along the wharves, "which I had never visited before since I had been in town."[15] As amazing as it sounds, this man, who lived in and served a waterfront neighborhood, not once had visited that waterfront during the first seven years of his ministry. He had visited a great number of homes and shared many a tea and a meal in shops, countinghouses, parlors, and dining rooms, but seven years went by before he condescended to go down to the waterfront itself, to see the sailors and laborers and artisans on their terms. To become a man of the people, for this man at least, was no small transformation. By March 1794, he was "deeply interested by a sympathy with the public" over the problems at sea, and he even recorded with apparent approval when a few months later the "people" of Salem celebrated French military victories with cannon fire from the wharves.[16] The man who had never visited the wharves had come to embrace the aspirations of the people who worked there.

His new identification with the nonelites surely was reinforced by his economic marginalization. Bentley was not poor, but neither was he rich. His salary was £160 per year—significantly less, for example, than the £250 that Barnard was receiving over at the North Church. He would continue to receive nothing from his father, who was still impoverished, and whatever inheritance he might have received from his maternal grandfather's estate disappeared when a conniving uncle talked the ailing miller into changing his will at the last moment.[17] Bentley's needs were few, but he did have room rent to pay and siblings to assist, which he did often and generously. Leftover funds went to the purchase of books, his one indulgence. So if he was being melodramatic when he wrote that he had merely "a pittance in my pocket to be called my own," it was only slightly so.[18]

And his ideological turn was likely hastened all the more by the continuing rejections he received from the liberals around him. The merchants of the town's western half by and large left him alone, preferring at tea and suppers the more refined company of Prince and Barnard.[19] He was invited to meet with the elite Monday Night Club immediately after his ordination, but only, it seems, that one time; Prince and Barnard continued to attend.[20] It was not simply that the elites would never accept a man of low birth: Prince, after all, was the son of an artisan as well. But Bentley was simply too different. Whether for reasons theological or personal, he was kept at arm's length from those with whom he had, intellectually, most in common. He took his hardest knocks from the younger generation of professionals who could respect in the Christian naturalist neither the prestige of the Arminian nor the piety of the evangelical. He once spent an evening with just such a group of leisured men, young doctors and lawyers all, who teased and taunted him. "Disgust soon succeeded to contempt," he wrote in his diary later that night, "expressions to emotions, and we parted early."[21] The sons of privilege against whom he had struggled as a tutor had now grown up, and they liked him no less in 1793 than they had a decade earlier. Nor did their fathers: Bentley's troublesome student John Pynchon was the son of William Pynchon, the host of the Monday Night Club.

Bentley's new political consciousness was real and truly political but it was also fundamentally theological. The particular aspect of theology was not, however, the familiar ones of mechanisms of individual salvation or the means of divine intervention or even the attributes of Christ. Rather, Bentley's new republicanism was grounded in his conception of the religious destiny of humanity itself.

His understanding of the chronology of human existence was derived from the Bible, which describes time as both linear and finite, a discrete path running from Creation to the Endtime, all tucked into an a-linear, infinite metaphysics. The Bible includes accountings of both ends of that line, in Genesis and in Revelation, respectively, believers in which, including Bentley, necessarily saw themselves living within it, for the biblical narration of human time suggests that humans live not on the forward edge of all time facing an infinite unfolding future but instead on the forward edge of experienced time facing the finite and shrinking gap that precedes the true end of linear existence. There is much to ponder about this. Generations before Bentley's wondered about the ontological difficulties of creation ex nihilo, and generations subsequent to his would wonder about the difficulties of geological and biological creation in only six days, but neither of these was the main concern of eighteenth-century Anglo-Americans. In fact, Bentley's generation hardly wondered about the ontological bookend moments at all. They were concerned instead with the theological stories just inside those moments: the Fall and the Second Coming. The stories were more important than the bookend moments because the stories were what gave meaning to the linear time that the moments merely bracketed. For Bentley no less than for any other Christian of his time, that meaning was humanity's need to reestablish in the millennium the divine favor lost in Eden. The Christian purpose of human existence, the *telos* of all life, is to get to that point, to return thereby to the righteousness of the very beginning. Time is linear, but the plot is circular.

But just how humanity will return to God depends on what pushed humanity away from him in the first place, and *that* depends on how one interprets the story of the pushing. All Anglo-American theological groups before Bentley, including moderate Arminians, accepted the literal truth of the Fall just as Genesis described it. Arminians challenged only the Augustinian interpretation of the Fall, not the literal truth of the event. Charles Chauncy, for example, published an extensive treatise on the subject of original sin, but his thesis—namely, that what Paul meant in Romans was that the Fall brought woeful imperfection rather than insuperable guilt—did not require doubting the Eden narrative itself. In fact, he asserted its literal veracity in the very first paragraph of his long work, and quite explicitly so: it was Genesis, not the "principles of mere reason," that described humanity's true origins, and in an account that was "solid and rational . . . that no one need be ashamed to own."[22] Little had changed even by 1799, when Thomas Barnard of Salem's North

Church was preaching and publishing the literal truth of early Genesis, though he did acknowledge that some passages "admit not of an easy explanation."[23]

Bentley also believed in the Fall. He too thought that humanity was created with an original goodness from which it declined and thereby anguished and alienated God. He believed in the narrative very much, only not literally.[24] He thought that the Eden story, while true allegorically, was true only allegorically.

And just what it was an allegory of, he learned from Jean-Jacques Rousseau. Bentley liked Rousseau. He frequently lent out copies of *Emile*, and sometime in 1792 or 1793—the specific entries in his commonplace book are not dated— he received a Genevan edition of Rousseau's oeuvre in thirty volumes, a set that he likely requested from a traveling merchant. The books were an important addition to his library, and though he was ambivalent about the moral qualities of their author, he approved of the ideas therein. "This strange man deserves attention," he wrote to himself in his commonplace book upon receiving them, "and tho' his character be not one to be imitated, he is one of those whose virtue checked the eccentricity of his mind, and whose works may be read with profit."[25] But it was the *Discourse on the Origins of Inequality* that made the deepest impression. In 1755, Rousseau had published the essay speculating on the causes of social hierarchy and locating them in early humanity's acquisition of luxurious property. The *Discourse* was not particularly popular in America— John Adams did not read it until 1794, and Benjamin Rush not until 1799—but Bentley read it in the 1780s, perhaps from his five-volume set of Rousseau's writings that preceded the thirty-volume set.[26] And he was persuaded. "We have learned to converse about this state with more judgment than it was formerly considered with," Bentley told listeners in what could have been a reference only to Rousseau's work before going on to describe, in terms that mirrored Rousseau's, what he thought the story of the Fall was trying to convey.

The figures of Adam and Eve stand in for humanity in its original state of creation, and their closeness to God for the righteousness of early humanity's obedience to their own consciences. Eden, in short, was an allegory for the state of nature, a paradise indeed because the absence of property ownership meant that few needs went unmet, few enemies brought war, and few barriers prevented the exercising of sympathies and benevolence. Humanity was materially equal, emotionally happy, and morally acute. God was truly pleased. At some point, however, these early peoples moved from the state of nature into a state of socialization. Possessions were consolidated among a few, and jealousy, misery, and social dislocation followed. God was aggrieved. Thus was the real fall from grace allegorized by the expulsion from Eden.[27]

But the "state of nature" theory did not by itself make Bentley a republican. Its consequent ideological conclusions could actually point in several directions, and indeed in the 1780s, the state of nature theory had allowed Bentley to argue that original sin was envy by the poor of the rich. In fact, the sermon in which Bentley first outlined his belief in it was one whose purpose was to criticize the poor for their resentments. And his interpretation of Mandeville in 1787 did indeed end in blaming the merchants, but not for being self-interested as much as for engaging in the kinds of commerce that rile up envy. In the 1780s, his social and economic liberalism allowed, even encouraged, this interpretation. But the experiences of the early 1790s required that new conclusions be drawn from the proposed state of nature. After 1794, the original sin allegorized by the expulsion from Eden was no longer the jealousy felt by the poor but the acquisitiveness and greed among the wealthy that fostered that jealousy. It was the pursuit of luxury, wealth, and the will to power that had driven humanity from the paradise of conscientiousness. In short, the true original sin was self-interest.

Reimagining the beginning of the narrative of human history meant reimagining its conclusion as well. Reading the Eden story as allegorical rather than literal truth did not change its theological function or lessen its theological weight, and Bentley felt no less strongly than did any other minister that his duty was to hasten humanity to the future paradise by eliminating the sinfulness that had ended the first one. He considered Revelation as much an allegory as was Genesis, but he believed deeply in what he thought it stood for, and although he did not share the urgency of many evangelicals' millennialism, he believed no less than they that a paradise waited ahead for a humanity that has cleansed itself.[28] His version of the future of humanity was in its details unlike anybody else's, but to the degree that he believed that with the passage of time and the spread of the gospel rightly understood humanity will recapture its original virtue and create of this world a final paradise that again pleases God, it was exactly like everyone else's.[29] In redefining original sin from the liberal conception to the Rousseauian one, he redefined what was necessary to eliminate it. After 1794, that is, the voice of conscience necessary both to the salvation of the soul and the salvation of humanity alike would speak less of restraint and submission and more of commonwealth and equality.

The embargo left hardly a mark on the larger political history of the decade, but to Bentley it was as important as the Birmingham riot. And for the same, or at least a parallel, reason. Birmingham had exposed the clerical liberals' self-interest; the embargo exposed that of the secular ones. The secular liberals, he now saw, were no more willing to act for the common good than were the ministers who urged the masses to persecute Priestley. And the secular leaders, like the clerical ones, were doing more than just choosing what they wanted. They were choosing what they wanted at a time when humanity needed something else. The power of self-interest is not merely to prefer what benefits oneself, but to do so even when there exists a greater, countervailing need. Merely wanting to profit was not the problem; choosing profit over commonwealth was.

But to understand the depth of his reaction, it is essential to see that Bentley's response is here, as it was to Birmingham, fueled by a sense of betrayal. To understand what he thought of the liberal elites before 1794, consider that when offering the prayer at the opening of a 1792 session of federal court, he experienced, so he wrote, "all the emotions of early youth, and the agitation was so great that I could not by the most diverting scenes of the country free myself from them the whole day."[30] Bentley was then thirty-three years old and a decade into his ministry, but this son of a ship carpenter was nonetheless still made nervous by having to speak in front of distinguished men. "All the emotions of early youth" is particularly telling. As late as 1792, Bentley was still operating in a mental world of social deference, still looking up to those with wealth and sophistication. And before 1794, he had seen no reason to do otherwise. But now, in 1794, those same men were proving themselves not so wise or virtuous after all. He took the news hard.

7

The Liberal Symbiosis

Whatever trust Bentley had put in liberal stewardship as a young man was shattered. Those whom he had thought manifestly fit to govern had failed to lead the people to the truth of rational Christianity, and they had failed to put aside their interests when the fate of human freedom was resting on the outcome of the French Revolution. In fact, the arenas of theology and of politics were rapidly collapsing on each other, and for the rest of the decade it would be hard to tell if it was Bentley's religious or his secular ideas that were cause for the suspicion directed toward him. Was it for reasons political or religious that the *Gazette* chose in 1792 to transcribe Burke's arguments against the English Unitarians' appeal for toleration?[1] And did David Tappan, Harvard's recently seated Hollis Professor of Divinity, draw any distinction between them when he denounced in 1793 not only the "popular anarchy and ferocity which have now spread a dark veil over the fair countenance of liberty" but also the "favorite *material system* of some literary and Christian characters of the present day"— meaning certainly Priestley and probably Bentley as well?[2] To classical liberals in both religion and politics, Jacobinism and Unitarianism were twin and related evils, radical theory and radical Christianity working together to undermine morality and social order. By 1794, ministers and merchants had come together, and Bentley would spend the rest of the decade fighting the dominant, even hegemonic, symbiosis that resulted.

It was as unsurprising then as it is now that behind the tectonic shift in New England's religious and political life was the pen of Thomas Paine. In a French prison, this greatest of revolutionary pamphleteers had turned his talents to religion and in 1794 presented the reading public with the century's clearest expression of deism. *The Age of Reason* presented natural religion without a trace of supernaturalism: Creation proved the existence of a Creator, conscience proved the obligations of morality, and common sense proved the necessity of justice conditional to behavior. Paine would believe in nothing else.

William Bentley hated deism. Bentley had in fact devoted the entirety of his 1788 Thanksgiving sermon to excoriating deists "from Lord Herbert to the lowest mortal, an Allen," the latter being a reference to Revolutionary War hero and known deist Ethan Allen. So he was enraged when he first saw what he called the "scandalous insult" that was Paine's work. *The Age of Reason*, he preached that week, was "imperfect, rash and malicious," a work of the "vilest language [and] meanest sophistry."[3] So capable is Paine, continued Bentley, "of making merry with his own nonsense, that to vent his spleen he can forsake common sense, insult the rights of man, and open as he thinks the age of reason with the greatest insult reason ever conceived."[4]

The theological differences between Paine's deism and Bentley's Christian naturalism bear repeating. Unlike the deists' Creator, Bentley's God was necessarily the God of the Bible, and unlike the deists themselves, Bentley did believe in the New Testament miracles. Reason could point to both an obligation to conscience and a supernatural place for divine justice, but only revelation implied that Jesus' instructions connect the two, and only the miracles within that revelation could prove that Jesus had God's permission to say so. And of those miracles, by far the most important was the Resurrection. The other miracles proved that Jesus was on a divine mission, but only the Resurrection proved that abiding by his message takes a soul to heaven. A literal acceptance of the Resurrection had to stay, and for Bentley it did. For Paine, famously, it did not. "Thomas did not believe the resurrection," Paine wrote of Saint Thomas and his doubts in lines often singled out by critics, "and, as they say, would not believe without having ocular and manual demonstration himself. *So neither will I*, and the reason is equally as good for me, and for every other person, as for Thomas."[5] So over and over in 1794 and 1795 Bentley went to his pulpit to explain the difference between a faith that accepts the Resurrection as proof of the supernatural consequences of behavior and a faith that does not.

For the first time, Bentley found himself on the orthodox side of a theological question. The same empirical spirit of the Enlightenment which had driven Bentley's redefinitions of so much of the inherited tradition now threatened what little remained, elements even he wanted to keep. But Bentley had precious little material on which to rest his defense of the Resurrection. He ended up using the only option he had, namely the testimony of witnesses.[6] Armed with the single fact that hundreds of people had laid eyes on Christ after the Resurrection, Bentley could assure his congregation that deists were wrong and that he, the Christian naturalist, was right, and for the next two years he would stay at it, delivering sermon after sermon on the witness evidence of Christianity and the scurrility of Thomas Paine.

This was the end of Bentley's redefining elements of the inherited faith. Paine had shown Bentley the limits of an empirical Christianity. There was nothing left to redefine and no reason to do so anyway. Bentley would remain a Christian naturalist but go no further, his days of theological pioneering behind him.

But although Paine's theological arguments had a profound effect on Bentley, they were in actuality not what made the book so important to others. Paine, after all, was no more heterodox than was Lord Herbert in the early seventeenth century or John Toland in the latter part or any of the other deists in the eighteenth. The power of *The Age of Reason*, rather, lay in a confluence of the skill of its author, the appreciation of that author by the lower sort, and the willingness of that lower sort to accept previously taboo ideas, all in addition to the ideas themselves. If those ideas were not new, no previous deist rendered them so accessible or spread them so widely as did Paine. With the same joyous iconoclasm that had made *Common Sense* such a hit, he was bringing to the masses what had before been an intellectual dalliance only of gentlemen. The North Church's Thomas Barnard was undoubtedly referring to Paine's success when he told the audience of the 1795 Dudleian Lecture that "the subjects of religion are now more freely conversed upon. It has ceased to be highly disreputable to attack them. It has become, in a degree, fashionable to treat them with less reverence."[7] And a writer to the Salem *Gazette* made explicit the source of his concern: he had, he wrote, been often "accosted" with what was "the grand inquiry of the present day . . . 'have you read the Age of Reason?'"[8]

And its popularity among the accosting people was, to liberals, exactly the problem. Because denying the infinitude of hell and the possibility of temporal punishment through special providence, as deism did, removed what liberals considered the most powerful restraints on popular misbehavior.[9] Without the fear of God's response in either this life or the next, what would keep the masses in line, particularly in an age of growing popular self-consciousness? Barnard had gone on to say as much when he lamented how Paine had also made it "fashionable" to "disregard the strictest commands of piety and virtue, as precise and superstitious."[10] For liberals, to allow popular deism to spread among the masses in the 1790s was to risk nothing less than the unraveling of the rules of behavior.

Some liberal Christians were concerned enough to respond in print, but all liberals were affected to one degree or another.[11] In fact, the success of *The Age of Reason* reshaped the very factions of the region's ecclesiastical politics. Paine, in short, made liberals willing to ally themselves with their old Calvinist opponents. Arminians were no more sympathetic to Calvinists in the mid-1790s than they had ever been, but the new desire to retain ongoing supernaturalism outweighed the older differences over the means of salvation. When considered in ontological terms, Arminians and Calvinists actually had a lot in common. There was, after all, no ontological difference between the Trinitarian Christ and the Arian one: both were preexistent and thus incarnated from the supernatural plane into the natural one, and though the Arian Jesus was "created" by God rather than "begotten" of God, the distinction had no direct bearing on the ongoing present of the eighteenth century. Nor was there any ontological difference between an orthodox belief in miracles and a latitudinarian belief in special providence: in both God was able to violate natural law—either as its own end or as seed event triggering the sequence that ends at the intended phenomenon—and in the 1790s, retaining God's ability to violate that law in punishing sinners, be they depraved or just immoral, was exactly what the orthodox and the liberals alike wanted to ensure.

By the same token, Bentley was moved into the same camp as Paine. Bentley was no deist, but his Christian naturalism did share with deism exactly the denial of an infinite hell and special providence that so concerned the liberals. That is, although Christian naturalism may have been *theologically* distinct from deism, it was *ontologically* no different, and as of 1795, ontology trumped theology.

Ontology mattered because it either did or did not allow God to intervene in the natural world, a power generally thought to be exercised in response to human behavior. Ontological claims were, in a word, political claims, and those who wanted to keep the threat of God's intervention and those who wanted to maintain every other kind of social restraint found much to like in each other. After 1794, as Bentley put it, the great bulk of the established Congregationalist ministry, liberal and orthodox alike, became "the tools of the Federalists."[12]

It was a good match for both secular and clerical Federalists, with each side giving the other a gift of incalculable worth. The clerical Federalists wanted and received from the secular ones a commitment to defend supernatural Christianity, insofar as they were able to by retaining the establishment. In return, the secular ones wanted and received from the clergy the reassurance that God approved of what they were doing. Claims of a covenantal relationship between God and New England, and, after 1783, between God and America, were standard fare, but these ministers in 1795 began to argue that God favored Federalist Americans above all others. They were fortunate that a broad national prosperity was available to allow such an interpretation, and they made the most of the opportunity: the dispersion of the whiskey rebels, the failure of the Genet mission, the successful suppression of the democratic societies, all this and more was claimed as empirical evidence that God manifestly approved of Federalist leadership. George Washington himself was now the "happy instrument" of providence, a secondary cause raised up by God to defeat enemies both foreign and domestic.[13] By 1795, that is, the old epistemological trick of phenomena "above" reason had become swept into the service of partisan politics.

Bentley, watching from the outside, condemned the whole bargain. His naturalism precluded claims to specially providential Federalist successes, and his already-extant opposition to the establishment was only hardened by his liberal peers' willingness to allow the state to enforce the supernaturalism he thought both false and detrimental to right religion. That the liberal clergy around him would use the secular power of Federalist leaders to push back the benevolent explorations of reasoning and moral Christians was to Bentley the local manifestation of the same clerical will to power demonstrated at Birmingham in 1791. And if the Massachusetts liberals were not going so far as to "stimulate the ignorant to burn meetinghouses, private buildings, and ruin families to gratify propensities they imbibe from the government," they were no less willing than their English peers to sacrifice the truth as Bentley understood it for their own power.[14]

Put another way, Bentley began to see claims of ongoing supernaturalism less as superstitions and more as corruptions. The shift in conception was important. Superstitions were those things believed by the masses who did not know better; corruptions were those things *claimed* by the empowered few who *did* know better. Now Bentley would place the blame not on the superstitious folk so much as on the "artful and ambitious" clergy who have "terrified mankind by their weakest passions to become the slaves of the most ungenerous purposes ever conceived by the most corrupt dispositions and most infernal resolutions."[15] Back in 1782, Priestley had published *History of the Corruptions of the Christian Church*, but Bentley in the 1780s was not ready to see Priestley's point. As with so much else, Bentley needed the experiences of the early 1790s to give political meaning to his theological convictions. By 1795, though, he had acquired that experience. He had always thought that irrationality breeds bewilderment and immorality; after 1795, he thought that it, when combined with party politics, breeds oppression as well.

He was now telling listeners that he and they could not "more successfully frustrate designing men than by enlightening the world," and in the second half of the decade he tried to do just that.[16] Whether he was in fact enlightening the world was not yet his to know, but he surely was frustrating some of the men in it. The decade's second half was one of more or less continual conflict between him and Salem's Federalists both clerical and secular.

One striking example of the contempt in which the liberal clergy now held Bentley was the hymnal edited by Jeremy Belknap and published in 1795. Belknap was minister over Boston's Federal Street Church, an acquaintance and contemporary of Bentley's and a typical member of the liberal generation between Charles Chauncy and William Channing. The hymnal he produced would become the one of choice for liberal churches, including the First and North Churches in Salem. A close comparison of Belknap's and Bentley's hymnals—for both men not only selected which hymns would be used but also edited, differently, the ones they did select—reveals the growing chasm between the moderate and the radical strains of liberal Christianity. Whereas Belknap's hymnal had the "thoughtless sons of Adam's race," for example, Bentley's version used "thoughtless sons of men"; whereas Belknap's singers would lament "wretched souls who strive in vain" to escape sin, Bentley's sang about the "wretched souls who still remain" in immorality.[17] But the difference was most clear in the distinction between Belknap's Arianism and Bentley's Socinianism. In some instances, Bentley had omitted a hymn that Belknap would keep. "The Word Made Flesh" is one such unsurprising example.[18] In other instances, they included the same hymn but incorporated different phrasings: where one of Belknap's read "Jesus to thee I breathe my prayer," the same hymn in Bentley's had "Great God to thee, I breathe my prayer," and in another, where Belknap's read "The Savior's gracious call obey," Bentley's had "The kind, the gracious call obey."[19] And in others yet, they changed whole verses: Belknap's singers would sing, but Bentley's would not, for example, that

> Vain are our fancies, airy flights,
> If faith be cold and dead;
> None but a living pow'r unites
> To Christ the living head.[20]

But even if most readers around Boston did not take time to compare hymnals— and likely some did—they could not have missed the purpose of Belknap's hymnal as laid out in the introduction. It was devoted to criticizing Bentley and Unitarianism with a sarcasm and stridency attributable only to the heightened fears of deism in the aftermath of Paine's work:

> It is humbly apprehended, that a grateful and affectionate address to the exalted Saviour of mankind, or a hymn in honour of the Eternal Spirit, cannot be disagreeable to the mind of God. To stigmatize such an act of devotion with the name of idolatry, is (to say the least) an abuse of language. It cannot be justly charged with derogating from the glory due to the ONE God and Father of all, because he is the ultimate object of the honour which is given to his Son and to his Spirit. In this selection those Christians, who do not scruple to sing praises to their Redeemer and Sanctifier, will find materials for such a sublime enjoyment; whilst others whose tenderness of conscience may oblige them to confine their addresses to the Father only will find no deficiency of matter suited to their idea of "the chaste and awful spirit of devotion."[21]

As far as Arians such as Belknap were concerned, Bentley's Socinian Jesus was no better than deism's human one; each version of Christ would lead an individual to hell as quickly as would the other. New political fears brought an end to silently accommodating the theological idiosyncrasies of Salem's East Church preacher.

Things settled down for a few years but flared up again in 1798 when, on a day of national thanksgiving, Federalist clergymen rose to denounce all for which France, reason, Freemasonry, and—by implication on all three accounts—William Bentley stood. But of all the preachers in Massachusetts that day, none made a bigger splash than Jedidiah Morse, who told two congregations and then the reading public about an international cadre of atheistic and revolutionary Freemasons conniving against Christian America. Morse was not the only one beating this drum, and Federalists everywhere were already suspicious of foreign ideas and peoples, but Morse claimed he had proof of a conspiracy of Illuminati, and he may well have had Bentley, a passionate defender of Masonry and a Freemason himself, in mind as one of the conspirators. Bentley had indeed published several Masonic discourses during the previous year, but he was no Illuminati; there *were* no Illuminati in America.[22] However emblematic Morse's charges may have been of a generalized Federalist paranoia, in his case he was also tapping into nearly a decade of his suspicions about Bentley, begun back in 1790 when he accused Bentley of editing a recent publication of the Englishman Thomas Emlyn's Unitarian *Extracts.*

Bentley's war with the secular Federalists was also out in the open. He had, since 1794, provided news summaries for the *Gazette*, but the further the paper moved towards Federalism, the more the summaries stood out in opposition, so much so that by 1797 U.S. Senator Benjamin Goodhue concluded that their author was part of the "pack of disorganizing plundering and murdering rascals" that was the Democratic-Republican party.[23] Soon after, Bentley was relieved of his position. He continued to submit pieces to the newspaper, but the owner and now editor, Thomas Cushing, would not publish them without adding his own editorial asides.[24] And on one occasion, when Cushing did agree to print one of Bentley's submissions—some criticisms of the English evangelical William Wilberforce by the English Unitarian Thomas Belsham—he printed only two paragraphs of it and put beside them a four-paragraph *defense* of Wilberforce borrowed from English journals.[25]

Whatever lines remained between sacred and secular were entirely erased in the conflicts over the works of the later, more radical Enlightenment that were making their way across the Atlantic. Bentley was only a lukewarm supporter of Mary Wollstonecraft and not one at all of William Godwin, but he stringently opposed attempts to squelch their ideas. He chafed at efforts to block the dissemination of Godwin's *Political Justice*, for example, and he was driven to outright protest over the liberals' reaction to the apparent spread of Wollstone-craftian feminism. In many ways Wollstonecraft posed a greater threat to liberal values than did the man who was her husband, biographer, and, to critics, apologist for her adultery. A poem in the *Gazette* in 1798 made sport of the recently deceased and scandalized Wollstonecraft who, it rhymed, had taught women to "assert their *rights* to eat and drink/Prove by themselves their sex *can* think/And dare maintain, that 'tis no treason/For wives and mothers to use reason!!"[26] But Bentley saw things differently, admiring what he called in one sermon "the generous affections of a modern lady—Wollstonecraft—towards her sex, and the ample proofs she has brought to the world of comprehensive wisdom."[27] Her arguments remained only abstractions, however, until local teacher Abigail Rogers gave them life. Sometime in 1800, it seems, a collection of privileged Salem girls formed small social groups with such names as the "Mosquito Fleet." The young women were Rogers's students, and before long liberal Salemites began to wonder just what lessons she was passing on to their daughters. The central accuser, who appeared in Boston's *Columbian Centinel* under the name "Latitudinarian," was likely the North Church's Thomas Barnard—certainly he had nothing nice to say about Wollstonecraft in a later sermon delivered to the Salem Female Charitable Society[28]—but others spoke up as well, charging these girls with casting aside decorum and delicacy and virtue, seeking to "come forth in defiance of order and authority and boldly assume 'the rights of woman,'" and contaminating other girls with such "satanic arts."[29] The girls were surely innocent of the charges, certainly of the more extreme ones, but they were decidedly partaking in *something* new, and their instructor was the likely prod of the novelty. But Bentley, for all his ambivalence about Wollstonecraft's personal life, came to Rogers's defense. He praised the students for thinking "mental improvement preferable to those pretty feminine airs and graces which have so endeared the sex to us," substituted in Rogers's classes when she was made ill by the ordeal, and finally, in classic form, canceled his subscription to the *Columbian Centinel*.[30]

Bentley defended even the German rationalists. He had a useful and sympathetic correspondence with Christoph Ebeling, useful for Ebeling in that his geography of America was much improved by the newspapers and magazines sent from Salem and useful for Bentley in that it was Ebeling who provided the material with which Bentley refuted Morse's charges of American Illuminatism, in large measure bringing the flare-up to an end. But Bentley's support for German intellectualism went further than this. The Enlightenment was a German phenomenon no less than an English or French one, and the Federalist *Gazette* was soon full of denunciations of what it called "philosophism," particularly at the University of Jena, where students were "almost to a man, *Republicans*." The problem was the books these students were reading, the authors of which—Fichte, Wieland, Schiller, and Kant—also came in for their share of abuse. Goethe was described as "one of those literati who contribute, by their writings, to deprave the minds of their countrymen."[31] Bentley, though, held his ground: Wieland and Goethe held "opinions which will not be universally received," he admitted, "but their genius will be revered"; and as for Kant, "upon no other system," Bentley wrote, "can the hopes of mankind be established."[32] Early in the nineteenth century, Boston's liberal elites would send four young students to Germany. The students would come to Bentley to get advice and letters of introduction, but once in Germany, far from picking up its radicalism, they simply became more reactionary. Even among the small group of Americans interested in German Higher Criticism, Bentley was alone. Any appreciation of German scholarship would have to wait for another generation.[33]

What emerges from this period is a sense of a struggle not only in print, but *over* print, as both parties tried to sway the newly empowered public to their side. The liberal, now Federalist, hope of keeping in check lower-sort passions meant, in the late 1790s, restricting access to books that might stir those passions. In contrast, Bentley held that free access to ideas was essential because only when a people can choose right from among options that include wrongs can they demonstrate the conscientiousness necessary for goodness. This was the spirit of the Bereans brought into politics and into the struggles over the printed word. So even when he did not agree with the ideas in a given book, as he often did not, he supported its publication. "Men should write and act freely," he declared even while criticizing Paine's *Age of Reason*. Or as he put it in his Thanksgiving sermon in 1795, "Some books have been written with an ill effect, but we are not to interrupt the stream."[34]

But not until nearly the end of the decade, with radical ideas in the air and war with France looming did Federalists try so vigorously to suppress dissent, most notably in a set of sedition laws aimed at suppressing Republican newspaper editors. The laws did not result in any prosecutions in Salem because there was as yet no Republican newspaper in town, but their spirit was nonetheless present, as when, for example, in November 1798, Chief Justice Francis Dana opened the Salem session of the commonwealth's Supreme Judicial Court by announcing his support for a local sedition law to prohibit the recurrence of a liberty pole like the one lately in Dedham whose builder was soon resting in the Salem jail.[35]

Naturally enough, Bentley was bothered by the sedition laws, but he was even more attuned to informal efforts to suppress dissent, campaigns of intellectual coercion not through legislation but through invocations of the greater inherent wisdom of the social elites. As he was well placed to know, the most pervasive of all assumptions of classical liberalism was that the wealthy class, in addition to being morally superior to the lower sort, was simply smarter than them as well. And in Salem before the 1790s, the lower sort had for the most part agreed. The middle of the decade had witnessed the beginnings of a sustained challenge to that assumption, and the liberals, now Federalists, at decade's end were scrambling to turn back the clock. As Bentley put it, the Federalist editors of the *Gazette* were trying nothing less than to "pervert the minds of common readers, so that as soon as they have read & begin to think, they are blusteringly arrested by some absolute decision upon the construction they ought to put."[36] The spectacle of a justice supporting a sedition law sent Bentley to his pulpit that Sunday to give what turned out to be a distillation of everything he had learned about the social causes of intellectual deference. "It is the power to seize the minds of men that gives such astonishing advantages to eloquence," he told his congregants. "It is the power to get into men's minds as they are and to lead them by their fears which gives such superior influence to men in other respects undeserving of the least regard."[37] Bentley knew what he was talking about. After all, back in the 1780s he had been one of those whose minds had been seized.

Just as Justice Dana's remarks in November of 1798 gave Bentley the opportunity to demonstrate how his intellectual republicanism had matured, the day of national thanksgiving in that same month provided Bentley the chance to demonstrate how his economic and political republicanism had come along as well. This was the same day that Morse levied his accusations of Masonic conspiracy and that John Prince gave a sermon over at Salem's First Church which would become his first publication.[38] It is good fortune that Prince's congregants thought enough of it to subsidize its printing, for there is no better example of what the classically liberal, now Federalist ideology had come to represent. He was concise. The goal of good government, Prince reiterated to an audience who had long thought the same, is in guaranteeing the "peaceable enjoyment of life and property under the protection of good laws," a goal met only when the masses submit to the will of those above them. This was liberalism brought forth into the 1790s, its original revolutionary quality now permanently stripped in the face of the decade's radical new ideas of equality and social justice. The specters of Paine, Godwin, and Wollstone-craft hovered over the piece, but more threatening yet, because more fundamental, was Rousseau. John Prince in fact took time to denounce the theory, then nearly fifty years old, of the origins of inequality. Liberals had by then had time to cultivate a counterargument of their own, and Prince held nothing back. The state of nature Rousseau had found so appealing was to Prince "rude" and "low," a condition whose dwellers were nearly "different orders of beings" from those properly socialized in mind and conduct. For Prince and the other liberals, society—the "refined and improved state"—was the cause of happiness, not of misery; indeed, it and only it could free the individual from his or her own darker passions that nature, if left to its devices, will only abet. For liberals, society, not nature, was the desired state. More exactly, it was society as *they* would have it governed and indeed as to that point they *had* governed it. But not, as Federalists could already see, for much longer.

Compare that to what Bentley was saying and doing about a half-mile to the east. By the late 1790s, Bentley was ready to become a Rousseauian in spirit as well as in letter. "Tribute to whom tribute is due," Prince had happily quoted Paul. "Custom to whom custom; fear to whom fear; honor to whom honor." But Bentley was through with such talk. By the late 1790s, he had come to reject not only liberal economics but also the liberal claims of the benevolence of hierarchy and submission. The Chain of Being had vanished. "No superiority of talents is universal," he now preached, and "no inferiority is absolute." Human societies, not natural creation, produced the inequalities within those societies. "A good friend of human nature should think that society has made the greatest part of this difference," he argued. The rich ought to ask themselves, when they see a pauper, "Had my education been as theirs, had my means been as slender, my acquaintance in life the same, what would be my hopes?"[39] This was no longer a man who could condemn the servant for resentment of the master; now, he preached that the good master was one who "wished to make his servant his friend" and would "lead him into all truth."[40] This was no longer a man who could tell congregants that the proper role for women and children was subservience to the patriarch; now he would say that "the head of a family is not a tyrant, but a father," and that a wife, far from submitting to their husband, has a right "to his care and to a share in his interest. Here she rises to every honor he can possess and partakes in every joy."[41] This was no longer a man who could defend the caging of vagrants as acceptable because it was legal; now he had experienced persecution under an unjust sedition law and could, when listing recent improvements to society, include in that list the "mildness of our laws."[42] This was no longer a man who could see the populace as simply too ignorant to recognize the right faith; now he saw them as the victims of manipulation by those who had gone halfway to that faith and who wanted others not to go at all. And this, finally, was no longer a man who could condemn antislavery activism. He had not experienced slavery from within, but he *had* learned of the biases inherent in liberal governance and could see racist double standards with new clarity. Several years later, for example, a Federalist lawyer in Boston shot and killed the son of the head of the local Republican Party to avenge a political insult. The jury brought back a verdict of manslaughter rather than premeditated murder. Republicans everywhere were enraged, but it was not partisanship that led Bentley to remark how, by comparison, "a negro for murdering a child finds no difficulty in his way to the gallows."[43]

Events of the 1790s had convinced him that Rousseau was right, and Bentley's future millennium would thenceforth be a return to Rousseau's past, a paradise marked by and guaranteed by the minimization if not elimination of the inequalities of wealth. Free from the hegemonic convergence of liberal Christianity and liberal social ethics, Bentley had moved into the realm of social radicalism. He no longer feared God's anger at questioning the social order; he no longer thought that the status quo was necessarily pious; he no longer was convinced that the values of the marketplace were necessarily those of greatest virtue. Bentley's desire for the masses' spiritual liberation, it seems, had, over the course of the 1790s, become a prospectus for their physical liberation as well. Bentley of course valued morality—more so, he would say, than did his opponents—but he had become convinced that the liberal version of morality was emphasized by liberals mostly to justify liberal success. Morality, he now saw, means more than moderation, prudence, discipline, and restraint. It means advocacy, charity, and defense of the defenseless as well.

So on that fast day in 1798, while Prince was holding forth at the First, Bentley at the East rose to extol the will of the people over the instituted authorities. "It is not in the administration we are to look for the greatest public happiness," he told them, "even when it is in the hands of the best men ... but in the hearts of the people.... In elections, the people should employ such men as discover a love of the people. Who will have the confidence of the people and who will regard the people in the laws?"[44] Six times, "the people." Bentley's political transformation, like his theological one, was complete. As awkward as it sounds, libertarian republicanism had made this liberal a democrat.

8

Republicanism Victorious

By 1800, Bentley was a republican in every economic, intellectual, spiritual, and cultural way. He opposed the union of church and state; he was suspicious of corruption and conspiracy by insiders; he insisted on a free press and the free exchange of ideas. Beneath each of these were hard lessons learned about the power of self-interest over conscientiousness. If others in America were becoming republican because of their agrarian interests or sectional sympathies or hostility toward Hamiltonian finance, Bentley's priorities lay in preserving the rights to information, ideas, and enlightenment, which he saw as the best sureties of the spread of morality and thus human happiness.[1] But although a republican, he had not yet become a Republican. At least not formally. The new year, however, would see him finally join the partisan struggles to which his life had been pointing him for the better part of a decade.

The extent of the economic and political power of Salem's merchants emerges from even a cursory glance at the town's recent political history. Every colonial community was dominated by its wealthy minority, but Salem particularly so. A small group of merchants had exercised nearly complete control over town affairs, occupying the seats of selectmen and other major town offices, sitting on the various courts, and serving as the town's representatives to the colonial legislative body, the General Court. Wealthy merchants all, they gave to Salem a notably conservative bent. So when the imperial crisis began after 1763, Salem under their leadership demonstrated precious little of the revolutionary spirit. The town meeting objected to the Stamp Act in 1765 but more so to the Boston mobs, and one suspects that even if Andrew Oliver, who was hanged in effigy and whose house was damaged after he became stamp officer, had not been the father of one of Salem's representatives to the General Court, the town would have found reason to protest "the subversion of laws—the terror of his Majesty's subjects—and the destruction of private property."[2] The next year they returned Tories to the legislature, and the year after that they rejected the Boston town meeting's resolution not to consume British goods, steadfastly maintaining their right to "avoid excess and licentiousness in every form."[3] To be sure, Tories fell from favor beginning in 1769. Voters that year scrapped all the loyalist selectmen and General Court representatives, and in 1771 they removed Tories even as overseers of the poor and members of the school committee.[4] But Tory numbers and influence stayed strong. In 1774, they held a ball to honor the departing Governor Thomas Hutchinson, and when his replacement moved the provincial government to Salem—itself an indication of where he felt most comfortable—more than a hundred Tories "and as many ladies" feted the newcomer.[5] Forty-eight men went even further and signed a letter of welcome which recommended Salem as a substitute for the closed port of Boston.[6] At a time when Bostonians were starving and British troops were marching, to sign was to make an unambiguous and public statement of loyalism to the Crown and indifference to the colonists. Some of the signers soon recanted, but others remained Tories to the end.[7] Andrew Oliver opted to ride out the war in Salem, as did the physician E. A. Holyoke and the lawyer William Pynchon—the latter of whom kept up appearances until a crowd broke his windows while celebrating Saratoga, and he with a brave face "contentedly" boarded them up—but most Tories thought it better to leave. Some went to Nantucket, others to inland towns, others to Newfoundland or Nova Scotia, and a few, the most vocal ones, all the way to England.[8]

Not that Salem became any more radical in their absence. The men who led Salem after 1769 were patriots rather than Tories, but patriots of a most conservative kind. Salem's leading Whigs were men such as Richard Derby Jr. and Timothy Pickering, men whose commitment to the patriot cause, such that it was, was pragmatic rather than ideological. Pickering, after all, had spent much of his youth unsuccessfully trying to ingratiate himself into what would become Tory circles, and Derby's opposition to the Crown was founded on the loss of a vessel to English warships in an earlier conflict, not to any particular republicanism. Whigs such as Derby and Pickering were the most reluctant of revolutionaries, and it is safe to speculate that it was only their own resentment of being on the periphery of Salem society that kept them from falling into the Tory camp altogether.[9] There were other patriots, too, of course, but they were no more radical than these. Some—to judge by the list of signers of a letter protesting the arrival of General Thomas Gage and with him martial law— were, like Derby and Pickering, up and coming men who had received neither social acceptance nor appointed positions in the judiciary or militia and who had little to lose by opposing the new mercantilism and much to gain from toppling the local Tory oligarchy. Others—including apothecary John Barton, who in 1771 was doing well enough to have a thousand pounds out on loan; shoemaker Peter Chever, who owned two slaves; and tanner Dudley Wood- bridge, who claimed two thousand feet of wharfage—were prosperous artisans who may have been willing to contest the actions of Parliament but surely did not wish to see the local social order upturned.[10] In short, Salem had noth- ing analogous to Boston's "Loyal Nine"—men such as Sam Adams, William Molineux, or Thomas Young, all middle-class, nonmercantile, ideologically radical Whigs. And so Salem, even under its new Whig leadership, slipped back into its old ways. When news arrived of Parliament's decision that the five justices of the Superior Court of Judicature would be paid out of customs revenues rather than money appropriated by the General Court, a widely re- sented measure because it removed from the colonists their ability to influence the judges through their salaries, Salem refused to respond to Sam Adams's call for a committee of correspondence. "I hear nothing of old Salem," the frustrated Adams wrote to Elbridge Gerry. "I fear they have had an opiate ad- ministered to them." Perhaps the town could afford to be sanguine because Salem's own Nathaniel Ropes was one of the justices, but in any case it was not until almost another year had passed, not until after the Boston Port Bill in the spring of 1774, that they finally agreed to a committee of correspondence.[11]

The Whig leadership did become bolder through the fall of 1774 and the spring of 1775, hosting an illegal meeting of the House of Representatives and then sending delegates to an equally illegal county meeting, but they could never be accused of overeagerness in defense of liberty. Pickering for one responded with inexplicable caution when called to lead Salem's militia to meet the British marching on Lexington and Concord, and a number of merchants, including Derby, continued to trade with the British in Nova Scotia.[12] And Salem's most ballyhooed unit, the company of well-to-do men who volunteered for an expe- dition to liberate Newport in 1778, signed on for all of three weeks, appointed as company captain a Tory shopkeeper, and enlisted in the first place only be- cause, as Benjamin Goodhue candidly explained, "the poorer kind insisted on our exerting ourselves in this affair."[13] They took no casualties and were soon back in Salem trading war stories.

With the shifting of the theater of war southward, Salem's role accordingly abated, and whatever revolutionary fervor still remained was extinguished for good. In 1778, the town meeting unanimously rejected the proposed state constitution, citing the objections of an Ipswich convention later expressed in the *Essex Result*, a preview of what the mercantile interest would look like in the new republic.[14] Indeed, the Tories and the conservative Whigs spent the latter part of the war mostly putting aside their differences and rediscovering their shared antagonism toward the lower sort and its radical Whig agenda. The stain of Toryism did not matter as early as 1780 when four of Salem's eight delegates to the state constitutional convention were men who in 1774 had signed the letter welcoming General Gage. Most Tory exiles came home to no resistance, at least none of the political kind. (Benjamin Pickman Jr. enjoyed an easy transition, thanks to his wife's prudent control of his affairs, and he would even serve as town treasurer from 1788 until 1803. Samuel Curwen, however, discovered that in his absence his wife had allowed her nephew to squander his fortune; after an unhappy nine months, Curwen left once again for London, from whence he instructed a friend in Salem not to allow his wife's body into the family tomb when she died, for he "should not be a little deranged in the Resurrection morning to find Abigail Curwen starting up at my side.")[15] It was in fact hard to guess from economic considerations who had been a Tory and who had been a Whig, since many of the prominent Whigs had done quite well for themselves during the war, outpacing even further the middling class they had so recently left behind: whereas blacksmiths received £24 for building gun carriages, for example, Derby received £146 for his warehoused gunpowder.[16] To outright Tories such as Pickman and Curwen and to conservative Whigs such as Derby and Pickering, it seemed clear that the two groups would be better served as allies than as opponents, joined together in a new commercial conservatism articulated most loudly by the political clique of North Shore elites called the Essex Junto, four members of which were Salem merchants—two Whigs and two Tories.[17]

Thus Salem entered the new republic with a unified upper class once again in complete control of town affairs. When Bentley arrived in 1783, they were back in uncontested power. Nor was it contested anytime during the rest of that decade, voters returning the same board of selectmen for five years running after 1782, the town's longest stretch of unchanged leadership.[18] And when the Shaysites spoke up in 1786, Salem responded with a single voice. Its merchants had good reason: they were the kinds of creditors against whom the Shaysites were chafing. Nearly half of the wealth of two of Salem's leading merchants, for example, was in the hands of debtors. The inventory taken at the death of Benjamin Pickman Sr. in 1773 tallied an estate worth £13,000, but when the last of the outstanding loans was finally collected in 1785, the total had jumped to £21,000. In 1786, the estate of Francis Cabot, including several pews in Salem's North Church, was worth £6,350, but the hundred outstanding notes added another £4,200, and the loan office certificates, state notes, and five shares of the Massachusetts Bank counted for more. And although executors accepted deck nails and wood as payment when necessary and wrote off eighteen people as "desperate," the great majority of borrowers were expected to pay in full and pay in cash.[19] For Pickman, Cabot, and merchants like them, anything less was robbery. So when the Shaysites erupted in western Massachusetts in late 1786, Salem's elites were eager to see them put down. Stephen Higginson, then in Boston, and Elias Hasket Derby contributed money to raise troops, and William Pynchon watched son John, Bentley's ersatz student at Harvard, lead a small band of men against the insurgents.[20] The Salem *Mercury* continually printed denunciatory letters and articles while keeping readers abreast of Benjamin Lincoln's soldiering through the western counties.[21] And when the next elections rolled around, Salem voted its fears even more than did the other commercial towns in the county. Voters in nearly all of Essex County supported John Hancock that year over incumbent Governor James Bowdoin who, they thought, had used too much force against the rebels; voters in Marblehead, Beverly, and Newburyport, for example, favored Hancock two to one. But Salem preferred Bowdoin. And in the race for lieutenant governor between Thomas Cushing and Benjamin Lincoln, who by then had returned from his march, those three towns and Boston preferred Cushing, but Salem went with Lincoln by a count of two hundred to nine.[22] The threat to property posed by the Shaysites was one of the bogeys hovering over the drafting and ratification of the United States Constitution later that year, and leading Salemites were well pleased with both the new foundation for government and its first administration.

There was little threat to Federalist control during the years of Washington's presidency. Although in the annual gubernatorial decision, Salemites went with Hancock from 1788 to 1793 and Samuel Adams in 1794 and 1795, these were candidates whose powerful personalities overrode partisanship. In other elections, voters went consistently Federalist, for example sending Benjamin Goodhue to the House of Representatives four times beginning in 1788, and with a 361-3 mandate in 1790.[23] No democratic society was formed in Salem, and though mobs formed in other towns protesting the English-favoring Jay Treaty, none did in Salem. In fact, the *Gazette* acidly suggested sending the Essex County militia to control unruly Bostonians.[24] In his town, Bentley knew, "the men who hold the securities under the government are sufficiently influential against the disquiets and angry expressions of more dependent people."[25] The opposition was entirely cowed. "Conversation on politicks," wrote Stephen Goodhue in Salem to brother Benjamin down in Philadelphia late in 1795, "hath almost wholly ceased here. It seems to be almost wholly worn out, [and] Jacobinism seems to be almost entirely at an end."[26] Election results bore him out. In the 1796 gubernatorial contest, Federalists were able to defeat Sam Adams in Salem even though Adams won the general election, and later that year, Salem voters preferred Federalist electors, 106–11, in the choice for president.[27]

Nor did the administration of John Adams bring much hint of change. In fact, the Federalist Party was stronger than ever because of the violence of the Boston Jay Treaty riots, the resignation of Sam Adams from the governorship, the XYZ affair, and the commencement of ship seizures by the French. The *Gazette* rang in 1798 with a special New Year's Day poem, 188 lines of rhyming Federalism, one section of which summarized all things French:

> On scepticism's waves afloat,
> France leaves right reason *sans culottes*,
> From truth's Bastille sets passion free,
> Sends pirates forth to scour the sea,
> A Meloch liberty enthrones,
> The Bible burns, and God disowns.
> But, readers kind, be not chagrin'd,
> Though every good be guillotin'd,
> Though many a scurvy trick she plays ye,
> Remember that the slut is *crazy*.[28]

Anti-French sentiment was reaching new heights, not least because Salem vessels were among those captured by the French, and in May of 1798, while Salem's own Timothy Pickering was serving as secretary of state, more than nine hundred Salemites signed the town's declaration of support for retaliation. "The Federalists are in triumph," wrote Bentley that month. "And [others] dare to speak."[29] All talk turned to war against France. Once again merchants armed their merchantmen and this time were also able to support a fledgling United States Navy by subscribing to support the *Essex*, a thirty-two-gun frigate then in the yards. Election results reflected this Federalist swell: Salem voted 138-2 for Increase Sumner in the 1797 gubernatorial race and 220-2 for Stephen Sewall in the 1798 congressional contest. In 1799, Salem's voters returned Sumner to the governorship with a 509-40 mandate, a victory twice as lopsided as in Boston.[30] The Tories would have been, and in some cases were, well pleased.

Yet not all power is reflected in electoral returns and newspaper pieces. Other kinds of power existed, too, kinds that operated outside the formal instruments of control and that went unreflected in the formal modes of expression. The lower sort of Salem well knew the power of the riot and the mob. Disenfranchised seamen in coastal towns had long protested impressment policies, and what John Adams called the "swarm of tumultuous people" in colonial Salem who celebrated Guy Fawkes Day each November 5 with bonfires and effigies gave men like Adams ample reason to be nervous.[31] The crisis years had provided a certain legitimacy to public discontentment, at least insofar as it was directed only against Tories. The people took up the offer, tarring and feathering suspected informants, destroying caskets of tea, and breaking the windows and hassling the rector of St. Peter's.[32] They broke down the door of the home of Nathaniel Ropes, whose court appointment a few years earlier had been met with such nonchalance by elite Salem, and threatened to drag him into the street, and they drove the tenant off of William Browne's property. But the most consequential act of all came in October of 1774, when someone struck a spark in the woodshed of noted Tory Peter Frye. What followed was the largest fire Salem had known, and though it ended up burning patriot property as well as Tory, that the newspaper listed Tory victims before patriot ones is perhaps not incidental.[33] But the fact that most Tories—the merchant ones if not the Anglican ones—were men of wealth meant that a concerned individual could never be entirely sure that the popular disgruntlements were being stirred by the Toryism and not by the wealth. In 1774, yet another variable entered the picture, at least for a season, when Salem underwent a minor smallpox outbreak. For years the debate over smallpox inoculation had divided elites who favored it from the masses who feared it, a suspicion literally brought home to Benjamin Lynde in 1752 when someone put an envelope containing infectious smallpox scabs on the windowsill of his kitchen.[34] Inoculation in 1774 combined those older tensions with the new imperial ones, leading mobs to attack the homes of the proprietors of the Marblehead hospital and set fire to the hospital itself, then later march to Salem, break open the jail, and release several of the arsonists.[35] Nathaniel Ropes in fact had been home with smallpox when the mob threatened. If it is not clear whether that mob was angry at his being allowed back into town or at his Toryism or at his wealth, the likelihood of overlapping motives is exactly the point. Popular conflation of anti-Toryism and antielitism is exactly why Salem's mercantile leaders had come together in spite of their differences in imperial loyalties. As if to make public their awareness of this, the wealthy Whigs of 1775, who stood as much to lose as did Tories from a populace less given to fine distinctions than was, say, the populace of 1767, enlarged the town's committee of safety, even adding

Tories, to guard not against British invasion but rather against their window-breaking, dung-daubing, and fire-starting neighbors of the lower sort.[36]

None of this agitation, however, had led to a lasting, systemic opposition. The war itself actually *unified* economically divided Salemites. Partially this was because the strangulation of trade had hurt Salemites of every station. In 1776, the town's citizens had been unable to reimburse Thomas Boylston for the ship hull they had scuttled in the harbor and had been unable even to pay their provincial taxes.[37] The British blockade and the loss of fishing grounds, Salemites explained in a letter to the General Court, had left "seamen and fishermen without employment, handcraftsmen without work, traders without goods;" the number of poor was rising, the almshouse and workhouse were full, and the town had to maintain the others with the little money it had remaining.[38] The difficult time had indeed been shared by all; even Thomas Barnard at the North Church had been forced to forgo his salary from 1776 to 1781 and get by on irregular contributions alone.[39] Partially, though, class discontent was suppressed because the war shifted hostilities from internal class tensions to rural-urban tensions after the feeling spread that, as William Pynchon reported, hoarding farmers were threatening to "starve the seaports" unless their increased prices were met. Exaggeration or not, soon Salemites were scuffling with Marbleheaders over what little bread was available, and by 1778 Pynchon was recording in his diary that "tradesmen and salary-men grumble at the countrymen's extortion, and threaten to join the [British] Regulars against them." The farmers had resentments of their own, of course. They had not forgotten the years of tax assessments that put the burden on acreage rather than on stock and shipping, they heard the rumors of merchants hoarding sugar and coffee, and they were not blind to the profits being made through privateering. No doubt these westerners could muster but little sympathy when Salem's town meeting complained again to the General Court how "when we see the produce of land increased not less than sixfold by means of the war and the land itself more than doubled in value while the proprietors suffer no losses and daily exhaust our interest for the necessaries of life . . . we feel ourselves grievously oppressed."[40] Resentments cut both ways indeed; as George Williams summed it up for Timothy Pickering, then away with the Continental Army, "the farmer is jellous of the marchant, the marchant of the farmer."[41] Indeed, the fact that the rural folk returned the hostilities the urban folk felt for them only exacerbated those hostilities. But the legitimacy of either side's argument aside, the point remains, in short, that Salem's lower sort during the war were too busy being angry at farmers to be angry at merchants.[42]

Nor did any sustained oppositionalism emerge in the rest of the 1780s, not least because workers no less than merchants benefited from the General Court continuing to place assessments on acreage rather than on polls or stock or ships. Even when workers did bristle, in 1787, it did not lead to any lasting political presence. Salem's elite and electoral response to Shays' Rebellion was absolute condemnation, but a look at the records of the town meeting in the spring of 1787 suggests a different and more sympathetic reaction among the nonvoting residents of Salem. The position of town treasurer had never before been difficult to fill; indeed it was something of an honor, and most treasurers served for a series of terms. But in 1787, nobody wanted to serve: the first appointee asked to be excused from service, as did the second, third, and fourth before finally someone agreed. Meanwhile, more than a *dozen* selectmen-elect asked to be excused and then refused to serve when their request was denied. More unappealing yet was the office of tax assessor, and even though voters lowered the assessment for the first time in years, they had to go through a long list of men before they found someone willing to take the job. Least attractive of all was tax *collector*, and not until the town allowed collectors to keep two and a half percent of what they brought in did they find volunteers.[43] Had the men in the meeting been hearing talk about resistance in their own town? Had the sailors and fishermen and laborers been grumbling about how they might take to their streets like the Shaysites had to the country roads? Had threats and rumors not extant in official records and newspapers been spreading among the wharves and taverns? Mercantile capital—warehouses, stores, ships, and homes—kindled as easily in 1787 as it had in 1774, and Salem's merchants, it seems, were taking no chances. But however nerve-fraying to elites were these murmurings, they were also, in tone and purpose, little different from the anti-Tory and anti-inoculation mobs of the late colonial period, and they, like their antecedents, led to no sustained politicization of the lower sort. As late as 1795, Bentley could comment on the ability of the security-holders to keep down the "disquiets and angry expressions of more dependent people."[44] And even that had not changed much by the end of the decade. The habits of deference were everywhere hard to break, but in few places were they more lasting or more powerful than in Salem.

But in 1800, those very people would find their voice. If before 1800, the spirit of dissent and discontentment had neither the language nor the vision nor the means to transfer oppositional energy into formal, systemic, and consistent political action, the turn of the century would bring exactly that. The Federalist Party, after all, was not the only party in the first party system. Opposition had coalesced in the form of the Democratic-Republicans, or just "Republicans," or even "Jeffersonians" in the spirit of their most prominent ideologue. This party had begun in Washington's first term, first in opposition to Hamilton's

plans and then, as the 1790s progressed, in continuing and growing opposition to whatever the Federalists put forth. It had not yet taken control of either
the executive or the legislative branches of government but was a party on the
rise. It drew much of its strength from the South and West, but in the northern
cities, the party was drawing to it the slightly empowered and the newly empowered, creating in Salem a coalition of social outsiders, shunned arrivistes,
and dispossessed urban and maritime workers, all unified against Federalist
hegemony in matters sacred and secular.[45]

Bentley was of course sympathetic but had, to date, refrained from overt
partisan activity. But the new year—the new decade and new century, too—saw
William Bentley become a party man. Since 1791 he had been preaching spiritual republicanism; since 1794 he had been preaching economic republicanism. Now he was ready to take his republicanism of both kinds down from the
pulpit altogether and use it to support, through writing, the party that shared
its name.

Back in 1796, Salem Republicans had drummed up 103 votes against the
Federalists' 190 in the presidential race, but they had been unorganized and
inarticulate, "not without men of firm minds," as Bentley commented then,
but not "qualified by education to plead or to write."[46] But all that had since
changed. Now, in 1800, they were ready to plead and to write, and to do it well
and in print. In April of that year, the Republicans got a newspaper of their
own. The *Impartial Register* was in fact quite partial, and its creation was, as
Bentley put it, a "subject of regret" to Federalists.[47] Its editor was William
Carlton, the old editor of the *Gazette* who, like Bentley, had been fired three
years earlier. The man who had let them go, Thomas Cushing, was still at the
Gazette, more Federalist than ever, and now Carlton was his equal, free to edit
and write as he wished for the Republican side. The first thing he did was
recruit Bentley to work with him. So Bentley wrote the same type of news
summaries at the *Register* that he had at the *Gazette*, though it is fair to suspect
that he had his hand in much else that appeared in its pages. Bentley's presence was everywhere, and his topics far-ranging. It was in the *Register*, for
example, that Bentley would soon be defending Abigail Rogers and Immanuel
Kant both.

His ministry at the East Church, meanwhile, was proving equally as important to the party. For the better part of a decade, he had been articulating the
ideology of republicanism, and in fact the 1796 campaign had hinted at the
importance of his contributions. Back then the *Gazette* was still printing oppositional submissions, and though some focused on social policy—to wit, the
Washington administration's disregard for sailors imprisoned by the British—
others had honed in on religious issues, namely the *Gazette*'s decisions to keep

reprinting English printer William Cobbett's attacks on Priestley. In fact, "David Jones" wrote on both topics. He may not have been the same person each time and indeed may not have been a sailor at all, but the choice of pseudonym suggests the emerging awareness of the common interests of all those who would question the elite leadership of a seaport town, for reasons spiritual as much as economic.[48] And now in 1800, Bentley's congregants were poised to join the party whose ideology he had been preaching for so long. His parish was peopled by exactly the seamen, artisans, and rising merchants drawn to the new language of natural rights, and it was those middling merchants and Bentley's good friends—men such as Benjamin Hodges and Edward Gibaut—who would make up the party's leadership. John Fiske was another such man. Fiske had been a privateer and naval commander during the Revolution and a merchant since. But he too knew what it was like to be an outsider and to feel the animosity of the liberal elites, for he was the son of the Rev. Samuel Fiske, who had been expelled from the First Church back in 1736 by what would become its liberal wing. Having moved to the East Church, John Fiske had since become one of its most visible and active members, among other things purchasing both the Diman and the Derby family pews.[49] John Fiske and Bentley were good friends: Bentley sermonized touchingly on the passing of Fiske's 17-year-old daughter, Lydia, in 1785; he rode in Fiske's sloop "Lydia" in 1792; and years later, when he assisted in moving some Fiske corpses to a new family tomb, he cut a piece of silk from the bow in Lydia's hair and brought it home.[50]

And it would be another of Bentley's congregants, a Crowninshield, who would become the most important *candidate* of the new party. The shipping company Crowninshield and Sons had done well during the 1790s. Formed by George Crowninshield, the business had started the decade modestly, with only three ships and all under 100 tons, but the middle years were good to the company, and soon it had built the 209-ton *Belisaurius* and bought the 266-ton *Minerva* and was sending them on regular trips to the Far East. The company was embarking on a new type of trade, one beyond the coastal and West Indian cod and rum runs, beyond even those to Africa and the Mediterranean. This was commerce for a new generation, with longer, riskier, and more profitable voyages for Sumatran pepper and Cantonese fabrics. George Crowninshield had five sons working with him, and together they excelled at the new venture, so that by the mid-1790s, the firm was among the most successful in town.[51] But for all their success, they remained outsiders and outcasts in Salem's political and social life. They were easterners, not westerners; none had gone to Harvard; they traded more with the French empire than the English empire; they were of German rather than English stock; and the patriarch was a rough-edged man who was resistant to the rules of polite behavior. Profit alone was not enough for membership in the cod aristocracy: the right family, education, and congregation all were necessary to allow one in or, in Crowninshield's case, to keep one out. William Bentley and the Crowninshields understood each other perfectly, and in fact it was to the home of a Crowninshield widow taking boarders that Bentley had moved back in 1791 and where he had lived contentedly ever since. By the end of the decade, all five brothers had retired from the sea. Now they could operate the business from land while hiring as captains other young men who were following their own paths upward. Jacob Crowninshield, the second oldest, had also turned his eye toward politics, and already in 1800 he was taking up the Republican cause on behalf of his family, his neighbors, and his minister.

Jacob Crowninshield ran in 1800 to fill the seat of a retiring congressman. Samuel Sewall had represented the Third Middle District since 1796, when he was elected to replace Benjamin Goodhue, who had resigned to run for the U.S. Senate in a seat left vacant when George Cabot retired. Sewall, Goodhue, and Cabot were Federalists—intense, committed, high Federalists—and Salem's voters had liked them that way. Nathan Read, the Federalist candidate against Crowninshield in 1800, was fully in this vein. If he lived in Danvers rather than Salem and was an apothecary rather than a merchant, still he had many of the requisite Federalist credentials. He was a Harvard graduate and tutor, an inventor of steam engine modifications with several patents to his name, a member of the American Academy of Arts and Sciences, and most recently an organizer of the Salem Iron Factory. In three separate elections that summer and fall, Read and Crowninshield squared off. Sewall had actually resigned before his term was complete, so the candidates ran once (and then a run-off) to fill that term and then once again in the regular election. The Federalists championed their man with rhetoric that was by then standard issue: Read's was the party of the Constitution, of Washington and Adams, and of the prosperity of the 1790s; it was, they said, the party that was the home of "all the friends of good order, of good government—all who have a regard for their religion, their laws, and their domestic enjoyments." And Read, they noted, was a man of education, an owner of sufficient property, and "(what is not very common at this day) a believer and public professor of his faith"—all evidence enough of his worth.[52] Moreover, their Republican opponents were "disorganizers and deists—men who feast themselves upon all that is odious— who wink at blasphemy, smile at murder, and burst into a broad laugh at atheism."[53] The comments about the Federalists' religious fidelity and the Republicans' infidelity were to some degree a reflection on Thomas Jefferson, the deistic Republican candidate for president that year; all Republicans were tarred with that brush. But the ubiquity of these remarks suggests that in Salem the Federalists were taking aim also at the ongoing ontological deism of Crowninshield's minister and intellectual patron.

For his part, Crowninshield had little with which to campaign. The party had never been in power on the national, state, or local level, and he personally had never even held office. Still, it was not just a lack of alternatives that led his side to play up the economic divisions in town. They presented Crowninshield as an advocate of the lower sort. "An Old Salt," "A Real Mechanic," "A Shoe Maker" from Lynn, and others explained in the *Register* how Crowninshield alone understood them and represented them, and "A Seaman" highlighted Crowninshield's efforts to release an impressed Salemite, reminding "ye Sons of Neptune" that "our Shipmate [rescued] you from the paw of the British Lion."[54] Since its founding, the *Register* had positioned itself as the party of the sailing interest, printing letters complaining of the ferocity of the English navy, the unfairness of the adjudication process in Halifax, and, most damningly, the unwillingness of Federalist politicians—including Salem's own Benjamin Goodhue—to help, but now they had an actual candidate to support.[55] So on it went in issue after issue of the *Register*, variations on the theme that Read was *"the rich man's candidate"* and Crowninshield was "the poor man's friend, who has clothed the naked and fed the hungry, many a time and oft."[56] Republicans from Georgia to Maine were selling themselves as the party of the poor and dispossessed, and in Salem at least did so with a level of class hostility not seen since the imperial crisis. The *Register* zinged with caustic letters impossible to imagine a few years previously. "An Old Salt," for example, appeared in its pages to vent on shipowners' occasional practice of refusing to pay the 5 per-cent of the proceeds due the master of a voyage because, so they said, the master had deviated from orders once at sea. "The rash curses of merchants are remembered," Bentley sympathized, "and their deeds of great injustice are recorded in the memory of the sufferers."[57] The criticism struck a chord with others as well. "New Salt" from Marblehead wrote to the *Register* with a sar-casm not previously heard in public debates. The first writer, he began, had seemed

> to insinuate that it is a CRIME for an OWNER to rob a *Master* of *two or three thousand dollars!!*—What an ignorant blockhead he must be to think so. Does not he know that *Masters* are *Slaves*, and that OWNERS are RICH? And does not he know that RICHES consti-tute POWER, and are, besides, a legal substitute for COMMON SENSE, HONOR, HONESTY, and RELIGION? And does he not know that an OWNER has a right to say how much his *slave* shall

make for him every voyage, and to stop his wages and commissions to make up any deficiency? And does not he know that the slaves are obliged to submit, and think themselves fortunate to get off with their lives? Does he not know that the RICH may of right rob, cheat, lie, murder, and do anything else to increase their RICHES—and that the poor who are so presumptuous as to err in judgment, are, and of right ought to be, deprived of "even that which they have"— dismissed from employment and made to starve in the streets?[58]

This was a virulence unarticulated in the 1790s, much less in the 1780s or before the Revolution, at least in public. It was of an angry underclass, urged on by the promise of a political voice, lashing out now in print rather than in mobs. It was republican rhetoric infused with the bitterness of oppression, and it had taken root quickly during the campaigning that summer and fall of 1800. "Vive la Republique," wrote James Winthrop to Bentley on the eve of one of the elections, but more than esprit was needed to get their man in office; Read won both the replacement and the regular elections.[59]

But the returns suggested that a change was indeed under way. Read won only in some of the eighteen other Essex and Middlesex towns. In Salem, Crowninshield won both times.[60] And if he did so only because he was from Salem and Read was not, he would not have that advantage next time. In 1802, Federalists would not renominate the incumbent, and Crowninshield would face a candidate who was also from Salem. But that was only the beginning of Crowninshield's problems.

Crowninshield's opponent this time was Salem's most experienced, most famous, and most ideologically extreme statesman. Other members of the first party system in Massachusetts may have been moderates, fearing more than feeding partisanship, but there was nothing centrist about this particular contest.[61] Here was pitted a Francophile arriviste backed by a Socinian preacher/publicist against a man whose name was by then practically synonymous with High Federalism. Son of a Tabernacle deacon, Timothy Pickering had inherited in spades his father's acute moral rigor and tendency to disputation. After Harvard, a rudimentary training in the law, and self-instruction in the fundamentals of militias, Pickering had risen from colonel of Salem's regiment to staff officer in the Continental Army and then, after the war, postmaster general, Indian commissioner, and, finally, secretary of state under Washington and Adams. He was the most powerful member of the Essex Junto, a man whose Federalist credentials more than matched those of Cabot, Higginson, and the other Boston and North Shore merchants. Though released from duty by Adams for obstructionism, Pickering was an asset to the Essex Junto, and friends quickly organized a subscription to purchase his Pennsylvania lands to allow him to return to Salem and to political life. In 1802, then, he was back and ready to run for Congress against the three-time loser Jacob Crowninshield. The two men and their platforms could hardly have been more different; here, there was no "revolutionary center." Here the candidates boasted, and voters would decide between, two very different visions for the future of the Republic.

It would be hard-fought, for Federalism was still powerful in Salem. Salemites had gone with Federalist Caleb Strong over Republican Elbridge Gerry in the past three gubernatorial races, and they had yet to vote a Republican slate into either the state Senate or the lower House, rejecting Crowninshield himself for both offices just that spring.[62] But even so, Republicans had reason to hope. Strong was indeed a formidable figure in Massachusetts politics, but the support he received was as much personal as it was ideological; that Salem voted for him was hardly an accurate reflection of broader Federalist leanings.

Most important, this time the Republicans had material. By then, Jefferson was president, and they had not only two years of Republican governance at the national level to highlight, but an opponent with a long and now vulnerable record. Pickering, the voters were reminded, had promoted a stamp tax, a sedition law, a larger standing army, federal borrowing at 8 percent to build a navy, bribes to Algerians, and even New England secessionism. Nothing in Pickering's career went unrecalled: he had hesitated to lead Salem's militia in April of 1775; he had been fired by the second president in May of 1800; and he had cared not a bit for the interests of the middling or lower sort. This son of a farmer was a mere pawn of the merchants, Republicans claimed, and unsympathetic, untalented, and unpleasant to boot.[63]

But Republicans had another weapon as well. Earlier that year, the Federalist *Gazette* had prophesized that the spring elections for local offices would depend on the virtuous freeholders in the rural districts rather than on the segment of the population it described as the "stews of a populous seaport or the sweepings of a vessel's hold."[64] Republicans pounced on the phrases as further evidence of the Federalists' contempt for the working class. The Federalist newspaper's words were reminiscent of Burke's famous dismissal of the "swinish multitude," a phrase that had been trotted out in 1800 by Republicans eager to remind the lesser sort, as if they needed reminding, of the snobbery in even enlightened conservatism. Over and over now, the *Register*'s readers were told how they were nothing but sweepings and stews in the minds of their Federalist neighbors.[65] The Federalists had blundered, to be sure, but the Republican reaction was more than mere opportunistic politicking. In taking offense, Republicans were signaling a new unwillingness of the underclass simply to take their lumps. They were putting their townspeople on notice that there would be no more quiet acceptance of this kind of dismissiveness. That wealth continued to be unequally distributed everyone knew, but that the poorer sort would simply accept a concomitant inferiority was something of the past.

Crowninshield won. And this time he won not only in Salem but in the rest of the district. The thirty-two-year-old parishioner of the East Church had beaten Essex County's highest ranking politician and was on his way to the new federal city of Washington.

Spurred by Bentley's pen, the Republican Party continued to grow.[66] Voters returned Crowninshield to the House of Representatives as long as he was available, and in 1804 went not only with a Republican gubernatorial candidate for the first time but also with Republican presidential electors over Federalist ones in a ratio greater than in the rest of the commonwealth.[67] Salem Republicans also won, for the first time, the races for the General Court, two years before that party had a majority in the legislature. This last victory was particularly sweet, for Federalists ran a ticket that included Salem's famous merchant William Gray and its famous mathematician Nathaniel Bowditch, but it lost anyway to two middling merchants and a Quaker schoolteacher.[68] But perhaps most important, Republicans took over the offices of town government. By then, party slates had replaced individual nominations, and voters in 1802 elected en masse an entirely new, and Republican, group of selectmen, a change that led one Salemite to write in a private journal simply: "Federalists weep. Died in this town, Federalism."[69] Indeed it had: Republicans retained the town offices each successive year and in ever growing numbers.

Bentley was not the only cause of Republican success, but some sense of his importance to it can be gained by a comparison with the party affiliations of other towns. It is true that Salem was not the only town even in Essex County drifting toward the Republican Party; the independent fishermen of Marblehead made it staunchly Republican, as did those of Gloucester. But that is all. There were no other Republican towns in the county. Lynn, though later Republican, was strongly Federalist in both 1800 and 1802. Danvers, on Salem's western border, naturally went with the local favorite Read in 1800, but it was only a little less Federalist in 1802, 60 percent instead of 62 percent of its votes, when Read was not in the race. The residents of Beverly, a seafaring town just across the North River, was also Federalist, with 88 percent going for Read in 1800 and 61 percent for Pickering in 1802. The best comparison of all is with Newburyport, a town up on the Merrimac River with a smaller population but the same social structure and economic diversity as Salem. And there, Federalism never wavered. They were in a different congressional district than

Salem and so did not participate in either of the Crowninshield races, but in their own contests they went 84 percent Federalist in 1800 and 74 percent in 1802.[70] The difference between Danvers, Beverly, and Newburyport on the one hand and Salem on the other was, it seems, Bentley.

His opponents clearly thought that he was responsible for the party's rise, enough so to regularly harangue him in the *Gazette* because of it. They mocked his writing style, and they fretted for his parishioners. They coined new names for him, the "Essex Clerical Illuminat and Electioneering Tool" in 1800 and the "learned bombadier," the "Arch-Spouter," and the "wise man of the East" in 1802.[71] Even Crowninshield thought that Bentley deserved the credit. He was at least grateful enough to persuade other congressmen in November of 1804 to elect Bentley chaplain of the House of Representatives, an honor Bentley declined.[72] And in a letter back to Salem, Crowninshield could hardly contain himself. "Your triumph seems to be almost complete," he gushed to his minister in words that inferred that the victory was more Bentley's than his own. "We ardently rejoice in your success. It exceeds all calculations. You have," he told his friend, "indeed done wonders."[73]

In 1805 Crowninshield introduced Bentley by letter to Thomas Jefferson himself. "Mr. Bentley himself is a very respectable citizen," Crowninshield wrote the president. "No man respects you more than that Gentleman. Our political opponents have lavished upon him all the venom of their rage, but the injury is nothing." Bentley, he concluded, was "a genuine republican with a reputation unspotted and a mind enlarged by the most generous feelings and talents far above the common lot of mortals."[74] It was high praise indeed and perhaps at least part of the cause for the invitation received soon after to become one of the instructors at the proposed college in Washington. Bentley, then forty-six years old, considered it carefully but finally declined, unable to leave the "affections of a little society" that had, for better or worse, been his home for so long.[75] Crowninshield was making quite a name for himself in Washington, and the next year he would be nominated by Jefferson to be secretary of the Navy, an appointment he turned down.[76] So if Bentley had done wonders, it was because he had good material with which to work. But it was he, not Jacob Crowninshield, who was in Salem, shaping the minds of Salem voters.

Perhaps the best indicator of Bentley's role in the party's success was the fact that when in 1806 both houses of the Massachusetts General Court were for the first time controlled by Republicans, their members invited William Bentley to give the annual Election Day sermon. Their appreciation in fact ran deeper than this, for they had been proposing him for that honor since 1803 but had been blocked by Federalist majorities, and they would also nominate him to be the legislative chaplain, though Bentley would withdraw his name.[77] He did agree to give the sermon, however. Each May, newly elected legislators attended a religious service as a benediction to their year of governance, the center of which was, of course, the sermon. Bentley's sermon was delivered to a jubilant crowd, for James Sullivan had been reelected governor (and had won in Salem), and the Republicans had swept the lower House (and had won in Salem). Massachusetts state government was for the first time entirely in Republican hands, and there was Bentley, addressing them as they began their duties.[78] He was, certainly, one of the very few local Republican Congregationalists— the chaplain was a Baptist, and the Election Day speaker the next year would have to come all the way from Pittsfield—but the choice was also an acknowledgment of Bentley's great contributions in cultivating the party in eastern Massachusetts, indeed in nursing the spirit of the party before the party itself even existed.

Liberal Arminians, now Federalists too, still circled inside the feedback loop of wealth and virtue and so remained as convinced as ever that their material success reflected a superior morality which in turn dictated that they, the talented and virtuous few, should continue to hold sway over the unfit and undeserving masses around them. The *Gazette*, for one, was mortified by the shift of town governance to the Republicans, sniffing that the victory had been announced in an "open town-meeting by a democratic shout resembling an Indian yell."[79] Soon after, a nearby Federalist wrote to a friend that "such a revolution of sentiment in so short a period I never suspected. Men whom we heretofore relied on for support, now appeared openly against us, and boldly espoused the Republican cause."[80] The comment is telling. The Republicans had openly dared to assert political rights over economic power. The Republicans had not only won political races but in so doing had liberated the demos from the assumption that one's social superior was a political superior as well. As Bentley wrote in 1803 about Federalist losses, "The country was to be a feast to this new nobility from which they are excluded with disgrace."[81]

The "revolution of sentiment," that is, was not only that the lower sort were voting Republican but that they were voting at all. Before 1800, voting had been a ritual of a narrow minority of those eligible. Salem's town records from the colonial or revolutionary periods rarely include the actual numbers of votes in a contest, but when Salemites in 1773 considered whether to allow a townsman to build an inoculation hospital—unquestionably a controversial and passionate issue—the proposal was acted on by only 240 voters in a year in which more than a thousand were eligible.[82] Low turnout rates plagued elections then as now, but the fact that three-quarters or more of the eligible voters did not exercise the right suggests that many members of the community were in the habit of leaving town affairs in what they assumed were hands more capable than theirs; it is not surprising, then, that when in 1765 the town considered a proposal that two members of the school committee should be "chosen of machanics," the vote failed.[83] The war, the confederation period, and even the 1790s had not expanded the use of the franchise. Only sixty-four voters had cast ballots in the governor's race in 1795, for example, and ninety-one in the congressional race of 1796. The rise of a second party, however, and particularly one so much closer in spirit to the masses, brought the people into the electoral process. The three congressional elections between Read and Crowninshield in 1800 were voted on by 622, 843, and 937 voters, respectively. The requirements for voting had not changed; what had changed were assumptions about the legitimacy and necessity of popular participation in the political arena.[84] With Crowninshield's victory, the days when the elite few controlled the formal mechanisms of public life had ended. The grip of the elites had been broken.

It was not in Salem alone that supporting the Jeffersonian Republican party symbolized a larger shedding of deference, but given the power of deference in Salem, the party's ascendancy there suggested that a fundamental corner had been turned. It may not be too much to say that to many Salemites, only in 1805 was the American Revolution finally, truly, won.

And Bentley had won his own revolution too against oppressive social deference. In April of 1803, Timothy Pickering assuaged his ego by suing the *Register*'s editor for libelous statements printed during the previous fall's campaign. The case was heard by Massachusetts's highest court, one presided over by Samuel Sewall, whose seat Crowninshield had competed for in 1800. Here was a Federalist ex-congressman determining whether a Federalist ex-secretary of state had been libeled by Bentley's friend and ally. As the case wore on, Bentley was called to testify against Carlton, but he simply refused to go. The man who once quivered in the presence of social power, who in fact once trembled from the very idea of speaking in front of such an audience, had become defiant of it.[85]

He had become as enthusiastic a believer in the Republican agenda as he had been in Unitarianism, and for the same reasons. The "struggle for liberty is deserved if it gives the soul only one breath more of the free air in which it lives," he wrote. "There is no life in a slave."[86] He was still, and would always be, most concerned to bring enlightenment to the people. On weekdays he worked at it through the Republican Party, and on Sundays he climbed into the pulpit. He was making progress; Salem had become a legitimate two-party town, in part because of Bentley's insistence on the right to inquiry, candor, and the free exchange of ideas. Later he would reflect back on just what the Republican victories had meant for the town. "While Salem was under the greatest aristocracy in New England," he then wrote, "few men thought and the few directed the many. Now the aristocracy is gone and the many govern."[87]

9

Vox Populi, Vox Dei

Bentley had accomplished something that nobody, even just a
few years earlier, could have imagined. Nor would the William Bentley
of, say, 1783 have been pleased by what he had come to think and
do in the years since. Bentley was not the only person involved in
the rise of the Republicans, but he had played a singularly important role in it. Largely because of his arguments from the pulpit and
in print, the classically liberal Federalists of Salem had been deposed.
But just why everyone who disagreed with the Federalists did agree
with Bentley was a different matter, for his was not the only kind of
republicanism in town. Salem was home to other kinds, too, and
though they ended up taking Bentley's side, they did so for reasons all
their own.

The economic agenda of Salem republicanism does not easily fit any
postindustrial ideology. Jacob Crowninshield had won by tapping
into the lower sort's resentment of their social superiors, but the actual republican hope was considerably more nuanced, and moderate,
than what was implied by the campaign rhetoric. In fact, Salem's
brand of republicanism was a voice not nearly as much for the profoundly dispossessed as for what the *Register* called the "great body
of the middle class of citizens," the artisans and ranking seamen
who wanted to use the liberating power of the market to break into real
prosperity.[1] Republicans were not opposed to hierarchy per se; they
did not want to level the social pyramid but to get a fair chance at

rising up it. Nor were they opposed to wealth so much as wealth not duly and fairly earned; "Capt. Crowninshield is as rich as any candidate," boasted his defenders in the *Register*, but he was "indebted only under God *to his industry* for all the wealth he possesses."[2] Nor were Republicans opposed to commercial capitalism as a system. In fact, they *supported* commercial capitalism as the system that provided the surest incentive to act on the manifest wisdom and benefits of natural morality. Like the liberal Federalists, they held that the free market maximized ethical behavior by rewarding the virtuous and punishing the vicious. Commercial wealth was unlike the landed wealth that had preceded it or the industrial wealth that would follow. In a free commercial market, they believed, the life course of a sailor (as mate, supercargo, captain, and then merchant) or of an artisan (as apprentice, journeyman, and then master) was determined above all by the virtues of the individual, with skill and discipline bringing happiness, and sloth and intemperance bringing misery. To Salem Republicans—in this sense of party identification as well as in the lower-case ideological commitment—an environment in which these causal relationships can be enacted was exactly the benefit of independence. Their spirit of '76 had aimed at unburdening themselves of the aristocracy, manor lords, and mercantilism that kept them down. In the 1790s, the Federalists had threatened to replace those older oppressions with their new one, but the Republicans had broken that hold as well, and now capitalism and the free market allowed free individuals to reap the rewards of whatever virtues they possessed.[3]

But at the same time, there were important differences between how the republicans and the classical liberals viewed that market. Republican capitalism was not *unrestrained* capitalism. For though they were committed to capitalism as the best way to organize a political economy, Republicans also insisted on allowing alternative values to guide the invisible hand and soften its blows when necessary, to interject into the market at least *some* of the moral imperatives that had been stripped from it by liberals' all-too-eager readings of Locke, Mandeville, and Smith. Though they desired success, that is, they also desired a political economy that paid at least some attention to those who failed to find it. For theirs was a new type of wealth, a wealth that had once been poor and that remembered the poor and that reached out to the poor. They had learned that not all poor were poor because of vice. Of course Bentley still held in utter contempt the foolish and the lazy and the drunken, and he would do little to help them, but now he saw that the virtuous can become impoverished from causes beyond their control. The man who once blamed the suffering of Marblehead fishermen on the fishermen themselves was now able to see that sometimes the lower sort suffer not from their own decisions but from decisions made by others. The high price of firewood, he now wrote, would "be a great oppression in the time of stagnation of all business."[4]

All this was akin to what historians of ideology have described as the "country" mentality arrayed against the "court" one, but in Salem, which had no rural self-identification and in fact positioned itself against rural values, a better context is the notion of a moral economy, an insistence that there does exist a place and a time for economic agents to take into consideration right and wrong as well as profit and loss. In late 1800, for example, a minor smallpox outbreak hit nearby Marblehead. Immediately, forestallers—individuals who would corner a market in foodstuffs brought in from rural areas—began to meet incoming farmers at Salem's town limits. They lied that smallpox had reached Salem, too, but happily, they would purchase the produce there on the spot. The grateful farmers sold, whereupon the forestallers took the food into Salem and set their price. The ruse did not last long, but long enough for both parties, or at least their quasi-formal party organs, to respond. The Federalist *Gazette* maintained the liberal line, arguing that the forestallers deserved the rewards of their risks, while the Republican *Register* condemned the deception and profiteering at the expense of well-meaning fear and ignorance.[5] Bentley's brand of republicanism did not begrudge the rewards that come from taking risks with capital, but it did oppose the taking advantage of the innocent weaknesses of others. This was an extension into political economy of the same theme he had been arguing for a decade, that those who possess knowledge are morally responsible to ameliorate, not exacerbate, the miseries suffered by those who do not possess knowledge.

In terms of religious alignments, Crowninshield's victory could hardly have come solely on the strength of the town's Christian naturalists. There simply were not that many of them. He received undoubtedly precious few votes from the liberal churches, both Federalist practically to a man. It seems likely, then, that he won largely because of the support given him by, of all people, the town's evangelicals.

Of these there were many. The Tabernacle was enjoying a remarkable renaissance under Nathaniel Whitaker's successor, Joshua Spaulding, a Connecticut native and Salem's first minister not to attend college. The liberal Arminians were not impressed when the rumor spread that the newcomer had risen from his bed in the middle of a dream about being an angel and jumped out of his window into a ditch.[6] But the Tabernacle members had liked him enough to extend a call. They then adopted a new covenant which returned the church from Presbyterianism back to Congregationalism, and the beleaguered church began to revive, enough so even by 1791 to build a second chapel.[7] Daniel Hopkins's South Church, in 1783 a sputtering congregation using the old town hall, had also grown, adding thirty-nine members in the decade that followed and more since.[8]

That Bentley was forced to ally with evangelicals surely did not sit well with him, but the evangelicals liked it no better, at least to judge by Bentley's complaint to Crowninshield about the difficulties of forging an alliance with those who "on all occasions denounce you as an enemy to the truth, or rather of their truth."[9] But the alliance would hold, at least during the campaign seasons, because although they were theologically different, they were ideologically in perfect agreement. Evangelicals, after all, had long believed in their *own* form of republicanism.

It was indeed the case that elsewhere in New England evangelicals were drawn to the Republican Party for reasons not specifically economic. Some of them, particularly dissenting ones, appreciated the party's opposition to the parish system.[10] But whatever the importance of dissent elsewhere, the issue was not a pressing one in Salem because there was no establishment from which *to* dissent, Bentley having dissolved the second of the two parishes back in the 1780s. Other evangelicals elsewhere appreciated the party's support for the French Revolution, something they believed in on the grounds that the destruction of Catholicism would hasten the return of Christ and the inauguration of the final paradise. Ebenezer Bradford of Rowley was one such millenarian, and in 1795 he published the only pro-Republican sermon to come that year from Essex County, but he had "suffered much" from his effort, as Bentley recorded it, and his influence quickly waned.[11] Joshua Spaulding at Salem's Tabernacle was another such example, even confident enough to identify the French Revolution as the "sixth trumpet" foretold in the Book of Revelation, but church members were so put off by it that they dismissed him in 1802 and called a Federalist as his successor.[12] And although Spaulding had enough supporters to start up Branch Church, the third evangelical congregation in town, it was a smaller congregation than the one he had left. Whatever Spaulding's influence over those who agreed with him, neither he nor his millenarianism shaped the party's public ideological positions.

What *did* matter to Salem evangelicals—of whatever congregation—was *economic* republicanism. And it had mattered to them for two generations. Ever since the Awakening, many evangelicals had been as suspicious of the ideology of liberal economics as of the theology of liberal Christianity; they had long held their neighbors to the bar of economic morality as Edwards, not Chauncy, understood it, all the more so in times that called for communalism rather than individualism.

One such time had been the imperial crisis and Revolution. Although strict correlations between the theological and the political identities of Revolution-era clergy have proved difficult to discern, in Salem there was no ambiguity.[13] For starters, the clergy of the two liberal churches were committed and public loyalists to the last minute. The First's Thomas Barnard Sr. was Tory enough to sign a public farewell letter to Thomas Hutchinson, and Asa Dunbar, full pastor after Barnard's death in 1776, could hardly have been very patriotic from Weston, to which he had prudently absented himself.[14] Dunbar's successor, John Prince, had assumed the pulpit only in 1779, so he avoided having to take a stand, but it says something of his tolerance of Toryism that, when John Appleton returned from exile in 1782, members of the First chose him as ruling elder. Meanwhile, over at the North, Thomas Barnard Jr. signed the Hutchinson farewell letter too—an act he was later forced to recant, requesting a "veil of charity and forgiveness" from the Committee of Safety[15]—and though he is credited with ending a standoff in 1774 between patriots and British Regulars, his willingness to negotiate and the British willingness to negotiate back reflect nothing so much as their mutual interests. No wonder that Salem's Anglicans went to the North after St. Peter's closed its doors.[16] Compare this to the South's Daniel Hopkins, who spent the war years in the Third Provincial Congress of Massachusetts, the General Court, and the Governor's Council, and whose congregation welcomed four transfers from the First who had left embittered by its loyalism.[17] And compare this particularly to the Tabernacle's Nathaniel Whitaker, who was the single most important mouthpiece and conscience of the radical patriot faction that emerged among the lower classes after 1769. It was ironic that his meetinghouse accidentally burned down in the anti-Tory fire of 1774 because it had been there that a crowd had met on the one-year anniversary of the Boston Massacre to listen as Whitaker "displayed the fatal effects of tyranny in its many hideous forms" in a performance thus described by Thomas Hutchinson.[18] And Whitaker had published in 1777 what became perhaps New England's best-known patriot sermon, *An Antidote against Toryism*. From the heart of one of the most Tory towns in America, Whitaker had ventured to demonize not only the overt Tories but also the neutrals, obstructionists, and silent sympathizers who abetted their cause.

Whitaker's pages practically dripped republican hostilities. The occasion of the anger was of course the political decision that some made of loyalism over rebellion, but the source of that anger was the corrupt economic motives behind that decision. The brunt of his fury fell in fact on all those who were putting their private interests ahead of the public cause, those who were "eagerly pursuing worldly gain and heaping up unrighteous mammon by cruel oppression and grinding the faces of the poor, while our country lies bleeding of her wounds."[19] At the end of the war—in fact, in May of 1783, the very month William Bentley had arrived in Salem—Whitaker had published a second anti-Tory sermon, this one on the dangers of allowing Tories back into town. By then he was haranguing Loyalists on a regular basis, at least according to Mehitabel Higginson, who complained to Timothy Pickering about the "torrent of curses that are vented on Sunday evenings" at the Tabernacle.[20] The published sermon showed Whitaker in full rhetorical flourish, pulling out the stops lamenting the patriot martyrs "in whose blood the Tories have stained their murdering hands; to whose tortures, cries and dying groans they have danced, as to the sweet sound of the viol." But again the core of his concern was economic, this time the ex-Tories' supposed plan to restore themselves to their former commercial power. The refugees, warned Whitaker,

> have doubtless formed their connections already with the merchants, and probably with the court of Britain, for a large supply of goods. By these means those murderers, who ought to suffer for treason, will get the start of all the friends of liberty who have not yet formed any connections there, will have the run of the trade, will sell below even the sterling cost to gain custom, sink the price of goods in the hands of our honest merchants which they procured at a high price, and so break them; stop all our home manufacturers; drain off all our money into the hands of Britain, except what sticks in the hands of Tories, and by which they will be able to influence our elections, rise in power and pervert our counsels.[21]

Commerce was the avenue to wealth, prestige, and place in Salem, whether one deserved it or, as Whitaker was convinced was usually the case, one did not.

The East Church, then under James Diman, had been predominantly patriotic. Diman himself had served as chaplain to the General Court when it met in Salem, but more tellingly, thirty-one members had signed the letter against Gage while none had signed the letter welcoming him. Bentley's congregation, that is, had their own sensitivities to the political corruptibility of liberal wealth, and, although not evangelical, they were in 1800 ready to ally with those who were and to accept in return the alliance of those who disagreed with them.

The one congregation of Christian naturalists and the two, later three, congregations of evangelicals shared nothing except the conviction that true Christianity lay in restoring conscientiousness over acquisitiveness. Salem's republicanism was a combination of the "rights of man" and "covenanted communalism," come together to resist the liberal claim that true virtue is demonstrated by the very possession of wealth and power. Wealth and power, they both knew, were human creations, not divine ones. For the evangelicals, God rewarded the faithful, but less for moderation and restraint than for humility before God and activism in the name of God, and the reward was bestowed in any event in heaven rather than on earth. For Bentley, God did not reward at all. To the degree that virtue creates wealth, it did so only by following the natural laws of creation, certainly not as a sign of salvation or a sanction for power. Salem republicanism, that is, was an alliance of the many who believed that God does not directly reward liberal values and the one who believed that God cannot.

These were strange bedfellows indeed, William Bentley and the evangelicals. But such was the nature of Republican oppositionalism in New England. Not too many years later, the *Gazette* published the text of a series of toasts given by a group of Salem Republicans and added to each a mocking and derisive postscript. In one such embellishment, the imaginary Republican toastmaster raised a glass to the "triumph of reason" and the death by guillotine of the clerics, reprieving "for their political services, viz. Parson Bentley, Parson Leland, Parson Allen, Elias Smith, and Tom Paine."[22] Excepting Paine, each man on the list was a Republican minister, though they had little else in common. John Leland was a Baptist preacher in the Berkshires whose Republican loyalties stemmed from both disestablishmentarianism and a friendship with Madison formed during an earlier residence in Virginia. Thomas Allen also lived in western Massachusetts, where, undaunted by seaboard merchants, he had carried his personal inclination to radicalism from the war years into the Jeffersonian party, even assisting his nephew in putting out the Republican *Pittsfield Sun*. Unlike Leland, however, Allen was a Congregationalist. And unlike Bentley, Allen was a Calvinist. Elias Smith, meanwhile, had broken with the Baptist church over the creeping formalism of the Boston Baptists and gone on to form his own sect, the "Christ-ian Church," which combined the pietistic and experiential faith he found lacking in Boston with an anti-Trinitarian, anti-creedal universalism. His was a pietist rationalism of a unique and improbable kind, and the synthesis did not hold; he won few adherents, and his church soon dwindled away. But not before his support for the Republicans was notorious among the Federalists.[23] This small group, then—an unlikely coalition of Baptists, ex-Baptist sectarians, Standing Order frontier Calvinists, and a Socinian rationalist—shared only an opposition to the entrenched social and economic power of the Federalists. It was an uncomfortable fit for Bentley, who had little admiration for Calvinists, less for Baptists, and none at all for sectarians, but it was the only way to break the Federalist grip on economic, political, and religious life in establishment Massachusetts.

The alliance, as odd as it was, was not without precedent. In many ways it was replicating the sixteenth-century alliance of European Anabaptists and rationalists—who shared nothing else—against the hegemonic Lutheran and

Calvinist establishments, only this time against Congregationalist Federalists.[24] But although not surprising, the alliance does raise a couple of interesting questions. If evangelical republicanism was so much older than rationalist republicanism, if indeed it was fully in place even well before the 1790s, why then did not a Republican Party emerge before 1800 and why, when it did emerge, did not an evangelical lead it? Part of the answer has to lie in the fact that there had been in the 1790s no voice comparable to Whitaker's in the 1770s. He was no longer in Salem, and his replacement at the Tabernacle, Spaulding, had none of his energy or interests; over at the South Church, meanwhile, Daniel Hopkins was quiet, too, the disinterestedness he was urging being more a theological than an economic one. Perhaps had there been such a figure, a party of evangelical republicanism might have emerged. But one suspects that in Salem, the Republican Party needed an ex-liberal, not an evangelical, to take the lead. At least the men who ended up running the party needed a liberal. They were lucky that in their town was a republican who also happened to be one.

A second question is why the evangelicals were willing to support a Christian rationalist congressman or for that matter a deist president. Again hard evidence is elusive, but it is tempting to think that the answer is tied up in the liberating power of the revolutionary era writ large. For although the Federalist clergy had indeed feared that the lower sort would run to deism, the lower sort themselves had no intention of doing so. And they saw such dire prediction for the snobbish paranoia it was. They felt none of the ministers' urgency for a state-sponsored religion to combat supposedly pernicious humanism, for their God did not need a government of Federalists to do his work. Of course they had opposed Paine's brand of deism, but they had not been afraid of it. And at the turn of the century, they knew that, Federalist doomsayers to the contrary, men such as Jacob Crowninshield and Thomas Jefferson were not going to destroy religious life in America. Their God would not allow it. Their God had a plan that would unfold just as he wished it to, regardless of which members of Creation occupied posts of secular power. Just as evangelical parents were taking their children to be baptized by Bentley even while disagreeing with him over just what was happening, so too would they elect Crowninshield and Jefferson even while disagreeing with them. The paradise at the end of the Christian narrative was always out there, in no way postponed by the misunderstandings of the unregenerate.

The established clergy were right to be nervous after all, but for the wrong reason. Lower-sort congregants did not reject God's warnings, but they did reject the clergy's.

IO

William Bentley and the Limits of Revolutionary Ideology

The social conservatism Bentley showed in the 1780s had become by the early 1790s a political oppositionalism and then, by the end of the decade, outright radicalism. The merchants' desire to trade with England while it was at war with the French Republic, their seeming apathy to impressments, and their valuing of commerce over commonwealth had taught Bentley to be suspicious of mercantile interests and accordingly sympathetic to popular interests. He was further schooled in oppositional politics by the liberal reaction to his dissemination of Unitarianism and then even more by the others' leap to Federalism upon the appearance of *The Age of Reason*, behavior that to Bentley reflected a failure of stewardship over the spirituality of the masses. He had kept his faith in the ideals of the French Revolution long after most Americans had lost theirs, and his solitary conviction of its liberating promise had guided him to leadership of a disparate and conflicted Republican Party in Salem. By then, after years of alienation and hostility from the elite liberals he had as a young man admired, Bentley had found a social conscience. And with it he sought to break the cycle of liberal self-justification that had served to keep low the lowly. The political rights inherent in natural creation, he saw at century's end, ought to be expanded to the social and economic realms as well, and he had devoted the first few years of the nineteenth century to making those rights more real through a new and ultimately victorious political party.

By 1805, Bentley had been working for twenty-two years on behalf of that vision of America and of Christianity. In some aspects he had been successful and in others less so, but in either case, and in both arenas of activity, his time and his usefulness had already come and gone.

William Bentley had created a new political party in Salem, one that had quickly risen to dominance. But Bentley's importance to it was already in 1805 on the wane. Even while Crowninshield was telling Jefferson about Bentley, and even while the Massachusetts legislature was acknowledging his contributions, Bentley's role in Salem Republicanism itself was diminishing. He was no longer needed to disseminate pamphlets by Dissenters, since Priestley's books were now available in Salem bookstores. Priestley had enjoyed the respite of Jefferson's presidency and had died in Pennsylvania in 1804, and soon Joseph Jr. was complaining to Bentley that he had on hand seven hundred copies of his father's *Discourses on Various Subjects*, two hundred and fifty copies of *General History of the Christian Church*, and two hundred copies of the *Notes on All the Books of Scripture* and *Socrates and Jesus Compared*, and was wondering if there was "a prospect of selling many copies by lowering the price?"[1] The moral urgency of proselytization had passed, and the days of handing out free copies were over; in 1805, Joseph Priestley Jr. had inventory to move. Bentley was being marginalized even at the *Register*, the newspaper he helped found. William Carlton's libel trial had ended in conviction, and he had been jailed for two months, emerging weak and sickly.[2] He died in July of 1805. In the void, Bentley had become acting editor, but the paper's owners had different plans for the long run. Bentley was not consulted when they considered a replacement, and he did not like the man they selected. They soon changed the paper's name from the *Salem Register* to the *Essex Register* (the change from "Impartial" to "Salem" having come not long after its creation), a move designed to appeal to county readers but also one that reflected the shrinking importance of its central town—and its central ideologue. Bentley still wrote summaries, but his role at the paper had shrunk to just that.[3]

His arguments in print, and in the pulpit, were no longer essential. Republicans now had a complex party machinery to do the work he used to do. Caucuses now chose the candidates, and committees at the county, ward, and district levels spread the message and drummed up the votes. "No neighborhood is without" the new structures, he reported from a distance.[4] The party leadership had moved beyond his reach as well. The small circle of leading Republicans at the East Church had by then dissolved, Benjamin Hodges Sr. having died and Edward Gibaut having moved away. John Fiske, Bentley's closest ally in Salem, had also died by then after sliding into a dementia that left him prone to wandering through the county dirty and destitute.[5] Even the Crowninshields were gone, with Jacob in Washington and his brothers living in New York and France to oversee the interests of their firm. And so new men had taken the lead in the party, men over whom Bentley had practically no influence. He was acquainted with such new Republican town officers as John Hathorne and Joseph Sprague, but he did not enjoy with them the close friendships he had had with Fiske, Hodges, and especially Crowninshield.

Bentley's brand of Republicanism—a rational, libertarian, Christian Republicanism—had come to an end. He had forged the party in the fire of persecution, but it had since become richer, more accepted, and more mainstream. The outsiders had become the insiders, and they no longer needed the fringe radical who was becoming something of an embarrassment. It had always been a party of middle-class aspirations; now it was the party *of* the middle-class. And the middle class was not radical. The new Republicans wanted to break the Federalist hold on power, not overturn the system's very assumptions. These Republicans were also liberals, and the aspect of liberalism they admired was the idea that their success was due to their own worth. What these new middle-class republicans wanted most of all was exactly what Bentley could not give them, namely a God who was pleased with their success. As Federalists, classical liberals may have lost, but as Arminians they won, even among the evangelicals. The Arminian conviction that God is made happy by material success (if earned by right morality, as every Arminian thought of his or her means) was perhaps the most lasting and influential contribution of New England liberal Christianity to America, and Bentley's small voice, coming as it did from one corner of a declining port town itself crammed up in the old corner of the country, was no match. His hope for Republicanism as avenue to a rationalist libertarianism of conscience had foundered on the reality that what these newly freed Americans really wanted was less the freedom to be equal than the freedom to be rich.

While Salem's Republicans were rejecting his radical vision, Salem's Christians were rejecting his rational one. He had had the congregation to himself since 1785, but after twenty years, it had all seemingly come to little. Attendance at church was irregular, for when winter storms were not keeping congregants homebound, summer sunshine was tempting them into carriage rides and island picnics.[6] Nor were those who did attend always pleased by what they heard. On one particularly unsuccessful Sabbath he sermonized in the morning on the progress of the parish and in the afternoon on dangers at sea, and the congregants naturally enough let him know what they thought. "One did not go to [one] meeting for arithmetic, and another to learn to swim," he wrote in his diary, recording the criticisms he had heard that day.[7] He had plenty of problems maintaining the choir, and then there were the irritants that just seem to go with the calling, as when he received the "bitterest reproaches" from a woman whose son was not invited to choir school and "another female drubbing" from a mother who ripped him with "odious comparisons, hearty threatenings, and a sufficient quantity of base reflections" because she felt that her departed son had been inadequately eulogized.[8]

More significant, and for Bentley more sad, the church itself was shrinking. Membership, mostly by attrition after the first year, traced a continuous downward arc. When Bentley began at the East, the church had around one hundred and fifty members, but within five years it had less than half that. By 1802 church membership was down to sixty-three, and by 1808 it had gone as low as sixty.[9] He had done all he could to open up membership as widely as possible, to remove as many barriers as possible, and yet he could not find anyone who wanted to join. On Communion days the irony was particularly painful and public. Sometimes there were no communicants at all. On Communion days, the sacrament was offered after the morning service was concluded, and those who would not take it were welcome to stay and watch those who would. But on more than one occasion, there was Bentley, alone, watching his parishioners watch him take Communion, by himself, from himself. He was angry, befuddled, and desperate. The sermon on the following Sabbath was inevitably an extended criticism of their reluctance to join him. "Enemies," he once warned, "may well now begin to complain that there are no fruits to our generous and Christian terms of communion."[10] After another such incident, he returned to preach on Elijah standing alone amid sinners and reminded members of the great benefit of a sacramental policy in which "nothing more is required to a worthy communion than a sober hope toward God of the resurrection to life by Jesus and a corresponding deportment in the world." Surely, he preached, they could have "no rational objections."[11] But objections they did have, and they stayed away. His vision of a Christian community willing to pursue a faith only of reasoned conscience was his alone.

All this while Salem itself was growing: from a population of less than seven thousand when Bentley arrived in 1783, Salem had grown to 9,457 in 1800 and would reach 12,613 in 1810.[12] And all this while church membership everywhere else in town was growing. In fact, Bentley's East Church was the *only* congregation that shrank.

The two Arminian churches, the First and the North, were thriving, and the North exceedingly so: begun in 1772, by 1803 it had 269 members and was the single most important community, outside the Federalist Party and the social clubs, for Salem's mercantile elites.[13] But if Bentley's vision of a rational republic never materialized, the reason was not the relatively few Christian liberals who refused to take the final step toward rationalism but the many, many more evangelicals who refused to go far along the journey. They were the ones over whom Bentley had hoped to exercise stewardship, but they had not let him, either in his liberal 1780s or his rational 1790s. The evangelical ascendancy was not sudden in 1805, but it did become especially apparent that year. The Second Great Awakening washed over Salem, and the effects were everywhere. By then, Daniel Hopkins's South Church—far from using the old assembly hall as it was when Bentley first came to town—had built a beautiful meetinghouse, one Bentley called "the best structure for public worship ever raised in Salem," and it had even called an assistant pastor.[14] Samuel Worcester was doing well over at his new post at the Tabernacle, and Joshua Spaulding was settling in nicely at the Branch Church over which he had just been installed. And those were just the Congregationalists. There were others, too. Lucius Bolles was spending summers immersing converts in the North River, creating as he went a congregation large enough by 1805 to warrant his ordination, the first of a Baptist in Salem. Methodism had so taken root in Lynn that the Methodists could hold their first big camp meeting in the area that summer. And Universalists had by then left the confines of Gloucester and begun preaching in Bentley's own neighborhood.[15] On one of the last days of December in 1805, looking back over a year that saw the arrival of the Baptists, Methodists, and Universalists, the formation of a new evangelical church, and the construction of two new evangelical meetinghouses, Bentley could only report sadly that the "sects are in all their glory. . . . They are as thick as the gulls upon our sandbar."[16] The next year, when it came time to pick a verse for his anniversary sermon, he found particular resonance in Jeremiah 25:3, which reads in part, "Even unto this day, that is the three and twentieth year, the word of the Lord hath come unto me, and I have spoken unto you, rising early and speaking; but ye have not listened." Surely a verse that uses twenty-three years as a marker was an irresistible choice on Bentley's own twenty-third anniversary as a minister, but the core of its point, and his selection of it, was the lament of its final phrase. In fact, he went home that night and added up his labors over those twenty-three years. He had given, he discovered, more than twenty-three hundred sermons, nearly thirteen hundred from texts written out in full and more than a thousand from outlines or notes, but could conclude only that it was proof "at least of diligence if nothing else." And indeed he thought it amounted to nothing else. The people of Salem, Bentley was convinced, had not listened. "Fanaticism," he concluded that night, "is triumphant."[17]

Bentley never saw the appeal. All he saw was what he considered their superstitions. Hopkinsians, he wrote, were "farmer metaphysicians" who had "infested" Congregationalism. Universalists were "illiterate, illiberal, and impudent"; their "stupid distinctions" were "involving Christianity in the thick darkness of mysticism." Methodists were characterized by "ignorance, superstition, and riot," and Baptists were "profligate, irregular, and ignorant," existing only "by an aversion to a tax and a previous inability to pay them" and led by a ministry who do nothing but "immerse their disciples in water and ignorance." He held them in utter and complete contempt. In fact, his analogy of sects to seagulls was a bit of an extended one: they were like gulls, he thought, in that they were "as hungry and as useless."[18] He never could see why people might be drawn to faiths such as these, different from his own because of their belief in ongoing supernaturalism.

But to understand that appeal can help explain why his project met with such limited success, something he also did not understand. It is commonplace now to suggest that some part of the appeal of evangelicalism was its efforts to meet the needs of the outsider and the powerless. Certainly this was true as far as race was concerned. Since the Great Awakening, evangelicalism had appealed to Africans and African Americans in ways that Puritanism and Arminianism never could. Perhaps the physicality and emotionalism of conversion echoed repressed cultural sensibilities of African rituals, or perhaps it was the Awakening's commitment to challenging a status quo that included unapologetic slave owning. Perhaps it was that revivalists were more likely to welcome blacks to the services, and their message more often and more explicitly invited black hearers to undertake the necessary journey from damnation to grace.[19] Perhaps it was that the revivalists took special care to inform unconverted slave owners of the eternity of torment that awaited them. By underscoring that the kingdom belongs to the unlikely—the poor, the servant, the least among them—evangelicals, albeit neither yet abolitionist nor free from racism, offered a particularly retributory future in which the Lord's bondsman and the Lord's freeman might swap places after all. So when there was a push in Salem in 1807 for the education of African-American children, it was Joshua Spaulding at the Branch Church, not William Bentley, who did the pushing.[20]

Women too were offered something that Bentley could not see. Even when he did try, his biases led him to the wrong conclusion. His urging of women's rights to education, after all, was still predicated on his assumption that women were intellectually inferior and thus morally vulnerable. And though he was convinced that all evangelicals were prone to taking the conversion moment to be license for subsequent misbehavior, he singled out female evangelicals as being particularly inclined to the sexual forms of that misbehavior, and he thought that revivals provided the opportunity for doing so. Revivals combined the worst parts of superstition, Sabbath-breaking, and sexual temptation, and it was in a sermon against this "cursed infection" that Bentley raved against Hutchinson.[21] Large and unruly crowds with individuals of both sexes acting on their primal passions were the chance, he thought, for women to "settle their concerns for both worlds at once."[22] And when these meetings were held at night, Bentley went apoplectic. It is one of the few fine literary moments in the diary when Bentley wrote about what happened to John Cleaveland's own daughter. "In the middle of night meetings," he wrote, she was "overtaken by temptation and fell."[23] Whatever his real intention with this phrase, his conflation of losing one's virginity with having a conversion perfectly captures his deeper fears about the causal connections of sexual impropriety and evangelicalism. So he was hardly surprised but thoroughly upset when one night, while passing some "beautiful girls" walking to a Baptist night lecture, he overheard nearby sailors refer to them as "candidates for another dipping," just the kind of remark that confirmed all his worst speculations about what really went on at such gatherings.[24] Perhaps Bentley was not entirely wrong, for revivals, with their ubiquitous talk of consummation and their orgiastic melees of conversions, may well have allowed women to tap into an otherwise unacknowledged sexuality.[25] But more important, these churches offered women a chance for fellowship and communion not available at Bentley's or the liberal ones. Consider the experience of Eleanor (Read) Emerson, who had undergone a conversion experience and then moved to Salem at the turn of the century, where she became a Baptist, married the assistant preacher of the Hopkinsian South, and, later, after dying, was eulogized by the pastor of the New Light Tabernacle.[26] This cross-fertilization is exactly the kind of public sphere that evangelicals labored to forge. She was organizationally connected to three houses of worship but spiritually part of one community, one that made women like Eleanor feel especially welcome.

But it was on the question of economic rather than racial or sexual inequality that evangelicals were most prepared to provide sustenance for believers. When Lucius Bolles gave the sermon at the dedication of the Baptists' brick meetinghouse in 1806, it was still bold to claim as he did that "it is of the least moment, what rank in society we sustain, or what our titles and distinctions are: whether we fill a throne or occupy a cottage, whether we are clothed in purple, or covered with rags, there exists a like infinite disparity between us and our Creator. The prince and the peasant are obligated to approach the Lord with equal sentiments of humility and submission." Nor were these mere words, for as Bolles went on to report, the proprietors of the Baptist meetinghouse had decided that because the poor—"whose salvation is of equal importance with others"—could not afford to purchase pews in the new building, the church would abandon pew proprietorship entirely and open up the pews to all comers, free of charge.[27]

Bentley had no more to offer those dispossessed by economics than he did to those dispossessed by race or sex. They certainly could not expect any relief in Bentley's version of heaven. He even modified his hymnal to make sure they did not get the wrong idea. Singers at his church sang a hymn titled "Blessed Are the Poor in Spirit," but they did not sing this verse, because Bentley had deleted it from his version:

> In vain the sons of wealth and pride
> Despise your lot, your hopes deride;
> In vain they boast their little stores,
> Trifles are theirs, a kingdom yours.[28]

He had to omit it. The naturalist God does not promise kingdoms and indeed does not promise anything at all; in the naturalist universe, the sons of wealth and pride win in death as they so often do in life. But the clearest articulation of a future retribution is of course the beatitudes. Both Matthew and Luke record versions of the beatitudes, but it was likely not accidental that Bentley chose Matthew 5:3 ("Blessed are the poor in spirit") rather than Luke 6:20 ("Blessed are the poor") to avoid the temporal radicalism of the Lukan phrasing. His modifications to the hymnal are particularly illuminating in this regard. His compilation included an Isaac Watts hymn based on the beatitudes, but whereas Watts's version ran to eight verses, Bentley's had only seven. He omitted this verse and this verse only:

> Blest are the meek, who stand afar,
> From rage and passion, noise and war;
> God will secure their happy state,
> And plead their cause against the great.[29]

Bentley's naturalist God does no pleading for anyone, for any purpose; the meek created by natural law, it seems, are left to fend for themselves. The verse had appeared not only in Watts but also in the Salisbury collection from which Bentley had modeled his hymnal; he alone could not abide its implication of divine justice for the poor. In his quest to make the mysterious more believable, he stripped from the beatitudes everything that made them so powerful a statement of equality. For those persons willing to accept the rationally unknowable and the outright irrational, real psychological relief could be gained from a conviction in the universality of the depraved immaterial soul and the promise of heavenly bliss for converted Christians regardless of station. By reconfiguring heaven as moral progress on this plane, however, Bentley eliminated some of Western culture's most enduring denunciations of unfair acquisition.

Secular critics following Marx might add that the beatitudes or other similar claims of heavenly justice were mere phantasms, offering nothing of tangible aid. But belief in supernatural interference did affect the real behavior of individuals toward their neighbors, at least to the extent that oppressors felt the cold eye of God watching their every move. The covenant had long been an agent of economic justice in New England, and extortion, usury, and the oppressiveness of unfettered mercantile capitalism had been near the top of every Puritan's list of threats to it. In fact, it was at Salem's First Church in 1663 that the minister reminded listeners that the town had been founded as "a plantation of religion, not a plantation of trade" in an election sermon that became the model for scores of subsequent jeremiads just like it.[30] Latitudinarianism would soon wean the First off that kind of gloom, but others in New England would pick up the point. And for many eighteenth-century evangelicals, too, God's wrath in this plane was caused by nothing so much as oppression of the poor. When the Tabernacle's Nathaniel Whitaker convened his church on the famous "dark day" in 1780, he explained that the sudden twilight was God's immediate response to the "extortion" committed by the wealthy of New England against its poor.[31] When Congress in 1783 was debating the salaries of officers of the Continental Army, Ipswich's John Cleaveland went to the press to argue for payments, not for the sake of public credit as had "Publicola" but rather because the soldiers had been promised as much, and a nation victorious thanks to God's good graces should not fail "sacredly to observe and faithfully to fulfill and perform the national treaties, covenants, compacts and promises" made during the war. Such a people, he wrote, "may reasonably expect to be punished by some signal judgment of Divine Providence."[32] So too in 1794, when David Osgood, a Calvinist, credited providence with "precipitating prosperous guilt from its lofty seat."[33] By invoking the covenant and the possibility of divine repercussion, Whitaker, Cleaveland, and Osgood were wielding the most powerful—and in some cases the only— weapon of the economically dispossessed. The covenant, in forms tangible or not, had made clear that great inequalities of wealth and maltreatment of the destitute were displeasing to God, but it had teeth only as long as one accepted that God could intervene in this world to express displeasure. So Bentley, by denying the covenant and special providence, had removed the most important means of tangible recourse and protection for the disaffected poor. Bentley read Osgood's sermon and dismissed it as "the holy revenge" of God, never seeing that for many of the impoverished, God's revenge was the only hope they had in this life.[34]

Bentley's elitism valued order over righteous agitation; his Arminianism denied the possibility of collective accountability; his liberalism emphasized freedom over justice and individual rights over communal demands; his rationalism removed the equality of souls, the threat of divine judgment, and the urgency, necessity, and confidence of reform. Bentley never saw that his Enlightenment ideal of tolerance, moderation, and virtue benefited and confirmed only those already empowered; he did not consider that defiance, extremity, and passion are sometimes the only means by which the powerless may be raised. He thought that faith in secondary causes and instruments was in fact just a failure of nerve, a retreat into supernaturalism by those unready to free themselves. By removing the threat of divine punishment, he had removed the paranoia, nosiness, and self-righteousness that fueled religious persecution. But in so doing, he also severed the last binding ties save conscience, a worthy motive of good and free agents but one that by itself was unlikely in the eighteenth century to effect social justice. Bentley himself could parlay his naturalism into a Rousseauian social conscience, but only in the 1790s and only after awakening to its potentiality by factors not inherent to Christian naturalism; devoid of social context, Christian naturalism itself had little to offer the poor.

It might be the case, however, that Christian naturalism failed as much for ideational reasons as for social ones. For starters, its condemnation of human emotionalism was a difficult case to make in a newly freed and energetic America. William Bentley was not an emotional man, and his diary is remarkable for the near absence of feelings of warmth. He seems almost incapable of deep personal affection, and more than once he came close to wondering if that were indeed the case. When he did, he wrote poetry. He wrote one such poem at the end of a day in which he had attended an island picnic and watched as a fiddler played and the partygoers danced and sang along. He returned home to record that the music had "furnished a pleasure which the happiness of ignorance may innocently occasion," and then he set down these lines:

> Hark,—his tortured catgut squeals
> He tickles every string, to every note
> He bends his pliant neck—
> The fond yielding Maid
> Is tweedled into Love.[35]

The verse fairly jumps with sexual imagery, what with all the squealing, tickling, bending, and tweedling into love, but its meaning (and sadness) emerges from his thoughts introducing the poem, that it was only the "happiness of ignorance"—something his life's work had forbidden him—that permitted such abandon. Bentley had been only a spectator to the revelry, neither dancing nor singing, prohibited by temperament more than office from sharing even the innocent emotional pleasures of his townsfolk. Few ministers would have jumped right in, and likely few parishioners wanted them to, but the point here is that the hyperintellectualism and elitism that delineated the boundaries of his religious faith not only kept him from experiencing real visceral joy but also kept the majority of his townspeople—those less afraid of human emotions—at bay. Bentley lived as well as preached a life of physical moderation and restraint, and though each week he invited listeners to join him on his journey of intellectual liberation, few were willing to amputate their passions and tag along.

Another such effort came close to being a love poem, except that the point will be that the narrator cannot actually feel the love he sees and rationally approves of in others. The first four verses are the response of a hypothetical priest to an inquirer about why the priest had not married. The concluding verse, though, shifts to the first person and is the author, Bentley, asking "sweet A—" to allow him more time to find his true love. The poem's touching melancholia, though, comes from the middle verses when Bentley as the priest explains that his solitude comes less by his vows than by his inability to forgo reason for the emotion that love requires.

> Said F.— to a priest one day,
> Priests should to men examples prove;
> Why neglect you then to marry,
> 'For happiness's allied to love.'
>
> The priest replied, Reason I followed,
> But without fire, Love's but a name:
> Reason is cool, deliberate, wise,
> Tis only passion fans the flame.
>
> Merit and beauty reason sees;
> Passion admires, to love inclined,
> Passion is warm, & soon pursues
> While reason always lags behind.
>
> Mr R.— yielded to his passion
> His choice my reason did approve:
> He gained the prize: Love's undivided,
> My part is to admire the Love.

> Yet my sweet A— grant a friend
> At modest distance, hours to spend,
> To form his choice—until he find
> A maid blessed with so pure a mind.[36]

Perhaps the Catholicism of the protagonist is apt, since the poem is really a confessional of sorts. When in the penultimate verse the priest describes watching yet another friend marry while he, the priest, can sadly, jealously, offer only intellectualized approval, it becomes clear that this is Bentley's admission, his fear, that his unlimited commitment to the rational life has left him unable to fall in love.

Bentley never did marry. Congregationalist ministers were free to woo and wed, and all the other ministers in town had done so: John Prince and Thomas Barnard enjoyed apparently happy unions, the thirty-seven-year-old Daniel Hopkins had married one of his school-age pupils, and Nathaniel Whitaker's home life is perhaps best summed up by his explanation to Eleazar Wheelock that he was going to England to escape the "hell" that was life with "Mrs. W."[37] But Bentley struggled with courtship. He was not above noticing "the most agreeable girl of the place" when visiting, but he was just not much of a romancer. He made a few timid stabs at it, usually during carriage rides between towns. In 1789, for example, he was introduced to a Mr. Carter's "amiable" daughter, and since he "wished for an acquaintance," he took advantage of the "favorable opportunity" to ride with her back to Boston, but nothing came of it. And the following year, when planning a trip with the Pickman family, he made "all those timorous approaches to gain the company of the eldest daughter for the journey which distinguishes old bachelors, and are commonly unsuccessful." Again he failed and returned home to take solace that "a man may approve of his own address, even when it fails of the end he professes." In fact, there is no suggestion that he was anything other than one of the "veterans in celibacy" that his friend Jeremy Belknap once said of him.[38]

He did, however, fall in love. It was late in his life, and she was thirty years younger than he. Hannah was a Crowninshield, the granddaughter of the woman with whom he boarded. He had baptized her when she was born in 1789. Through her teens she had gone with him on day trips to the beach and the Neck, and by 1810, when she was twenty-one, she had become his "favorite pupil." Soon they were traveling together, he and "my Hannah," on small trips through Essex County, lodging, he was careful to note, in separate quarters. In 1815, he escorted her to Harvard's commencement; two years later they enjoyed the first steamboat rides around Salem Harbor; he even bequeathed to her his silver.[39] In perhaps the most moving passage of the entire diary, he writes in

1819 of performing the wedding between Hannah and a naval officer from Virginia. It was "the most interesting scene of my life," he wrote. "The event is not from my wishes or at my will. The sympathy was beyond description. The hundred I have united never gave such emotions." Bentley's heart had broken. "I hope H. will be happy," he concluded his diary entry that night. "It will be my happiness."[40]

Or perhaps Christian naturalism failed because it required of people what they were not yet ready to give. Most people, for one, were less confident than was Bentley in what was supposedly induced from empiricism, and they were certainly not yet secure enough to abandon the Bible for these inductions. Few Christians were willing to surrender their belief in mystery and supernaturalism in Bentley's era, especially since "science" was not yet able to offer credible alternative explanations. In 1806, he felt it necessary to devote a sermon to counteracting parishioners' fears of an impending eclipse, and not long after, a local diviner would borrow a Bible to help locate buried treasure on the Neck. "What progress have we made while we still have our conjurers &c. in full credit?" he wondered to his diary.[41] For the vast majority of men and women in the eighteenth century, science needed to prove that it accorded with religion, not religion with science. Newton's laws had helped explain heavenly motion but left much room for religiosity as well, and such fields as geology and anthropology, which would confront the biblical tradition in the nineteenth century, were in the eighteenth concerned more with classification than with explanation of change. Besides, exposure to the arguments of the Enlightenment was itself hardly universal. Not everyone in Salem had been to Harvard, read the *Principia*, or compared parallel texts of Scripture. For them, Enlightenment theories were an option rather than "truth" and in many cases made a weaker showing than did the inherited Biblicism. Individuals who held to the Eden story, for example, could easily argue that the proposed state of nature was just a guess, too. State-of-nature theorists pointed to native peoples as empirical evidence, but theists like Bentley further speculated that such a state had been God's original plan, which makes the theory as speculative as was Genesis. And contemporaries might well have thought that the writer of a letter to the *Essex Gazette* in 1772 defending the miraculousness of the Deluge was more "reasonable" than were those who used natural philosophy to explain it (away) with secondary causes. When the writer finished his survey of the empirical hypotheses then in vogue and concluded that "the most rational supposition is that there was a miraculous supply of water, and perhaps a miraculous removal of it," the juxtaposition of the "rational" and the "miraculous" was made without a hint of paradox, irony, or confusion, for until science could do better than underground lakes and comets, that writer was opting to believe, as a reasonable thinker would, in the simpler explanation of the direct will of God.[42] No, science—the province of the elites in Salem—held little sway indeed over the pietistic masses. For why would a person accept new rationalist theories over ones that were thousands of years old, had the endorsement of untold numbers of believers, and were authored by the Holy Spirit itself? The burden of proof in the eighteenth century lay on rationalism, not on evangelicalism, and the natural philosophers were not yet up to the task.

To strive to have both reason and revelation meant the sacrifice of one or the other. As much as Bentley might think he could have both, when faced in the pulpit with the real pressures of being both Christian and rationalist, he inevitably struggled. There simply was no good way, for example, for a person to account for Old Testament miracles with entirely natural causes. The results of the efforts were, to say the least, awkward. His full description of Old Testament angels, to take one example, was that they were "expressions of the divine purpose by human forms or voice, as well as all other manners of a divine revelation, whether by the elements, unthinking substances, or animal forms. These are representations of the deity, not of his person, but of his purposes, and power."[43] On the Flood, to take another, he tried to convince listeners that at creation, "the supreme power may have established any intercourse with the creatures different from the present apparent course of Nature, and that may be as really the then-present course of Nature as a different one may be to us."[44] To be a Christian naturalist in the eighteenth century was to try to understand through new rational criteria phenomena that for centuries had been accepted as true despite their irrationality. To dismiss them as lies was to be a deist; to accept them at face value was to abandon one's criteria; and to walk the middle way through vague special providence was to burden oneself with stilted language and tortured logic. To lay claim to a faith of both reason and revelation was easy for a layperson who has the luxury of glossing over the difficult parts, but for an eighteenth-century minister called to explain the meaning of every part of Scripture and committed to doing so in ways that were both "rational" and "religious," it was a more difficult task.

Or, finally, it may be that Christian naturalism simply failed at providing what the faithful seek from their faith. Whatever their worth as guides to reading Scripture with rational consistency, Bentley's epistemological criteria stripped the Bible of much of the power that believers ascribed to it. The orthodox interpretation of Scripture may have insisted on things that did not accord with sensory evidence about the natural world, but the rationalist interpretation removed much of the ability that Scripture *does* have to instruct, console, and, indeed, enlighten. Nonrationalists read their Bibles literally, but also within the larger typological framework of the broad Christian narrative: the Fall actually happened as written, but it also looks forward to the necessity of Christ; the Deluge actually happened as written, but it also symbolizes a later and stronger covenant; the stayed sacrifice of Isaac actually happened as written, but it also previews the Crucifixion. For evangelicals and liberals alike, God acts within as well as above history to give it all meaning, and accepting Scripture as true despite apparent conflicts with the laws of nature was a small price to pay for the comfort of purpose. A Christian naturalist such as Bentley read his Bible as a collection of stories, sometimes literally true and sometimes only allegorically so, but in all cases valuable only insofar as the truth of the events as written could be determined. For evangelicals and liberals, the literal truth of Creation and the Incarnation and the Apocalypse allowed them to deduce figurative conclusions, whereas Bentley was concerned more to argue that Eden did not exist than that it symbolizes human pride, more to argue that Satan is a myth than that he embodies the irrationality of evil in this world, and more to argue that Abraham had "proof" for what he did than that the command to sacrifice Isaac represents the difficulties that confront the faithful servants of a sometimes incomprehensible sovereign. What to Bentley reflected only superstition, emotion, and irrationality offered to those who did believe the promise of equality, justice, and home.

And his definition of what constituted a church was likewise not that of his neighbors. Perhaps it was exactly because he had removed all experiential or intellectual requirements for membership that so few people wanted to become a member; they could see no reason, it seems, to join a group bound only by vague notions of natural morality. And perhaps it was exactly because he had removed supernaturalism from Communion that so few people cared enough to participate: they could see no reason, it seems, to commune with a God who does not commune back.

What Bentley was calling faith was a faint shadow of their understanding of that word. As he preached quite bluntly in an early sermon at the East, "We are not to conceive that faith becomes acceptable when it has no evidence, or that it deserves the name when set in competition with sense and demonstration. Our mind must discern, or our senses perceive the evidence, and we must assent in proportion to its clearness, for as soon as we give up our judgment, we give up our religion."[45] He said this as part of a sermon delivered during his candidacy in 1783 on the subject of Abraham's sacrifice of Isaac. It was already an uncomfortable passage for liberals, since it seemed to teach faith over works (unless one chose to emphasize, as did liberals, James's interpretation over Paul's), and it seemed to teach the primacy of God's immediate commands over the moral laws of Creation, points not lost on the antinomians and enthusiasts who had variously cited it to justify claims of their own direct experiences with the divine. But Bentley's ontological banishment of God from the present world left him with few such difficulties because it left him with little to say at all. He argued that Abraham had been justified in carrying out the order because he had proof that the voice was indeed God's, but that they, the members of the East Church, would not be justified, for they can hear no such voice, can receive no such order. "We cannot have his evidence and therefore not his faith, nor can we be subjects of special instructions, but we have enough for faith to execute." The faith he offered was not that of Abraham nor of the evangelicals nor even that of the moderate Arminian liberals. What he offered instead was faith solely in the goodness of Creation as it is, without the least possibility of special interventions, the work of a loving God who placed in that Creation—at the moment *of* Creation—laws both natural and moral which make manifest that love.

And this is exactly the problem. The universe, after all, does not always seem so benevolent. And in such times, Bentley had little comfort to add. Accounting for evil and suffering in a universe superintended by God was the intellectual core of pastoral counseling. But as a good Newtonian, Bentley would feign no hypotheses, no speculation about God and God's purposes. Hardly able to explain *how* God works in this world, that is, the Christian naturalist had absolutely nothing at all to say about *why*, and so abdicated what is perhaps the single most important contribution of the Christian faith to human peace of mind.

Establishing a theodicy had posed little problem for Calvinists, who learned the lesson taught to Job that the Creator need not explain himself to those he created. But for the eighteenth-century Christian who had redefined God as benevolent *and* reasonable, the problem was a difficult one. The various factions of New England Christianity had developed solutions that accorded with their theologies, and the return of peace in the 1780s gave representatives the chance to take them to the public. The Presbyterian clergyman John Murray in Newburyport offered his opinion in 1785 that God allows evil because evil is not a thing itself but rather an absence of good and therefore out of God's control. Chauncy's liberal view, published just the previous year, was that God's goodness "necessarily inheres in him, i.e. independently of his own choice," but that "his benevolent exertions in all instances and all kinds are perfectly voluntary." And the Hopkinsians, uniquely concerned to maintain God's absolute omnipotence, argued that sin is not merely allowed by God but is in fact *caused* by God, although assuredly for some larger, unknown, greater good. All three positions were vulnerable to critics in the other camps: Murray, it was said, limited God's power, Hopkinsians limited God's benevolence, and Chauncy just begged the question. It is impossible, of course, to provide an entirely satisfactory theodicy that preserves both divine power and divine goodness, and so these men were left to run in the circles which Enlightenment theodicy must always run, pleading finally that they, like everyone else, see through the glass but darkly.[46]

Bentley's theodicy, however, was bound by the ontological restrictions inherent in Christian naturalism. Because Bentley's God does not intervene in the ongoing, postbiblical present, the question of theodicy became one of justifying the evil allowed by natural law. This was what Bentley considered the real—and useful—purpose of the Job text, assuming as he did that the framing plot moments were fictional Jewish additions and the body of the book only poetry, true only insofar as poetry can be. For Bentley, God was responsible for any one particular sorrow—say, a death by epidemic or storm—only to the degree to which God had included epidemics and storms in Creation and then stepped back and allowed them to do what epidemics and storms naturally do. The question of whether sufferings from epidemics or storms or other sources were truly necessary was answered by the very existence of their causes, since a good God would not have included in the universe an *unnecessary* evil. And just *why* that suffering and evil are necessary was exactly what was inscrutable and must be accepted on faith.

Christian naturalism led to no conclusion other than this one, but even Bentley came to it only gradually. When in November of 1783 he had to give the sermon at the funeral of his most auspicious parishioner, Richard Derby Sr., he preached, improving on Job, that in the execution of divine law, God "assumes no other than his unalienable prerogative," an ambiguous phrasing typical of moderate Arminians. But he would later give equal power to divine will and divine law, telling smallpox patients in 1792 that "God does as he pleases. That is true. But he must do right." Soon only law remained.

Christian naturalism, that is, did indeed provide Bentley with a theodicy, one that was no more or less logical than any other. But how soothing could it have been for the widows and orphans to hear him preach that "when God is said to be a father, it is not intended by any instruments beyond the established course of nature" and that orphans were orphans to "teach them more to depend upon themselves" and widows were widows because *someone* had to raise the children, and it is easier for a woman to muster the necessary reason than for a man to scrape up the necessary sympathy?[47] In fact, life in Salem was a dangerous one for everybody, even without the countless risks of a life spent at sea. Winter storms blew elderly ladies into the icy water, children slipped into necessaries and suffocated, sailors broke their necks falling from the rigging onto the wharf, wagon wheels crushed young boys, and smallpox struck down the just and unjust alike. Few people in Salem did not know tragedy and did not grieve, and one suspects that for many people, the consoling power of Christian naturalism was a small one. In fact, one suspects too that Bentley's insistence on the goodness of Creation was for many people itself unconvincing. To many of his townspeople, Bentley's claims about the benevolence of God's superintendency simply did not fit with their existence. For them, Christ served more as a guarantor of the sympathy and justice they craved than as a model of morality for the already contented. Their world remained one of mysteries—the work of Jehovah rather than of the Author—and in the mystery of God's will was their consolation for the losses and sadness that marked so much of their lives. This is what Jonathan Edwards Jr. meant at the ordination of Timothy Dwight in 1783 when he argued that liberals were wrong to think that the happiness of Creation implies the happiness of its creatures. "Nothing is more evident," Edwards pointed out, than that if God aimed at the greatest happiness of each individual, God failed, "inasmuch as individuals, even in this life, are extremely miserable."[48] He was referring as always to the metaphysical misery of depravity, but it was also an acknowledgment of the pain and poverty in a world only fools could consider the best of all those possible. Apparently the people of Bentley's Salem agreed.

All questions of salvation are, in the end, empirically unknowable, and so different individuals find different ways to console themselves about the death that will someday come. But in this life, Christians want other things from their Christianity. The dispossessed want some sense of dignity here and the promise of retribution elsewhere, and the privileged want the power of the faith to maintain the social order that they consider their just reward for faith rightly followed. Bentley's Christianity offered neither. Put another way: although Christianity was fundamentally about the necessary steps to reconnect with God in death, ideally it served its believers in this life as well, soothing anger, assuaging grief, explaining loss, providing community, easing uncertainty, and preparing the mind for death. Peace, comfort, and security of mind were important to the believer, and the degree to which Calvinists, evangelicals, Arminians, or the lone Christian naturalist could provide these was the degree to which they were successful among a populace newly able to decide from among them.

By 1805, Bentley had been at the East Church for twenty-two years and was preaching to his second generation of parishioners. It was long enough for the infants whom he had baptized early on to have since become adults, some of whom were now presenting Bentley with children of their own to be baptized.

Bentley had baptized Benjamin Hodges back in 1785 when he and Diman were alternating tasks, and in the years since, Hodges had studied with Bentley, graduated from Harvard, and begun preparing for a career in the ministry. His unexpected death in 1804 was one of the saddest moments in Bentley's ministry.[49] Of grief and joy alike he had seen much. But he had seen, and done, more than that. A Christian naturalist bound to social liberalism in the 1780s, he became a radical Unitarian in the 1790s and a rational Republican beyond.

His efforts at spiritual reform were largely frustrated. In changing his church from an established congregation with a Calvinist theology to a voluntarist one with a Christian naturalist theology, he had forced at least this small group of Americans to confront the prospect of a universe governed by a God unable or unwilling to help them. It was not an arbitrary godless universe Bentley showed them, but one even more difficult to understand: a benevolent universe created by a benevolent Creator who, after sending one final revelation in the wisdom of Jesus Christ, had then withdrawn from its operations to allow the world to return to benevolence on its own. It was the only way Bentley could make sense of both Scripture and nature together, and he—and, in New England, he alone—tried to persuade others to see it that way, too. But they could not, and so he could not.

He *had* been successful in leading his congregants—and their evangelical opponents—toward a new political vision. He of course was not the only one working toward this goal; by 1805, the Republican Party was firmly in the ascendancy not only in Salem but across the country. But it was no longer the party he had once envisioned. It was no longer a party forged in the crucible of persecution and no longer committed to a paradise of reason. By 1805, the Republicans had little place for radical rationalism and dreams of a millennium of conscience.

The second generation of his parishioners was also the second generation of Americans, and they were living in an America more permanent and more stable and more prosperous than the one they had known two decades earlier. William Bentley had become a minister in the first year of that nation's uncontested existence, and he and it had matured together. Now it had passed him by. He would continue to preach in Salem for the rest of his life, but his most dynamic years were behind him.

Epilogue

William Bentley imagined an America of freedom, benevolence, tolerance, reason, and charity. Through rational faith and republican governance, Americans could be kinder, more conscientious, indeed more Christian people, leading the rest of the world to that future paradise promised in the text that remained the best of all books. America, however, rejected that vision. In the first two decades of the early Republic, American culture set the course on which it would sail, guided by the conviction that property and the market are the best guarantees of economic security and public morality. When, in the next generation, those values diffused through that culture during what historians call the Market Revolution, Bentley's Rousseauian vision entirely vanished. And for the most part, Americans remained committed to a Christianity full of ongoing supernaturalism. Convinced that God pays special attention to them and that the fear of God is necessary to good governance, Americans continued to put Christianity—supernatural Christianity—at the center of their public and private lives. Though the liberal version thrived among its small but influential audience, and a multitude of evangelical versions were carried to the farthest corners of the growing nation, Christian naturalism never spread much beyond Salem's East Church.

Bentley never reconciled with the economic imperatives of classical liberals or with the men who claimed them. He could gain some satisfaction that although those merchants continued to do well, they would not again have the power and prominence they possessed during the early decades of his ministry. The harbor, perfect for the coastal exchanges, was too small for the larger vessels and more ambitious commerce of the nineteenth century. The town's one claim—and no minor one—was its dominance of the East India trade, the fruits of which still delight visitors to the town's Peabody Essex Museum. But even so, Salem's significance was steadily diminishing. Of course, the whole country was growing, and not primarily toward the northeast. The center of the nation was moving southward and westward, and the mercantile life of towns like Salem no longer loomed so large or important in the American mind. Even Bentley's news summaries shifted to the west, as befit the imagination and interest of his readers; he was more likely now to lead his column with Lewis and Clark than with Napoleon.

Nor, more important, did Bentley reconcile with the liberal clergy from whom he had split in the 1790s. Their churches were doing well. In Salem they were thriving, and Prince and Barnard continued to remain friends until Barnard's death in 1814. (Prince would die in 1836.)[1] Both would be pleased to know that the North Church later merged back into the First, and that the First Church still exists and still serves the people around Chestnut Street, a Federalist Row of sorts laid out in 1796 as a haven from the Republican bustle of the eastern neighborhoods, a serene and orderly grid of a neighborhood that is still there, the moderate Enlightenment in brick and mortar. Boston's liberal churches were just as healthy, for although John Eliot was still at the New North, John Lathrop still at the Second, and Bentley's friend James Freeman still at King's Chapel, a new and promising generation had taken up in some of the other congregations: Joseph Buckminster now stood in Cooper's old pulpit at Brattle Street, William Ellery Channing in Belknap's at Federal Street, and William Emerson in Chauncy's at the First. Old and new, in Boston as in Salem, liberal Christians were poised to carry their moderate Arminian latitudinarianism through the nineteenth century, armed with William Paley's *Natural Theology* and Scottish moral sense philosophy which together would keep at bay old-school Presbyterians, ever-schismatic evangelicals, Concord Transcendentalists, and, beginning in 1859, Darwinians.[2]

Bentley's marginalization from these men was apparent on a number of fronts. He had written a history of Salem, for example, which he published in 1799 in the proceedings of the Massachusetts Historical Society, a group to which he had been elected in 1796. But his celebrations of Salem democracy were promptly critiqued by Federalist readers, and Bentley ended the relationship. (So it came as a laugh in 1808 when he received a bill for twelve years' worth of dues. "So much," he said, disregarding the notice, "for the Historical Society.")[3] He had even cut ties with his beloved Harvard. The break came in

1803 when the university rejected for admission a young member of the Crowninshield family whom Bentley had been tutoring. "My connections with Cambridge cease," he fumed, and he was relieved upon hearing of his student's happy settlement at the College of William and Mary.[4] By the time Harvard elected a theological liberal to succeed David Tappan as the Hollis Chair of Divinity in 1805, Bentley had nothing to do with the school. But he was caught up in the event nonetheless. When Tappan took the chair, his pastorate called as a successor one Joseph Richardson, but not before a particularly nasty schism and controversy at the bottom of which was animosity toward the new man by Jedidiah Morse and his circle of orthodox Congregationalist Federalists. Perhaps not surprisingly, then, the minister who was asked to deliver the sermon at Richardson's ordination was William Bentley. Salem is on the North Shore of Boston Harbor, Hingham on the South Shore, but apparently there was nobody closer willing to welcome a Jeffersonian into the ministry. So down Bentley went to Hingham to deliver the sermon. It was published, and that year's *Monthly Anthology*, the literary organ of Boston's Federalist liberals, included a review. Bentley had to know it would not be well received, but even he could not have been prepared for this. "We notice this sermon," began the review, "because having read it through for that purpose, we do not choose to have so much labor lost." And later, "after forcing our way a little farther through the miserable brushwood of half-grown ideas," the reviewer congratulated himself that "no one will deny us praise, when, as drudges in the cause of literature, we have toiled through fifteen pages like this," adding that "if we were to judge from this production, we should conclude, that its author had not an whole idea in his mind."[5] And again the following year, in reviewing Bentley's election sermon before the gathered state government, the *Anthology* wrote:

> Mr. Bentley early obtained, and had long enjoyed, the reputation of a
> great scholar. He had holden a distinguished rank among the Amer-
> ican literati; and a democratick congress considered themselves as
> paying a compliment to learning, when they chose for their chaplain
> the *Minister of the second church in Salem*. But whence was this
> fame derived? What evidence have the world ever received of the su-
> perior talents of Bentley? This question is not easily answered. The
> reputation for great parts is very oddly acquired in this country, where
> all our geese are swans, and our swans, alas! too often turn out geese.[6]

Bentley was cut off completely from his liberal colleagues, isolated, ridiculed, and despised. He would live for thirteen years after that summary in 1806, and the schism would never close. (It was hardly consolation when in 1819 Harvard awarded him an honorary doctorate, since he suspected, perhaps rightly, that doing so was merely an attempt to ensure that his enormous personal library be donated to the school. In any case, it came too late: just that May, Bentley had rewritten his will to bequeath the theological and classical volumes to Allegheny College in Meadville, Pennsylvania, and the rest to the American Antiquarian Society in Worcester, Massachusetts, recently formed by his friend Isaiah Thomas.)

The decision by Harvard to choose an Arian symbolized something else as well: the return of theology over ontology as the main determinant of clerical tension in New England. From 1795 to 1805, the fear of ongoing naturalism, in either its deistic or its Christian naturalistic forms, had kept the supernaturalists together. But by 1805, that fear had passed, supernatural Christianity seemed again secure, and the liberals and the orthodox could go back into theological opposition. That this time it would be over Christology and not soteriology is less important than that each side once again saw itself primarily in opposition rather than alliance with the other.

It is as good an indicator as any of the fading memory of the 1790s that by 1819 the Arian liberals were willing to call themselves "Unitarians."[7] The immediate cause of the term's revitalization came in 1815, when Bentley's old nemesis Jedidiah Morse excerpted and printed a chapter from Thomas Belsham's *Memoirs of the Life of the Rev. Theophilus Lindsey* about Bentley's and Freeman's attempts to disseminate English Unitarianism in America. Morse's intention was to expose *all* Boston liberals as devotees of Unitarianism, or Socinianism, even though the other liberals had been Arians, not Unitarians, and they had decidedly not participated in the network of transatlantic radicalism. Drawing this distinction was exactly the point made in rebuttal by William Ellery Channing, by then one of Boston's leading liberal pastors. Channing addressed precisely the issue of preexistence when he pointed out that he and his colleagues "believe that Jesus Christ is more than man, that he existed before the world, that he literally came from heaven to save our race, that he sustains other offices than that of a teacher and witness to the truth, and that he still acts for our benefit, and is our intercession with the Father."[8] This was Arianism, not Unitarianism, and even though Channing would in 1819 adopt the "Unitarian" name, he and his peers retained, and throughout most of the nineteenth century would continue to retain, an Arian Christology that compromised where Bentley, beginning back in 1785, could not. Channing's 1819 sermon has come down as one of the programmatic statements of American Unitarianism, but in truth, he was saying nothing that Bentley had not been saying for thirty-six years. In fact, he was saying less.

Meanwhile, evangelicalism grew even stronger after 1805. The Universalist John Murray had moved from Gloucester to Boston, where he set up a new congregation, but he came up to Salem on some occasions, and George Richards came down from Portsmouth on other ones, until finally in 1808 the cornerstone was laid in Salem for a Universalist meetinghouse.[9] The non-Baptist evangelical ministers protested when Baptist minister Lucius Bolles began to immerse adults whom they had already sprinkled as children, but there was little to be done.[10] The Baptist church kept on growing. Founded in 1804 with twenty-three members, by 1810 it had another one hundred and fifty.[11] The Baptists had even splintered into factions, in Protestantism a sure sign of success. Bolles's congregation of Closed Communion Baptists was soon joined by Elias Smith's Free Will Baptists, and immediately the two began arguing. Bentley thought each new group worse than the previous one, and of the Free Willers he could not imagine a sect "in a lower state of degradation in point of talents, converts, and superstitious violence." But both groups prospered: Bolles's congregation soon had a nice new brick meetinghouse for itself, and Smith's Free Willers built one as well (surely not the "shed" that Bentley described). The Baptist ministerial association chose Salem as a meeting place in 1807, and that same year even Bentley's own choir director absented himself one Sunday to attend the public baptisms. Thus there was, Bentley reported, no singing that morning at the East Church.[12]

And 1810 would bring the greatest harvest of all. Salem now hosted a pantheon of notable evangelical preachers: Samuel Worcester at the Tabernacle, Daniel Hopkins and Brown Emerson at the South, Joshua Spaulding at the Branch, Edward Turner at the Universalist house, Bolles at the Closed Communion Baptist, and Smith at the Free Will Baptist. All these came together in the spring of 1810 to lead an "immense Awakening," attracting on some evenings an estimated two thousand people to their churches.[13] The Branch Church admitted seventy-four new members that year—fifty-one in March alone—and the Baptist congregation grew by one hundred and twenty-five, sometimes as many as ten in a single Sabbath.[14]

On the political front, too, Bentley's day had passed. The Republican Party in Salem was growing ever stronger, sending Republican members to the General Court, going with Republican James Sullivan in the next three gubernatorial elections, and returning Jacob Crowninshield to Congress in 1806 for a third term.[15] Outside the polling places, Republicans took over the Essex militia, initiated their own civic parades and ceremonials, and even began their own bank. Federalism had hardly died out completely, and Jefferson's Embargo of 1807 helped resuscitate the party there as it did in many New England ports. Even so, Salem stayed as Republican as any coastal town could have during the slowdown, keeping town offices in their hands and even voting down the Boston selectmen's request to protest the embargo.[16]

Bentley continued to be a Republican and to support all these developments, but never again was he as important as he was before 1805. The most influential member of the party in Salem was now Joseph Story, a Marblehead native who had moved to Salem only in 1801. Story's Republicanism was true enough: he too had publicly defended the local Wollstonecraftian Abigail Rogers, and he had gotten into "fisty cuffs" with Hearsey Derby over some electioneering insult or another. Salem's "Republican lawyer"—as Story was known—had risen quickly through the ranks, even giving the keynote address at the 1804 Fourth of July celebration at the East Church.[17] But even so, he and Bentley never warmed to each other. By all rights, Story should have been a Federalist. He was a Harvard graduate, an Arminian liberal, and a future justice of the United States Supreme Court, a man made Republican by his Marblehead origins but the kind of Republican later to become a Whig and the kind who saw nothing to admire in the old radical down in the waterfront parish.[18] And if Story was the new intellect of the party, the new money came from William Gray, reputedly the wealthiest merchant in America. An ex-Federalist, Gray had become Republican only during the Embargo and only, so cynical friends thought, because he profited from the sudden shortages therein. Either way, Gray now seemed committed, but he, like Story, owed nothing of his ideology to Bentley. Theirs was a Republicanism based *on* self-interest, not against it, and the party was following their lead, not Bentley's. Worst of all, in 1808, Jacob Crowninshield died. Two days after his body arrived in Salem harbor, the Republicans held a caucus to pick a nominee to fill his seat. They chose Joseph Story. Bentley was, again, alone, rejected this time by those he made powerful. He hardly knew the candidate they ran in the regular election that fall.

In a town full of evangelical Republicans and liberal Federalists, William Bentley fit in nowhere. He continued to rent the room in the Crowninshield house. He continued to collect books, enough so that when he died, his personal library was one of the largest in the country, perhaps second in size behind only Thomas Jefferson's.[19] He continued to follow politics, writing his news summaries and avidly supporting war when it came in 1812. But mostly he continued to preach, now from notes rather than full texts, to whoever came to his East Church on Sundays.

So it was that he passed through the first and second decades of the nineteenth century, a shrunken man in a shrinking town. In the last year of that decade, just two weeks after Hannah Crowninshield was married, Bentley's father died. Not that William was upset. He had fallen out of touch with his family after the dispute over his grandfather's will. His mother had passed away in 1804, and his father and he had then lost almost all contact. Joshua wrote on occasion, usually when he needed money for firewood, in one note reminding "Billy" that "the hand of Providence is hard when ones friends are shy." Joshua was no theologian, but he knew that friends as well as storm fronts could be secondary causes, and their uncharitableness could be as hurtful. It was ironic that he sent this to one of the few men in New England who did not believe in special providence. But Bentley did believe in charity as part of God's universal will for humanity set at Creation, so he sent money when he could. He would not kid himself—as he would have put it—that he was an instrument of God's contingent will, but he did see it as acting in accordance with conscience and thus in abidance with God's moral law. To send the money was still the right thing to do, he thought, as a son and as a Christian. But father and son had had little else to do with each other; when Joshua Bentley died, William did not attend the funeral.[20]

And in December of that year, 1819, William Bentley died, too. He was sixty years old. Edward Everett gave the funeral sermon, and then Bentley was buried in Salem's Howard Street Burying Ground. Parishioners later erected a memorial at Harmony Grove Cemetery and may have had his body moved there; the exact location of his remains is uncertain. The loner who struggled his entire life for a secure place in Salem would appreciate that.[21]

Notes

LIST OF ABBREVIATIONS

AHR	*American Historical Review*
AQ	*American Quarterly*
BTR	*Records of the Boston Town Commissioners* (Boston Town Records)
ECPR	Essex County Probate Records, Massachusetts State Archives, Boston
EG	*Essex Gazette*
EIHC	*Essex Institute Historical Collections*
IR	[Salem] *Independent Register*
MA	Massachusetts Archives Collection, Massachusetts State Archives, Boston
MHSC	*Collections of the Massachusetts Historical Society*
MHSP	*Proceedings of the Massachusetts Historical Society*
NEGHR	*New England Genealogical and Historical Register*
NEQ	*New England Quarterly*
PCSM	*Publications of the Colonial Society of Massachusetts*
SHG	John Langdon Sibley and Clifford K. Shipton, *Biographical Sketches of Graduates of Harvard University* [*Sibley's Harvard Graduates*]. 17 vols. (Boston: Massachusetts Historical Society, 1873–1975)
SG	*Salem Gazette*
SR	*Salem Register*
STR	Salem Town Records, handwritten copy in the Phillips Library, Peabody Essex Museum, Salem

TPP   Timothy Pickering Papers, microfilm copies of originals at
              Massachusetts Historical Society, Boston
WBP   William Bentley Papers. American Antiquarian Society
WBPT   William Bentley Papers. Tufts University Archives
WBS   William Bentley Sermons. Tufts University Archives
WMQ   *William and Mary Quarterly*, third series

INTRODUCTION

1. "East Church, miscellaneous manuscripts, 1717–1804."

2. For midcentury Arminianism, see Conrad Wright, *The Beginnings of Unitarianism in America* (Boston: Beacon Press, 1955; repr. New York: Archon, 1976), and "Rational Religion in Eighteenth-Century America," in his *The Liberal Christians: Essays on American Unitarian History* (Boston: Beacon Press, 1970).

3. WBP, box 2, folder 2.

4. Though a minor figure on the national scene, he is not unknown to students of the early Republic. Richard D. Brown has nicely recounted Bentley's efforts to effect an educated citizenry, and a number of other historians have made passing references to his theological or political ideas. See Brown's *Knowledge Is Power: The Diffusion of Information in Early America, 1700–1865* (New York: Oxford University Press, 1989): 197–217. The *Essex Institute Historical Collections* has published a variety of articles on Bentley's life in Salem, including several by Louise Chipley: " 'The Best Instruction of the People': William Bentley on the Congregational Clergy and the Republic, 1783–1819," *EIHC* 127 (1991): 194–210; " 'Enlightened Charity': William Bentley on Poor Relief in the Early Republic, 1783–1819," *EIHC* 128 (1992): 162–79; "The Enlightenment Library of William Bentley," *EIHC* 122 (1986): 2–29; "The Financial and Tenure Anxieties of New England's Congregational Clergy during the Early National Era: The Case of William Bentley, 1783–1819," *EIHC* 127 (1991): 277–96; "William Bentley, Journalist of the Early Republic," *EIHC* 123 (1987): 331–47. See also the biographical sketches in *MHSP* 1 (1791–1855): 320–23; William Sprague, ed., *Annals of the American Pulpit: Commemorative Notices of Distinguished American Clergy of Various Denominations* (New York, 1857–1869), VIII: 154–57; Samuel A. Eliot, ed., *Heralds of a Liberal Faith* (Boston: American Unitarian Association, 1910), I: 149–59.

5. For Arminians of Bentley's time or slightly before, see Charles W. Akers, *Called unto Liberty: A Life of Jonathan Mayhew, 1720–1766* (Cambridge, Mass.: Harvard University Press, 1964), and *The Divine Politician: Samuel Cooper and the American Revolution in Boston* (Boston: Northeastern University Press, 1982); Edward M. Griffin, *Old Brick: Charles Chauncy of Boston, 1705–1787* (Minneapolis: University of Minnesota Press, 1980); Charles Lippy, *Seasonable Revolutionary: The Mind of Charles Chauncy* (Chicago: Nelson Hall, 1982); Edmund S. Morgan, *The Gentle Puritan: A Life of Ezra Stiles, 1727–1795* (New Haven, Conn.: Yale University Press, 1962); Robert J. Wilson, *The Benevolent Deity: Ebenezer Gay and the Rise of Rational Religion in New England, 1696–1787* (Philadelphia: University of Pennsylvania Press, 1984).

6. To list just those touching on liberal rather than evangelical Christianity, in addition to Wright's, other important works include Philip Greven, *The Protestant Temperament: Patterns of Child-Rearing, Religious Experience, and the Self in Early America* (Chicago: University of Chicago Press, 1977), particularly part 4, "The Genteel: The Self Asserted"; Alan Heimert, *Religion and the American Mind: From the Great Awakening to the Revolution* (Cambridge, Mass.: Harvard University Press, 1966); Harry S. Stout, *The New England Soul: Preaching and Religious Culture in Colonial New England* (New York: Oxford University Press, 1986); Bruce Kuklick, *Churchmen and Philosophers: From Jonathan Edwards to John Dewey* (New Haven, Conn.: Yale University Press, 1985): 80–94. Although its coverage is of the liberal ministry in the nineteenth century, Daniel Walker Howe's *The Unitarian Conscience: Harvard Moral Philosophy, 1805–1861* (Cambridge, Mass.: Harvard University Press, 1970) should be mentioned here as one of the essential works on the group as a whole.

7. See William G. McLoughlin, *New England Dissent, 1630–1883: The Baptists and the Separation of Church and State*, 2 vols. (Cambridge, Mass.: Harvard University Press, 1971), and his collection of essays, *Soul Liberty: The Baptists' Struggle in New England, 1630–1833* (Hanover, R.I.: Brown University Press, 1991); and C. C. Goen, *Revivalism and Separatism in New England, 1740–1800: Strict Congregationalists and Separate Baptists in the Great Awakening* (New Haven, Conn.: Yale University Press, 1962). But also see Stephen A. Marini, *Radical Sects in Revolutionary New England* (Cambridge, Mass.: Harvard University Press, 1982); and Carla Gardina Pestana, *Quakers and Baptists in Colonial Massachusetts* (Cambridge: Cambridge University Press, 1991).

8. On the American side, many works have looked at the beliefs of deists Jefferson and Franklin. Overviews are in G. Adolph Koch, *Republican Religion: The American Revolution and the Cult of Reason* (New York: Henry Holt, 1933); Herbert M. Morais, *Deism in Eighteenth-Century America* (New York: Columbia University Press, 1934); Kerry S. Walters, *Rational Infidels: The American Deists* (Wolfeboro, N.H.: Longwood, 1992). For deists in New England, see A. Owen Aldridge, "Natural Religion and Deism in America before Ethan Allen and Thomas Paine," *WMQ* 54 (1997): 835–48; Roderick A. French, "Elihu Palmer, Radical Deist, Radical Republican: A Reconsideration of American Free Thought," *Studies in Eighteenth-Century Culture* 8 (1978): 87–108; Pauline Maier, "Reason and Revolution: The Radicalism of Dr. Thomas Young," *AQ* 28 (1976): 229–49; Darlene Shapiro, "Ethan Allen: Philosopher-Theologian to a Generation of American Revolutionaries," *WMQ* 21 (1964): 236–55. Larger studies of Allen and Paine include Michael A. Bellesiles, *Revolutionary Outlaws: Ethan Allen and the Struggle for Independence on the Early American Frontier* (Charlottesville: University Press of Virginia, 1993); and Eric Foner, *Tom Paine and Revolutionary America* (New York: Oxford University Press, 1976). James Turner has written the most authoritative analysis of deism's influence into the nineteenth century: *Without God, Without Creed: The Origins of Unbelief in America* (Baltimore: Johns Hopkins University Press, 1985).

9. A list of even the important works on political ideology in the revolutionary period is a very long one, but an excellent starting point to consider the overlap of

ideology with religious concerns is James Kloppenberg, "The Virtues of Liberalism: Christianity, Republicanism, and Ethics in Early American Political Discourse," *Journal of American History* 74 (1987): 9–33. Other works are listed in the endnotes for relevant parts of this text.

10. Christopher Grasso, *A Speaking Aristocracy: Transforming Public Discourse in Eighteenth-Century Connecticut* (Chapel Hill: University of North Carolina Press, 1999); Wilson Kimnach's introduction to Jonathan Edwards, *Sermons and Discourses 1720–1723*, ed. Wilson H. Kimnach (New Haven, Conn.: Yale University Press, 1992); Donald Weber, *Rhetoric and History in Revolutionary New England* (New York: Oxford University Press, 1988); Stout, *New England Soul.*

11. Jürgen Habermas, *The Structural Transformation of the Public Sphere: An Inquiry into a Category of Bourgeois Society* (Cambridge: MIT Press, 1991); a more concise description of the central concept, in Habermas's own words, is "The Public Sphere," in *Rethinking Popular Culture: Contemporary Perspectives in Cultural Studies*, ed. Chandra Mukerji and Michael Schudson (Berkeley: University of California Press, 1991): 398–404. Perhaps more helpful still in providing an introduction are the essays in Craig Calhoun, ed. *Habermas and the Public Sphere* (Cambridge: MIT Press, 1992). For these ideas in America, the best analysis remains Michael Warner, *Letters of the Republic: Publication and the Public Sphere in Eighteenth-Century America* (Cambridge, Mass.: Harvard University Press, 1990). Jay Fliegelman has argued instead that oral culture was still the dominant mode of discourse into the nineteenth century: *Declaring Independence: Jefferson, Natural Language, and the Culture of Performance* (Stanford, Calif.: Stanford University Press, 1993). For the evangelical use of the public sphere, see Timothy D. Hall, *Contested Boundaries: Itinerancy and the Reshaping of the Colonial American Religious World* (Durham, N.C.: Duke University Press, 1994); Frank Lambert, *"Pedlar in Divinity": George Whitefield and the Transatlantic Revivals, 1737–1770* (Princeton, N.J.: Princeton University Press, 1994); T. H. Breen and Timothy D. Hall, "Structuring Provincial Imagination: The Rhetoric and Experience of Social Change in Eighteenth-Century New England," *AHR* 103 (1998): 1411–38.

12. Henry F. May, *The Enlightenment in America* (New York: Oxford University Press, 1976). On the later Enlightenment in America, see Donald H. Meyer, *The Democratic Enlightenment* (New York: Putnam's, 1976); and Daniel Boorstin, *The Lost World of Thomas Jefferson* (New York: Henry Holt, 1958).

13. On the symbiosis of Christian and economic liberalisms, two recent works bear mention here: Jonathan D. Sassi, *A Republic of Righteousness: The Public Christianity of the Post-Revolutionary New England Clergy* (New York: Oxford University Press, 2001); and Peter S. Field, *The Crisis of the Standing Order: Clerical Intellectuals and Cultural Authority in Massachusetts, 1780–1833* (Amherst: University of Massachusetts Press, 1998).

14. E. Brooks Holifield, *Theology in America: Christian Thought from the Age of the Puritans to the Civil War* (New Haven, Conn.: Yale University Press, 2003); Mark A. Noll, *America's God: From Jonathan Edwards to Abraham Lincoln* (New York: Oxford University Press, 2002).

15. Oliver to Bentley, June 16, 1790. Misc. Manuscript Collection, American Philosophical Society.

16. William Bentley, *The Diary of William Bentley, D.D. Pastor of the East Church, Salem, Massachusetts*, 4 vols. (Salem, Mass.: Essex Institute, 1905–1914; repr. Gloucester, Mass.: Peter Smith, 1962): I: 7. Citations of this work are from the latter edition and are hereafter cited as Bentley, *Diary*.

17. Marquis de Chastellux, *Travels in North America in the Years 1780, 1781, and 1782*, trans. Howard C. Rice Jr., 2 vols. (Chapel Hill: University of North Carolina Press, 1963), II: 495.

18. *Salem, April 5, [1783]. By the Ship Astrea, Captain John Derby, who arrived here yesterday, in 22 days from France* (Salem, 1783), [broadside]. Two weeks earlier, a vessel had brought to Philadelphia the first news of the preliminary peace. What Derby carried and Hall printed in Salem was an early copy of the declaration of cease-fire written to the American public by John Adams, Benjamin Franklin, and John Jay. Derby was an old hand at transatlantic news runs. Eight years earlier, he had been the first to take to England the announcement of the war's opening rounds. Reports of the battles at Lexington and Concord had needed some context, some interpretation, and both the British and the colonists rushed to get their side of the story back to London. The Provincial Congress quickly collected affidavits swearing that the shot heard 'round the world had come from a British musket and that the American response was self-defense, and it directed Richard Derby Jr., one of Salem's leading merchants, to hurry the affidavits to Benjamin Franklin in London. Derby sent his brother John in the *Quero*, and although an English packet ship had cleared Boston Harbor four days earlier carrying the British version of events, Derby's schooner was faster, and the Americans' tale had already spread through England when the *Sukey* finally heaved up. The documents that Derby took to Franklin in 1775 are reprinted in Peter Force, ed., *American Archives* (Washington, 1839), 4th ser., II: 486–501.

19. Sprague, *Annals*, VIII: 128–32; Samuel A. Eliot, *Heralds of a Liberal Faith*, I: 141–48. William Ware, ed., *American Unitarian Biography* (Boston, 1850) I: 101–18; Charles W. Upham, *Memoir of Rev. John Prince, L.L.D.* (Boston, 1836).

20. At the time of its formation in 1628, the only other church in New England was in Plymouth, and the Pilgrims had come over as an existing Separatist body. For notices of the importance of Salem's First Church in covenant and congregational polity, see Daniel Appleton White, *New England Congregationalism in its Origin and Purity; Illustrated by the Foundation and Early Records of the First Church in Salem* (Salem, 1861); and Williston Walker, *The Creeds and Platforms of Congregationalism* (1893; repr. Boston: Pilgrim Press, 1960): 97–122.

21. Bernard Bailyn and Lotte Bailyn, *Massachusetts Shipping 1697–1714* (Cambridge, Mass.: Harvard University Press, 1959): 79, 83, 97; Daniel Vickers, *Farmers and Fishermen: Two Centuries of Work in Essex County, Massachusetts, 1630–1850* (Chapel Hill: University of North Carolina Press, 1994): 157; Donald Warner Koch, "Income Distribution and Political Structure in Seventeenth-Century Salem, Massachusetts," *EIHC* 105 (1969): 58, 61; William I. Davisson, "Essex County Wealth Trends: Wealth and Economic Growth in Seventeenth-Century Massachusetts," *EIHC* 103 (1967): 291–342; Edward M. Cook Jr., *The Fathers of the Towns: Leadership and Community Structure in Eighteenth-Century New England* (Baltimore: Johns Hopkins University Press, 1976): 66.

22. Charles Francis Adams, ed., *The Works of John Adams, Second President of the United States* (Boston, 1850), II: 198.

23. *SHG*, 16: 457–63; Asa Dunbar, "Diary, 1771–1778."

24. *SHG*, 16: 316–22; Sprague, *Annals*, VIII: 16–18; Samuel A. Eliot, *Heralds of a Liberal Faith*, I: 131–40.

25. Samuel Williams, *A Sermon, Preached January 13, 1773* (Salem, 1773): 28.

26. Benjamin Guild, "Diary." Harvard University Archives.

27. Franklin Bowditch Dexter, ed., *The Literary Diary of Ezra Stiles* (New York: Charles Scribner's Sons, 1901), I: 230. Between 1745 and 1765, 159 persons joined what would become the Tabernacle, whereas 102 joined the First; ministers at the evangelical church performed 575 baptisms, whereas 403 were performed at the First. "Tabernacle Church, Record Book, 1743–1833"; "Records of the First Church of Salem, 1736–1875."

28. Since his call in 1718, Fiske's ministry had been going along just fine, highlighted by New England's first centennial celebration in 1729 and an invitation to preach the court's election sermon in 1731. But one of Fiske's duties was to provide midweek lectures to those parishioners whose appetite for pastoral wisdom was not sated by the two Sabbath-day sermons. Apparently, his flock was well enough fed, for poor attendance and poorer compensation soon compelled Fiske to discontinue the lectures. His parishioners, though, wanted their minister to provide a lecture even if they chose neither to attend nor to subsidize it. Fiske refused to do so without adequate compensation, and in 1732 he turned the tables on the congregation, accusing them of failing to live up to the promise they made back in 1718 to attend and fund the lectures. The members remembered no such vote, and when they examined the record book, they were surprised to find the notation wedged awkwardly into a narrow blank space and in ink only a day or two old. So began a controversy that would polarize ministers across Massachusetts, require the intervention of the governor, and split the First Church. See Pierce, ed., *Records of the First Church*, 266. The Fiske affair has been retold a number of times, most recently in James F. Cooper, *Tenacious of Their Liberties: The Congregationalists in Colonial Massachusetts* (New York: Oxford University Press, 1999): 188–93. See also *SHG* 5: 415–22; and James Duncan Phillips, *Salem in the Eighteenth Century* (New York: Houghton Mifflin, 1937): 102–12.

29. The exact number of people who attended in Salem is unclear. The original edition of this, the "Seventh Journal," put the number at two thousand, a figure repeated in Whitefield's 1756 edition. But Benjamin Franklin's 1741 edition puts it at seven thousand, and Benjamin Lynde wrote that there were "supposed near 6000." In any case, it was no doubt the largest crowd then assembled in Salem. [Whitefield], *George Whitefield's Journals* (London: Banner of Truth Trust, 1960): 465; Whitefield, *Journal* (London, 1756): 397; *A Continuation of the Reverend Mr. Whitefield's Journal* (Philadelphia, 1741): 78; *The Diaries of Benjamin Lynde and Benjamin Lynde Jr.* (Boston, 1880): 161.

30. Whitefield, *A Continuation*, 85–86.

31. *Diaries of Benjamin Lynde*, 98–99.

32. Chauncy, *Seasonable Thoughts on the State of Religion in New England* (Boston, 1743): 1–18. The most that the compiler of the *Christian History* could tout of Salem was

John Higginson's shopworn line about New England being "originally a plantation of religion, not a plantation of trade"; [Thomas Prince], *The Christian History* (Boston, 1744): 68. Whitefield's 1745 tour is in "An Unpublished Journal," in *George Whitefield's Journals*.

33. *A Letter from a Gentleman in Salem, to his friend in Boston, Oct. 25, 1745* (broadside, distributed with the *Boston Evening Post*, Nov. 4, 1745).

34. George F. Dow, ed., *The Holyoke Diaries, 1709–1856* (Salem, Mass.: Essex Institute, 1911): 74; *Diaries of Benjamin Lynde*, 199; Whitaker, *A Funeral Sermon, on the Death of the Reverend George Whitefield* (Salem, 1770).

35. "Tabernacle Church, Record Book, 1743–1833."

36. South Church, untitled record book, Tabernacle Church Archives. The Timothy Pickering Papers includes a number of documents—including an offer of "120 fish-hogsheads" for the Pickering pew at the Tabernacle—relating to Whitaker and the formation of the South. Sketches of Hopkins's life are in Sprague, *Annals*, I: 581–84; Franklin B. Dexter, ed., *Biographical Sketches of the Graduates of Yale College* (New York, 1896), II: 533–35. For the basic tenets of Hopkinsianism, or the New Divinity, see Douglas A. Sweeney, *Nathaniel Taylor, New Haven Theology, and the Legacy of Jonathan Edwards* (New York: Oxford University Press, 2003); Joseph A. Conforti, *Samuel Hopkins and the New Divinity Movement: Calvinism, the Congregational Ministry, and Reform in New England between the Great Awakenings* (Grand Rapids, Mich.: Eerdmans, 1981); Mark Valeri, *Law and Providence in Joseph Bellamy's New England: The Origins of the New Divinity in Revolutionary America* (New York: Oxford University Press, 1994); and William K. Breitenbach, "The Consistent Calvinism of the New Divinity Movement," *WMQ* 41 (1984): 241–64. John Cleaveland was a New Light rather than a Hopkinsian, but Christopher Jedrey's study speaks to the lives of many of Bentley's evangelical contemporaries: *The World of John Cleaveland: Family and Community in Eighteenth-Century New England* (New York: Norton, 1979).

37. Thirty-six members signed the East's original covenant in 1718, but one hundred and seventy men were taxed for the minister's salary that year. And in the 1770s, the church had about twenty-five male members but sixty male pew proprietors and some two hundred and fifty male heads of household in the parish. Not all attended every week, but the point remains that membership figures alone do not reflect the community's participation in the affairs of the church. See Pierce, *Records of the First Church*, 263; "East Church. Record Book, 1717–1757"; "East Church. Record Book, 1757–1793"; and "Valuation of Pews in East Meeting House, 1774," in Crandall, "Salem Tax Lists," reel 9.

38. John Gardner, "Diary, 1771–1779." Gardner Family Papers, PEM.

PROLOGUE

1. Annie Haven Thwing, *The Crooked and Narrow Streets of the Town of Boston, 1630–1822* (Boston: Marshall Jones Company, 1920): 26–77.

2. Bentley, *Diary*, II: 118–19.

3. Joseph A. Goldenberg, *Shipbuilding in Colonial America* (Charlottesville: University Press of Virginia, 1976).

4. *BTR* 14: 228, and 19: 78; Robert Francis Seybolt, *The Town Officials of Colonial Boston, 1634–1775* (Cambridge, Mass.: Harvard University Press, 1939).

5. Fred Anderson, *A People's Army: Massachusetts Soldiers and Society in the Seven Years' War* (Chapel Hill: University of North Carolina Press, 1984): 60.

6. He was then their only child. An elder son, Joshua Jr., had died at four months.

7. Gary B. Nash, *The Urban Crucible: Social Change, Political Consciousness, and the Origins of the American Revolution* (Cambridge, Mass.: Harvard University Press, 1979): 421–22, 255–56.

8. He was apparently not the most conscientious of tradesmen. The Boston selectmen served him in 1763 with a copy of a provincial law that regulated wheat standards "for preventing abuses by millers." A subsequent inspection led to the formation of a committee to remedy "the inconveniences the Town now labours under for want of faithful management in said Mills," and the committee threatened sanctions if Paine failed to weigh the incoming grain or the outgoing meal. *BTR*, 19: 259; 16: 147.

9. Bettye Hobbs Pruitt, ed., *The Massachusetts Tax Valuation List of 1771* (Boston: Hall, 1978): 4. "New Brick Church. Boston Records, 1722–1775," *NEHGR* 19 (1865): 233–34. Elizabeth Paine had been baptized there in 1738, and she and Joshua were married there before switching over to Joshua's church, the New North. See Bentley, *Diary* II: 120.

10. "Tax and Valuation Lists, 1771." Massachusetts Archives, 132: 95.

11. The Boston Latin School was founded in the seventeenth century. When the North Grammar School, the one Bentley attended, began in 1713, Boston Latin became known as the South Grammar School to distinguish between the two. It remained so until the North Grammar School closed in 1789, at which time the South Grammar again became known as the Boston Latin School. Although Bentley taught at the Latin School (when it was the South Grammar School), he was never a student there. Pauline Holmes, *A Tercentenary History of the Boston Public Latin School, 1635–1935*, Harvard Studies in Education, Vol. 25 (Cambridge, Mass.: Harvard University Press, 1935); and Henry F. Jenks, *Catalogue of the Boston Public Latin School, with an Historical Sketch* (Boston, 1886), although Jenks lists incorrect dates for Bentley's tenure as master at the North Grammar School. For the proportion of students who went on to the grammar school, see Robert Francis Seybolt, *The Public Schools of Colonial Boston, 1635–1775* (Cambridge, Mass.: Harvard University Press, 1935): 64. The contemporary curriculum is quoted in William B. Fowle, comp., "Schools of the Olden Time in Boston," *Common School Journal* 12: 311–12.

12. Nash, *Urban Crucible*, 342–43. See also Jayne E. Triber, *A True Republican: The Life of Paul Revere* (Amherst: University of Massachusetts Press, 1998): 7–71.

13. Alan Day and Katherine Day, "Another Look at the Boston Caucus," *Journal of American Studies* 5 (1971): 32–33; Elbridge Henry Goss, *The Life of Colonel Paul Revere* (Boston, 1891) I: 188–89; David Hackett Fischer, *Paul Revere's Ride* (New York: Oxford University Press, 1994): 103–105, 301–307; Esther Forbes, *Paul Revere and the World He Lived In* (Boston: Houghton Mifflin, 1942): 255–56.

14. Bentley, *Diary*, III: 149.

15. Untitled copybook, WBPT. His outside reading at Harvard, at least that which he charged from the college library as a junior and senior, reflect this predilection. Like other students, Bentley read Hugo Grotius's *De Veritate Religionis Christianæ* and Mosheim's *Ecclesiastical History*, but more than most of his peers he focused on linguistics. He particularly enjoyed the *Historical Connection of the Old and New Testaments* (1716–1718), a study of the period between the two testaments by Humphrey Prideaux, an English orientalist and Anglican minister. More influential yet was Edward Pococke, another English orientalist whose interests in languages and in manuscript collection may have served as a model for the Harvard undergraduate. After editing the Arabic portion of the Pentateuch for a polyglot Bible and doing his part to convert Muslims by publishing an Arabic version of Grotius's *De Veritate*, Pococke turned his attention to the Old Testament's minor prophets, writing commentaries that Bentley charged again and again from the college library. Library Charging Records, Harvard University Archives.

16. *Massachusetts Soldiers and Sailors of the Revolutionary War* (Boston, 1896) I: 980.

17. Bentley, *Diary*, II: 120.

18. Samuel E. Morison, *Three Centuries of Harvard, 1636–1936* (Cambridge, Mass.: Harvard University Press, 1936): 149. Bentley's preaching success is noted in his *Diary*, III: 209.

19. Harvard University, *Proceribus Politiae Massachusettensis* (Boston, 1777); Henry N. Blake, "Harvard Soldiers and Sailors in the American Revolution," *Harvard Graduates' Magazine* 28 (1919): 258; Sheldon S. Cohen, "Harvard College on the Eve of the American Revolution," in *Sibley's Heir: A Volume in Memory of Clifford Kenyon Shipton* (Boston: Colonial Society of Massachusetts, 1982): 173–90.

20. *BTR*, 25: 45, 52.

21. *BTR*, 25: 88; Harvard University, Corp. Rec. (April 4, 1780; March 20, 1781) 3: 74, 110. Volume and page numbers in citations of the Corporation Records refer to electroprint copies in the Harvard University Archives.

22. Harvard University, Corp. Rec. (June 10, 1778; March 10, 1779) 3: 2, 32.

23. Bentley, *Diary*, IV: 415.

24. Fitch Edward Oliver, ed., *The Diary of William Pynchon, Salem: A Picture of Salem Life, Social and Political, A Century Ago* (Boston: Houghton Mifflin, 1890): 68–72; "Lists of Temporary Students at Harvard College, 1639–1800," in the Harvard University Archives; Harvard University, Faculty Records, 4: 217–18, 280, 289, and 5: 8, 50; Samuel E. Morison, *Harrison Gray Otis, 1765–1848: The Urbane Federalist* (Boston: Houghton Mifflin, 1969): 36.

25. WBP, vol. 4.

26. *Assessors' "Taking Books" of the Town of Boston, 1780* (Boston: Bostonian Society, 1912): 10; *Acts and Resolves, Public and Private, of the Province of the Massachusetts Bay* (Boston, 1922) 21: 574.

27. WBP, vol. 4.

28. Gallatin's requests that Bentley help settle his accounts are in WBP, box 1, folder 4. Bentley sometimes volunteered to help Winthrop in the college library, superintending in October of 1780 when Winthrop went to Penobscot Bay to view an

eclipse and the next year contracting to paste the Harvard seal into the library's books: Harvard University, Corp. Rec. (Sept. 15, Oct. 11, 1780; Nov. 13, 1781) 3: 94–97, 133.

29. Bentley, *Diary*, I: 91–92; III: 489.

30. Harvard University, Corp. Rec. (April 1, 1783) 3: 164–65.

31. "East Church, miscellaneous manuscripts, 1717–1804"; *Journals of the House of Representatives of Massachusetts* (Boston, 1921) II: 121, 186, 203; Richard D. Pierce, ed., *The Records of the First Church in Salem, Massachusetts 1629–1736* (Salem, Mass.: Essex Institute, 1974): 262–67.

32. *SHG*, 5: 647–68; 7: 371–74.

33. Dexter, *Literary Diary of Ezra Stiles*, I: 257–58.

34. Williams, *A Sermon, Preached January 13, 1773*, 39.

35. Samuel Williams, *The Influence of Christianity on Civil Society* (Boston, 1780): 28–32. Capitalization in the original.

36. Guild, "Diary."

37. John Lathrop, *A Sermon, Preached at the Ordination of William Bentley* (Salem, 1783): 22; Oliver, *Diary of William Pynchon*, 124; *SG*, Sept 25, 1783.

CHAPTER 1

1. WBP, box 5, folder 11; Bentley, *Diary*, I: 1.

2. WBP, box 1, folder 4; *SG*, Sept. 25, 1783.

3. Diman's Charge is part of John Lathrop, *Sermon Preached at the Ordination of William Bentley*: 26.

4. *SG*, Aug. 2, 1785; Diman, *A Sermon, Preached at Salem, January 16, 1772. Being the Day on which Bryan Sheehan was Executed, for Committing A Rape on the Body of Abial Hollowell, the Wife of Benjamin Hollowell, of Marblehead* (Salem, 1772). Sheehan's execution was the first in Salem since the witch trials. He was executed on Salem Neck in front of as many as twelve thousand witnesses. James D. Phillips, *Salem in the Eighteenth Century*, 347; *Essex Gazette*, Jan. 16, 1772; *Diaries of Benjamin Lynde*, 201; *Holyoke Diaries*, 78.

5. *The testimony and advice of an Assembly of Pastors* (Boston, [1743]): 14; Samuel Gardner, "Diary for the Year 1759," *EIHC* 49 (1913): 4. He was what historians would call an Old Light Calvinist, a term given to those clergy who tried to maintain the faith against both the theologically liberal changes of the Arminians (like Bentley) and the socially radical changes of the evangelicals.

6. It should be remembered that some evangelicals—namely Wesleyan Methodists—would become Arminian too, but their brand of Arminianism should not be confused with this one. Both versions of Arminianism constituted rejections of election, but they went in very different directions about exactly what kind of human behavior has saving power.

7. WBS, #238.

8. WBS, #99.

9. WBS, #197.

10. WBS, #35.

11. WBS, #41.

12. [William Bentley, comp.], *Extracts from Doctor Priestley's Catechism* (Salem, 1785): 4; *The New-England Primer Improved* (Portsmouth, 1789). He learned this universalism from Charles Chauncy, perhaps while transcribing the manuscript of Chauncy's four-hundred-page *Mystery Hid from Ages and Generations* (London, 1784) before it was sent to England for publication, in case it was lost in the passage. But in any event, Chauncy's scheme was the one "most agreeable to divine goodness," Bentley thought, and he told his listeners in 1787, in a sermon following Chauncy's death, that about Chauncy's plan, "I acquiesce." Bentley, *Diary*, IV: 350; WBS, #296. For Chauncy's universalism in particular, see Griffin, *Old Brick*, 168–76, and Lippy, *Seasonable Revolutionary*, 107–23.

13. Two couples went to Daniel Hopkins's church, five women to the Tabernacle, and one woman to the First. (Diman's daughters, wrote Bentley bitterly, went "among those who happen to ask them to dine, of whatever persuasion.") Bentley, *Diary*, I: 26. Of the women, nothing is known; of the two men, only a little: Thomas Safford had joined in 1770, but he was not a proprietor. He was a man of average wealth, with total assessed property of £150. He did not vote at Bentley's ordination; perhaps he had already left before the vote was held. John Ingersoll was neither a member nor a proprietor. The 1785 tax record shows him to be quite poor, with less than £100 in combined real and personal estates.

14. Bentley, *Diary*, I: 347.

15. *SG*, June 14, 1785.

16. WBS, #75.

17. WBS, #339.

18. WBS, #108. David D. Hall, *Worlds of Wonder, Days of Judgment* (Cambridge, Mass.: Harvard University Press, 1989), particularly pp. 152–62, helped shape my understanding of the role of the sacraments in New England. But see also E. Brooks Holifield, *The Covenant Sealed: The Development of Puritan Sacramental Theology in Old and New England, 1570–1720* (New Haven, Conn.: Yale University Press, 1974); Robert G. Pope, *The Half-Way Covenant: Church Membership in Puritan New England* (Princeton, N.J.: Princeton University Press, 1969); and, on Stoddard, Grasso, *A Speaking Aristocracy*, 120–28.

19. WBP, box 5, folder 1; copied into Bentley, *Diary* I: 20–21.

20. Bentley, *Diary*, I: 22–24

21. Bentley, *Diary*, I: 24.

22. WBS, #156, #192, #194.

23. WBS, #171.

24. WBS, #184.

25. WBS, #194.

26. WBP, box 1, folder 15. The letter is undated, but the writer is probably the John Gunnison who was listed as a carpenter in 1785 in Bentley, *Diary*, I: 11.

27. Richard Joseph Morris, "Wealth Distribution in Salem, Massachusetts, 1759–1799: The Impact of Revolution and Independence," *EIHC* 114 (1978): 93–95, a summary of his "Revolutionary Salem: Stratification and Mobility in a Massachusetts

Seaport, 1759–1799" (Ph.D. diss., New York University, 1975). For the lives of fishermen, see Vickers, *Farmers and Fishermen*; for laborers, see Billy G. Smith, *"The Lower
Sort": Philadelphia's Laboring People, 1750–1800* (Ithaca, N.Y.: Cornell University Press,
1990); for mariners, see Marcus Rediker, *Between the Devil and the Deep Blue Sea:
Merchant Seamen, Pirates, and the Anglo-American Maritime World, 1700–1750* (Cambridge: Cambridge University Press, 1987).

   28. Figuring out the demographics of the church community is not as simple as
it seems. Bentley's diary has a number of lists of different kinds taken at different
times. For the number of parishioners: his diary begins with a list of the parish's heads
of households (though he calls them "members") written sometime between late 1783
and early 1785. Other names were added at unknown times, but the original list
had 202 names (143 men, 59 women; Bentley, *Diary*, I: 7–15). Those two-hundred-odd
households comprised some eleven hundred to twelve hundred individuals, or parishioners of all ages. (Bentley, *Diary*, I: 222; see also Bentley, *Diary*, I: 222–27, 332–38
for lists in 1790 and 1792.) For the number of proprietors: the early list has 52 proprietors (39 men, 13 women); a second list, made in 1788, had 59 names (40 men,
19 women) (Bentley, *Diary*, I: 49–50). For the number of members: in 1788, he copied
into his diary a list made by Diman back in 1778, a list that had 122 names (99 women
and 23 men). Of them, 41 had died between 1778 and 1788 and 9 more had moved
away, leaving 72. But 28 more individuals had joined in the same period (24 women
and 4 men, including Bentley), three of whom had since died, leaving a total of 97
members in 1788. If we assume a steady decline in membership from 1778 to 1788,
that is, from 122 to 97, then approximately 105 members would have been present
in 1785. (Bentley, *Diary*, I: 95–97.) Finally, there were eight men members voting at
Bentley's ordination in 1783. So, in sum and in round numbers and excluding considerations of overlap, there were a hundred members (more than nine-tenths female),
fifty pew proprietors (almost four-fifths male), and two hundred parishioner families with twelve hundred people in them under Bentley's care in the early years of
his ministry.

   29. Bentley, *Diary*, I: 346.
   30. Bentley, *Diary*, IV: 113–14.
   31. Bentley, *Diary*, IV: 100; I: 183.
   32. Bentley, *Diary*, I: 358.
   33. Bentley, *Diary*, II: 168.
   34. "Salem, Mass. Tax Valuation 1784–1785," microfilm #55, reel 1, Phillips Library.
   35. Bentley, *Diary*, I: 7–15.
   36. Bentley, *Diary*, III: 34, 339; IV: 383, 475, 515. For privateering in Salem, see
Gardner Weld Allen, *Massachusetts Privateers of the Revolution* (Cambridge, Mass.:
Harvard University Press, 1927); James D. Phillips, *Salem in the Eighteenth Century*,
392–442; Ronald N. Tagney, *The World Turned Upside Down: Essex County during
America's Turbulent Years, 1763–1790* (W Newbury, Mass.: Essex County History, 1989):
225–42.
   37. "Salem, Mass. Tax Valuation 1784–1785."
   38. WBP, box 5, folder 1; copied into Bentley, *Diary*, I: 20–21.

39. The congregation's desire to have Bentley rather than Diman baptize their children is borne out in statistics. Diman baptized the children of the church in 1784 because he would not allow Bentley to do so. But in the spring of 1785, the church allowed parents to pick the minister they preferred. So there were some months before that that only Diman could have baptized, and some months after Diman's exit in late October in which only Bentley could have baptized, and an unknown number of months in the middle in which the choice would have reflected preference. Were the two men's standards equally preferred, one would predict an equal distribution. But Bentley that year baptized twenty-four babies, and Diman baptized only seventeen. Bentley, *Diary*, I: 348.

40. Acts and Resolves of Massachusetts, 1782–1783, chap. 9, 503–504; WBP, box 5, folder 11.

41. Compare Rom. 4 and James 2, respectively.

42. Diman, *A Sermon*, 8.

43. John Huntington, *Sermons on Important Subjects* (Boston, 1767): 9–10. Italics in the original.

44. *SG*, June 14, Aug. 2, Oct. 4, 1785; Bentley, *Diary*, I: 24, 28, 106–107, 122, 135–38, 141, 176, 192–94, 201–204, 236, 251, 256, 354; WBS, #198, #394; Edwin R Dimond, *The Genealogy of the Dimond or Dimon Family* (Albany, 1891): 115–18.

CHAPTER 2

1. For the historiography of these questions, begin with Niebuhr's *The Social Sources of Denominationalism* (New York: Henry Holt, 1929). Then John C. Miller, "Religion, Finance, and Democracy in Massachusetts," *NEQ* 6 (1933): 29–58, for the progressive view supporting Niebuhr; and Edwin S. Gaustad, "Society and the Great Awakening in New England," *WMQ* 11 (1954): 566–77, for the "consensus" rebuttal. For more quantitative studies, see Richard L. Bushman, *From Puritan to Yankee: Character and the Social Order in Connecticut, 1690–1765* (Cambridge, Mass.: Harvard University Press, 1967): 187–92; J. M. Bumsted, "Revivalism and Separatism in New England: The First Society of Norwich, Connecticut, as a Case Study," *WMQ* 24 (1967): 588–612; Bumsted, "Religion, Finance, and Democracy in Massachusetts: The Town of Norton as a Case Study," *JAH* 57 (1971): 817–31; Gerald F. Moran, "Conditions of Religious Conversion in the First Society of Norwich, Connecticut, 1718–1744," *Journal of Social History* 5 (1972): 331–41; James Walsh, "The Great Awakening in the First Congregational Church of Woodbury, Connecticut," *WMQ* 28 (1971): 543–62; William Willingham, "Religious Conversion in the Second Society of Windham, Connecticut 1723–1743: A Case Study," *Societas* 6 (1976): 109–19; Peter S. Onuf, "New Lights in New London: A Group Portrait of the Separatists," *WMQ* 37 (1980): 627–43. For similar inquiries for the early Republic, see Mary Kupiec Cayton, "Who Were the Evangelicals? Conservative and Liberal Identity in the Unitarian Controversy in Boston, 1804–1833," *Journal of Social History* 31 (1997): 85–107; and Anne C. Rose, "Social Sources of Denominationalism Reconsidered: Post-Revolutionary Boston as a Case Study," *AQ* 38 (1986): 243–64.

2. By 1765, members of the Orne, Pickman, Lynde, Gardner, and Cabot families owned 40 percent of Salem's fifty-four fishing vessels and 40 percent of the town's thirty-five vessels engaged in trade with foreign ports. To take another measure, at a time when a mere 7 percent of men left estates worth more than £2,000, Samuel Gardner's was valued at £20,929, and Timothy Orne's at £27,980. "List of Salem Vessels in 1765," *EIHC* 62 (1926): 8–11; Jackson Turner Main, *Social Structure of Revolutionary America* (Princeton, N.J.: Princeton University Press, 1965): 41–42; Harrison Ellery and C. P. Bowditch, *The Pickering Genealogy* (privately printed, 1897) I: 94–97. The socializing fills the diary of E. A. Holyoke's wife in Dow, ed., *The Holyoke Diaries, 1709–1856.*

3. Pruitt, *Massachusetts Tax Valuation*, 130–54; "North Church Proprietors' Records, 1773–1836."

4. The North Church, *The First Centenary of the North Church and Society* (Salem, 1873).

5. Williams, *A Sermon, Preached January 13, 1773*: 28.

6. *EG*, Jan. 19, 1773; *Boston News-Letter*, June 3, 1773.

7. Unbound papers, in Records of the North Church.

8. Crandall, "Massachusetts Local Tax Lists"; "Tabernacle Record Book, 1743–1833"; "First Church, Proprietors' Records, 1746–1816"; Pruitt, *Massachusetts Tax Valuation*, 130–54.

9. Third Congregational Church [Salem, Mass.], *Rev. Sir, Our Destitute State* [Salem, 1775]; Samuel M. Worcester, *A Memorial of the Old and New Tabernacle* (Boston, 1855): 21; "Church Sketches—Tabernacle Church, Salem, MS," *Congregational Year-Book* (1857): 156–68.

10. Guild, "Diary."

11. Bentley, *Diary*, I: 346; "East Church, Record Book, 1717–1757"; "East Church Record Book, 1757–1793"; "Records of the First Church, 1736–1875"; "First Church, Proprietors Records, 1746–1816"; Crandall, "Massachusetts Local Tax Lists"; Pierce, *Records of the First Church*, 263; Pruitt, *Massachusetts Tax Valuation*, 130–54.

12. Bentley, *Diary*, I: 126; 269; II: 157.

13. WBS, #183. The standard work on the Chain of Being remains Arthur O. Lovejoy, *The Great Chain of Being: A Study in the History of an Idea. The William James Lectures Delivered at Harvard University, 1933* (Cambridge, Mass.: Harvard University Press, 1948).

14. Bentley, *A Collection of Psalms and Hymns*, hymn 17.

15. WBS, #375.

16. WBS, #127.

17. For the era's Cosmic Toryism, see Basil Willey, *The Eighteenth Century Background: Studies on the Idea of Nature in the Thought of the Period* (1940; repr. Beacon Press, 1961): 43–57. Many works on eighteenth-century English thought discuss the conservative quality of its assumptions about nature and natural law, but the ones most directly relevant here are A. M. C. Waterman, *Revolution, Economics, and Religion: Christian Political Economy, 1798–1833* (Cambridge: Cambridge University Press, 1991); Jacob Viner, *The Role of Providence in the Social Order* (Princeton, N.J.:

Princeton University Press, 1972); Ernst Cassirer, *The Philosophy of the Enlightenment*, trans. Fritz C. A. Koelln and James P. Pettegrove (1932; repr. Princeton, N.J.: Princeton University Press, 1951); and Sir Leslie Stephen, *History of English Thought in the Eighteenth Century*, 2 vols. (1876; repr. New York: Harcourt, Brace, and World, 1962). For the social conservativeness of midcentury Arminians, see, in addition to the theological works on Arminians, John Corrigan, *The Hidden Balance: Religion and the Social Theories of Charles Chauncy and Jonathan Mayhew* (Cambridge: Cambridge University Press, 1987); and Dale S. Kuehne, *Massachusetts Congregationalist Political Thought, 1760–1790: The Design of Heaven* (Columbia: University of Missouri Press, 1996).

18. WBS, #82.

19. Simeon Howard, *A Discourse Occasioned by the Death of Mrs. Elizabeth Howard* (Boston, 1777): 27; see also Charles Chauncy, *The Blessedness of the Dead* (Boston, 1749): 26–27. For the economic marginalization of women and for the idealization of Proverbs 31, see Laurel Thatcher Ulrich, *Good Wives: Image and Reality in the Lives of Women in Northern New England, 1650–1750* (New York: Knopf, 1980): 24–30, and passim; C. Dallett Hemphill, "Women in Court: Sex-Role Differentiation in Salem, Massachusetts, 1636–1683," *WMQ* 39 (1982): 164–75.

20. WBS, #174.

21. Chauncy, *Seasonable Thoughts*, xii.

22. WBS, #307, #379. On the memory of Hutchinson, see Amy Schrader Lang, *Prophetic Woman: Anne Hutchinson and the Problem of Dissent in the Literature of New England* (Berkeley: University of California Press, 1987).

23. John Murray, *A Welcome to the Grave* (Newburyport, 1781).

24. Mary Beth Norton, *Liberty's Daughters: The Revolutionary Experience of American Women, 1750–1800* (Boston: Little, Brown, 1980): 165–70.

25. *EG*, Oct. 25, 1768, and May 2 and June 27, 1769; the theological stance of each minister is from my own compilations. See Laurel Thatcher Ulrich, "'Daughters of Liberty': Religious Women in Revolutionary New England," in *Women in the Age of the American Revolution*, ed. Ronald Hoffman and Peter J Albert (Charlottesville: University Press of Virginia, 1989): 211–43; and Linda Kerber, "'History Can Do It No Justice': Women and the Reinterpretation of the American Revolution," in *Toward an Intellectual History of Women: Essays by Linda Kerber* (Chapel Hill: University of North Carolina Press, 1997): 85–87.

26. WBS, #174.

27. In 1764, the Boston selectmen reported that the "Negro fellow belonging to Mr. Payne the Miller" had smallpox. In 1771, Paine was taxed for two slaves. *BTR*, 20: 46.

28. WBS, #233.

29. Charles W. Akers, "'Our Modern Egyptians': Phillis Wheatley and the Whig Campaign against Slavery in Revolutionary Boston," *Journal of Negro History* 60 (1975): 410.

30. STR, March 3, 1755 (box 4, folder 4, 307–308).

31. Samuel Hopkins, *Dialogue Concerning the Slavery of the Africans* (Norwich, 1778): 8. For more on Hopkinsianism, see the works listed in note 36 of the Introduction.

32. The phrase is from David Grimsted, "Anglo-American Racism and Phillis Wheatley's 'Sable Veil,' 'Length'ned Chain,' and 'Knitted Heart,'" in *Women in the Age of the American Revolution*, ed. Ronald Hoffman and Peter J. Albert (Charlottesville: University Press of Virginia, 1989): 388. The more famous opposition of the Quakers was rooted in their desire to withdraw from the dominant culture and in their condemnation of the violence of the trade and the avarice of slave owning, for which see Jack D. Marietta, *The Reformation of American Quakerism, 1748–1783* (Philadelphia: University of Pennsylvania Press, 1984): 111–28. The literature on the relationship between Christianity and slavery is enormous, but David Brion Davis's books are particularly helpful; see his *The Problem of Slavery in Western Culture* (Ithaca, N.Y.: Cornell University Press, 1966), and *The Problem of Slavery in the Age of Revolution, 1770–1823* (Ithaca, N.Y.: Cornell University Press, 1975).

33. Pruitt, *Massachusetts Tax Valuation*, 130–54, compared with "Tabernacle Record Book, 1743–1833"; "First Church, Proprietors' Records, 1746–1816"; "East Church Record Book, 1757–1793."

34. As a minister, James Diman was exempt from the 1771 tax assessment from which the other slave-owning identities were drawn. But the 1785 town tax record includes a separate "Negro List" on which are the names "Caesar Diman" and "Sampson Diman." In 1792, Bentley casually entered into his diary that one "Caesar Orne Diman," age 79, had entered the almshouse. When it is recalled that James Diman's wife was from the prosperous Orne family, one can only conclude that Caesar Orne (then Diman) was a slave he acquired in the marriage. Nothing is known of when or how he acquired Sampson. Bentley, *Diary*, II: 354; "Salem, Mass. Tax Valuation 1784–1785."

35. "Salem, Mass. Tax Valuation 1784–1785."

36. Charles Chauncy, *The Appeal to the Public Answered* (Boston, 1768): 117.

37. Pruitt, *Massachusetts Tax Valuation*, 130–54.

38. ECPR, 354: 270, 485; 355: 84, 122.

39. ECPR, 354: 176–77.

40. Oliver, *Diary of William Pynchon*, 103.

41. *Diaries of Benjamin Lynde*, 208.

42. ECPR, 356: 367. The Quock Walker decision, handed down just weeks before Bentley arrived in Salem, was not universally understood as setting precedent. Important discussions of the Walker suit are Arthur Zilversmit, *The First Emancipation: The Abolition of Slavery in the North* (Chicago: University of Chicago Press, 1967): 113–15; William O'Brien, "Did the Jennison Case Outlaw Slavery in Massachusetts?" *WMQ* 17 (1960): 219–41; John D. Cushing, "The Cushing Court and the Abolition of Slavery in Massachusetts: More Notes on the 'Quock Walker Case,'" *American Journal of Legal History* 5 (1961): 118–44; and Robert M. Spector, "The Quock Walker Cases (1781–1783)—Slavery, Its Abolition, and Negro Citizenship in Early Massachusetts," *Journal of Negro History* 53 (1968): 12–32.

43. *SG*, Jan. 16, 1783.

44. *SG*, May 1, 1783.

45. *SG*, May 29, 1783. As late as 1787, Joshua and Joseph Grafton were repeatedly outfitting the *Africa* and the *Gambia* for the trade, although Joshua died later that year,

if he is the same Joshua Grafton of "professed deistical opinions" who openly flaunted an affair "in contempt of his lawful wife" and to whose deathbed Bentley was called only to receive insults and escape "in the greatest confusion"; this Joshua Grafton's will committed his children to his lover and left his wife and mother at the mercy of the poorhouse. Joseph slit his own throat in 1794. Elizabeth Donnan, ed, *Documents Illustrative of the History of the Slave Trade to America* (1932; repr. New York: Octagon Books, 1969), III: 80–81, and IV: 479–80, 491–92; James A. Rawley, *The Transatlantic Slave Trade: A History* (W. W. Norton, 1981): 351–53. For the fate of the Graftons, see Bentley, *Diary*, I: 77–78, 105, and II: 116.

46. Bentley, *Diary*, I: 104. Captains received slaves as part of their wages. A remarkable example of such instructions written in 1785 from a Salem owner to a slaving captain is printed in Felt, *Annals of Salem*, II: 289–90 and reprinted in Donnan, *Documents*, III: 78–80.

47. WBS, #392; Bentley, *Diary*, I: 105–106.

48. Bentley, *Diary*, I: 123.

49. Bentley, *Diary*, I: 123–24; [William Bentley, comp.], *Record of the Parish List of Deaths, 1785–1819* (Salem, Mass.: Essex Institute, 1882): 8. A letter from the captain's son also on board to his mother is in Donnan, *Documents*, III: 82–83.

50. Donnan, *Documents*, III: 84–99; Bentley, *Diary*, I: 385–86; WBS, #513; *SG*, July 3–17, 1792; the confusions over jurisdiction and federalism regarding the slave trade are discussed in Donnan, "The New England Slave Trade after the Revolution," *NEQ* 3 (1930): 253. As late as 1802, Bentley would note news about Salemites engaged in the slave trade: Bentley, *Diary*, II: 439, 442, 453.

51. STR, March 14, 1785 (box 5, folder 77, 644).

52. STR, Dec. 6, 1790 (box 6, folder 2, 92–95).

53. United States Bureau of the Census, *Heads of Families at the First Census of the United States Taken in the Year 1790* (Baltimore: Genealogical Publishing, 1966): 9.

54. STR, July 6, 1791 (box 6, folder 2, 120–30).

55. Bentley, *Diary*, II: 34, 38.

56. WBS, #599.

57. Fredrika Teute Schmidt and Barbara Ripel Wilhelm, "Early Proslavery Petitions in Virginia," *WMQ* 30 (1973): 139, 146.

58. WBS, #500.

59. Chauncy, *Benevolence of the Deity*, v.

60. WBS, #26; WBP, box 3, folder 2.

61. Bentley, *Diary*, I: 147.

62. WBS, #26.

63. WBS, #146.

64. WBS, #50.

65. Bentley, *Diary*, I: 288–89, 291; *SG*, Aug. 23–30, 1791.

66. In 1792, for example, forty of the forty-two recipients of the Thanksgiving day charities were widows; the other two were Uncle Diman and a blind man. There were two men on the list in 1801, he noted, but neither was actually a parishioner, "one being with a daughter at Marblehead and the other a Huguenot from France." In 1804,

the thirty-nine recipients included thirty-two widows, three wives "unprovided for," three maidens, and one "infirm old man." WBP, 33: 338; Bentley, *Diary*, I: 414; III: 81.

67. Conrad Edick Wright, *The Transformation of Charity in Postrevolutionary New England* (Boston: Northeastern University Press, 1992): 29, 41.

68. Bentley, *Diary*, I: 388.

69. Bentley, *Diary*, III: 200–201.

70. The important early work is Louis Hartz, *The Liberal Tradition in America: An Interpretation of American Political Thought in Revolutionary America* (New York: Harcourt, Brace, and World, 1955). The list of works on Revolutionary-era liberalism is a long one, but Joyce Appleby's *Capitalism and a New Social Order: The Republican Vision of the 1790s* (New York: New York University Press, 1984) is a good starting point. See also her *Liberalism and Republicanism in the Historical Imagination* (Cambridge: Harvard University Press, 1992).

71. Nicholas Phillipson, "Adam Smith as Civic Moralist," in *Wealth and Virtue: The Shaping of Political Economy in the Scottish Enlightenment*, ed. Istvan Hont and Michael Ignatieff (Cambridge: Cambridge University Press, 1983); V. M. Hope, *Virtue by Consensus: The Moral Philosophy of Hutcheson, Hume, and Adam Smith* (Oxford: Clarendon Press, 1989).

72. Anne Rowe Cunningham, *Letters and Diary of John Rowe, Boston Merchant* (Boston: W. B. Clarke, 1903): 162.

73. WBS, #279, #283, #291, #302.

74. WBS, #47.

CHAPTER 3

1. Watts, *Psalms of David*, 123.

2. Jonathan Parsons, *Sixty Sermons on Various Subjects* (Newburyport, 1779): 10.

3. Thomas Barnard Sr., *The Christian Salvation* (Portsmouth, 1757): 13. A good introduction to the various interpretations of the Atonement is G. Aulén, *Christus Victor: An Historical Study of the Three Main Types of the Idea of the Atonement* (New York: Macmillan, 1957 [Am. ed.]). For the Arminians' adoption of the Grotian version, see Wright, *Beginnings of Unitarianism in America*, 185–99; Frank Hugh Foster, *A Genetic History of the New England Theology* (1907; repr. New York, 1963): 189–223, 316–39; Joseph Haroutunian, *Piety Versus Moralism: The Passing of the New England Theology* (New York: Henry Holt, 1932): 131–76.

4. Wright, *Beginnings of Unitarianism in America*, 200–209.

5. Still useful as an introduction to this form of anti-Trinitarianism are Earl Morse Wilbur's *A History of Unitarianism: Socinianism and Its Antecedents* (Cambridge, Mass.: Harvard University Press, 1945), and *A History of Unitarianism: In Transylvania, England, and America* (Cambridge, Mass.: Harvard University Press, 1952).

6. WBS, #381.

7. See, for example, *The New-England Primer Improved* (Salem, 1784).

8. WBS, #165.

9. [William Bentley, comp.], *Extracts from Doctor Priestley's Catechism* (Salem, 1785): 11; Bentley, *Diary*, I: 21, 69, 124; WBP, 17: 211.

10. [William Bentley, comp.], *A Collection of Psalms and Hymns for Publick Worship* (Salem, [1788]).

11. And he thought the various internal typologies—Old Testament predictions of a therefore already-existent Christ—superfluous to right faith, no matter how much they "employ the ingenious and entertain the curious." WBS, #247, #332.

12. WBS, #121, #332.

13. In fact, his friend James Freeman became a Socinian, too, but Freeman was an Episcopalian rather than a Congregationalist. Freeman's importance is discussed in chapter 5.

14. For the seventeenth-century radicals, see Philip F. Gura, *A Glimpse of Sion's Glory: Puritan Radicalism in New England, 1620–1660* (Middletown, Conn.: Wesleyan University Press, 1984): 311–12. Briant was accused in John Porter, *A Vindication of a Sermon* (Boston, 1751): 46n. For Mayhew, see Akers, *Called unto Liberty*, 115–22. The Boston publication was Thomas Emlyn, *An Humble Inquiry into the Scripture-Account of Jesus Christ* (Boston, 1756).

15. Chauncy, *Benevolence of the Deity* (Boston, 1784): 166; Joseph Willard, *A Sermon Preached May 11, 1785* (Salem, 1785): 18; Timothy Hilliard, *A Sermon Preached Oct. 24th 1787 at the Ordination of the Rev. Henry Ware* (Salem, 1788): 6. Hilliard said this during the ordination sermon of Hingham's Henry Ware; ironically, it was the 1805 appointment of Ware to the Hollis Chair of Divinity that would mark the beginning of Harvard's so-called "Unitarian" phase.

16. Eliot to Hazlitt, July 1, 1789; *Christian Reformer* 6 (1839): 23.

17. For English deism at the turn of the century, see Robert E. Sullivan, *John Toland and the Deist Controversy: A Study in Adaptations* (Cambridge, Mass.: Harvard University Press, 1982).

18. Questions of salvation are closer to the core of the ministry than are questions of divine power, so it was the "Arminian" name rather than the "latitudinarian" one that was most commonly used to describe them. For the English latitudinarians, see Gerard Reedy, *The Bible and Reason: Anglicans and Scripture in Late Seventeenth-Century England* (Philadelphia: University of Pennsylvania Press, 1985); John Redwood, *Reason, Ridicule, and Religion: The Age of Enlightenment in England, 1660–1750* (London: Thames and Hudson, 1976); Gerard R. Cragg, *From Puritanism to the Age of Reason* (Cambridge: Cambridge University Press, 1966), and *Reason and Authority in the Eighteenth Century* (Cambridge: Cambridge University Press, 1964); and Roland N. Stromberg, *Religious Liberalism in Eighteenth-Century England* (Oxford: Oxford University Press, 1954). More recent works include Frederick C. Beiser, *The Sovereignty of Reason: The Defense of Rationality in the Early English Enlightenment* (Princeton, N.J.: Princeton University Press, 1996); Alan P. F. Sell, *John Locke and the Eighteenth-Century Divines* (Cardiff: University of Wales Press, 1997); and B. W. Young, *Religion and Enlightenment in Eighteenth-Century England: Theological Debate from Locke to Burke* (Oxford: Clarendon Press, 1998). For the Boyle Lectures in particular, see Margaret C. Jacob, *The Newtonians and the English*

Revolution, 1689–1720 (Ithaca, N.Y.: Cornell University Press, 1976): 143–200. For this early generation of clergymen in New England, see John Corrigan, *The Prism of Piety: Catholick Congregational Clergy at the Beginning of the Enlightenment* (New York: Oxford University Press, 1991); and James W. Jones, *The Shattered Synthesis: New England Puritanism before the Great Awakening* (New Haven, Conn.: Yale University Press, 1973).

19. See for example a footnote tacked onto the published version of Thomas Barnard Sr.'s Dudleian Lecture of 1768: "The proposition, 'I am,' is intuitively certain," he premised. "And to argue 'I think therefore I am' is trifling logick." Thomas Barnard Sr., *The Power of God, the Proof of Christianity* (Salem, 1768): 8n.

20. Thomas Barnard Sr., *The Power of God, the Proof of Christianity.*

21. Another phrase, "supernatural rationalism," was offered by Conrad Wright in *Beginnings of Unitarianism in America*, 135–60.

22. WBS, #30, #95. On the importance of the Deluge in eighteenth-century latitudinarianism, see, in addition to general works on the latitudinarians, Don Cameron Allen, *The Legend of Noah: Renaissance Rationalism in Art, Science, and Letters* (Urbana: University of Illinois Press, 1963); Norman Cohn, *Noah's Flood: The Genesis Story in Western Thought* (New Haven, Conn.: Yale University Press, 1996); and Rhoda Rappaport, *When Geologists Were Historians, 1665–1750* (Ithaca, N.Y.: Cornell University Press, 1997).

23. WBS, #95.

24. WBS, #4.

25. WBS, #19.

26. WBS #15, #75. In fact, one of the best examples of the self-editing of his early performances was in the sermon on the sacraments given during his probationary period. Bentley had originally written that baptism has "carried many souls to heaven" but then crossed it out and said instead that baptism has "promoted much virtue." WBS #14; cf. also WBS #108.

27. Charles Chauncy, *Five Dissertations on the Scripture Account of the Fall* (London, 1785): 248; Timothy Hiliard, *A Sermon Preached Oct. 24th 1787* (Salem, 1788): 6.

28. WBS, #313.

29. Chauncy and Mayhew, for example, had called their townsmen to repent for the sinfulness to which the burning of Boston was God's rightful response. See Chauncy, *Earthquakes a Token of the Righteous Anger of God* (Boston, 1755); and Mayhew, *God's Hand and Providence to be Religiously Acknowledged in Public Calamities* (Boston, 1760): 28. WBS, #396.

30. WBS, #51; John Murray, *Jerubbaal, or Tyranny's Grove Destroyed* (Newburyport, 1784): 11; Henry Cumings, *A Sermon Preached in Billerica* (Boston, 1784): 7; Joseph Willard, *A Thanksgiving Sermon Delivered at Boston* (Boston, 1784): 10.

31. WBS, #383.

CHAPTER 4

1. For the Baptists, see the works listed in note 7 of the Introduction.

2. The town's Quakers and Anglicans had long been exempted from parish laws. In 1777, census-takers listed 24 Quakers in a population of 1,193 males over the age

of 16; see Greene and Harrington, *American Population*, 31. The Anglican (soon to be Episcopal) Church was still recovering from its association with Toryism, under new rector Nathaniel Fisher, for which see Harriett Silvester Tapley, "St. Peter's Church in Salem before the Revolution," *EIHC* 80 (1944): 229–60, 334–67; 81 (1945): 66–82, reprinted as *St. Peter's Church Before the Revolution* (Salem, Mass.: Essex Institute, 1944). For sketches of Fisher's career, see Shipton, ed., *Sibley's Harvard Graduates* 15: 387–92. In the First Parish, the Fiske controversy had played havoc with the question of parish taxes, for with one faction in possession of the meetinghouse and the other in possession of the pastor, it was not clear just which congregation was established and which was dissenting; for nearly a generation *both* groups continued to call themselves the "First Church." In 1752, First Parish residents petitioned the General Court to allow each group to raise money through pew taxes rather than parish assessments, and when the request was granted, the First Parish was thereby dissolved. *Acts and Resolves*, 3: 604–605, 705–706.

3. John Cleaveland, *Infant Baptism "From Heaven," and Immersion, as the Only Mode of Baptism* (Salem, 1784); Benjamin Foster responded with *Primitive Baptism Defended, in a Letter to the Reverend Mr. Cleaveland* (Salem, 1784).

4. *SG*, Sept. 28, 1790. The title of Cleaveland's earlier work deserves full citation: *An Attempt to Nip in the Bud the Unscriptural Doctrine of Universal Salvation, and some other dangerous errors connected with it; which a certain stranger, who calls himself John Murray, has of late, been endeavouring to spread in the First Parish of Gloucester, to draw away disciples after him* (Salem, 1776). For more on Murray's struggle, see Russell E. Miller, *The Larger Hope: The First Century of the Universalist Church in America, 1770–1870* (Boston: Unitarian Universalist Association, 1979); Ann L. Bressler, "Popular Religious Liberalism in America, 1770–1880: An Interpretation of the Universalist Movement" (Ph.D. diss., University of Virginia, 1992); Paul Ivar Chestnut, "The Universalist Movement in America, 1770–1803" (Ph.D. diss., Duke University, 1973); McLoughlin, *New England Dissent*, I: 653–59; and John D. Cushing, "Notes on Disestablishment in Massachusetts, 1780–1833," *WMQ* 26 (1969): 169–90.

5. *SM*, Dec. 2–23, 1788.

6. *SG*, Oct. 5, 1790. Bentley wrote anonymously. That he was the author is made clear in his *Diary*, I: 202, 213.

7. Bentley, *Diary*, I: 162–66, 188.

8. Bentley, *Diary*, I: 150, 384–87.

9. Bentley, *Diary*, I: 24–26.

10. Bentley, *Diary*, II: 22, 76; North Church, *First Centenary*, 166–67. The First and North would adopt home baptisms in 1794, nine years after Bentley did.

11. Bentley, *Diary*, I: 150.

12. "Tabernacle Record Book, 1743–1833."

13. "Records of the First Church," 41. (The typed transcript erroneously puts the date at 1779, but the original volume, also in the First Church archives, has it in 1792.)

14. Bentley, *Diary*, I: 386–87.

15. Bentley, *Diary*, I: 378–85. The man brought another child to Bentley in 1797 and then his nephews in 1799, for which see WBP, 23: 557, and 33: 62.

16. Bentley, *Diary*, I: 255.

17. Bentley, *Diary*, I: 316–17. Translation of this and other Latin passages by Professor Emily McDermott, Department of Classics, University of Massachusetts, Boston.

18. Bentley, *Diary*, I: 163, 261; II: 294–95.

19. WBP, 23, 287.

20. Bentley, *Diary*, II: 295.

21. Tabulated from James A. Emmerton, "Salem Baptisms," *Historical Collections of the Essex Institute* 22 (1885): 177–92, 241–56; 23 (1886): 1–16, 81–96, 161–84, 241–80.

22. Bentley, *Diary*, I: 341, 348.

23. Bentley, *Diary*, II: 23–26, 28.

24. WBS, #345.

25. WBS, #208.

CHAPTER 5

1. The literature on the Rational Dissenters individually and as a group is substantial, but the works most relevant to this discussion are Anthony Lincoln, *Some Political and Social Ideas of English Dissent 1763–1800* (Cambridge: Cambridge University Press, 1938); Caroline Robbins, "Honest Heretic: Joseph Priestley in America, 1794–1804," *Proceedings of the American Philosophical Society* 106 (1962); Lloyd W. Chapin Jr., "The Theology of Joseph Priestley: A Study in Eighteenth-Century Apologetics" (Th.D. diss., Union Theological Seminary, 1967); C. B. Cone, *The English Jacobins: Reformers in Late Eighteenth-Century England* (New York: Scribner's, 1968); Colin Bonwick, *English Radicals and the American Revolution* (Chapel Hill: University of North Carolina Press, 1977); H. T. Dickinson, *Liberty and Property: Political Ideology in Eighteenth-Century Britain* (London: Holmes and Meier, 1977); Albert Goodwin, *The Friends of Liberty: The English Democratic Movement in the Age of the French Revolution* (Cambridge, Mass.: Harvard University Press, 1979); J. C. D. Clark, *English Society, 1688–1832* (Cambridge: Cambridge University Press, 1985); James E. Bradley, *Religion, Revolution, and English Radicalism: Nonconformity in Eighteenth-Century Politics and Society* (Cambridge: Cambridge University Press, 1990); and Knud Haakonssen, ed., *Enlightenment and Religion: Rational Dissent in Eighteenth-Century Britain* (Cambridge: Cambridge University Press, 1996); as well as Isaac Kramnick, "Religion and Radicalism: English Political Thought in the Age of Revolution," *Journal of Political Theory* 5 (1977): 505–34; Margaret Canovan, "The Un-Benthamite Utilitarianism of Joseph Priestley," *Journal of the History of Ideas* 45 (1984): 435–50; John Seed, "Gentlemen Dissenters: The Social and Political Meaning of Rational Dissent in 1770s and 1780s," *Historical Journal* 28 (1985): 299–325; Martin Fitzpatrick, "Heretical Religion and Radical Political Ideas in Late Eighteenth-Century England," in *The Transformation of Political Culture: England and Germany in the Late Eighteenth Century*, ed. Eckhart Hellmuth (London: Oxford University Press, 1990): 339–74; G. M. Ditchfield, "Anti-Trinitarianism and Toleration in Late Eighteenth-Century British Politics: The Unitarian Petition of 1792," *Journal of Ecclesiastical History* 42 (1991): 39–67; and

the many good articles in *Enlightenment and Dissent*, formerly the *Price-Priestley Newsletter*. For their connection to America, see Richard J. Twomey, *Jacobins and Jeffersonians: Anglo-American Radicalism in the United States, 1790–1820* (New York: Garland Publishers, 1989); and Paul Conkin, "Priestley and Jefferson: Unitarianism as a Religion for a New Revolutionary Age," in *Religion in a Revolutionary Age*, ed. Ronald Hoffman and Peter J. Albert (Charlottesville: University Press of Virginia, 1994): 290–307.

2. William Hazlitt, *An Essay on the Justice of God* (London, 1773), and *Human Authority in Matters of Faith Repugnant to Christianity* (London, 1774).

3. Bentley, *Diary*, I: 35.

4. Bentley, *Diary*, I: 34–35.

5. The actual charges were not listed in the published controversy, but they and the four testimonials on which they were based are extant in the Tabernacle's manuscript records. Together they suggest just what was being discussed on the streets about Nathaniel Whitaker. One man accused Whitaker of spending a Sunday working on a privateer, and a second avowed that Whitaker had suggested to the owners of a privateer a plan whereby another minister would travel to Bermuda and with Whitaker's help infiltrate the island under false pretenses and confiscate Tory property. A different kind of claim came from a female parishioner who testified that Whitaker had led her on a walk to an unspecified but apparently notorious location where "from his conduct then, she believed his intention to be bad, and that she viewed him as a very bad man." And then, from another young woman, another such story:

> Dr. N Whitaker came to our house on the evening of ___ that I took the candle
> to light him upstairs as we lived up chamber and made a motion for him
> to walk up first, but he refused. My mother then went up first and I followed
> her with the candle in my hand, the Dr. following after catched hold of my
> ancle as I ascended the stairs, after we entered the chamber he immediately
> catched hold of me and put his hand in my bosom, I in a passion called him
> a damn son of a Bitch, with that he replied oh! you wicked girl.

Together the testimonials provided enough evidence for angry church members to charge him with "lascivious language and behavior, expressive of an intention, if not a procedure, to the last freedoms," and to these they added his "haughty, supercilious, and overbearing temper and conduct" and set in motion the process that ended with his ousting.

What makes this case interesting is the possibility that Whitaker was being framed by Tories. His anti-Tory sermons had made enemies of powerful men, and William Pynchon, for one, followed Whitaker's troubles and gleefully kept his exiled friends abreast of the situation (Oliver, *Diary of William Pynchon*, 171, 179; Ward, *Journal and Letters of Samuel Curwen*, 398, 400, 402). They had good reason to stay informed, since their return in many ways depended on silencing Whitaker. And in a cryptic moment, Samuel Curwen was advised by an anonymous writer in June of 1783, the month after Whitaker's second anti-Tory sermon, to "let your patience and fortitude continue a month or two longer, and I believe that you may safely leave faction and party rage to spend their utmost spite without harm" (Ward, *Journal and Letters of Samuel Curwen*, 383). There was ample precedent for a frame, since evangelical ministers leading night meetings with adolescent girls were easy targets, and such charges were not uncommonly brought by disgruntled parishioners or neighbors; Whitaker had even predicted in his second patriot sermon that some of his opponents might "suborn false witness against him to put him out of the way" (Whitaker, *The Reward of Toryism* (Newburyport, 1777): [4]). Once the accusations were made, he was seemingly confident enough in his innocence to sue his accusers for slander and to make countercharges of accepting bribes to commit perjury. And the scribe of the ecclesiastical council called by the association of ministers was a Tory sympathizer (Heimert, *Religion and the American Mind*, 506–507).

Still, the evidence is not convincing. Pynchon and Curwen clearly celebrated Whitaker's troubles, but at no time did they take responsibility for what they were witnessing. The prediction of false testimonials may have been a preemptive strike against rumors that were already spreading, and when those accused of accepting bribes challenged him to name names, he refused, leaving the guilty party "to the stings of his own conscience" (Whitaker, *Mutual Care*, 26). He lost the defamation suit, and by the audience's applause at the decision it appears that he had already lost the public's support (Oliver, *Diary of William Pynchon*, 171). James Winthrop was not alone in thinking Whitaker "an accomplished son of licentiousness" (WBP, box 1, folder 4). And as for the council that recommended his resignation, the scribe was indeed a Tory sympathizer, but the other five members, including the moderator, were ardent patriots (Eli Forbes, *The Christian Ambassador* [Salem, (1784)]). Indeed, to accept the bribe theory is to accept that the six council members, who voted unanimously on all questions, were either duped or also in the setup, but considering that the council included four New Lights—three from Whitaker's Princeton—and not a single Arminian, it is hard to imagine a group less disposed to participate, even unwittingly, in framing an evangelical. The possibility remains, of course, that they were taken in, but surely they would have been aware of Whitaker's political enemies and would have made every effort not to convict him falsely of charges to which they too were susceptible. In either case, Whitaker then moved to Canaan in Maine, where in the spring of 1789 he was *again* accused of assaulting a woman in his congregation. This time he went to trial but was acquitted for lack of evidence. The Canaan church, like the Tabernacle, then reverted back to Congregationalism.

Whitaker's continuing fall from grace arced through Salem in 1790, when he arrived "emaciated and dressed in a very beggarly manner." His indiscretions had taken their toll, Bentley wrote: "That gracefulness of person and air of confidence which once distinguished him are lost.... The bitter execrations of the people in Maine follow him." Whitaker passed through and out of town and died in Virginia a few years later (Bentley, *Diary*, I: 176). The rough outline of this controversy can be discerned through Forbes, *Christian Ambassador*; Whitaker, *A Brief History of the Settlement of the Third Church in Salem, in 1769* (Salem, 1784); John Cleaveland, *The Rev. Dr. N. Whitaker's Neighbour is come, and Searcheth Him* (Salem, 1784); Whitaker, *The Mutual Care the*

Members of Christ's body Owe to each Other (Salem, 1785). The four testimonials and the articles of complaint are in the collection of manuscripts at the Tabernacle Church. For Whitaker's visits with noted midwife Martha Ballard, see Laurel Thatcher Ulrich, *A Midwife's Tale: The Life of Martha Ballard, Based on Her Diary, 1785–1812* (New York: Vintage Books, 1990): 123. See also the biographical sketch in the Undergraduate Alumni Files, box 3, Seeley G. Mudd Manuscript Library, Princeton University.

6. Ernest J. Moyne, ed., *The Journal of Margaret Hazlitt: Recollections of England, Ireland, and America* (Lawrence: University Press of Kansas, 1967); Moyne, "The Reverend William Hazlitt: A Friend of Liberty in Ireland during theAmerican Revolution," *WMQ* 21 (1964): 288–97; Moyne, "The Reverend William Hazlitt and Dickinson College," *Pennsylvania Magazine of History and Biography* 85 (1961): 289–302. For his lectures, see *Massachusetts Centinel*, Jan. 19, 1785; *SG*, Jan. 11, 1785; "Belknap Papers," *MHSC*, 6th ser., 4 (1891): 285. For related studies on the spread of post-1793 revolutionary ideals via migration to America, see David A. Wilson, *United Irishmen, United States: Immigrant Radicals in the Early Republic* (Ithaca, N.Y.: Cornell University Press, 1998); Michael Durey, *Transatlantic Radicals and the Early American Republic* (Lawrence: University Press of Kansas, 1997); Richard J. Twomey, *Jacobins and Jeffersonians: Anglo-American Radicalism in the United States, 1790–1820* (New York: Garland Publishers, 1989).

7. Quoted in Moyne, *Journal of Margaret Hazlitt*, 148n.

8. "Belknap Papers," *MHSC*, 6th ser., 4 (1891): 274, 308; 5th ser., 3 (1877): 169.

9. "Belknap Papers," *MHSC*, 5th ser., 2 (1877): 370–71. Italics in the original.

10. Joseph P. Felt, *Annals of Salem* [2nd ed.; Salem, 1845–49], II: 605.

11. John Cleaveland Sr., *Gospel-Ministers Must be Wise, Faithful, and Exemplary* (Newburyport, [1785]): 18, 36.

12. Bentley, *Diary* I: 17, 20–21.

13. WBS, #6, #54. In the earlier of the two he also insisted on the Holy Spirit's reality as a supernatural force. "Our access to God," he told his congregants during the probation, "is through the prevalency of his [the Holy Spirit's] intercession."

14. WBS, #101, #121.

15. WBS, #247, #273, #332, #374, #396.

16. Bentley, *Diary*, I: 19, 40. The publication, *Appeal to the Serious and Candid Professors of Christianity* (Philadelphia, 1784), appended another one by Priestley titled *General View of the Arguments for the Unity of God* and also *Triumph of Truth*, an anonymous account of an English Unitarian's trial on charges of blasphemy. Hazlitt's sermon was *A Thanksgiving Discourse* (Boston, 1786).

17. Hazlitt as "Philalethes" wrote against the Thirty-Nine Articles in the *American Herald* of November 1, 1784. As "A New Testament Christian," Hazlitt disputed against Samuel Parker of Trinity Church ("Elakistoteros") in the October and November 1784 issues of *Boston Magazine* and in the January and February 1785 issues of the *American Herald*. For the changes at King's Chapel, see Margaret Barry Chinkes, *James Freeman and Boston's Religious Revolution* (Glade Valley, NC.: Glade Valley Books, 1991); Henry Wilder Foote, *James Freeman and King's Chapel, 1782–87: A Chapter in*

the Early History of the Unitarian Movement in New England (Boston, 1873), and *Annals of King's Chapel* (Boston, 1882–1896); and Thomas Belsham, *Memoirs of the Late Reverend Theophilus Lindsey* (London, 1812): 238–45.

18. The first congregation in America to use the Unitarian name was the Unitarian Society of Portland, a small group of Episcopalians in Maine who were aided by copies of Freeman's revised liturgy. Freeman to W. B., March 19, 1792. James Freeman Papers, bMS Am 1569.5 (2).

19. WBP, folio vol. 4. By 1795, Freeman was sending cash directly to Johnson in London, for which see WBP, box 1, folder 19.

20. Freeman to Hazlitt, Nov. 20, 1787. *Christian Reformer* 6 (1839): 16; W. B, to Freeman, April 26, 1788. James Freeman Papers, bMS Am 1569.5 (12), in Papers of James Freeman Clarke, Houghton Library.

21. WBP, 2: 61–62; box 1, folder 12.

22. His notes on *A Collection of Hymns for Public Worship: on the general Principles of Natural and Revealed Religion* (Salisbury, 1778) are in WBP, 16: 20–23; 18: 231. WBS, #165.

23. Bentley, *Diary*, I: 293.

24. Freeman to Hazlitt, June 3, 1789. *Christian Reformer* 6 (1839): 21.

25. Bentley, *Diary*, I: 21.

26. WBS, #259.

27. "Social Library Records Charge Book, 1760–1768," in PEM. The degree to which early-eighteenth-century colonial latitudinarianism had been the result of imported books or of covenanted Calvinism's internal inconsistencies is a matter of debate. For the argument, contra Perry Miller, that the dissolution of Calvinism was generated by imported works rather than Calvinism's internal inconsistency, see Norman Fiering's "Will and Intellect in the New England Mind," *WMQ* 29 (1972): 515–58, and "The First American Enlightenment: Tillotson, Leverett, and Philosophical Anglicanism," *NEQ* 54 (1981): 307–44.

28. John Eliot, *A Biographical Dictionary* (Boston, 1809): 46.

29. "Social Library Records Charge Book"; Harriet Silvester Tapley, *Salem Imprints, 1768–1825: A History of the First Fifty Years of Printing in Salem, Massachusetts* (Salem, Mass.: Essex Institute, 1927): 230–37. Similar libraries with similar catalogs existed in other towns in the colonies: David Lundberg and Henry F. May, "The Enlightened Reader in America," *AQ* 28 (1976): 262–93.

30. Priestley, *Appeal to the Serious and Candid*, 16, 28.

31. WBP, 2: 61–62; box 2, folder 12.

32. WBS, #259.

33. "Belknap Papers," *MHSC*, 6th ser., 4 (1891): 145, 201, 203.

34. Bereanus Theosebes [pseudonym for Hazlitt], *A Discourse on the Apostle Paul's Mystery of Godliness Being Made Manifest in the Flesh* (Falmouth, 1786).

25. WBS #247, #249. Both verses had been favorably cited in Hazlitt, *Human Authority in Matters of Faith Repugnant to God* (London, 1774).

36. Bentley to Freeman, April 26, 1788. James Freeman Papers, bMS Am 1569.5 (12).

37. Neither *Letters to the Right Honourable Edmund Burke* (New York, 1791) nor *Description of a New Chart of History* (New Haven, 1792) was predominantly religious.

38. WBP, 2: 147–57; Social Library [Salem, Mass.], *Bylaws and regulations of the Incorporated Proprietors of the Social Library in Salem* (Salem, 1797).

39. Bentley, *Diary*, I: 62, 78, 88, 103.

40. *SM*, Dec. 8, 1789; John Dabney, *Catalogue of Books, for Sale and Circulation* (Salem, 1791); Dabney, *Additional Catalogue of Books* (Salem, 1794). In Boston, Freeman, too, distributed works that were otherwise unavailable. Neither Disney's writings nor Priestley's *General View*, for example, appear in any of Boston booksellers' catalogs in the eighteenth century. One bookseller advertised Priestley's *Appeal to the Serious and Candid* before 1791, but by then, Bentley and Freeman had spent half a decade making these works available to the public. See for example, William Martin, *Catalogue of Martin's Circulating Library* (Boston, 1786); Benjamin Guild, *A Catalogue of a large assortment of books* (Boston, 1787), and *Addition to a Catalogue* (Boston, 1787); and John Folsom, *Catalogue of Books* (Boston, 1788). Folsom was the only one to list Priestley's *Appeal* until Isaiah Thomas advertised it at his Worcester and Boston stores; cf. Thomas, *The Friends of Literature* (Worcester, 1791).

41. Bentley, *Diary*, I: 77, 82.

42. Freeman to Hazlitt, Nov. 20, 1787. *Christian Reformer* 6 (1839): 16.

43. WBS, #265.

44. WBS, #332.

45. On the landlady, see Bentley, *Diary*, I: 212, 215, 231–32; his father's criticisms are in Bentley, *Diary*, I: 114–15.

46. Bentley, *Diary*, I: 251. It would be printed in Boston as *A Sermon, Preached at the Stone Chapel* (Boston, 1790).

47. Such as the time in 1786 when, in a private letter, he complained that he had "no literary men" in his church. Somehow word got back, because that Sunday he felt compelled to improve on Ecclesiastes 12:12 (which reads in part, "much study is a weariness of the flesh") to defend what he called "the literary mind." Bentley, *Diary* I: 37; WBS, #244.

48. Diman, *A Sermon, Preached at Salem*. See also Wilson Kimnach's introduction to Jonathan Edwards, *Sermons and Discourses 1720–1723*.

49. WBS, #189.

50. Lathrop, *Sermon Preached at the Ordination of William Bentley*, 24.

51. Samson Occom, *A Sermon, Preached at the Execution of Moses Paul* (New Haven, 1772), preface.

52. Bentley, *Diary*, I: 380.

53. WBS, #259.

CHAPTER 6

1. There are numerous discussions of the Americans' early response to the French Revolution, but a recent overview is in Stanley Elkins and Eric McKitrick, *The Age of Federalism: The Early American Republic, 1788–1800* (New York: Oxford University

Press, 1993): 303–73. Salem, too, was supportive at first: the *Gazette* noted with approval Richard Price's discourse to the Revolution Society in 1789 and celebrated the "liberality" of the French National Assembly in 1791, "anything in Burke's pamphlet to the contrary notwithstanding." *SG*, March 9, 1790; Aug. 16, Dec. 6, 1791.

2. *SG*, July 10, 1792.

3. *SG*, Oct. 9, 1792.

4. *SG*, Jan. 29, 1793. Italics and capitalization in the original.

5. Bentley, *Diary*, I: 310.

6. [William Bentley], "Washington's Birth-Day Oration, at Salem, Mass., February 22, 1793," *Historical Magazine*, 2nd ser., 7 (1870): 5; *SG*, Feb. 26, 1793.

7. Bentley, *Diary*, II: 13; WBP, 23: 117.

8. WBS, #533.

9. Bentley, *Diary*, II: 15.

10. WBS, #667.

11. WBS, #285; the execution sermon was Joshua Spaulding, *The Prayer of a True Penitent for Mercy* (Salem, 1787).

12. "Social Library Records Charge Book, 1760–1768," PEM.

13. Bentley, *Diary*, II: 87, 92.

14. Bentley, *Diary*, I: 387.

15. Bentley, *Diary*, I: 140.

16. Bentley, *Diary*, II: 85, 102.

17. The estate was worth more than £2,300 and included several properties in Boston and Charlestown as well as the mansion on Prince Street. The slighted heirs pleaded their case before the probate judge of Suffolk County but to no avail. Soon rumors and ill feelings circulated, and "every branch of the family [was] at variance." By 1791, Joshua Bentley had lost his job as one of Boston's surveyors of boards and shingles and was trying to take even what little had been allotted William in the will that was probated. He continued to urge Bentley to return to court, but Bentley would not. In 1794, the heirs retained attorney Harrison Gray Otis, but by then William had had enough and quit his claims in return for £50 lawful. Bentley, *Diary*, I: 44–48, 51–57, 164, 252; WBP, 23: 141, 200–201, 306, 322; *Independent Chronicle*, Nov. 9, 1786; *Boston Gazette*, Nov. 6, 1786; *Massachusetts Centinel*, Nov. 4, 1786; Suffolk County Probate Court Record Books, 1st ser., 85: 733–34, 86: 28, and 88: 610.

18. Bentley, *Diary*, I: 295. Barnard's salary is in North Church, "Proprietor's Records, 1773–1836."

19. Dow, *Holyoke Diaries*, 138.

20. Oliver, ed., *Diary of William Pynchon*, 163, 170.

21. Bentley, *Diary*, I: 260, 419, 212, 391; II: 125. The decline of the ministry relative to the other professions is the subject of Donald M. Scott, *From Office to Profession: The New England Ministry, 1750–1850* (Philadelphia: University of Pennsylvania Press, 1978). Bentley's humble origins and controversial theological ideas made a bad situation worse.

22. Chauncy, *Five Dissertations*, 1, 79.

23. Thomas Barnard, *A Sermon, Preached December 29, 1799* (Salem, 1800): 9.

24. Children using the Watts catechism learned that the Bible was the "holy word," but Bentley's catechists learned that it was a book written by "good men." [Bentley], *Extracts*, 5; *New-England Primer*, unpaginated. See also WBS, #35, #249.

25. WBP, 19: 159; 4: 313–34.

26. WBP, 19: 159. For the general unpopularity of the work, see Paul M. Spurlin, *Rousseau in America, 1760–1809* (University: University of Alabama Press, 1969): 41–45. For the specific readings, see Zoltán Haraszti, *John Adams and the Prophets of Progress* (Cambridge, Mass: Harvard University Press, 1952): 80–92; and Dagobert D. Runes, ed., *Selected Writings of Benjamin Rush* (New York: Philosophical Library, 1947): 164–65.

27. WBS, #157, #238.

28. WBS, #121, #247.

29. The literature on the role of evangelical millenarianism in the early Republic is substantial, but important recent works include Donald Weber, *Rhetoric and History*; Ruth Bloch, *Visionary Republic: Millennial Themes in American Thought, 1756–1800* (Cambridge: Cambridge University Press, 1985); John F. Berens, *Providence and Patriotism in Early America, 1640–1815* (Charlottesville: University Press of Virginia, 1978); James West Davidson, *The Logic of Millennial Thought: Eighteenth-Century New England* (New Haven, Conn.: Yale University Press, 1977); Nathan O. Hatch, *The Sacred Cause of Liberty: Republican Thought and the Millennium in Revolutionary New England* (New Haven, Conn.: Yale University Press, 1977); Ernest Lee Tuveson, *Redeemer Nation: The Idea of America's Millennial Role* (Chicago: University of Chicago Press, 1968). Nor, for that matter, did Bentley share Priestley's brand of millenarianism, for which see Jack Fruchtman Jr., "The Apocalyptic Politics of Richard Price and Joseph Priestley: A Study in Late Eighteenth-Century English Republican Millennialism," *Transactions of the American Philosophical Society* 73 (1983); and Clarke Garrett, "Joseph Priestley, the Millennium, and the French Revolution," *Journal of the History of Ideas* 34 (1973): 51–66.

30. Bentley, *Diary*, I: 391.

CHAPTER 7

1. *SG*, Sept. 4–11, 1792.

2. David Tappan, *A Sermon Delivered to the First Congregation in Cambridge* (Boston, 1793): 17, 27–28. Italics in the original.

3. Bentley, *Diary*, II: 107.

4. WBS, #699.

5. Thomas Paine, *The Age of Reason*, ed. Philip S. Foner, (Secaucus: Citadel Press, 1948; repr. 1974): 54. Italics in the original.

6. Other liberals also relied on internal prophecies to defend the Resurrection, but Bentley had long before claimed that such prophecies were true only if understood allegorically rather than literally. WBS, #29.

7. Thomas Barnard Jr., *A Discourse on Natural Religion* (Boston, 1795).

8. *SG*, Dec. 30, 1794.

9. Empirical logic allowed inducing an arena of divine justice but not the traditional Christian versions of heaven and hell. Early in *The Age of Reason*, Paine laid out the basics of his deism, and with a wording that is instructive. He "believed" in God, he wrote, and he "believed" in the duties of conscience, but he "hoped" to go to heaven, or what he called "happiness beyond this life." The difference between belief and hope may seem minute, but in fact it carries great weight. What Paine meant by belief in God and moral obligation was his confidence in the proofs of their existence through design and the seeming universality of conscience, respectively. His hope, on the other hand, was what he felt for what reason cannot prove. That he would prefer to go to the place of happiness is neither surprising nor the issue at hand; the point here is that he could not know about heaven, or for that matter hell, in the way that he *could* know about God or morality. Paine, *Age of Reason*, 50.

10. Barnard, *Discourse on Natural Religion*.

11. Jeremy Belknap, *Dissertations on the Character, Death, and Resurrection of Jesus Christ* (Boston, 1795); John Clarke, *An Answer to the Question, "Why Are You a Christian?"* (Boston, 1795).

12. Bentley, *Diary*, II: 129; see also Sassi, *Republic of Righteousness*, 75–83. For other views on Paine's influence on clerical partisanship, see Gary B. Nash, "The American Clergy and the French Revolution," *WMQ* 22 (1965): 392–412; Anson E. Morse, *The Federalist Party in Massachusetts to the Year 1800* (Princeton, N.J.: Princeton University Press, 1909): 88–139.

13. Tone, not thesis, distinguished, for example, David Osgood's *A Discourse, Delivered February 19, 1795* (Boston, 1795) from Thomas Barnard's *A Sermon, Delivered on the Day of National Thanksgiving, February 19, 1795* (Salem, 1795).

14. WBS, #533.

15. WBS, #637.

16. WBS, #637.

17. [Bentley], *Collection of Psalms and Hymns*, hymns 137 and 104; Jeremy Belknap, *Sacred Poetry. Consisting of Psalms and Hymns* (Boston, 1795): 3, 82.

18. Belknap, *Sacred Poetry*, 28.

19. [Bentley], *Collection of Psalms and Hymns*, hymns 107 and 103; Belknap, *Sacred Poetry*, 321, 40.

20. [Bentley], *Collection of Psalms and Hymns*, hymn 102; Belknap, *Sacred Poetry*, 178.

21. Belknap, *Sacred Poetry*, v.

22. Jedidiah Morse, *A Sermon, delivered at the New North Church in Boston* (Boston, 1798); Bentley's Masonic discourses include *A Discourse, Delivered at Amherst* (Amherst, 1797), *A Discourse, Delivered in Roxbury* (Boston, 1797), and *A Charge Delivered Before the Morning Star Lodge* (Worcester, 1798). A good discussion of freemasonry in the early Republic is Steven C. Bullock, *Revolutionary Brotherhood: Freemasonry and the Transformation of the American Social Order, 1730–1840* (Chapel Hill: University of North Carolina Press, 1996).

23. Benjamin Goodhue to Stephen Goodhue, Jan. 28, 1797; Goodhue Family Papers, box 1, folder 6.

24. WBP, 33: 110; SG, Sept. 13, 1799; Bentley, *Diary*, II: 290.

25. *SG*, Nov. 30, 1798.

26. *SG*, Jan. 1, 1798. Italics in the original.

27. WBS, #837.

28. Thomas Barnard, *A Sermon Preached Before the Salem Female Charitable Society* (Salem, 1803): 14.

29. *SG*, Oct. 14, 1800, Feb. 10, 1801; *IR*, Dec. 15, 1800, Feb. 12–23, and March 26, 1801. On the Rogers episode, see Elysa Engelman, "Wollstonecraft and Needlecraft: A Case Study of Women's Rights and Education in Federal-Period Salem, Massachusetts," in *Painted with Thread: The Art of American Embroidery*, ed. Paula Richter (Salem, Mass.: Peabody Essex Museum, 2000): 141–47. For Wollstonecraft in the early Republic, see Chandos Michael Brown, "Mary Wollstonecraft, or, the Female Illuminati: The Campaign against Women and 'Modern Philosophy' in the Early Republic," *Journal of the Early Republic* 15 (1995): 389–424; R. M. Janes, "On the Reception of Mary Wollstonecraft's *A Vindication of the Rights of Woman*," *Journal of the History of Ideas* 39 (1978): 293–302; and Rosemarie Zagarri, "The Rights of Man and Woman in Post-Revolutionary America," *WMQ* 55 (1998): 203–30.

30. *IR*, March 26, 1801; Bentley, *Diary*, II: 364–65; WBP, box 2.

31. *SG*, Aug. 5, 1800, and Aug. 13 and Nov. 12, 1802.

32. *IR*, Aug. 11, 1800; *SR*, Nov. 15, 1802. For the correspondence, see William Coolidge Lane, ed., "Letters of Christoph Daniel Ebeling," *Proceedings of the American Antiquarian Society* 35 (1925): 272–451, plus unpublished letters from Ebeling to Bentley in the Papers of Christoph Ebeling, Houghton Library. Ebeling's work was *Erdbeschreibung und Geschichte von Amerika. Die vereinten Staaten von Nordamerika*, 7 vols. (Hamburg, 1783–1816). Volume 7, *Virginia*, is dedicated to Samuel Miller, Samuel Latham Mitchell, Henry St. George Tucker, and Bentley.

33. Jerry Wayne Brown, *The Rise of Biblical Criticism in America, 1800–1870: The New England Scholars* (Middletown, Conn.: Wesleyan University Press, 1969). See also Philip F. Gura, *The Wisdom of Words: Language, Theology, and Literature in the New England Renaissance* (Middletown, Conn.: Wesleyan University Press, 1981), and William Charvat, *The Origins of American Critical Thought, 1810–1835* (New York: A. S. Barnes and Co., 1961). Bentley's German connection is discussed in Russel Blaine Nye, *The Cultural Life of the New Nation* (New York: Harper and Bros., 1960): 235–36; Henry Pochmann, *German Culture in America: Philosophical and Literary Influences, 1600–1900* (Madison: University of Wisconsin Press, 1957); Carl Diehl, *Americans and German Scholarship, 1770–1870* (New Haven, Conn.: Yale University Press, 1978); Robert E. Cazden, *A Social History of the German Book Trade in America to the Civil War* (Columbia, S.C.: Camden House, 1984): 37–40. But see also Harold S. Jantz, "German Thought and Literature in New England, 1620–1820," *Journal of English and German Philology* 41 (1942): 31–45; and Elisabeth Hurth, "Sowing the Seeds of 'Subversion': Harvard's Early Gottingen Students," in *Studies in the American Renaissance*, ed. Joel Myerson, Vol. 16 (Charlottesville: University Press of Virginia, 1992).

34. WBS, #699, #806.

35. Bentley, *Diary*, II: 289; *SG*, March 29, 1799. For more on newspapers, the sedition laws, and republican commitments to a free press, see Jeffrey L. Pasley, *"The*

Tyranny of Printers": Newspaper Politics in the Early American Republic (Charlottesville: University Press of Virginia, 2001); Jeffery A. Smith, *Printers and Press Freedom: The Ideology of Early American Journalism* (New York: Oxford University Press, 1988); Leonard W. Levy, *Legacy of Suppression: Freedom of Speech and Press in Early American History* (Cambridge: Harvard University Press, 1960); Donna Lee Dickerson, *The Course of Tolerance: Freedom of the Press in Nineteenth-Century America* (Westport, Conn.: Greenwood Press, 1990); Richard Buel Jr., "Freedom of the Press in Revolutionary America: The Evolution of Libertarianism, 1760–1820," in *The Press and the American Revolution*, ed. Bernard Bailyn and John Hench (Worcester, Mass.: American Antiquarian Society, 1980): 59–78; James Morton Smith, *Freedom's Fetters: The Alien and Sedition Laws and American Civil Liberties* (Ithaca, N.Y.: Cornell University Press, 1956).

36. Bentley, *Diary*, II: 291.

37. WBS, #1099.

38. John Prince, *A Discourse, Delivered at Salem, on the Day of the National Fast* (Salem, 1798).

39. WBS, #996.

40. WBS, #903.

41. WBS, #903, #1136.

42. Bentley, *Diary*, III: 269.

43. Bentley, *Diary*, III: 266.

44. WBS, #1050.

CHAPTER 8

1. The sole evidence of Bentley's opinion of Hamilton's plan on the public credit suggests that he exceedingly disapproved. In November of 1792, Bentley made this passing comment in a sermon: "Shocking indeed that this defenseless state should be deprived of its little share of blessing. Depraved indeed is the man who can add to his treasures from the scanty stock of one that is but a pensioner on the bounty of his fellow mortals." But even so, opposition to Hamiltonian finance was not at all central to his developing republicanism. WBS, #530.

2. STR, Oct. 21, 1765 (box 4, folder 6, 543–44).

3. STR, Nov. 23–Dec. 7, 1767 (box 4, folder 7, 641–42); *Boston Evening-Post*, Dec. 28, 1767, and Jan. 11, 1768.

4. STR, May 27, 1769 (box 4, folder 8, 737–39), and March 11, 1771 (box 4, folder 9, 818–23).

5. Dow, *Holyoke Diaries*, 83; *EG*, June 7, 1774.

6. *EG*, June 14, 1774.

7. *EG*, Sept. 13, 1774.

8. Oliver, *Diary of William Pynchon*, 42, 85; Sydney W. Jackman, ed., "Letters of William Browne, an American Loyalist," *EIHC* 96 (1960): 1–46; George Atkinson Ward, ed., *The Journal and Letters of Samuel Curwen, An American in England, from 1775 to 1783* (Boston, 1864).

9. For similar "reluctant revolutionaries" elsewhere, see Thomas M. Doerflinger, *A Vigorous Spirit of Enterprise: Merchants and Economic Development in Revolutionary Philadelphia* (Chapel Hill: University of North Carolina Press, 1986).

10. *EG*, June 14–21, 1774; Pruitt, *Massachusetts Tax Valuation*, 130–54.

11. James T. Austin, *The Life of Elbridge Gerry* (Boston, 1829), I: 21; STR, June 7, 1773 (box 4, folder 9, 933–44), and May 17, 1774 (box 4, folder 10, 1000).

12. TPP, 17: 33, 242.

13. TPP, 17: 206.

14. STR, June 8, 1778 (box 5, folder 3, 287).

15. *Diary of William Pynchon*, 195, 199; Dow, *Holyoke Diaries*, 111–12.

16. TPP, 54: 53–67; STR, Feb. 5 and April 27, 1776 (box 5, folder 1, 97; folder 2, 119).

17. David H. Fischer, "The Myth of the Essex Junto," *WMQ* 21 (1964): 191–235.

18. Election results from 1780 to 1788 are recorded in the Salem Town Records as follows: 1780: March 31, Sept. 4 (box 5, folder 4, 362–63, 404–406); 1781: March 12, April 2, May 22 (box 5, folder 5, 429–33, 441–42, 453); 1782: March 11 (box 5, folder 5, 488–91, 503); 1783: March 10, April 7 (box 5, folder 6, 539–41, 552–53); 1784: March 8, April 5 (box 5, folder 6, 580–83, 595); 1785: March 14, April 4, May 9 (box 5, folder 7, 631–34, 652–53, 658–59); 1786: March 13, April 3, May 15 (box 5, folder 7, 687–89, 700; folder 8, 701, 703); 1787: March 12, April 2, May 10 (box 5, folder 8, 723–41; 737–38, 748); 1788: March 10, April 7, May 5 (box 5, folder 8, 782–85, 797–800, folder 9, 803–804).

19. ECPR, 358: 171–78; 359: 156–66.

20. David P. Szatmary, *Shays' Rebellion: The Making of an Agrarian Insurrection* (Amherst: University of Massachusetts Press, 1980): 106; J. F. Jameson, ed., "Letters of Stephen Higginson, 1783–1804," *Annual Report of the American Historical Association for the Year 1896* (Washington, D.C., 1897), I: 719–25, 732–33; Massachusetts Archives, 189: 65–66; Oliver, *Diary of William Pynchon*, 260.

21. *SM*, Nov. 18, 1786; Feb. 3, 1787.

22. STR, April 2, 1787 (box 5, folder 8, 737–38); *SM*, April 7, 1787.

23. Election results from 1789 to 1796 are recorded in the Salem Town Records as follows: 1789: April 6, May 11 (box 6, folder 1, 22–23, 32); 1790: March 8, April 5, May 10 (box 6, folder 1, 57–59, 65, folder 2, 72, 78); 1791: March 14, April 4, May 9 (box 6, folder 2, 98–99, 107, 118); 1792: March 5, April 2, May 14 (box 6, folder 2, 135; folder 3, 146–47, 150); 1793: April 1, May 6 (box 6, folder 3, 181, 187); 1794: March 10, April 7, May 5, Nov. 3 (box 6, folder 4, 215–16, 226–27, 232, 262–63); 1795: March 9, April 6 (box 6, folder 4, 268–69, 280); 1796: March 14, April 4, May 2, Aug. 1, Sept. 12, Nov. 7 (box 6, folder 5, 308–309, 329–30, 332–33, 335, 340, 344–47).

24. Bentley, *Diary*, II: 84; *SG*, Sept. 15, 1795.

25. Bentley, *Diary*, II: 146.

26. Stephen Goodhue to Benjamin Goodhue, Dec. 30, 1795. Goodhue Family Papers, Vol. 1.

27. STR, Nov. 7, 1796 (box 6, folder 5, 346–47); *SG*, Nov. 8, 1796.

28. *SG*, Jan. 1, 1798.

29. Bentley, *Diary*, II: 269; see also James Duncan Phillips, "Salem's Part in the Naval War with France," *NEQ* 16 (1943): 543–66.

30. In 1799, Boston voters returned Sumner with eighteen hundred votes, six times more than the three hundred they gave Heath. Salem's Federalist votes, by contrast, were twelve times as many as their Republican votes. *SG*, April 2, 1799. Election results from 1797 to 1799 are in the Salem Town Records as follows: 1797: March 13, April 3, May 1 (box 6, folder 6, 358–59, 373–74, 381–82); 1798: March 12, April 2, May 7, Nov. 5 (box 6, folder 6, 420, 437–38, 443–44, 467–68); 1799: March 11, April 1, May 6 (box 6, folder 7, 473–74, 485–87, 499).

31. *Works of John Adams*, II: 201.

32. *EG*, Sept. 6–13, 1768; July 19, Oct. 4–11, 1774; *Boston Gazette*, July 25 and Aug. 1, 1768; Dow, *Holyoke Diaries*, 69; *Diaries of Benjamin Lynde*, 192; Oliver, *Diary of William Pynchon*, 22, 42.

33. *EG*, Oct. 11, 1774.

34. *Diaries of Benjamin Lynde*, 175–76.

35. George A. Billias, "Pox and Politics in Marblehead, 1773–1774," *EIHC* 92 (1956): 43–58; Gerald H. Clarfield, "Salem's Great Inoculation Controversy, 1773–1774," *EIHC* 106 (1970): 277–96.

36. STR, March 13, 1775 (box 5, folder 1, 25–26). For discussions of Revolutionary mobs such as these, see Gordon Wood, "A Note on Mobs in the American Revolution," *WMQ* 23 (1966): 635–42; Jesse Lemisch, "Jack Tar in the Streets: Merchant Seamen in the Politics of Revolutionary America," *WMQ* 25 (1968): 371–407; Dirk Hoerder, *Mobs and People: Crowd Action in Massachusetts during the Revolution 1765–1780* (Berlin: Free University of Berlin, 1971); Hoerder, "Boston Leaders and Boston Crowds, 1765–1776," in *The American Revolution: Explorations in the History of American Radicalism*, ed. Alfred F. Young (DeKalb: Northern Illinois University Press, 1976): 233–71; Gary B. Nash, "Social Change and the Growth of Prerevolutionary Urban Radicalism," in *The American Revolution*, ed. Alfred F. Young (DeKalb: Northern Illinois University Press, 1976): 3–36; Gary B. Nash, "Artisans and Politics in Eighteenth-Century Philadelphia," in *The Origins of Anglo-American Radicalism*, ed. Margaret C. Jacob and James R. Jacob (1984; repr. Atlantic Highlands, N.J.: Humanities Press International, 1991): 258–78; Barbara Clark Smith, "Food Rioters and the American Revolution," *WMQ* 51 (1994): 3–38; Hermann Wellenreuther, "Labor in the Era of the American Revolution: A Discussion of Recent Concepts and Theories," *Labor History* 22 (1981): 573–600; Gary B. Nash, Billy G. Smith, and Dirk Hoerder, "Laboring Americans and the American Revolution," *Labor History* 24 (1983): 414–39; and Hermann Wellenreuther, "Rejoinder," *Labor History* 24 (1983): 440–54.

37. STR, June 26, 1776 (box 5, folder 2, 159).

38. Massachusetts Archives, 180: 275.

39. "North Church Proprietors' Records, 1773–1836."

40. Massachusetts Archives, 184: 141–45.

41. [Williams], "Revolutionary Letters," 120.

42. Oliver, *Diary of William Pynchon*, 24, 29, 52.

43. STR, March 12, 1787 (box 5, folder 8, 723–41).

44. Bentley, *Diary*, II: 146.

45. For an introduction to the Massachusetts Republicans as social and political outsiders, see Paul Goodman, *The Democratic-Republicans of Massachusetts: Politics in a Young Republic* (Cambridge: Harvard University Press, 1964); James M. Banner Jr., *To the Hartford Convention: The Federalists and the Origins of Party Politics in Massachusetts, 1789–1815* (New York: Alfred A. Knopf, 1970): 182–83; Ronald P. Formisano, *The Transformation of Political Culture: Massachusetts Parties, 1790s–1840s* (New York: Oxford University Press, 1983): 149. The values of artisanal republicanism are the subject of many good works, but some of the crucial ones are, *Urban Crucible*; Sean Wilentz, *Chants Democratic: New York City and the Rise of the American Working Class, 1788–1850* (New York: Oxford University Press, 1984); Howard B. Rock, *Artisans of the New Republic: The Tradesmen of New York City in the Age of Jefferson* (New York: New York University Press, 1984); and Billy G. Smith, *"The Lower Sort."* Most directly relating to Salem's laborers is Vickers's *Farmers and Fishermen*.

46. Bentley, *Diary*, II: 176.

47. Bentley, *Diary*, II: 335.

48. *SG*, July 5–15 and Aug. 10–19, 1796.

49. Bentley, *Diary*, I: 136–38; II: 105–106.

50. WBS, #187; Bentley, *Diary* I: 22, 381; II: 142.

51. Bentley, *Diary*, II: 205; John H. Reinoehl, "The Impact of the French Revolution and Napoleon upon the United States as Revealed by the Fortunes of the Crowninshield Family of Salem," (Ph.D. diss., Michigan State University, 1953); David L. Ferguson, *Cleopatra's Barge: The Crowninshield Story* (Boston: Little, Brown, 1976).

52. *SG*, Aug. 15–22 and Oct. 17, 1800.

53. *IR*, Aug. 21 and Oct. 16, 1800.

54. *IR*, Nov. 3, 1800.

55. *IR*, June 30 and July 3–31, 1800.

56. *IR*, Aug. 25, Oct. 13, Nov. 3, and Oct. 27, 1800. Italics in the original.

57. Bentley, *Diary*, II: 353.

58. *IR*, Oct. 16, 1800. Italics and capitalization in the original.

59. WBP, box 2, folder 11.

60. The election returns for 1800 are in the Salem Town Records as follows: March 10, April 7, May 5, Aug. 25, Oct. 20, Nov. 3 (box 6, folder 8, 539–41, 552–54; box 7, folder 1, 3–4, 16–17, 21–24); see also *IR*, Aug. 28–Sept. 1, Oct. 23, Nov. 6, 1800.

61. That is the interpretation of men like Caleb Strong and Elbridge Gerry offered in Formisano, *The Transformation of Political Culture*, 57–83.

62. STR, April 7, 1800 (box 6, folder 8, 552–54); April 6, 1801 (box 7, folder 1, 55–56); April 5, 1802 (box 7, folder 2, 130–31).

63. The *Register* dropped "Impartial" in January of 1802 and was then the *Salem Register*, so *SR*, Oct. 7–18, 1802. The Federalist side is in *SG*, Oct. 12–29, 1802.

64. *SG*, March 16, 1802.

65. *IR*, Aug. 25, 1800; *SR*, March 18–29, April 5, Oct. 7, 1802. When the *Gazette* later said of the seaports that "they are the reservoirs of the worthless part of the community," Republicans added that to their list of insults: *SG*, March 23, 1802.

66. Election results between 1801 and 1805 are recorded in the Salem Town Records as follows: 1801: March 9, April 6 (box 7, folder 1, 35–36, 55–56); 1802: March 8, April 5, May 3, Nov. 1 (box 7, folder 2, 109, 130–31, 141, 160); 1803: March 14, April 4, Nov. 1 (box 7, folder 2, 160, 171, 184; folder 3, 280); 1804: March 12, April 2, May 15 (box 7, folder 3, 201, 214, 224, 235–40); 1805: April 1, May 16 (box 7, folder 3, 255, 292). County and district results for 1801 to 1803 are from the following sources: the 1802 Congressional race is in *SG*, Nov. 2–5, 1802, and the gubernatorial races are in *SG*, April 9, 1801; *SR*, April 8, 1802; *SG*, April 5, 1803.

67. James Banner, *To the Hartford Convention*, 361–62. U.S. senators were still chosen by the state legislatures.

68. Bentley, *Diary*, III: 86.

69. "Diary of Benjamin Blanchard, 1800–1819," PEM.

70. A nice introduction to the political culture of these towns is in Formisano, *Transformation of Political Culture*, 161–62. For Lynn, see also Paul G. Faler, *Mechanics and Manufacturers in the Early Industrial Revolution: Lynn, Massachusetts, 1780–1860* (Albany: State University of New York Press, 1981). For Marblehead and Gloucester, see also Vickers, *Farmers and Fishermen*. For Newburyport, see also Benjamin Labaree, *Patriots and Partisans: The Merchants of Newburyport, 1764–1815* (Cambridge, Mass.: Harvard University Press, 1962).

71. *SG*, Oct. 10, 1800; Feb. 12, March 19, May 11, Oct. 26, 1802.

72. Bentley, *Diary*, III: 122; WBP-PEM, folder 4.

73. Jacob Crowninshield to William Bentley, Nov. 26, 1804, in Jacob Crowninshield Papers, Crowninshield Family Papers, box 3, folder 4, PEM.

74. Jacob Crowninshield to Thomas Jefferson, July 19, 1805. Typescript in Jacob Crowninshield Papers.

75. Bentley, *Diary*, III: 206–207, 209–10.

76. Bentley, *Diary*, III: 154. See William T. Whitney Jr., "The Crowninshields of Salem, 1800–1808: A Study in the Politics of Commercial Growth," *EIHC* 94 (1958): 1–36.

77. Bentley, *Diary*, III: 71, 141, 215, 229, 272, 297.

78. It was published as *A Sermon, Before the Governor, the Honorable Council, and both Branches of the Legislature of the Commonwealth of Massachusetts* (Boston, 1807).

79. *SG*, Nov. 2, 1802.

80. *SR*, Nov. 11, 1802.

81. Bentley, *Diary*, III: 15.

82. STR, Oct. 27, 1773 (box 4, folder 9, 962–63).

83. STR, March 11, 1765 (box 4, folder 6, 521). As elsewhere in the province before 1780, the franchise in General Court elections was extended only to those males over twenty-one who had been a resident in town for one year and who owned either enough real estate to generate rents of 40 shillings annually or property of any type worth £40 sterling. The franchise in elections of town leaders in such towns as Salem where taxes were assessed by the selectmen themselves required residency and an estate of at least £20 in the provincial currency. But calculations of franchise rates using tax assessments are complicated by the facts that property was often assessed at

perhaps one-sixth or one-eighth of its value, town assessors underestimated the assessments to reduce subsequent revenue demands from the General Court, distinctions were seldom made between property ownership and renting, and the value of local currencies in relation to sterling was in constant flux. But my analysis of the 1765 tax list showed that 94 percent of the taxpayers paid a tax on real or personal estates (rather than just a poll tax), suggesting that even with room for variability, the great majority of Salem's taxable males, if residents for one year, could vote. For the debate over colonial suffrage, see Robert E. Brown, *Middle Class Democracy and the Revolution in Massachusetts, 1691–1780* (Ithaca, N.Y.: Cornell University Press, 1955); John Cary, "Statistical Method and the Brown Thesis on Colonial Democracy, with a Rebuttal by Robert E. Brown," *WMQ* 20 (1963): 258; J. R. Pole, "Suffrage and Representation in Massachusetts: A Statistical Note," *WMQ* 14 (1957): 560–92; David Syrett, "Town Meeting Politics in Massachusetts, 1776–1786," *WMQ* 21 (1964): 352–66; Michael Zuckerman, "The Social Context of Democracy in Massachusetts," *WMQ* 25 (1968): 523–44.

84. The census of 1800 reported 950 free white males between the ages of sixteen and twenty-six. The number of those over age twenty-one would be approximately half, or 475, which, when added to the 1,334 white men over age twenty-six, gives a total of 1,809 adult free white men in Salem. Of those, 937 (52 percent) voted that year in the Read/Crowninshield election with the highest turnout. The elections for governor between 1805 and 1808 brought out between fourteen hundred and seventeen hundred voters in Salem, which, if examined with the 1810 census count of 2,718 adult white males, gives a rate between 52 percent and 62 percent. *Return of the Whole Number of Persons within the Several Districts of the United States* (1800) : 8; and *Aggregate Amount of each Description of Persons within the United States of America* (Washington, 1811). The expansion of suffrage is part of most discussions of Jeffersonianism in the Bay State. See, for example, Formisano, *Transformation of Political Culture*, 30–33, 128–43; Goodman, *Democratic Republicans*, 136–40; James H. Robbins, "The Impact of the First American Party System on Salem Politics," *EIHC* 107 (1971): 254–67; and James Banner, *To the Hartford Convention*, 359–60, who found similar results for the state as a whole.

85. Bentley was held in contempt of court; the charge was later dismissed. Bentley, *Diary*, II: 457–58, III: 20–24, 28, 33, 58; *SR*, April 25–May 2, 1803.

86. Bentley, *Diary*, III: 234.

87. Bentley, *Diary*, III: 265.

CHAPTER 9

1. *IR*, Oct. 27, 1800.

2. *SR*, March 25, 1802. Italics in the original.

3. The complex attitudes of Republicans toward capitalism is the subject of Drew McCoy, *The Elusive Republic: Political Economy in Jeffersonian America* (Chapel Hill: University of North Carolina Press, 1980).

4. Bentley, *Diary*, III: 334.

5. *SG*, Nov. 28, 1800; *IR*, Nov. 20, 1800.

6. Bentley, *Diary*, I: 58–59; Oliver, ed., *Diary of William Pynchon*, 275.

7. *Articles and Covenant Adopted by the Tabernacle Church* (Salem, 1804); *Diary*, I: 268.

8. South Church, untitled record book. Tabernacle Church Archives. Samuel Hopkins preached there in 1791, not long before his *System of Doctrines* was published in Boston backed by hundreds of subscribers across New England—including Bentley himself, whose subscription, it seems clear, speaks to his bibliophilia rather than his agreement. Samuel Hopkins, *The System of Doctrines* (Boston, 1793).

9. Bentley to Crowninshield, Feb. 11, 1805, in Jacob Crowninshield Papers, Crowninshield Family Papers, box 3, folder 4, PEM.

10. James Banner, *To the Hartford Convention*, 197–215; Formisano, *Transformation of Political Culture*, 154–59.

11. Bentley, *Diary*, II: 129, 156; Ebenezer Bradford, *The Nature and Manner of Giving Thanks to God* (Boston, 1795). See also David Tappan's response, *Christian Thankfulness Explained and Enforced* (Boston, 1795), and Bradford's reply, *The Nature of Humiliation* (Boston, 1795).

12. Joshua Spaulding, *Sentiments, Concerning the Coming and Kingdom of Christ* (Salem, 1796): 51–53; Spaulding's millenarianism is discussed in Bloch, *Visionary Republic*, 141–44. The ostensible grievance of Spaulding's parishioners was once again Presbyterianism, but Bentley knew that the real problem was listeners' resentment against what even Bentley thought was "ignorant and unseasonable political bawling" in favor of the Republicans. Bentley, *Diary*, II: 267–69.

13. In 1961, Alan Heimert challenged the supposed patriotism of liberal clerics, an older argument based largely on Jonathan Mayhew's 1750 *Discourse Concerning Unlimited Submission* and Charles Chauncy's later concerns over a proposed Anglican bishopric in America. Though the alignment of the two theologies into political camps proved problematic—a spectrum of positions were taken even by such a narrow group as the liberals of eastern Massachusetts, from Samuel Cooper (and Mayhew surely, had he lived) on the patriot side to Thomas Barnard Sr. on the Tory side—insofar as Salem was concerned, Heimert's thesis was exactly and entirely correct. See Heimert, *Religion and the American Mind*. For an introduction to the debate, see Philip Goff, "Revivals and Revolution: Historiographic Turns since Alan Heimert's *Religion and the American Mind*," *Church History* 67 (1998): 695–721. The older argument was articulated most notably in Alice M. Baldwin, *The New England Clergy and the American Revolution* (Durham, N.C.: Duke University Press, 1928). Many of the works cited in the introduction notes also touch on this issue, as do three important articles: William G. McLoughlin, "Enthusiasm for Liberty: The Great Awakening as the Key to the Revolution," *Proceedings of the American Antiquarian Society* 87 (1977): 69–95; Harry S. Stout, "Religion, Communications, and the Ideological Origins of the American Revolution," *WMQ* 34 (1977): 519–41; and Edmund S. Morgan, "The Puritan Ethic and the American Revolution," *WMQ* 24 (1967): 3–43.

14. Force, *American Archives*, 4th ser., III: 675; "Pastor's Record, 1772–1779."

15. *The New England Chronicle*, June 1, 1775.

16. Oliver, ed., *Diary of William Pynchon*, 32.

17. William Lincoln, ed., *The Journals of Each Provincial Congress of Massachusetts* (Boston, 1838). That members left the First is in "Pastor's Record, 1772–1779," First Church Records.

18. Thomas Hutchinson, *The History of the Colony and Province of Massachusetts-Bay*, ed. Lawrence Shaw Mayo (Cambridge, Mass.: Harvard University Press, 1936), III: 241.

19. Whitaker, *An Antidote against Toryism* (Newburyport, 1777): 20. For another work with the same theme, see Newburyport's John Murray, *Nehemiah, or the Struggle for Liberty Never in Vain* (Newburyport, 1779).

20. TPP, 18: 134, 160; 5: 316.

21. Whitaker, *The Reward of Toryism* (Newburyport, 1783): 21, 27.

22. *SG*, July 8, 1808.

23. Lyman H. Butterfield, "Elder John Leland, Jeffersonian Itinerant," *Proceedings of the American Antiquarian Society* 62 (1952): 155–242; Richard D. Birdsall, "The Reverend Thomas Allen: Jeffersonian Calvinist," *NEQ* 30 (1957): 147–65; McLoughlin, *New England Dissent*, II: 745–50.

24. George H. Williams, *The Radical Reformation* (Philadelphia: Westminster Press, 1962).

CHAPTER 10

1. WBP, box 3, folder 6. For Priestley's years in America, see Jenny Graham, "Revolutionary in Exile: The Emigration of Joseph Priestley to America, 1794–1804," in *Transactions of the American Philosophical Society* 85, pt. 2 (Philadelphia: American Philosophical Society, 1995).

2. Bentley, *Diary*, III: 28; *SR*, April 25–May 2, 1803.

3. Bentley, *Diary*, III: 244, 305, 310–11.

4. Bentley, *Diary*, III: 394.

5. Bentley, *Diary* II: 161, 167–68, 238, 240.

6. Bentley, *Diary*, I: 286, 355.

7. Bentley, *Diary*, I: 276.

8. Bentley, *Diary*, I: 339, 387.

9. Bentley, *Diary*, I: 26, 95–97,;II: 408; III: 277, 382–83, 473; WBS, #852.

10. WBS, #293.

11. WBS, #395.

12. Bentley, *Diary*, I: 7; *Return of the Whole Number of Persons within the Several Districts of the United States* (Philadelphia, 1791): 24; *Return of the Whole Number of Persons within the Several Districts of the United States* (Washington, 1801): 8; *Aggregate Amount of each Description of Persons within the United States of America, and the Territories thereof* (Washington, 1811; repr. New York, Norman Ross Publishing, 1990): 10.

13. North Church, *First Centenary*, 157–60.

14. Bentley, *Diary*, III: 132.

15. Bentley, *Diary*, III: 5, 67, 75–76, 123, 134, 145–46, 173, 201, 207, 251.

16. Bentley, *Diary*, III: 207.

17. Bentley, *Diary*, III: 251.

18. Bentley, *Diary*, I: 196, 269, 275, 363; III: 173, 207, 292, 443.

19. William D. Piersen, *Black Yankees: The Development of an Afro-American Subculture in Eighteenth-Century New England* (Amherst: University of Massachusetts Press, 1988): 49–61, 74–86.

20. Bentley, *Diary*, II: 252, 309.

21. WBS, #307.

22. Bentley, *Diary*, III: 516.

23. Bentley, *Diary*, I: 123.

24. Bentley, *Diary*, III: 516.

25. Christine Leigh Heyrman, *Commerce and Culture: The Maritime Communities of Colonial Massachusetts 1690–1750* (New York: W. W. Norton, 1984): 381–85.

26. Linda Kerber, *Toward an Intellectual History of Women: Essays by Linda Kerber* (Chapel Hill: University of North Carolina Press, 1997): 210–11.

27. Lucius Bolles, *A Sermon, Delivered to the Baptist Church and Society in Salem* (Salem, 1806): 6, 17.

28. [Bentley], *Collection of Psalms and Hymns*, hymn 108.

29. Watts, *Psalms of David*, 147; [Bentley], *Collection of Psalms and Hymns*, hymn 127.

30. John Higginson, *The Cause of God and his People in New-England* (Cambridge Mass., 1663): 10. For a discussion of how this sermon was a model for the jeremiad, see Perry Miller, *The New England Mind: From Colony to Province* (1953; repr. Boston: Beacon Press, 1961): 30, and Bernard Bailyn, *The New England Merchants in the Seventeenth Century* (Cambridge, Mass.: Harvard University Press, 1955): 140–42.

31. Oliver, *Diary of William Pynchon*, 63.

32. *SG*, Aug. 14–28, 1783.

33. David Osgood, *The Wonderful Works of God* (Boston, 1794): 9.

34. WBP, 23: 256.

35. Bentley, *Diary*, I: 267.

36. Bentley, *Diary*, I: 82–83.

37. Leon Burr Richardson, *History of Dartmouth College* (Hanover, N.H.: Dartmouth College Publications, 1932), I: 52.

38. Bentley, *Diary* I: 117, 170; WBP, box 2, folder 3.

39. WBP-PEM, folder 7.

40. Bentley, *Diary*, IV: 583–84.

41. Bentley, *Diary*, III: 235, 358–59.

42. *EG*, Nov. 24, 1772. For a similar argument, see Turner, *Without God, Without Creed*, 44–46.

43. WBS, #441.

44. WBS, #29.

45. WBS, #30.

46. Chauncy, *Benevolence of the Deity*, 30; John Murray, *The Origin of Evil* (Newburyport, 1785); Noah Worcester, *Some Difficulties Proposed for Solution* (Newburyport, 1786).

47. WBS, #648.

48. Jonathan Edwards Jr., *The Faithful Manifestation of the Truth* (New Haven, 1783).

49. Bentley, *Diary*, III: 81, 153; Benjamin Hodges's passing was one of the more difficult of the many deaths Bentley had witnessed in his tenure: Bentley, *A Funeral Discourse, Delivered in the East Meeting House, Salem* (Salem, 1804).

EPILOGUE

1. Prince naturally enough delivered the sermon at Barnard's funeral: John Prince, *A sermon, preached before the North Church and society in Salem, October 16, 1814* (Salem, 1814). When Prince passed on, his remains were mistakenly placed in the Barnard family tomb; see Samuel A. Eliot, *Heralds of a Liberal Faith*, 142.

2. For what Henry May calls the "Didactic Enlightenment," see *Enlightenment in America*, 341–57. Also, critically, see Daniel Walker Howe, *The Unitarian Conscience*, passim; and Turner, *Without God, Without Creed*, 96–104.

3. Bentley, *Diary*, II: 176, 377; III: 381. Bentley, "A Description and History of Salem," *MHSC*, 1st ser., 6 (1799): 212–88; "Remarks on 'A History of Salem,'" *MHSC*, 1st ser., 7 (1800); and "Remarks upon Remarks," *MHSC*, 1st ser., 8 (1801): 1–4.

4. Bentley, *Diary*, III: 14, 40, 87; IV: 612–13; WBP-PEM, folder 7.

5. *Monthly Anthology* 5 (1806): 656–57; Bentley, *Diary*, III: 217, 230–31, 237–38. The controversy can be traced in Bentley, *A Sermon, Delivered July 2, 1806, at the Ordination of Mr. Joseph Richardson* (Boston, 1806); First Church and Parish in Hingham (Mass.), *A Vindication of the Proceedings of the First Church and Parish* (Boston, 1807); Thomas Thaxter, *A Narrative of the Proceedings in the North Parish of Hingham* (Salem, 1807).

6. *Monthly Anthology* 6 (1807): 336. For a discussion of this publication as an expression of Brahmin culture, see Field, *Crisis of the Standing Order*, 82–110.

7. What historians call the "Unitarian controversy" at Harvard after 1805 was really a schism over Arianism, not Unitarianism proper, but in any event it is covered in a variety of studies and essays, including Field, *Crisis of the Standing Order*, 47–81; Conrad Wright, *The Unitarian Controversy: Essays on American Unitarian History* (Boston: Skinner House Books, 1994); and Conrad Edick Wright, ed., *American Unitarianism, 1805–1865* (Boston: Massachusetts Historical Society and Northeastern University, 1989).

8. William Ellery Channing, *A Letter to the Rev. Samuel C. Thacher on the Aspersions Contained in a Late Number of the Panoplist* (Boston, 1815): 7. The title referred to a positive and extended review of Morse's publication, *American Unitarianism, or a Brief History of the Progress and Present State of the Unitarian Churches in America*, in the orthodox magazine.

9. Bentley, *Diary*, III: 5, 67, 75–76, 123, 134, 145–46, 173, 201, 207, 251; "First Universalist Society in Salem, Massachusetts, Records, 1806–1955" (bms 342, box 1, folder 1) in Andover-Harvard Theological Library

10. Bentley, *Diary*, III: 501; Worcester, *Serious and Candid Letters to the Rev. Thomas Baldwin* (Salem, 1807).

11. *Members First Constituted into a Baptist Church in Salem, Mass* [broadside, 1810].

12. Bentley, *Diary*, III: 295, 312–18.

13. *Diary of William Pickman*, 188.

14. Branch Church Record Book; *Members First Constituted into a Baptist Church.*

15. Election results between 1806 and 1808 are recorded in the Salem Town Records as follows: 1806: box 7, folder 4, 374, 394, 420; 1807: box 7, folder 5, 432, 449; 1808: box 7, folder 5, 488, 500, 517, 520–21, 546–47.

16. Bentley, *Diary*, III: 349, 380, 383, 391–92.

17. Bentley, *Diary*, III: 16–18, 360. For his years in Salem, see William W. Story, ed., *Life and Letters of Joseph Story, Associate Justice of the Supreme Court of the United States* (Boston, 1851).

18. Bentley, *Diary*, III: 449.

19. Richard D. Brown, *Knowledge Is Power*, 207. See also Chipley, "The Bibliomania of the Reverend William Bentley, D.D."

20. WBP, Box 3, folder 5; Bentley, *Diary*, IV: 586–88.

21. His church no longer exists as a distinct entity. In 1899, it merged with the Barton Square Church to form the Second Church, and in 1923 the Second Church merged back into the First, the church from which it had come two hundred years earlier.

Bibliography

BENTLEY'S PAPERS

From his ordination in 1783 through December of 1799, Bentley wrote out his sermons in full, and retained them with his papers, ordered and numbered 1–1,203. He kept separate lists of these sermons with the date that each one was delivered. These are now housed in the Digital Collections and Archives of Tufts University, Medford, Massachusetts. Beginning in 1800, he most often drafted only outlines or abstracts for his sermons, only occasionally writing them out in full. The majority of these post-1800 sermons are no longer extant, although the American Antiquarian Society in Worcester, Mass., owns four volumes of abstracts from 1808 to 1813, and the Tufts archives has a volume from 1814 and 1815. The Tufts archives includes various miscellaneous manuscripts, but the great bulk of Bentley's papers is at the Antiquarian Society, a collection of more than forty volumes and six boxes, including his diary, correspondence, commonplace books, and financial papers. His diary, edited by George F. Dow, was published as *The Diary of William Bentley, D.D.*, 4 vols. (Salem, 1905–1914; repr. Gloucester, Mass: Peter Smith, 1962). That Dow was the editor is in his *Two Centuries of Travel in Essex County, Massachusetts* (Topsfield, Mass.: Topsfield Historical Society, 1921): 103.

MANUSCRIPT COLLECTIONS

American Antiquarian Society
    William Bentley Papers, 1666–1819

American Philosophical Society
  Joseph Priestley Papers, 1771–1803

Andover-Harvard Theological Library
  First Universalist Society in Salem, Massachusetts. Records, 1806–1955

First Church of Salem
  First Church Collection
    Records, 1629–1736
    "Records of the First Church of Salem, 1736–1875" (typed transcript)
    Records, 1736–1831
    Deacons' Records, 1713–1847
    Proprietors' Records, 1746–1816
    Proprietors' Records, 1756–1817
    Pastor's Record, 1772–1779
    unbound papers
  North Church Collection
    Proprietors' Records, 1773–1836
    Treasurers' Records, 1773–1828
    Treasurers' Records, 1796–1805
    Treasurers' Records, 1804–1832
    Deacons' Records, 1805–1810
    Account Book, 1786–1808
    unbound papers

Harvard University Archives
  Bentley, William, Papers, 1783–1815
  Harvard University Corporation Records
  Library Charging Records
  Minutes of the Faculty, 1725–1870+ (Fac. Rec.)
  Winthrop, James, Papers

Houghton Library, Harvard University
  Clarke, James Freeman, Papers, 1647–1937
  Ebeling, Christoph, Papers

Massachusetts State Archives
  Essex County Probate Records
  Massachusetts Archives Collection

Phillips Library at the Peabody Essex Museum
  Bentley, William, Papers
  Blanchard, Benjamin, "Diary, 1800–1819"
  Branch Church, Record Book, 1805–1848
  Crowninshield Family Papers, 1757–1934, 1697–1909, 1756–1864
  Curwen Family Manuscript Collection, 1637–1808
  Derby Family Papers, 1716–1921

East Church, Account Book of charitable contributions, 1791–1829
East Church, Baptisms, deaths and marriages, 1782–1824
East Church, misc. manuscripts, 1717–1804
East Church, misc. papers, 1717–1897
East Church, misc. papers, 1762–1897
East Church, pew tax list, 1783–1790
East Church, pew tax list, 1783–1800
East Church, pew tax list, 1800–1827
East Church, record book, 1717–1757
East Church, record book, 1757–1793
East Church, record book, 1783–1845
East Church, treasurers' book, 1762–1812
East Church, treasurers' book, 1783–1829
East Church, treasurers' book, 1786–1865
East Church, valuation lists, 1781–1791
First Baptist, account book, 1805–1835
First Baptist, account book and pew rentals, 1809–1828
First Baptist, membership lists, 1804–1861
Fiske Family Papers, 1719–1906
Gardner Family Papers, 1761–1889
Goodhue Family Papers, 1684–1858
Gray, William, Papers, 1781–1840
North Church, Records
Pickman, Benjamin, Papers, 1698–1904
Prince Family Papers, 1732–1839
Salem Athenaeum Records, 1760–1889
Salem Town Records
Social Library Records Charge Book, 1760–1768
South Church, misc. papers, 1774–1860
South Church, misc. papers, 1815–1915
Tabernacle Church, Records, 1781–1887
Tax Valuation and Collection Books, 1759–1799
Tabernacle Church Archives. Salem, Mass.
South Church, untitled record book
Tabernacle Church, "Record Book, 1743–1833"

Digital Collections and Archives, Tufts University
    William Bentley Papers
    William Bentley Sermon Collection

NEWSPAPERS

[Salem, Mass.] *Essex Gazette*
Salem Gazette
[Salem, Mass.] *Independent Register*

Salem Mercury
Salem Register

MAJOR PUBLISHED WORKS BY BENTLEY

An Address, Delivered in the Essex Lodge, Upon the Festival of St. John the Evangelist.
    Salem, 1799.
A Charge Delivered Before the Morning Star Lodge, in Worcester, Massachusetts. Worcester,
    1798.
[comp.]. *A Collection of Psalms and Hymns for Public Worship.* Salem, 1789. 2nd ed.,
    1795; 3rd ed., 1814.
"A Description and History of Salem." *Collections of the Massachusetts Historical Society,*
    1st ser., 6 (1799): 212–88.
*A Discourse, Delivered at Amherst, August 10, 1797; Before the Most Worshipful Nathaniel
    Adams, of the Grand Lodge of New Hampshire.* Amherst, 1797.
*A Discourse delivered in the East Meeting-House in Salem, September 2, 1807: at the
    Annual Meeting of the Salem Female Charitable Society.* Salem, 1807.
*A Discourse, Delivered in Roxbury, October 12, 5796; Before the Grand Lodge of Free
    and Accepted Masons in the Commonwealth of Massachusetts.* Boston, 1797.
[comp.]. *Extracts from Doctor Priestley's Catechism.* Salem, 1785.
*A Funeral Discourse, Delivered in the East Meeting House, Salem, on the Sunday after the
    Death of Major-General John Fiske.* Salem, 1797.
*A Funeral Discourse, Delivered in the East Meeting House, Salem, on Sunday, 15th April,
    1804.* Salem, 1804.
*A Sermon, before the Governor, the honorable Council, and both branches of the Legislature
    of the Commonwealth of Massachusetts: on the day of the General Election, May 27,
    1807.* Boston, 1807.
A Sermon, Delivered in the East Meeting-House, Salem, on Sunday Morning, March 13.
    Salem, 1791.
A Sermon delivered July 2, 1806 at the Ordination of Mr. Joseph Richardson. Boston,
    1806.
A Sermon, Preached at the Stone Chapel in Boston, September 12, 1790. Boston, 1790.
A Sermon, Preached Before the Ancient and Honourable Artillery Company in Boston.
    Boston, 1796.

MISCELLANEOUS WORKS BY BENTLEY

"Letter from Rev. Mr. Bentley to the Corresponding Secretary [Concerning the Abbe
    de Mably]." *Collections of the Massachusetts Historical Society,* 1st ser., 4 (1795):
    157–58.
Record of the Parish List of Deaths, 1785–1819. Salem, Mass.: Printed for the Essex
    Institute, 1882.
"Selections from Dr. W. Bentley's correspondence." *New England Historical and
    Genealogical Register* 27 (1873): 351–60.

"Selections from the papers of Rev. William Bentley, D. D., of Salem, Massachusetts." *Historical Magazine*, 2nd ser., 8 (1870): 339–42; 10: 102–113; 3rd ser., 2 (1873): 244–252, 305–307, 364–67.

"Washington's Birth-Day Oration, at Salem, Mass., February 22, 1793." *Historical Magazine*, 2nd ser., 7 (1870): 3–8.

PUBLISHED OR MICROFILMED PRIMARY SOURCES

[Belknap, Jeremy]. "Belknap Papers." *Collections of the Massachusetts Historical Society*, 5th ser., 2 (1877): 1–500; 5th ser., 3 (1877): 1–371; 6th ser., 4 (1891): 1–632.

Belsham, Thomas, ed. *Memoirs of the Late Reverend Theophilus Lindsey*. London, 1812.

Crandall, Ruth, comp. "Salem Tax Lists." In *Massachusetts Local Tax Lists Before 1776*. Harvard University Library, microfilm reels 8–9.

[Curwen, Samuel]. *Journal and Letters of Samuel Curwen: Judge of Admiralty, etc., An American Refugee in England from 1775–1784*, edited by George A. Ward, New York: C. S. Francis and Co., 1842. More recent edition, *The Journal of Samuel Curwen, Loyalist*, edited by Andrew Oliver, Cambridge, Mass.: Harvard University Press, 1972.

Dexter, Franklin Bowditch, ed. *The Literary Diary of Ezra Stiles, DD., L.L.D.* New York: Charles Scribner's Sons, 1901.

The Diaries of Benjamin Lynde and Benjamin Lynde Jr. Boston: privately printed, 1880.

Donnan, Elizabeth, ed. *Documents Illustrative of the History of the Slave Trade to America*. 1932; repr. New York: Octagon Books, 1969.

Dow, George F., ed. *The Holyoke Diaries, 1709–1856*. Salem, Mass.: Essex Institute, 1911.

[Ebeling, Christoph Daniel]. "Glimpses of European Conditions from the Ebeling Letters." *Proceedings of the Massachusetts Historical Society* 59 (1925–1926): 324–76.

———. "Letters of Christoph Daniel Ebeling." Edited by William Coolidge Lane. *Proceedings of the American Antiquarian Society* 35 (1925): 272–451.

Emmerton, James A. "Salem Baptisms." *Historical Collections of the Essex Institute* 22 (1885): 177–92, 241–56; 23 (1886): 1–16, 81–96, 161–84, 241–80.

[Hazlitt, William]. "The Hazlitt Papers." *Christian Reformer* 5 (1838): 505–12, 697–707, 756–64; 6 (1839): 15–24.

[Higginson, Stephen]. "Letters of Stephen Higginson, 1783–1804." Edited by J. F. Jameson. *Annual Report of the American Historical Association for the Year 1896*. Washington: Government Printing Office, 1897: 704–841.

Moyne, Ernest J., ed. *The Journal of Margaret Hazlitt; Recollections of England, Ireland, and America*. Lawrence: University of Kansas Press, 1967.

[Pickering, Timothy]. "Papers of Timothy Pickering." Massachusetts Historical Society. Microfilm.

[Pickman, Benjamin]. *The Diary and Letters of Benjamin Pickman, 1740–1819, with a Biographical Sketch and Genealogy of the Pickman Family*. Edited by George F. Dow. Newport, R.I.: Wayside Press, 1928.

Pierce, Richard D., ed. *The Records of the First Church in Salem, Massachusetts, 1629–1736*. Salem, Mass.: Essex Institute, 1974.

[Price, Richard]. "The Price Letters." *Proceedings of the Massachusetts Historical Society,* 2nd ser., 17 (1903): 262–378.

[Priestley, Joseph]. "Letters of Joseph Priestley." *Proceedings of the Massachusetts Historical Society,* 2nd ser., 3 (1888): 11–40.

Pruitt, Bettye Hobbs, ed. *The Massachusetts Tax Valuation List of 1771*. Boston: Hall, 1978.

[Pynchon, William]. *The Diary of William Pynchon, Salem: A Picture of Salem Life, Social and Political, A Century Ago*. Edited by Fitch Edward Oliver. Boston: Houghton Mifflin, 1890.

United States Bureau of the Census. *Heads of Families at the First Census of the United States Taken in the Year 1790: Massachusetts*. Baltimore: Genealogical Publishing, 1966.

Vital Records of Salem, Massachusetts, to the End of the Year 1849. 6 vols. Salem, Mass.: Essex Institute, 1916–1925.

Walker, Williston, ed. *The Creeds and Platforms of Congregationalism*. 1893; repr. Boston: Pilgrim Press, 1960.

SELECTED SECONDARY SOURCES

Ahlstrom, Sydney E. *Theology in America: The Major Protestant Voices from Puritanism to Neo-Orthodoxy*. Indianapolis: Bobbs-Merrill, 1967.

Ahlstrom, Sydney E., and Jonathan S. Carey, eds. *An American Reformation: A Documentary History of Unitarian Christianity*. Middletown, Conn.: Wesleyan University Press, 1985.

Akers, Charles W. *Called unto Liberty: A Life of Jonathan Mayhew, 1720–1766*. Cambridge, Mass.: Harvard University Press, 1964.

———. *The Divine Politician: Samuel Cooper and the American Revolution in Boston*. Boston: Northeastern University Press, 1982.

———. "Religion and the American Revolution: Samuel Cooper and the Brattle Street Church." *William and Mary Quarterly* 35 (1978): 477–98.

Albanese, Catherine L. *Sons of the Fathers: The Civil Religion of the American Revolution*. Philadelphia: Temple University Press, 1976.

Aldridge, A. Owen. "Natural Religion and Deism in America before Ethan Allen and Thomas Paine." *William and Mary Quarterly* 54 (1997): 835–48.

Almond, Philip C. *Heaven and Hell in Enlightenment England*. Cambridge: Cambridge University Press, 1994.

Appleby, Joyce. *Capitalism and a New Social Order: The Republican Vision of the 1790s*. New York: New York University Press, 1984.

———. *Liberalism and Republicanism in the Historical Imagination*. Cambridge, Mass: Harvard University Press, 1992.

Applewhite, Harriet B., and Darline G. Levy, eds *Women and Politics in the Age of the Democratic Revolution*. Ann Arbor: University of Michigan Press, 1990.

Ashworth, John. "The Jeffersonians: Classical Republicans or Liberal Capitalists?" *Journal of American Studies* 18 (1984): 425–35.

Bailyn, Bernard. *The Ideological Origins of the American Revolution.* Cambridge, Mass.: Harvard University Press, 1967.

———. "Religion and Revolution: Three Biographical Studies." *Perspectives in American History* 4 (1970): 85–169.

Baldwin, Alice M. *The New England Clergy and the American Revolution.* Durham, N.C.: Duke University Press, 1928.

Banner, James M. *To the Hartford Convention: The Federalists and the Origins of Party Politics in Massachusetts, 1789–1815.* New York: Knopf, 1970.

Banner, Lois. "Religious Benevolence as Social Control: A Critique of an Interpretation." *Journal of American History* 60 (1973): 23–41.

Banning, Lance. "Jeffersonian Ideology Revisited: Liberal and Classical Ideas in the New American Republic." *William and Mary Quarterly* 43 (1986): 3–19.

———. *The Jeffersonian Persuasion: Evolution of a Party Ideology.* Lawrence: University Press of Kansas, 1978.

———. "The Republican Interpretation: Retrospect and Prospect." *Proceedings of the American Antiquarian Society* 102 (1992): 153–79.

Barrow, Julia Paxton. "William Bentley: An Extraordinary Boarder." *Essex Institute Historical Collections* 97 (1961): 129–50.

Batchelor, George. "The Ecclesiastical and the Secular Origins of Unitarianism in Salem." *Social Equilibrium* (1887): 259–86.

Beiser, Frederick C. *The Sovereignty of Reason: The Defense of Rationality in the Early English Enlightenment.* Princeton, N.J.: Princeton University Press, 1996.

Bender, Thomas. *Community and Social Change in America.* New Brunswick, N.J.: Rutgers University Press, 1978.

Bercovitch, Sacvan. *The American Jeremiad.* Madison: University of Wisconsin Press, 1978.

———. *The Puritan Origins of the American Self.* New Haven, Conn.: Yale University Press, 1975.

Berens, John F. *Providence and Patriotism in Early America, 1640–1815.* Charlottesville: University Press of Virginia, 1978.

Berk, Stephen E. *Calvinism Versus Democracy: Timothy Dwight and the Origins of American Evangelical Orthodoxy.* Hamden, Conn.: Archon Books, 1974.

Berman, Mildred. "Salem's Maritime Activities: A Bentley-Eye View." *Essex Institute Historical Collections* 119 (1983): 18–27.

Berthoff, Rowland. "Independence and Attachment, Virtue and Interest: From Republican Citizen to Free Enterpriser, 1787–1837." In *Uprooted Americans: Essays to Honor Oscar Handlin,* edited by Richard L. Bushman, Neil Harris, David Rothman, Barbara Miller Solomon, and Stephan Thernstrom. Boston: Little, Brown, and Company, 1979: 97–124.

Bilhartz, Terry D. "Sex and the Second Great Awakening: The Feminization of American Religion Reconsidered." In *Belief and Behavior: Essays in the New*

Religious History, edited by Philip R. Vandermeer and Robert P. Swierenga. New Brunswick, N.J.: Rutgers University Press, 1991: 117–35.

———. *Urban Religion and the Second Great Awakening: Church and Society in Early National Baltimore*. Rutherford, N.J.: Fairleigh Dickinson University Press, 1986.

Billias, George A. "Pox and Politics in Marblehead, 1773–1774." *Essex Institute Historical Collections* 92 (1956): 43–58.

Birdsall, Richard D. "The Reverend Thomas Allen: Jeffersonian Calvinist." *New England Quarterly* 30 (1957): 147–65.

———. "The Second Great Awakening and the New England Social Order." *Church History* 39 (1970): 345–64.

Blau, Joseph L., ed. *American Philosophic Addresses 1700–1900*. New York: Columbia University Press, 1946.

Bloch, Ruth H. "American Feminine Ideals in Transition: The Rise of the Moral Mother, 1785–1815." *Feminist Studies* 4 (1978): 101–26.

———. "The Gendered Meanings of Virtue in Revolutionary America." *Signs* 13 (1987): 37–58.

———. *Visionary Republic: Millennial Themes in American Thought, 1756–1800*. Cambridge: Cambridge University Press, 1985.

Blumin, Stuart M. *The Emergence of the Middle Class: Social Experience in the American City, 1760–1900*. Cambridge: Cambridge University Press, 1989.

Bödeker, Hans Erich. "Journals and Public Opinion: The Politicization of the German Enlightenment in the Second Half of the Eighteenth Century." In *The Transformation of Political Culture: England and Germany in the Late Eighteenth Century*, edited by Eckhart Hellmuth. London: Oxford University Press, 1990: 423–46.

Bonomi, Patricia U. "'A Just Opposition': The Great Awakening as a Radical Model." In *The Origins of Anglo-American Radicalism*, edited by Margaret C. Jacob and James R. Jacob. 1984; repr. Atlantic Highlands, N.J.: Humanities Press International, 1991: 226–39.

———. *Under the Cope of Heaven: Religion, Society, and Politics in Colonial America*. New York: Oxford University Press, 1986.

Bonomi, Patricia U., and Peter R. Eisenstadt. "Church Adherence in the Eighteenth-Century British American Colonies." *William and Mary Quarterly* 39 (1982): 245–86.

Bonwick, Colin. *English Radicals and the American Revolution*. Chapel Hill: University of North Carolina Press, 1977.

Boorstin, Daniel. *The Lost World Of Thomas Jefferson*. New York: Henry Holt, 1958.

Botein, Stephen. "Income and Ideology: Harvard-Trained Clergymen in the Eighteenth Century." *Eighteenth-Century Studies* 13 (1979–80): 396–413.

———. "Religious Dimensions of the Early American State." In *Beyond Confederation: Origins of the Constitution and American National Identity*, edited by Richard Beeman, Stephen Botein, and Edward C. Carter II. Chapel Hill: University of North Carolina Press, 1987: 315–32.

Boyer, Paul S., and Stephen Nissenbaum. *Salem Possessed: The Social Origins of Witchcraft*. Cambridge, Mass.: Harvard University Press, 1974.

Boylan, Anne M. *The Origins of Women's Activism: New York and Boston, 1797–1840*. Chapel Hill: University of North Carolina Press, 2002.

Bradley, James E. *Religion, Revolution, and English Radicalism: Nonconformity in Eighteenth-Century Politics and Society*. Cambridge: Cambridge University Press, 1990.

Brauer, Jerald C. "Conversion from Puritanism to Revivalism." *Journal of Religion* 58 (1978): 227–43.

Breen, T. H. "'Baubles of Britain': The American and Consumer Revolutions of the Eighteenth Century." *Past and Present* 119 (1988): 73–104.

———. *The Character of the Good Ruler: Puritan Political Ideas in New England, 1630–1730*. New Haven, Conn.: Yale University Press, 1970.

———. "Narrative of Commercial Life: Consumption, Ideology, and Community on the Eve of the American Revolution." *William and Mary Quarterly* 50 (1993): 471–501.

Breen, T. H., and Timothy Hall. "Structuring Provincial Imagination: The Rhetoric and Experience of Social Change in Eighteenth-Century New England." *American Historical Review* 103 (1998): 1411–38.

Breitenbach, William K. "The Consistent Calvinism of the New Divinity Movement." *William and Mary Quarterly* 41 (1984): 241–64.

———. "Unregenerate Doings: Selflessness and Selfishness in New Divinity Theology." *American Quarterly* 34 (1982): 479–502.

Bridenbaugh, Carl. *Cities in Revolt: Urban Life in America, 1743–1776*. New York: Knopf, 1955.

Brooke, John L. "Ancient Lodges and Self-Created Societies: Voluntary Association and the Public Sphere in the Early Republic." In *Launching the "Extended Republic": The Federalist Era*, edited by Albert Hoffman and Peter J. Albert. Charlottesville: University Press of Virginia, 1996: 273–380.

———. *The Heart of the Commonwealth: Society and Political Culture in Worcester County, Massachusetts, 1713–1861*. Cambridge: Cambridge University Press, 1989.

Brown, Chandos Michael. "Mary Wollstonecraft, or, the Female Illuminati: The Campaign against Women and 'Modern Philosophy' in the Early Republic." *Journal of the Early Republic* 15 (1995): 389–424.

Brown, Jerry Wayne. *The Rise of Biblical Criticism in America, 1800–1870: The New England Scholars*. Middletown, Conn.: Wesleyan University Press, 1969.

Brown, Richard D. *Knowledge Is Power: The Diffusion of Information in Early America, 1700–1865*. New York: Oxford University Press, 1989.

———. *The Strength of a People: The Idea of an Informed Citizenry in America, 1650–1870*. Chapel Hill: University of North Carolina Press, 1996.

Brown, Robert E. *Middle Class Democracy and the Revolution in Massachusetts, 1691–1780*. Ithaca, N.Y.: Cornell University Press, 1955.

Buchanan, John G. "The Justice of America's Cause: Revolutionary Rhetoric in the Sermons of Samuel Cooper." *New England Quarterly* 50 (1977): 101–24.

Buel, Richard, Jr. "Democracy and the American Revolution: A Frame of Reference."
    William and Mary Quarterly 21 (1964): 165–90.
———. "Freedom of the Press in Revolutionary America: The Evolution of
    Libertarianism, 1760–1820." In *The Press and the American Revolution*, edited
    by Bernard Bailyn and John Hench. Worcester, Mass.: American Antiquarian
    Society, 1980: 59–78.
———. *Securing the Revolution: Ideology in American Politics, 1789–1815.* Ithaca, N.Y.:
    Cornell University Press, 1973.
Buell, Lawrence. *New England Literary Culture: From Revolution through Renaissance.*
    Cambridge: Cambridge University Press, 1986.
Bullock, Steven C. *Revolutionary Brotherhood: Freemasonry and the Transformation of the
    American Social Order 1730–1840.* Chapel Hill: University of North Carolina
    Press, 1996.
Bushman, Richard. *From Puritan to Yankee: Character and the Social Order in
    Connecticut, 1690–1765.* Cambridge, Mass.: Harvard University Press, 1967.
Butler, Jon. *Awash in a Sea of Faith: Christianizing the American People.* Cambridge,
    Mass.: Harvard University Press, 1990.
Canovan, Margaret. "Paternalistic Liberalism: Joseph Priestley on Rank and Inequal-
    ity." *Enlightenment and Dissent* 2 (1983): 23–37.
———. "The Un-Benthamite Utilitarianism of Joseph Priestley." *Journal of the History
    of Ideas* 45 (1984): 435–50.
Cassirer, Ernst. *The Philosophy of Enlightenment.* Translated by Fritz A. Koelln and
    James P. Pettegrove. Princeton, N.J.: Princeton University Press, 1951.
Cayton, Mary Kupiec. "Who Were the Evangelicals? Conservative and Liberal Identity
    in the Unitarian Controversy in Boston, 1804–1833." *Journal of Social History*
    31 (1997): 85–107.
Cazden, Robert E. *A Social History of the German Book Trade in America to the Civil War.*
    Columbia, SC.: Camden House, 1984.
Chable, Eugene Roberts. "A Study of the Interpretation of the New Testament in
    New England Unitarianism." Ph.D. diss., Columbia University, 1955.
Chapin, Lloyd W, Jr. "The Theology of Joseph Priestley: A Study in Eighteenth-Century
    Apologetics." Th.D. diss, Union Theological Seminary, 1967.
Chipley, Louise. "'The Best Instruction of the People': William Bentley on the
    Congregational Clergy and the Republic, 1783–1819." *Essex Institute Historical
    Collections* 127 (1991): 194–210.
———. "'Enlightened Charity': William Bentley on Poor Relief in the Early Republic,
    1783–1819." *Essex Institute Historical Collections* 128 (1992): 162–79.
———. "The Enlightenment Library of William Bentley." *Essex Institute Historical
    Collections* 122 (1986): 2–29.
———. "The Financial and Tenure Anxieties of New England's Congregational Clergy
    during the Early National Era: The Case of William Bentley, 1783–1819." *Essex
    Institute Historical Collections* 127 (1991): 277–96.
———. "William Bentley, Journalist of the Early Republic." *Essex Institute Historical
    Collections* 123 (1987): 331–47.

Clarfield, Gerald H. "Salem's Great Inoculation Controversy, 1773–1774." *Essex Institute Historical Collections* 106 (1970): 277–96.

Clarfield, Gerald H. *Timothy Pickering and American Diplomacy, 1795–1800.* Columbia: University of Missouri Press, 1969.

———. *Timothy Pickering and the American Republic.* Pittsburgh: University of Pittsburgh Press, 1980.

Clark, Christopher. *The Roots of Rural Capitalism: Western Massachusetts, 1780–1860.* Ithaca, N.Y.: Cornell University Press, 1990.

Clark, J. C. D. *English Society, 1688–1832* Cambridge: Cambridge University Press, 1985.

———. *The Language of Liberty, 1660–1832: Political Discourse and Social Dynamics in the Anglo-American World.* Cambridge: Cambridge University Press, 1994.

Combs, Jerald A. *The Jay Treaty.* Berkeley: University of California Press, 1970.

Cone, C. B. *The English Jacobins: Reformers in Late Eighteenth-Century England.* New York: Scribner's, 1968.

Conforti, Joseph A. "Samuel Hopkins and the New Divinity: Theology, Ethics, and Social Reform in Eighteenth-Century New England." *William and Mary Quarterly* 34 (1977): 572–89.

———. *Samuel Hopkins and the New Divinity Movement: Calvinism, the Congregational Ministry, and Reform in New England between the Great Awakenings.* Grand Rapids, Mich.: Eerdmans, 1981.

Conkin, Paul K. "Priestley and Jefferson: Unitarianism as a Religion for a New Revolutionary Age." In *Religion in a Revolutionary Age,* edited by Ronald Hoffman and Peter J. Albert. Charlottesville: University Press of Virginia, 1994: 290–307.

Constantin, Charles. "The Puritan Ethic and the Dignity of Labor: Hierarchy vs. Equality." *Journal of the History of Ideas* 40 (1979): 543–61.

Cook, Edward M., Jr. *The Fathers of the Towns: Leadership and Community Structure in Eighteenth-Century New England.* Baltimore: Johns Hopkins University Press, 1976.

Cooper, James F. *Tenacious of Their Liberties: The Congregationalists in Colonial Massachusetts.* New York: Oxford University Press, 1999.

Corrigan, John. *The Hidden Balance: Religion and the Social Theories of Charles Chauncy and Jonathan Mayhew.* Cambridge: Cambridge University Press, 1987.

———. *The Prism of Piety: Catholick Congregational Clergy at the Beginning of the Enlightenment.* New York: Oxford University Press, 1991.

Cott, Nancy F. *The Bonds of Womanhood: "Woman's Sphere" in New England, 1780–1835.* New Haven, Conn.: Yale University Press, 1977.

———. "Young Women in the Second Great Awakening in New England." *Feminist Studies* (1975): 15–29.

Cragg, Gerald R. *From Puritanism to the Age of Reason.* Cambridge: Cambridge University Press, 1966.

———. *Reason and Authority in the Eighteenth Century.* Cambridge: Cambridge University Press, 1964.

Crane, Elaine Forman. *Ebb Tide in New England: Women, Seaports, and Social Change, 1630–1800.* Boston: Northeastern University Press, 1998.

Crowley, John E. *"This Sheba, Self": The Conceptualization of Economic Life in Eighteenth-Century America.* Baltimore: Johns Hopkins University Press, 1974.

Cushing, John D. "Notes on Disestablishment in Massachusetts, 1780–1833." *William and Mary Quarterly* 26 (1969): 169–90.

Darnton, Robert. "In Search of the Enlightenment: Recent Attempts to Create a Social History of Ideas." *Journal of Modern History* 42 (1971): 113–32.

Davidson, Cathy. *Revolution and the Word: The Rise of the Novel in America.* New York: Oxford University Press, 1986.

Davidson, James West. *The Logic of Millennial Thought: Eighteenth-Century New England.* New Haven, Conn.: Yale University Press, 1977.

Davis, David Brion. *The Problem of Slavery in the Age of Revolution, 1770–1823.* Ithaca, N.Y.: Cornell University Press, 1975.

———. *The Problem of Slavery in Western Culture.* Ithaca, N.Y.: Cornell University Press, 1966.

Davisson, William I. "Essex County Wealth Trends: Wealth and Economic Growth in Seventeenth-Century Massachusetts." *Essex Institute Historical Collections* 103 (1967): 291–342.

D'Elia, Donald J. "Benjamin Rush: Philosopher of the American Revolution." *Transactions of the American Philosophical Society* 64 (1974).

Dickinson, H. T. *Liberty and Property: Political Ideology in Eighteenth-Century Britain.* London: Holmes and Meier, 1977.

Dickson, Charles Ellis. "Jeremiads in the New American Republic: The Case of National Fasts in the John Adams Administration." *New England Quarterly* 60 (1987): 187–207.

Diehl, Carl. *Americans and German Scholarship, 1770–1870.* New Haven, Conn.: Yale University Press, 1978.

Diggins, John P. *The Lost Soul of American Politics: Virtue, Self-Interest, and the Foundations of Liberalism.* New York: Basic Books, 1984.

Ditchfield, G. M. "Anti-Trinitarianism and Toleration in Late Eighteenth-Century British Politics: The Unitarian Petition of 1792." *Journal of Ecclesiastical History* 42 (1991): 39–67.

Doherty, Robert. *Society and Power: Five New England Towns 1800–1860.* Amherst: University of Massachusetts Press, 1977.

Douglas, Ann. *The Feminization of American Culture.* New York: Knopf, 1977.

Downey, James. *The Eighteenth-Century Pulpit: A Study of the Sermons of Butler, Berkeley, Secker, Sterne, Whitefield, and Wesley.* Oxford: Clarendon Press, 1969.

Durey, Michael. *Transatlantic Radicals and the Early American Republic.* Lawrence: University Press of Kansas, 1997.

East, Robert A. "The Massachusetts Conservatives in the Critical Period." In *The Era of the American Revolution: Studies Inscribed to Evarts Boutell Greene,* edited by Richard B. Morris. New York: Columbia University Press, 1939: 349–92.

Elkins, Stanley, and Eric McKitrick. *The Age of Federalism: The Early American Republic, 1788–1800.* New York: Oxford University Press, 1993.

Elliott, Emory. *Power and the Pulpit in Puritan New England.* Princeton, N.J.: Princeton University Press, 1975.

———. *Revolutionary Writers: Literature and Authority in the New Republic, 1725–1810.* New York: Oxford University Press, 1982.

Ellis, Richard E. *The Jeffersonian Crisis: Courts and Politics in the Young Republic.* New York: Oxford University Press, 1971.

Endy, Melvin B., Jr. "Just War, Holy War, and Millennialism in Revolutionary America." *William and Mary Quarterly* 42 (1985): 3–25.

Essig, James D. *The Bonds of Wickedness: American Evangelicals against Slavery, 1770–1808.* Philadelphia: Temple University Press, 1982.

Faler, Paul G. *Mechanics and Manufacturers in the Early Industrial Revolution: Lynn, Massachusetts, 1780–1860.* Albany: State University of New York Press, 1981.

Farber, Bernard. *Guardians of Virtue: Salem Families in 1800.* New York: Basic Books, 1972.

Farnam, Anne. "Dr. Bentley's Account Books: Documentation for the Creation of a Historical Setting." *Essex Institute Historical Collections* 116 (1980): 206–22.

———. "A Society of Societies: Associations and Voluntarism in Early Nineteenth-Century Salem." *Essex Institute Historical Collections* 113 (1977): 181–90.

Felt, Joseph B. *Annals of Salem.* 2 vols. Salem, Mass.: W. and S. B. Ives, 1845, 1849.

———. "A List of Congregational and Presbyterian ministers who have been settled in the county of Essex, Mass. from its first settlement to the year 1834." *American Quarterly Register* 7 (1834–35): 246–61.

Ferguson, David L. *Cleopatra's Barge: The Crowninshield Story.* Boston: Little, Brown, 1976.

Field, Peter S. *The Crisis of the Standing Order: Clerical Intellectuals and Cultural Authority in Massachusetts, 1780–1833.* Amherst: University of Massachusetts Press, 1998.

Fiering, Norman S. "The First American Enlightenment: Tillotson, Leverett, and Philosophical Anglicanism." *New England Quarterly* 54 (1981): 307–44.

———. *Jonathan Edwards's Moral Thought and Its British Context.* Chapel Hill: University of North Carolina Press, 1981.

———. "President Samuel Johnson and the Circle of Knowledge." *William and Mary Quarterly* 28 (1971): 199–236.

———. "The Transatlantic Republic of Letters: A Note on the Circulation of Learned Periodicals to Early Eighteenth Century America." *William and Mary Quarterly* 33 (1976): 642–60.

———. "Will and Intellect in the New England Mind." *William and Mary Quarterly* 29 (1972): 515–58.

Fischer, David H. "The Myth of the Essex Junto." *William and Mary Quarterly* 21 (1964): 191–235.

Fitzpatrick, Martin. "Heretical Religion and Radical Political Ideas in Late Eighteenth-Century England." In *The Transformation of Political Culture: England and Germany in the Late Eighteenth Century*, edited by Eckhart Hellmuth. London: Oxford University Press, 1990: 339–74.

———. "Toleration and Truth." *Enlightenment and Dissent* 1 (1982): 3–31.

Flaherty, David H. "Crime and Social Control in Provincial Massachusetts." *Historical Journal* 24 (1981): 339–60.

Fliegelman, Jay. *Declaring Independence: Jefferson, Natural Language, and the Culture of Performance*. Stanford, Calif.: Stanford University Press, 1993.

Foner, Eric. *Tom Paine and Revolutionary America*. New York: Oxford University Press, 1976.

Foote, Henry Wilder. *James Freeman and King's Chapel, 1782–87: A Chapter in the Early History of the Unitarian Movement in New England*. Boston: L. C. Bowles, 1873.

Forman, Benno M. "Salem Tradesmen and Craftsmen Circa 1762: A Contemporary Document." *Essex Institute Historical Collections* 107 (1971): 62–81.

Formisano, Ronald P. *The Transformation of Political Culture: Massachusetts Parties 1790s–1840s*. New York: Oxford University Press, 1983.

Forrer, Richard. *Theodicies in Conflict: A Dilemma in Puritan Ethics and Nineteenth-Century American Literature*. Westport, Conn.: Greenwood Press, 1986.

Fowler, William M. "The Massachusetts Election of 1785: A Triumph of Virtue." *Essex Institute Historical Collections* 111 (1975): 290–304.

French, Roderick A. "Elihu Palmer, Radical Deist, Radical Republican: A Reconsideration of American Free Thought." *Studies in Eighteenth-Century Culture* 8 (1978): 87–108.

Fruchtman, Jack, Jr. "The Apocalyptic Politics of Richard Price and Joseph Priestley: A Study in Late Eighteenth-Century English Republican Millennialism." *Transactions of the American Philosophical Society* 73 (1983).

Garrett, C. "Joseph Priestley, the Millennium, and the French Revolution." *Journal of the History of Ideas* 34 (1973): 51–66.

Gascoigne, John. "Anglican Latitudinarianism, Rational Dissent, and Political Radicalism in the Late Eighteenth Century." In *Enlightenment and Religion: Rational Dissent in Eighteenth-Century Britain*, edited by Knud Haakonssen. Cambridge: Cambridge University Press, 1996: 219–40.

Gay, Peter. *The Enlightenment: An Interpretation*. 2 vols. New York: Alfred A. Knopf, 1967, 1978.

Geffen, Elizabeth M. *Philadelphia Unitarianism, 1796–1861*. Philadelphia: University of Pennsylvania Press, 1961.

Geib, Susan. "Landscape and Faction: Spatial Transformation in William Bentley's Salem." *Essex Institute Historical Collections* 113 (1977): 163–80.

Geissler, Suzanne. *Jonathan Edwards to Aaron Burr, Jr.: From the Great Awakening to Democratic Politics*. New York: E. Mellen Press, 1981.

Gilchrist, David T., ed. *The Growth of the Seaport Cities, 1790–1825*. Charlottesville: University Press of Virginia, 1967.

Gildrie, Richard P. *Salem, 1626–1683: A Covenant Community*. Charlottesville: University Press of Virginia, 1975.

Gilmore, William J. *Reading Becomes a Necessity of Life: Material and Cultural Life in Rural New England, 1780–1835*. Knoxville: University of Tennessee Press, 1989.

Goen, C. C. *Revivalism and Separatism in New England, 1740–1800: Strict Congregationalists and Separate Baptists in the Great Awakening*. New Haven, Conn.: Yale University Press, 1962.

Goodman, Paul. *The Democratic Republicans of Massachusetts*. Cambridge, Mass.: Harvard University Press, 1964.

———. "Ethics and Enterprise: The Values of a Boston Elite, 1800–1860." *American Quarterly* 18 (1966): 437–51.

Goodwin, Albert. *The Friends of Liberty: The English Democratic Movement in the Age of the French Revolution*. Cambridge, Mass.: Harvard University Press, 1979.

Goodwin, Gerald J. "The Myth of Arminianism-Calvinism in Eighteenth-Century New England." *New England Quarterly* 41 (1968): 213–37.

Gould, Philip. "New England Witch Hunting and the Politics of Reason in the Early Republic." *New England Quarterly* 68 (1995): 58–82.

Graham, Jenny. "Revolutionary in Exile: The Emigration of Joseph Priestley to America, 1794–1804." *Transactions of the American Philosophical Society* 85 (1995).

Grasso, Christopher. *A Speaking Aristocracy: Transforming Public Discourse in Eighteenth-Century Connecticut*. Chapel Hill: University of North Carolina Press, 1999.

Greene, Evarts B., and Virginia D. Harrington. *American Population before the Federal Census of 1790*. New York: Columbia University Press, 1932.

Greven, Philip, Jr. *Four Generations: Population, Land, and Family in Colonial Andover, Massachusetts*. Ithaca, N.Y.: Cornell University Press, 1970.

———. *The Protestant Temperament: Patterns of Child-Rearing, Religious Experience, and the Self in Early America*. New York: Knopf, 1977.

Griffin, Edward M. *Old Brick: Charles Chauncy of Boston, 1705–1787*. Minneapolis: University of Minnesota Press, 1980.

Gura, Philip F. *The Wisdom of Words: Language, Theology, and Literature in the New England Renaissance*. Middletown, Conn.: Wesleyan University Press, 1981.

Haakonssen, Knud, ed. *Enlightenment and Religion: Rational Dissent in Eighteenth-Century Britain*. Cambridge: Cambridge University Press, 1996.

Habermas, Jürgen. *The Structural Transformation of the Public Sphere: An Inquiry into a Category of Bourgeois Society*. Cambridge: MIT Press, 1991.

Halévy, Elie. *The Growth of Philosophic Radicalism*. Translated by Mary Morris. Boston: Beacon Press, 1955.

Hall, David D. *Cultures of Print: Essays in the History of the Book*. Amherst: University of Massachusetts Press, 1996.

———. *The Faithful Shepherd: A History of the New England Ministry in the Seventeenth Century*. Chapel Hill: University of North Carolina Press, 1972.

———, ed. *Needs and Opportunities in the History of the Book: America, 1639–1876*. Worcester, Mass.: American Antiquarian Society, 1987.

————. *Worlds of Wonder, Days of Judgment: Popular Religious Belief in Early New England.* Cambridge, Mass.: Harvard University Press, 1989.

Hall, Peter Dobkin. "Family Structure and Economic Organization: Massachusetts Merchants, 1700–1850." In *Family and Kin in Urban Communities,* edited by Tamara K. Haraven. New York: New Viewpoints, 1977: 38–61.

Hall, Timothy D. *Contested Boundaries: Itinerancy and the Reshaping of the Colonial American Religious World.* Durham, N.C.: Duke University Press, 1994.

Hall, Van Beck. *Politics without Parties: Massachusetts, 1780–1791.* Pittsburgh: University of Pittsburgh Press, 1972.

Handlin, Oscar, and Mary Handlin. *Commonwealth: A Study of the Role of Government in the American Economy: Massachusetts 1774–1861.* New York: New York University Press, 1947.

Haraszti, Zoltán. *John Adams and the Prophets of Progress.* Cambridge, Mass.: Harvard University Press, 1952.

Haroutunian, Joseph. *Piety Versus Moralism: The Passing of the New England Theology.* New York: Henry Holt, 1932.

Hartz, Louis. *The Liberal Tradition in America: An Interpretation of American Political Thought in Revolutionary America.* New York: Harcourt, Brace, and World, 1955.

Hatch, Nathan O. *The Democratization of American Christianity.* New Haven, Conn.: Yale University Press, 1989.

————. "The Origins of Civil Millennialism in America: New England Clergymen, War with France, and the Revolution." *William and Mary Quarterly* 31 (1974): 407–30.

————. *The Sacred Cause of Liberty: Republican Thought and the Millennium in Revolutionary New England.* New Haven, Conn.: Yale University Press, 1977.

Heimert, Alan. *Religion and the American Mind from the Great Awakening to the Revolution.* Cambridge, Mass.: Harvard University Press, 1966.

Hench, John B. "The Newspaper in a Republic: Boston's *Centinel* and *Chronicle,* 1784–1801." Ph.D. diss., Clark University, 1979.

Henretta, James A. "Economic Development and Social Structure in Colonial Boston." *William and Mary Quarterly* 22 (1965): 75–92.

————. *The Origins of American Capitalism.* Boston: Northeastern University Press, 1991.

Heyrman, Christine Leigh. *Commerce and Culture: The Maritime Communities of Colonial Massachusetts 1690–1750.* New York: W. W. Norton, 1984.

————. "The Fashion among More Superior People: Charity and Social Change in Provincial New England, 1700–1740." *American Quarterly* 34 (1982): 107–24.

Hindus, Michael Stephen. *Prison and Plantation: Crime, Justice, and Authority in Massachusetts and South Carolina, 1767–1878.* Chapel Hill: University of North Carolina Press, 1980.

Hoecker, James. "Joseph Priestley and Utilitarianism in the Age of Reason." *Enlightenment and Dissent* 3 (1984): 55–64.

Hoerder, Dirk. *Mobs and People: Crowd Action in Massachusetts during the Revolution 1765–1780.* Berlin: Free University of Berlin, 1971.

Hoffman, Ronald, and Peter J. Albert, eds. *The Transforming Hand of Revolution: Reconsidering the American Revolution as a Social Movement.* Charlottesville: University Press of Virginia, 1995.

Holbrook, Clyde A. "Original Sin and the Enlightenment." In *The Heritage of Christian Thought: Essays in Honor of Robert Lowry Calhoun,* ed. Robert E. Cushman and Egil Grislis. New York: Harper and Row, 1965.

Hole, Robert. *Pulpits, Politics, and Public Order in England, 1760–1832.* Cambridge: Cambridge University Press, 1989.

Holifield, E. Brooks. *The Covenant Sealed: The Development of Puritan Sacramental Theology in Old and New England, 1570–1720.* New Haven, Conn.: Yale University Press, 1974.

———. "On Toleration in Massachusetts." *Church History* 38 (1969): 1–13.

———. *Theology in America: Christian Thought from the Age of the Puritans to the Civil War.* New Haven, Conn.: Yale University Press, 2003.

Hont, Istvan, and Michael Ignatieff, eds. *Wealth and Virtue: The Shaping of Political Economy in the Scottish Enlightenment.* Cambridge: Cambridge University Press, 1983.

Hope, V. M. *Virtue by Consensus: The Moral Philosophy of Hutcheson, Hume, and Adam Smith.* Oxford: Clarendon Press, 1989.

Horwitz, Robert H. *The Moral Foundations of the American Republic.* Charlottesville: University Press of Virginia, 1979.

Howe, Daniel Walker. "The Decline of Calvinism: An Approach to Its Study." *Comparative Studies in Society and History* 14 (1972): 306–27.

———. *Making the American Self: Jonathan Edwards to Abraham Lincoln.* Cambridge, Mass.: Harvard University Press, 1997.

———. *The Unitarian Conscience: Harvard Moral Philosophy, 1805–1861.* Cambridge, Mass: Harvard University Press, 1970.

Howe, John R. "Republican Thought and the Political Violence of the 1790s." *American Quarterly* 19 (1967): 147–65.

Jacob, Margaret C. *The Newtonians and the English Revolution, 1689–1720.* Ithaca, N.Y.: Cornell University Press, 1976.

———. *The Radical Enlightenment: Pantheists, Freemasons, and Republicans.* London: George Allen and Unwin, 1981.

Jaffee, David. "The Village Enlightenment in New England, 1760–1820." *William and Mary Quarterly* 47 (1990): 327–46.

Jedrey, Christopher. *The World of John Cleaveland: Family and Community in Eighteenth-Century New England.* New York: Norton, 1979.

Jones, Douglas Lamar. "The Strolling Poor: Transiency in Eighteenth-Century Massachusetts." *Journal of Social History* 8 (1975): 28–54.

———. *Village and Seaport: Migration and Society in Eighteenth-Century Massachusetts.* Hanover, N.H.: University Press of New England, 1981.

Jones, James W. *The Shattered Synthesis: New England Puritanism before the Great Awakening.* New Haven, Conn.: Yale University Press, 1973.

Jordan, Winthrop. *White over Black: American Attitudes toward the Negro, 1550–1812.* Chapel Hill: University of North Carolina Press, 1968.

Joyce, William L., et al., eds. *Printing and Society in Early America*. Worcester, Mass.: American Antiquarian Society, 1983.

Juster, Susan. *Disorderly Women: Sexual Politics and Evangelicalism in Revolutionary New England*. Ithaca, N.Y.: Cornell University Press, 1994.

Kantrow, Alan Mitchell. "Anglican Custom, American Consciousness." *New England Quarterly* 51 (1979): 307–25.

Kerber, Linda K. *Federalists in Dissent*. Ithaca, N.Y.: Cornell University Press, 1970.

———. *Toward an Intellectual History of Women: Essays by Linda Kerber*. Chapel Hill: University of North Carolina Press, 1997.

———. *Women of the Republic: Intellect and Ideology in Revolutionary America*. Chapel Hill: University of North Carolina Press, 1980.

Ketcham, Joyce. "The Bibliomania of the Reverend William Bentley, D.D." *Essex Institute Historical Collections* 58 (1972): 275–303.

Keyssar, Alexander. "Widowhood in Eighteenth-Century Massachusetts: A Problem in the History of the Family." *Perspectives in American History* 8 (1974): 83–119.

Kloos, John M., Jr. *A Sense of Deity: The Republican Spirituality of Dr. Benjamin Rush*. Brooklyn: Carlson Publishing, 1991.

Kloppenberg, James. "The Virtues of Liberalism: Christianity, Republicanism, and Ethics in Early American Political Discourse." *Journal of American History* 74 (1987): 9–33.

Koch, Donald Warner. "Income Distribution and Political Structure in Seventeenth-Century Salem, Massachusetts." *Essex Institute Historical Collections* 105 (1969): 50–71.

Koch, G. Adolph. *Republican Religion: The American Revolution and the Cult of Reason*. New York: Henry Holt, 1933. Reprinted as *Religion of the American Enlightenment*. New York: Crowell, 1968.

Kornblith, Gary John. "Artisan Federalism: New England Mechanics and the Political Economy of the 1790s." In *Launching the "Extended Republic": The Federalist Era*, edited by Albert Hoffman and Peter J. Albert. Charlottesville: University Press of Virginia, 1996: 249–72.

———. "The Rise of the Mechanic Interest and the Campaign to Develop Manufacturing in Salem, 1815–1830." *Essex Institute Historical Collections* 12 (1985): 44–65.

Kramnick, Isaac. *Bolingbroke and His Circle: The Politics of Nostalgia in the Age of Walpole*. Cambridge, Mass.: Harvard University Press, 1968.

———. *Republicanism and Bourgeois Radicalism: Political Ideology in Late Eighteenth-Century England and America*. Ithaca, N.Y.: Cornell University Press, 1990.

Kuehne, Dale S. *Massachusetts Congregationalist Political Thought, 1760–1790: The Design of Heaven*. Columbia: University of Missouri Press, 1996.

Kuklick, Bruce. *Churchmen and Philosophers: From Jonathan Edwards to John Dewey*. New Haven, Conn.: Yale University Press, 1985.

Kulikoff, Allan. "The Progress of Inequality in Revolutionary Boston." *William and Mary Quarterly* 28 (1971): 375–412.

La Vopa, Anthony J. "Conceiving a Public: Ideas and Society in Eighteenth-Century Europe." *Journal of Modern History* 64 (1992): 79–116.

Labaree, Benjamin. "The Making of an Empire: Boston and Essex County, 1790–1850." In *Entrepreneurs: The Boston Business Community, 1700–1850*, edited by Conrad E. Wright and Katheryn P. Viens. Boston: Massachusetts Historical Society, 1997: 343–63.

———. *Patriots and Partisans: The Merchants of Newburyport 1764–1815.* Cambridge, Mass.: Harvard University Press, 1962.

Lambert, Frank. *"Pedlar in Divinity": George Whitefield and the Transatlantic Revivals, 1737–1770.* Princeton, N.J.: Princeton University Press, 1994.

Lang, Amy Schrader. *Prophetic Woman: Anne Hutchinson and the Problem of Dissent in the Literature of New England.* Berkeley: University of California Press, 1987.

Lasser, Carol S. "A 'Pleasingly Oppressive' Burden: The Transformation of Domestic Service and Female Charity in Salem, 1800–1840." *Essex Institute Historical Collections* 116 (1980): 156–75.

Lause, Mark A. "The Unwashed Infidelity: Thomas Paine and Early New York City Labor History." *Labor History* 27 (1986): 385–409.

Lemay, J. A. Leo, ed. *Deism, Masonry, and the Enlightenment: Essays Honoring Alfred Owen Aldridge.* Newark: University of Delaware Press, 1987.

Lemisch, Jesse. "Jack Tar in the Streets: Merchant Seamen in the Politics of Revolutionary America." *William and Mary Quarterly* 25 (1968): 371–407.

Lerner, Ralph. "Commerce and Character: The Anglo-American as New-Model Man." *William and Mary Quarterly* 36 (1979): 3–26.

———. *Revolutions Revisited: Two Faces of the Politics of Enlightenment.* Chapel Hill: University of North Carolina Press, 1994.

Levy, Leonard W. *Legacy of Suppression: Freedom of Speech and Press in Early American History.* Cambridge, Mass.: Harvard University Press, 1960.

Lewis, Jan. "The Republican Wife: Virtue and Seduction in the Early Republic." *William and Mary Quarterly* 44 (1987): 689–721.

Lincoln, Anthony. *Some Political and Social Ideas of English Dissent 1763–1800.* Cambridge: Cambridge University Press, 1938.

Link, Eugene P. *Democratic-Republican Societies, 1790–1800.* New York: Columbia University Press, 1942.

Lippy, Charles H. *Seasonable Revolutionary: The Mind of Charles Chauncy.* Chicago: Nelson Hall, 1982.

———. "The 1780 Massachusetts Constitution: Religious Establishment or Civil Religion?" *Journal of Church and State* 20 (1978): 533–50.

Logue, Barbara J. "In Pursuit of Prosperity: Disease and Death in a Massachusetts Commercial Port, 1660–1850." *Journal of Social History* 25 (1991): 309–43.

Love, William Deloss. *The Fast and Thanksgiving Days of New England.* Boston: Houghton Mifflin, 1895.

Lovejoy, David S. "'Desperate Enthusiasm': Early Signs of American Radicalism." In *The Origins of Anglo-American Radicalism*, edited by Margaret C. Jacob and James

R. Jacob. 1984; repr. Atlantic Highlands, N.J.: Humanities Press International, 1991: 214–25.

———. "Samuel Hopkins: Religion, Slavery, and the Revolution." *New England Quarterly* 40 (1967): 227–43.

Lowrance, Mason I., Jr. *The Language of Canaan: Metaphor and Symbol in New England from the Puritans to the Transcendentalists.* Cambridge, Mass.: Harvard University Press, 1980.

Lundberg, David, and Henry F. May. "The Enlightened Reader in America." *American Quarterly* 28 (1976): 262–93.

Lynd, Staughton. *The Intellectual Origins of American Radicalism.* New York: Pantheon Books, 1968.

Maas, David Edward. *The Return of the Massachusetts Loyalists.* New York: Garland Press, 1989.

Maier, Pauline. "Reason and Revolution: The Radicalism of Dr. Thomas Young." *American Quarterly* 28 (1976): 229–49.

Main, Gloria L. "Gender, Work, and Wages in Colonial New England." *William and Mary Quarterly* 51 (1994): 39–66.

———. "Inequality in Early America: The Evidence from Probate Records of Massachusetts and Maryland." *Journal of Interdisciplinary History* 7 (1977): 559–81.

———. "Widows in Rural Massachusetts on the Eve of the Revolution." In *Women in the Age of the American Revolution,* edited by Ronald Hoffman and Peter J. Albert. Charlottesville: University Press of Virginia, 1989: 67–90.

Main, Jackson Turner. *The Social Structure of Revolutionary America.* Princeton, N.J.: Princeton University Press, 1965.

Malmsheimer, Lonna M. "New England Funeral Sermons and Changing Attitudes toward Women, 1672–1792." Ph.D. diss., University of Minnesota, 1972.

Marini, Stephen A. *Radical Sects in Revolutionary New England.* Cambridge, Mass.: Harvard University Press, 1982.

Marty, Martin E. *Religion, Awakenings, and Revolution.* Wilmington, N.C.: Consortium Press, 1977.

Masson, Margaret W. "The Typology of the Female as a Model for the Regenerate: Puritan Preaching, 1690–1730." *Signs* 2 (1976): 304–15.

Matthews, Richard K. *Virtue, Corruption, and Self-Interest: Political Values in the Eighteenth Century.* Bethlehem, Pa.: Lehigh University Press, 1994.

May, Henry F. *The Enlightenment in America.* New York: Oxford University Press, 1976.

McCalman, Iain. "New Jerusalems: Prophecy, Dissent, and Radical Culture in England, 1786–1830." In *Enlightenment and Religion: Rational Dissent in Eighteenth-Century Britain,* edited by Knud Haakonssen. Cambridge: Cambridge University Press, 1996: 312–35.

McCoy, Drew R. *The Elusive Republic: Political Economy in Jeffersonian America.* Chapel Hill: University of North Carolina Press, 1980.

McKey, Richard Haskayne, Jr. "Elias Hasket Derby, Merchant of Salem, Massachusetts, 1739–1799." Ph.D. diss., Clark University, 1961.

McLachlan, H. J. *Socinianism in Seventeenth-Century England.* Oxford: Oxford University Press, 1951.

McLoughlin, William G. *New England Dissent, 1630–1883: The Baptists and the Separation of Church and State.* 2 vols. Cambridge, Mass.: Harvard University Press, 1971.

———. *Revivals, Awakenings, and Reform: An Essay on Religion and Social Change in America, 1607–1977.* Chicago: University of Chicago Press, 1978.

———. *Soul Liberty: The Baptists' Struggle in New England, 1630–1833.* Hanover, N.H.: University Press of New England, 1991.

Mead, Sidney E. "Denominationalism: The Shape of Protestantism in America." *Church History* 23 (1954): 291–320.

———. "The Rise of the Evangelical Conception of the Ministry in America, 1607–1850." In *The Ministry in Historical Perspectives,* edited by H. Richard Niebuhr and Daniel Williams. New York: Harper, 1956: 207–49.

Melish, Joanne Pope. *Disowning Slavery: Gradual Emancipation and "Race" in New England, 1780–1960.* Ithaca, N.Y.: Cornell University Press, 1998.

Meyer, Donald. "The Dissolution of Calvinism." In *Paths of American Thought,* edited by Arthur M. Schlesinger and Morton White. Boston: Houghton Mifflin, 1963: 71–85.

Meyer, Donald H. *The Instructed Conscience: The Shaping of the American National Ethic.* Philadelphia: University of Pennsylvania Press, 1972.

———. *The Democratic Enlightenment.* New York: Putnam's, 1976.

Meyer, Jacob C. *Church and State in Massachusetts from 1740 to 1833: A Chapter in the History of the Development of Individual Freedom.* Cleveland, Ohio: Western Reserve University Press, 1930.

Middlekauff, Robert. "Piety and Intellect in Puritanism." *William and Mary Quarterly* 22 (1965): 457–70.

Miller, Perry. "From the Covenant to the Revival." In *Religion in American Life,* Vol. 1: *The Shaping of American Religion,* edited by James Ward Smith and A. Leland Jamison. Princeton, N.J.: Princeton University Press, 1961: 322–68.

———. *The Life of the Mind in America: From the Revolution to the Civil War.* New York: Harcourt, Brace, and World, 1965.

———. *The New England Mind: From Colony to Province.* Cambridge, Mass.: Harvard University Press, 1953.

Morais, Herbert M. *Deism in Eighteenth-Century America.* New York: Columbia University Press, 1934.

Morgan, Edmund S. "The American Revolution Considered as an Intellectual Movement." In *Paths of American Thought,* edited by Morton White and Arthur M. Schlesinger Jr. Boston: Houghton Mifflin, 1963: 11–33.

———. *The Gentle Puritan: A Life of Ezra Stiles, 1727–1795.* New Haven, Conn.: Yale University Press, 1962.

———. "The Puritan Ethic and the American Revolution." *William and Mary Quarterly* 24 (1967): 3–43.

Morison, Samuel Eliot. *The Maritime History of Massachusetts, 1783–1860.* Boston: Houghton Mifflin, 1921.

————. *Three Centuries of Harvard, 1636–1936.* Cambridge, Mass.: Harvard University Press, 1936.

Morris, Richard Joseph. "Revolutionary Salem: Stratification and Mobility in a Massachusetts Seaport, 1759–1799." Ph.D. diss., New York University, 1975.

————. "Urban Population Migration in Revolutionary America: The Case of Salem, Massachusetts, 1759–1799." *Journal of Urban History* 9 (1982): 3–30.

————. "Wealth Distribution in Salem, Massachusetts, 1759–1799: The Impact of Revolution and Independence." *Essex Institute Historical Collections* 114 (1978): 87–102.

Morse, Anson E. *The Federalist Party in Massachusetts to the Year 1800.* Princeton, N.J.: Princeton University Press, 1909.

Moss, Richard J. *The Life of Jedidiah Morse: A Station of Peculiar Exposure.* Knoxville: University of Tennessee Press, 1995.

————. "Republicanism, Liberalism, and Identity: The Case of Jedidiah Morse." *Essex Institute Historical Collections* 126 (1990): 209–36.

Murdock, Kenneth. *Literature and Theology in Colonial New England.* Cambridge, Mass.: Harvard University Press, 1949.

Murphy, Susan. "In Remembrance of Me: Sacramental Theology and Practice of Colonial New England." Ph.D. diss., University of Washington, 1978.

Nash, Gary B. "The American Clergy and the French Revolution." *William and Mary Quarterly* 22 (1965): 392–412.

————. "Artisans and Politics in Eighteenth-Century Philadelphia." In *The Origins of Anglo-American Radicalism*, edited by Margaret C. Jacob and James R. Jacob. 1984; repr. Atlantic Highlands, N.J.: Humanities Press International, 1991: 258–78.

————. *The Urban Crucible: Social Change, Political Consciousness, and the Origins of the American Revolution.* Cambridge, Mass.: Harvard University Press, 1979.

————. "Urban Wealth and Poverty in Pre-Revolutionary America." *Journal of Interdisciplinary History* 6 (1976): 545–84.

Newlin, Claude M. *Philosophy and Religion in Colonial America.* New York, 1962; repr. Westport, Conn.: Greenwood Press, 1968.

Niebuhr, H. Richard. *The Social Sources of Denominationalism.* New York: Henry Holt, 1929.

Noll, Mark A. *America's God: From Jonathan Edwards to Abraham Lincoln.* New York: Oxford University Press, 2002.

Norton, Mary Beth. *Liberty's Daughters: The Revolutionary Experience of American Women, 1750–1800.* Boston: Little, Brown, 1980.

Norton, Susan L. "Marital Migration in Essex County, Massachusetts, in the Colonial and Early Federal Periods." *Journal of Marriage and the Family* 35 (1973): 406–18.

Pasley, Jeffrey L. *"The Tyranny of Printers": Newspaper Politics in the Early American Republic.* Charlottesville: University Press of Virginia, 2001.

Patterson, Stephen. *Political Parties in Revolutionary Massachusetts.* Madison: University of Wisconsin Press, 1973.

Peters, Ronald M. *The Massachusetts Constitution of 1780: A Social Compact*. Amherst: University of Massachusetts Press, 1978.

Phillips, James Duncan. *Salem in the Eighteenth Century*. New York: Houghton Mifflin, 1937.

——. *Salem and the Indies: The Story of the Great Commercial Era of the City*. Boston: Houghton Mifflin, 1947.

Phillips, Joseph W. *Jedidiah Morse and New England Congregationalism*. New Brunswick, N.J.: Rutgers University Press, 1983.

Philp, Mark. "Rational Religion and Political Radicalism in the 1790s." *Enlightenment and Dissent* 5 (1986): 35–44.

Piersen, William D. *Black Yankees: The Development of an Afro-American Subculture in Eighteenth-Century New England*. Amherst: University of Massachusetts Press, 1988.

Pocock, J. G. A. "Virtue and Commerce in the Eighteenth Century." *Journal of Interdisciplinary History* 3 (1972): 119–34.

——. *Virtue, Commerce, and History: Essays on Political Thought and History, Chiefly in the Eighteenth Century*. New York: Cambridge University Press, 1985.

Pole, J. R. "Enlightenment and the Politics of American Nature." In *Enlightenment in National Contexts*, edited by Roy Porter and Mikulas Teich. Cambridge: Cambridge University Press, 1981: 192–214.

Pope, Robert G. *The Half-Way Covenant: Church Membership in Puritan New England*. Princeton, N.J.: Princeton University Press, 1969.

Price, Jacob M. "Economic Function and the Growth of American Port Towns in the Eighteenth Century." *Perspectives in American History* 8 (1974): 121–86.

Prochaska, Franklyn K. "Thomas Paine's *The Age of Reason* Revisited." *Journal of the History of Ideas* 33 (1972): 561–76.

Rediker, Marcus. *Between the Devil and the Deep Blue Sea: Merchant Seamen, Pirates, and the Anglo-American Maritime World, 1700–1750*. Cambridge: Cambridge University Press, 1987.

Redwood, John. *Reason, Ridicule, and Religion: The Age of Enlightenment in England, 1660–1750*. Cambridge, Mass.: Harvard University Press, 1976.

Reedy, Gerard. *The Bible and Reason: Anglicans and Scripture in Late Seventeenth-Century England*. Philadelphia: University of Pennsylvania Press, 1985.

Reinoehl, John H. "The Impact of the French Revolution and Napoleon upon the United States as Revealed by the Fortunes of the Crowninshield Family of Salem." Ph.D. diss., Michigan State University, 1953.

Robertson, John. "The Scottish Enlightenment at the Limits of the Civic Tradition." In *Wealth and Virtue: The Shaping of Political Economy in the Scottish Enlightenment*, edited by Istvan Hont and Michael Ignatieff. Cambridge: Cambridge University Press, 1983: 137–78.

Robbins, Caroline. *The Eighteenth-Century Commonwealth Man: Studies in the Transmission, Development, and Circumstance of English Liberal Thought from the Restoration of Charles II until the War with the Thirteen Colonies*. Cambridge, Mass.: Harvard University Press, 1959.

————. "Honest Heretic: Joseph Priestley in America, 1794–1804." *Proceedings of the American Philosophical Society* 106 (1962).

Robbins, James H. "The Impact of the First American Party System on Salem Politics." *Essex Institute Historical Collections* 107 (1971): 254–67.

Robinson, David. *The Unitarians and the Universalists.* Westport, Conn.: Greenwood Press, 1985.

Rock, Howard B. *Artisans of the New Republic: The Tradesmen of New York City in the Age of Jefferson.* New York: New York University Press, 1984.

Rose, Anne C. "Social Sources of Denominationalism Reconsidered: Post-Revolutionary Boston as a Case Study." *American Quarterly* 38 (1986): 243–64.

Roth, Randolph A. *The Democratic Dilemma: Religion, Reform, and the Social Order in the Connecticut River Valley of Vermont, 1791–1850.* Cambridge: Cambridge University Press, 1987.

Saillant, John. "Slavery and Divine Providence in New England Calvinism: The New Divinity and a Black Protest, 1775–1805." *New England Quarterly* 68 (1995): 584–608.

Sandoz, Ellis. *A Government of Laws: Political Theory, Religion, and the American Founding.* Baton Rouge: Louisiana State University Press, 1990.

Sanford, Charles B. *The Religious Life of Thomas Jefferson.* Charlottesville: University Press of Virginia, 1984.

————. *Thomas Jefferson and His Library: A Study of His Literary Interests and of the Religious Attitudes Revealed by Relevant Titles in His Library.* Hamden, Conn.: Archon Books, 1977.

Sassi, Jonathan D. *A Republic of Righteousness: The Public Christianity of the Post-Revolutionary New England Clergy.* New York: Oxford University Press, 2001.

Saunders, Alan. "The State as Highwayman: From Candour to Rights." In *Enlightenment and Religion: Rational Dissent in Eighteenth-Century Britain,* edited by Knud Haakonssen. Cambridge: Cambridge University Press, 1996: 241–71.

Schechner, Sara J. "John Prince and Early American Scientific Instrument Making." *Colonial Society of Massachusetts Publications* 59 (1982): 431–503.

Schlesinger, Arthur M. *The Colonial Merchants and the American Revolution, 1763–1776.* New York: Atheneum, 1919.

Schmotter, James W. "Ministerial Careers in Eighteenth-Century New England: The Social Context, 1700–1760." *Journal of Social History* 9 (1975): 249–67.

Schofield, Robert E. *The Enlightened Joseph Priestley: A Study of His Life and Work from 1773 to 1804.* University Park: Pennsylvania State University Press, 2004.

————. *The Enlightenment of Joseph Priestley: A Study of His Life and Work from 1733 to 1773.* University Park: Pennsylvania State University Press, 1997.

Schultz, Ronald. *The Republic of Labor: Philadelphia Artisans and the Politics of Class, 1720–1830.* New York: Oxford University Press, 1993.

Scott, Donald M. *From Office to Profession: The New England Ministry, 1750–1850.* Philadelphia: University of Pennsylvania Press, 1978.

Seed, John. "Gentlemen Dissenters: The Social and Political Meaning of Rational Dissent in 1770s and 1780s." *Historical Journal* 28 (1985): 299–325.

———. "'A set of men powerful enough in many things': Rational Dissent and Political Opposition in England, 1770–1790." In *Enlightenment and Religion: Rational Dissent in Eighteenth-Century Britain,* edited by Knud Haakonssen. Cambridge: Cambridge University Press, 1996: 140–68.

Sell, Alan P. F. *John Locke and the Eighteenth-Century Divines.* Cardiff: University of Wales Press, 1997.

Shalhope, Robert E. "Republicanism, Liberalism, and Democracy: Political Culture in the Early Republic." *Proceedings of the American Antiquarian Society* 102 (1992): 99–152.

Shapiro, Darlene. "Ethan Allen: Philosopher-Theologian to a Generation of American Revolutionaries." *William and Mary Quarterly* 21 (1964): 236–55.

Sharp, James Roger. *American Politics in the Early Republic: The New Nation in Crisis.* New Haven, Conn.: Yale University Press, 1993.

Shea, Daniel B., Jr. *Spiritual Autobiography in Early America.* Princeton, N.J.: Princeton University Press, 1968.

Shepherd, James F., and Gary M. Walton. "Economic Change after the American Revolution: Pre- and Post-War Comparisons of Maritime Shipping and Trade." *Explorations in Economic History* 13 (1976): 397–422.

Shiels, Richard D. "The Feminization and Americanization of American Congregationalism, 1730–1835." *American Quarterly* 33 (1981): 46–62.

Shipton, Clifford K., and John Langdon Sibley. *Sibley's Harvard Graduates: Biographical Sketches of those who attended Harvard College.* 14 vols. Boston: Massachusetts Historical Society, 1873–1968.

Simpson, Lewis P. *The Federalist Literary Mind: Selections from the "Monthly Anthology and Boston Review," 1803–1811.* Baton Rouge: Louisiana State University Press, 1962.

Smelser, Marshall. "The Federalist Period as an Age of Passion." *American Quarterly* 10 (1958): 391–419.

Smith, Billy G. *"The Lower Sort": Philadelphia's Laboring People, 1750–1800.* Ithaca, N.Y.: Cornell University Press, 1990.

Smith, H. Shelton. *Changing Conceptions of Original Sin.* New York: Scribner's, 1955.

Smith, James Morton. *Freedom's Fetters: The Alien and Sedition Laws and American Civil Liberties.* Ithaca, N.Y.: Cornell University Press, 1956.

Smith, Jeffery A. *Franklin and Bache: Envisioning the Enlightened Republic.* New York: Oxford University Press, 1990.

Smith, Philip Chadwick Foster. "William Bentley on Trade and the Marine Artificers." *Essex Institute Historical Collections* 113 (1977): 204–15.

Smith, Timothy L. "Congregation, State, and Denomination: The Forming of an American Religious Structure." *William and Mary Quarterly* 25 (1968): 155–76.

Smylie, James H. "Clerical Perspectives on Deism: Paine's *The Age of Reason* in Virginia." *Eighteenth-Century Studies* 6 (1972–73): 203–20.

Snyder, Alan K. "Foundations of Liberty: The Christian Republicanism of Timothy Dwight and Jedidiah Morse." *New England Quarterly* 56 (1983): 382–97.

Spalding, Samuel Jones. "The History of the Essex North Association, with Sketches of Its Members." *Congregational Quarterly* 6 (1864): 161–75.

Spellman, W. M. *John Locke and the Problem of Depravity*. Oxford: Clarendon Press, 1988.

Sprague, William B., ed. *Annals of the American Pulpit: Commemorative Notices of Distinguished American Clergy of Various Denominations*. 9 vols. New York: Robert Carter and Bros., 1857–1869.

Stauffer, Vernon. *New England and the Bavarian Illuminati*. New York: Columbia University Press, 1918.

Steffen, Charles G. *The Mechanics of Baltimore: Workers and Politics in the Age of Revolution, 1763–1812*. Urbana: University of Illinois Press, 1984.

Steiner, Bruce E. "New England Anglicanism: A Genteel Faith?" *William and Mary Quarterly* 27 (1970): 122–35.

Stephen, Leslie. *English Thought in the Eighteenth Century*. New York: Harcourt, Brace, and World, 1962.

Stewart, Donald H. *The Opposition Press of the Federalist Period*. Albany, N.Y.: State University Press, 1969.

Stewart, Robert C. "Reading Dr. Bentley: A Literary Approach to a Historical Diary." *Essex Institute Historical Collections* 113 (1977): 147–62.

Stout, Harry S. *The Divine Dramatist: George Whitefield and the Rise of Modern Evangelicalism*. Grand Rapids, Mich.: William B. Eerdmans, 1991.

———. *The New England Soul: Preaching and Religious Culture in Colonial New England*. New York: Oxford University Press, 1986.

———. "Religion, Communications, and the Ideological Origins of the American Revolution." *William and Mary Quarterly* 34 (1977): 519–41.

Stout, Harry S., and D. G. Hart, eds. *New Directions in American Religious History*. New York: Oxford University Press, 1997.

Stromberg, Roland N. *Religious Liberalism in Eighteenth-Century England*. New York: Oxford University Press, 1954.

Sullivan, Robert E. *John Toland and the Deist Controversy: A Study in Adaptations*. Cambridge, Mass.: Harvard University Press, 1982.

Sweet, Leonard I., ed. *Communication and Change in American Religious History*. Grand Rapids, Mich.: Eerdman's, 1993.

Syrett, David. "Town Meeting Politics in Massachusetts, 1776–1786." *William and Mary Quarterly* 21 (1964): 352–66.

Szatmary, David P. *Shay's Rebellion: The Making of an Agrarian Insurrection*. Amherst: University of Massachusetts Press, 1980.

Tapley, Harriet Silvester. *Salem Imprints, 1768–1825: A History of the First Fifty Years of Printing in Salem, Massachusetts*. Salem, Mass.: Essex Institute, 1927.

———. "St. Peter's Church in Salem before the Revolution." *Essex Institute Historical Collections* 80 (1944): 229–60, 334–67; 81 (1945): 66–82.

Tapper, Alan. "Priestley on Politics, Progress, and Moral Theology." In *Enlightenment and Religion: Rational Dissent in Eighteenth-Century Britain*, edited by Knud Haakonssen. Cambridge: Cambridge University Press, 1996: 272–86.

Thompson, E. P. "The Moral Economy of the English Crowd in the Eighteenth Century." *Past and Present* 50 (1971): 76–136.

Toulouse, Teresa. *The Art of Prophesying: New England Sermons and the Shaping of Belief.* Athens: University of Georgia Press, 1987.

Triber, Jayne E. *A True Republican: The Life of Paul Revere.* Amherst: University of Massachusetts Press, 1998.

Turner, James. *Without God, Without Creed: The Origins of Unbelief in America.* Baltimore: Johns Hopkins University Press, 1985.

Tuveson, Ernest Lee. *Redeemer Nation: The Idea of America's Millennial Role.* Chicago: University of Chicago Press, 1968.

Twomey, Richard J. "Jacobins and Jeffersonians: Anglo-American Radical Ideology, 1790–1810." In *The Origins of Anglo-American Radicalism*, edited by Margaret C. Jacob and James R. Jacob. 1984; repr. Atlantic Highlands, N.J.: Humanities Press International, 1991: 313–28.

———. *Jacobins and Jeffersonians: Anglo-American Radicalism in the United States, 1790–1820.* New York: Garland Publishers, 1989.

Tyler, John W. *Smugglers and Patriots: Boston Merchants and the Advent of the American Revolution.* Boston: Northeastern University Press, 1986.

Ulrich, Laurel Thatcher. "'Daughters of Liberty': Religious Women in Revolutionary New England" In *Women in the Age of the American Revolution*, edited by Albert Hoffman and Peter J. Albert. Charlottesville: University Press of Virginia, 1989: 211–43.

———. *Good Wives: Image and Reality in the Lives of Women in Northern New England, 1650–1750.* New York: Knopf, 1980.

———. "Vertuous Women Found: New England Ministerial Literature, 1668–1735." *American Quarterly* 28 (1976): 20–40.

Valeri, Mark. *Law and Providence in Joseph Bellamy's New England: The Origins of the New Divinity in Revolutionary America.* New York: Oxford University Press, 1994.

Van de Wetering, Maxine. "Moralizing in Puritan Natural Science: Mysteriousness in Earthquake Sermons." *Journal of the History of Ideas* 43 (1982): 417–38.

Vickers, Daniel. *Farmers and Fishermen: Two Centuries of Work in Essex County, Massachusetts, 1630–1850.* Chapel Hill: University of North Carolina Press, 1994.

———. "An Honest Tar: Ashley Bowen of Marblehead." *New England Quarterly* 69 (1996): 531–53.

Viner, Jacob. *The Role of Providence in the Social Order: An Essay in Intellectual History.* Princeton, N.J.: Princeton University Press, 1972.

Vinovskis, Maris A. "Mortality Rates and Trends in Massachusetts before 1860." *Journal of Economic History* 32 (1972): 184–213.

Wade, Herbert T. "The Essex Regiment in Shays' Rebellion–1787." *Essex Institute Historical Collections* 90 (1954): 317–49.

Walker, D. P. *The Decline of Hell: Seventeenth-Century Discussions of Eternal Torment.* Chicago: University of Chicago Press, 1964.

Walters, Kerry S., ed. *The American Deists: Voices of Reason and Dissent in the Early Republic.* Lawrence: University Press of Kansas, 1992.

———. *Rational Infidels: The American Deists.* Wolfeboro, N.H.: Longwood, 1992.

Walzer, Michael. "Puritanism as a Revolutionary Ideology." *History and Theory* 3 (1964): 59–90.

———. *The Revolution of the Saints: A Study in the Origins of Radical Politics.* Cambridge, Mass.: Harvard University Press, 1965.

Warden, G. B. "Inequality and Instability in Eighteenth-Century Boston: A Reappraisal." *Journal of Interdisciplinary History* 6 (1976): 585–620.

Warner, Michael. *Letters of the Republic: Publication and the Public Sphere in Eighteenth-Century America.* Cambridge, Mass.: Harvard University Press, 1990.

Waterman, A. M. C. "The Nexus between Theology and Political Doctrine in Church and Dissent." In *Enlightenment and Religion: Rational Dissent in Eighteenth-Century Britain*, edited by Knud Haakonssen. Cambridge: Cambridge University Press, 1996: 193–218.

———. *Revolution, Economics, and Religion: Christian Political Economy, 1798–1833.* Cambridge: Cambridge University Press, 1991.

Watts, Steven. *The Republic Reborn: War and the Making of Liberal America, 1790–1820.* Baltimore: Johns Hopkins University Press, 1987.

Webb, R. K. "Rational Piety." In *Enlightenment and Religion: Rational Dissent in Eighteenth-Century Britain*, edited by Knud Haakonssen. Cambridge: Cambridge University Press, 1996: 287–311.

Weber, Donald. *Rhetoric and History in Revolutionary New England.* New York: Oxford University Press, 1988.

Welter, Barbara. "The Feminization of American Religion: 1800–1860." In *Clio's Consciousness Raised: New Perspectives on the History of Women*, edited by Mary S. Hartman and Lois Banner. New York: Harper and Row, 1974: 137–57.

West, John G., Jr. *The Politics of Revelation and Reason: Religion and Civic Life in the New Nation.* Lawrence: University Press of Kansas, 1996.

Wheeler, William Bruce. "Urban Politics in Nature's Republic: The Development of Political Parties in the Seaport Cities in the Federalist Era." Ph.D. diss., University of Virginia, 1967.

White, Morton. *The Philosophy of the American Revolution.* New York: Oxford University Press, 1978.

Whitlock, Marta Nevampaa. "Voluntary Associations in Salem, Massachusetts, before 1800." Ph.D. diss., Ohio State University, 1972.

Whitney, William T., Jr. "The Crowninshields of Salem, 1800–1808: A Study in the Politics of Commercial Growth." *Essex Institute Historical Collections* 44 (1958): 1–36, 79–118.

Wilbur, Earl Morse. *A History of Unitarianism: Socinianism and Its Antecedents.* Cambridge, Mass.: Harvard University Press, 1945.

———. *A History of Unitarianism in Transylvania, England, and America.* Cambridge, Mass: Harvard University Press, 1952.

Wilentz, Sean. *Chants Democratic: New York City and the Rise of the American Working Class, 1788–1850.* New York: Oxford University Press, 1984.

Wiley, Basil. *The Eighteenth-Century Background: Studies on the Idea of Nature in the Thought of the Period*. London: Chatto and Windus, 1940.

Wilson, David A. *Paine and Cobbett: The Transatlantic Connection*. Kingston, Ontario: McGill-Queen's University Press, 1988.

———. *United Irishmen, United States: Immigrant Radicals in the Early Republic*. Ithaca, N.Y.: Cornell University Press, 1998.

Wilson, Douglas L., ed. *Jefferson's Literary Commonplace Book*. Princeton, N.J.: Princeton University Press, 1989.

Wilson, Robert J. *The Benevolent Deity: Ebenezer Gay and the Rise of Rational Religion in New England, 1696–1787*. Philadelphia: University of Pennsylvania Press, 1984.

Wintersteen, Prescott B. *Christology in American Unitarianism: An Anthology of Nineteenth and Twentieth Century Unitarian Theologians*. Boston: Unitarian Universalist Christian Fellowship, 1977.

Wolford, Thorp L. "Democratic-Republican Reaction in Massachusetts to the Embargo of 1807." *New England Quarterly* 15 (1942): 36–61.

Wood, Gordon S. *The Creation of the American Republic*. Chapel Hill: University of North Carolina Press, 1969.

Wright, Conrad. *The Beginnings of Unitarianism in America*. 1955; repr. New York: Archon, 1976.

———. *The Liberal Christians: Essays on American Unitarian History*. Boston: Beacon Press, 1970.

Wright, Conrad Edick, ed. *American Unitarianism, 1805–1865*. Boston: Massachusetts Historical Society and Northeastern University Press, 1989.

———. *The Transformation of Charity in Postrevolutionary New England*. Boston: Northeastern University Press, 1992.

Young, Alfred F., ed. *The American Revolution: Explorations in the History of American Radicalism*. DeKalb: Northern Illinois University Press, 1976.

———. *The Democratic Republicans of New York: The Origins, 1763–1797*. Chapel Hill: University of North Carolina Press, 1967.

Young, B. W. *Religion and Enlightenment in Eighteenth-Century England: Theological Debate from Locke to Burke*. Oxford: Clarendon Press, 1998.

Young, Christine Alice. *From "Good Order" to Glorious Revolution: Salem, Massachusetts, 1628–1689*. Ann Arbor: UMI Research Press, 1980.

Youngs, J. William T., Jr. *God's Messengers: Religious Leadership in Colonial New England, 1700–1750*. Baltimore: Johns Hopkins University Press, 1976.

Ziff, Larzer. *Writing in the New Nation: Prose, Print, and Politics in the Early United States*. New Haven, Conn.: Yale University Press, 1991.

Zuckerman, Michael. *Peaceable Kingdoms: New England Towns in the Eighteenth Century*. New York: Knopf, 1970.

———. "The Social Context of Democracy in Massachusetts." *William and Mary Quarterly* 25 (1968): 523–44.

Zvesper, John. *Political Philosophy and Rhetoric: A Study of the Origins of American Party Politics*. Cambridge: Cambridge University Press, 1977.

Index

Abraham and Isaac, story of, 70,
    175–176
Adams, Abigail, 93
Adams, John, 11, 115, 138–139,
    144–146, 193
Adams, Samuel, 135, 137–138
African-Americans
    Bentley on, 55–56, 129–130
    and evangelicalism, 166
    See also slavery
alien and sedition laws, 128–130,
    147
Allegheny College, 184
Allen, Ethan, 100, 120
Allen, Thomas, 159
American Antiquarian Society, 184
American Revolution, 16–17, 75
    Bentley during, 23
    privateering in, 41–42
    providence in, 75
    and women, 49–50
    and slavery, 52
Anabaptists, 79
angels, 174
Anglicans, 79
Arianism, 64–65, 92, 122, 124–125,
    184

Arminianism, 4, 33–36, 42–44,
    61–65
    and classical liberalism, 45–60
    and the Fall, 114–115
    and Methodism, 198 n. 6
    and the poor, 56–59
    and slavery, 51–52
    and wealth, 58–59
Arminius, Jacobus, 4
Athanasian Creed, 63–64

baptism, 36–37, 41, 73, 83–86, 201
Baptists, 79–81, 89, 165–167, 185
Barnard, Thomas Jr., 12, 86–87,
    172, 182
    at Bentley's ordination, 31
    on the Fall, 114–115
    on Paine, 121–122
    ordination, 26, 46
    salary, 113, 140
    and Socinianism, 93, 101
    toryism of, 157
    on Wollstonecraft, 126–127
Barnard, Thomas Sr., 12, 59, 64,
    69, 157
Belknap, Jeremy, 93, 99, 124–125,
    172, 182

Belsham, Thomas, 126
Bentley, Joshua, 20–24, 101, 187
Bentley, William
  on African-Americans and slavery,
    53–56, 130
  call to the East Church, 31–44
  childhood, 20–22, 196 n. 11
  on Christology, 65–67, 94–104
  classical liberalism of, 48–60
  death and burial, 187
  as Democratic-Republican, 142–143,
    147–150, 162–163
  emotional life, 170–173
  on freedom of print, 127–128
  at Harvard, 22–25, 197 n. 15
  library of, 183–184, 186
  and news summaries, 126, 142
  on Paine, 120–122
  on poverty, 56–59, 112–113
  print exchanges, 95–204
  on the sacraments, 72–73,
    83–87
  salary, 113
  sermon style of, 102–103
  social marginalization of, 113
  on toleration and dissent,
    80–89
  on women, 49–50, 130
  See also Christian naturalism
Bereans, 99, 128
Bolles, Lucius, 165, 167–168, 185
Bowditch, Nathaniel, 148
Bowdoin, James, 137
Bradford, Ebenezer, 156
Branch Church, 156, 185
Briant, Lemuel, 67
Brown, Moses, 55
Buckminster, Joseph, 182
Burke, Edmund, 89, 102, 119, 147

Cabot, George, 144
Calvinism, 32–36, 42–44, 65
Carlton, William, 142, 151, 162
Catholicism, 81–82
Channing, William, 8, 182, 184
Charles I, 109

Chauncy, Charles
  Arianism of, 67
  on conversions, 73
  on the Fall, 114
  on poverty, 57
  Seasonable Thoughts, 14
  on theodicy, 176
  on women, 49–50
  universalism of, 81, 98–99
  writings, 96
Christian naturalism
  defined, 4
  theology of, 67–77, 87–88
  reasons for failure, 163–179
  See also Bentley, William
Clarke, Samuel, 97
classical liberalism. See liberalism,
    classical
Cleaveland, John, 32, 80–81, 167,
    169
Cleveland, Stephen, 54–55
Communion, 36–37, 72–73, 164, 175
Cooper, Samuel, 31, 51, 93, 182
covenant, 169–170
Crowninshield
  George, 40, 143–144
  Hannah, 172–173
  Jacob, 144–156, 160, 162–163,
    185–186
  and Sons, 143–144
Cumings, Henry, 75
Curwen, Samuel, 136
Cushing, Thomas, 126, 137, 142

Dabney, John, 100
deism, 68–69, 71, 96, 100–101,
    120–125
Deluge, the, 70, 173–175
Democratic-Republican Party,
    141–152
Derby, Elias Hasket, 137
Derby, John, 10
Derby, Richard Jr., 134–136, 177,
    193, n. 18
Descartes, 69
Dickinson College, 93

Diman, James, 52, 61
  baptism numbers, 86
  and Bentley, 31–44
  problems at East Church, 26–27
  sermon style, 103
disestablishment. *See* dissent
Disney, John, 92, 98
dissent, 79–84
Dudleian Lectures, 69
Dunbar, Asa, 12, 17, 26, 157
Dwight, Timothy, 61, 178

East Church
  demographics, 38–41, 164, 195,
    200, n. 28
  ecclesiastical rules, 39–40
  history, 26, 230 n. 21
  patriotism, 158–159
  physical structure, 3
  wealth, 47
Ebeling, Christoph, 127
Edwards, Jonathan, 15, 61, 156
Edwards, Jonathan Jr., 178
Eliot, John, 67, 93, 97–99, 182
Embargo of 1807, 185
Emerson, William, 182
Emlyn, Thomas, 67, 101, 125
Essex Junto, 136, 146
Essex Result, 136
Evangelicalism
  and republicanism, 155–160
  and African-Americans and slavery,
    51, 166
  success of, 185
  theology of, 12–13
  and women, 50, 166–167
  See also Tabernacle; South Church
Everett, Edward, 187

Federalism, 122, 137–138, 141–142,
  147–149
Federalist Party. *See* Federalism
First Church, 97, 182
  history of, 11–14, 209 n. 2
  sacramental policy of, 84
  slaveowning at, 51–52

success of, 164–165
wealth of, 45–46
See also Prince, John
Fiske, John, 40, 143, 162–163
Fiske, Samuel, 13–14, 194 n. 28
Flood. *See* Deluge, the
Franklin, Benjamin, 7–8, 74, 193
Freeman, James, 95–96, 101, 182, 184
Freemasonry, 125, 127
French and Indian War. *See* Seven
  Years' War
French Revolution, 102, 107–109

Gage, Thomas, 135–136, 158
Gallatin, Albert, 25, 197 n. 28
Gardner, John, 16–17
Germany, 127
Gerry, Elbridge, 135, 147
Godwin, William, 126
Goethe, Johann Wolfgang von, 127
Goodhue, Benjamin, 126, 135, 137–138,
  144–145
Gordon, William, 25
Grafton, Joshua, 100–101
Gray, William, 148, 186
Great Awakening, the First, 13–14, 79,
  166
Great Awakening, the Second, 165–185
Great Chain of Being, 48
Grotius, Hugo, 58, 64

Half-Way Covenant, 36–37
Hall, Samuel, 10
Hamilton, Alexander, 89, 220 n. 1
Hancock, John, 75, 137
Harvard, 22–25, 182
Hazlitt, William, 91–104
Hoadly, Benjamin, 97
Higginson, Stephen, 137
Hilliard, Timothy, 67, 73
Holyoke, E. A., 46, 134
Holy Spirit, 63–65, 72–73, 213 n. 13
Hopkins, Daniel, 15, 47, 51, 157, 160.
  See also South Church
Hopkins, Samuel, 15, 51, 55, 226 n. 8
Hopkinsianism, 15, 166, 176–177

Howard, Simeon, 49
Huntington, John, 43–44
Hutcheson, Francis, 59
Hutchinson, Anne, 49–50, 167
Hutchinson, Thomas, 22, 134, 157

Impartial Register, 142, 145, 162
impressment, 112, 142, 145
interpositions. *See* miracles

Jay Treaty, 137–139
Jebb, John, 92
Jefferson, Thomas, 147, 149, 160, 162
    elections of 1800, 144–145
    as libertarian, 88–89
    library of, 186
    opposition to, 108
Jeffersonians. *See* Democratic-Republican
    Party
Johnson, Joseph, 95
Kant, Immanuel, 127, 142

King's Chapel, 95

Lathrop, John, 31, 182
latitudinarianism, 68–73, 76
Lear, Tobias, 24
Leavitt, Daniel, 46
Leland, John (Eng.) 97
Leland, John, 159
Lewis and Clark, 182
liberalism, classical, 45–60, 102–104, 111
Lincoln, Benjamin, 137
Lindsey, Theophilus, 91–92, 95, 184
Locke, John, 58, 61, 154
Louis XVI, 108–109
loyalists, 133–136, 139–140
Lynde, Benjamin, 52, 139

de Mandeville, Bernard, 111, 116, 154
Massachusetts Historical Society, 182
Mather, Cotton, 26
May, Henry, 6, 8
Mayhew, Jonathan, 49, 67
Methodists, 165, 166
millenarianism, 116, 156

miracles, 66–67, 70–72, 74–76, 120
mobs and mob behavior, 139–141
Morse, Jedidiah, 125, 129, 183–184
Murray, John (of Gloucester), 81, 185
Murray, John (of Newburyport), 50, 75,
    92, 176

Niebuhr, H. Richard, 45
Newton, Isaac, 66, 67–68, 173
North Church, 45, 51, 137, 182
    history of, 12
    success of, 164–165
    wealth of, 46
    See also Barnard, Thomas Jr.

Occum, Sampson, 14, 103
Oliver, Andrew, 7–8, 134
Osgood, David, 169
Otis, Harrison Gray, 23–24

Paine, Thomas, 102, 109, 120–125, 159
Paine, William, 21, 113, 196 n. 8
Paley, William, 182
Parsons, Jonathan, 64
Pemberton, Ebenezer, 22
Pickering, Timothy Jr., 134–136, 138,
    146–147, 151, 158
Pickering, Timothy Sr., 51
Pickman, Benjamin, 12, 136
Pope, Alexander, 48, 97
poverty, 56–59, 112–113, 124–130, 167–170
Presbyterianism, 14–15
Price, Richard, 92, 102
Priestley, Joseph
    in America, 162
    and Birmingham riot, 102–104,
        116–117, 123
    Federalists against, 119, 143
    and Unitarianism, 91–102
Priestley, Joseph Jr., 162
Prince, John, 11–12, 44, 172, 182
    on baptism, 84, 86–87
    at Bentley's ordination, 31
    as liberal Federalist, 129–130
    ordination of, 26–27
    on Socinianism, 93, 101

toryism of, 157
    See also First Church
print and print culture, 95–101, 127–128
    catechism and hymnal, 96–97
    transatlantic networks of, 95–97
    and deism, 100–101
privateering, 41–42
prophecy, internal, 71
providence, 67–68, 74–76, 122–123.
    See also miracles
Pynchon, John, 24, 113, 137
Pynchon, William, 28, 113, 134,
    137, 140

Quakers, 79, 208 n.2

rationalism, 62
Read, Nathan, 144–146, 151
republicanism
    and capitalism, 153–155
    defined, 110
    and the embargo of 1794, 109–112,
        116–117
    and evangelicalism, 155–160
    and theology, 113–116
    social marginalization of, 113
Republican Party. *See*
    Democratic-Republican Party
Revere, Paul, 22, 23
Richardson, Joseph, 183
Rogers, Abigail, 126–127, 142, 186
Ropes, Nathaniel, 135, 139–140
Rousseau, Jean-Jacques, 115, 129–130
Rush, Benjamin, 115

Salem
    and the American Revolution, 136–140
    Congregationalist churches in, 10–15
    East India trade, 182
    and the imperial crisis, 133–135
    physical layout of, 10
    population of, 164
    social structure of, 38–41
Salem *Gazette*, 108, 142–143
Second Great Awakening. *See* Great
    Awakening, the Second

Servetus, Michael, 101
Seven Years' War, 19–21
Sewall, Samuel, 144, 151
Sewall, Stephen, 22, 24
sexuality and evangelicalism, 166
Shays' Rebellion, 59–60, 108, 136–137,
    140–141
Sherlock, William, 97
Sinclair, Joseph, 54–55
slavery
    and the American Revolution, 52
    and Arminianism, 51–52
    Bentley on, 21, 51–55
    and Diman, 204 n.34
    in Salem, 51–55
    See also African-Americans
smallpox, 139, 155
Smith, Adam, 59, 154
Smith, Elias, 159, 185
Social Library, 97, 99–100, 111
Socinianism, 65–67, 124, 125. *See also*
    Unitarianism
South Church, 34, 52, 155–156
    history of, 14–15
    success of, 165
    wealth of, 47
    See also Hopkins, Daniel
Spaulding, Joshua, 155–156, 160,
    165, 166
St. Peter's Church, 139, 157, 208–209 n.2
Stamp Act, 134
Stiles, Ezra, 26
Story, Joseph, 186
Strong, Caleb, 147
suffrage, 224–225 n. 83
Sullivan, James, 150, 185

Tabernacle, 34, 51, 155–156
    history of, 13–14
    sacramental policy of, 84, 86–87
    wealth of, 46–47
    See also Whitaker, Nathaniel
Tappan, David, 119, 183
Taylor, Jeremy, 97
Tennent, Gilbert, 13–14
theodicy, 176–177

Thoreau, Henry David, 12
Tileston, John, 21–22
Tillotson, John, 97
Tindal, Matthew, 100
Tories. *See* loyalists
Toulmin, Joshua, 92
Trinitarianism, 62–67, 93–94. *See also*
    Arianism, Socinianism,
    Unitarianism, Holy Spirit
typology, 207 n. 11

Unitarian Society of Portland, Maine,
    214 n. 18
Unitarianism
    and English rationalists, 91–104
    liberal reaction against,
        101, 125
    in nineteenth century, 184–185
    and print, 95–102
    See also Socinianism
Universalism, 81–82, 165–166

Warburton, William, 97
warning-out, 55–56
Washington, George, 108, 123, 146
Wheelock, Eleazar, 172

Whiston, William, 97
Whitaker, Nathaniel, 14–15, 51, 155,
    169, 172
    dismissal of, 211–213 n. 5
    and Hazlitt, 92–93
    patriotism of, 157–158
    See also Tabernacle
Whitefield, George, 13–15, 194 n. 29
Wigglesworth, Edward, 22, 24
Wilberforce, William, 126
Willard, Joseph, 25, 67, 75
William and Mary, College of, 183
Williams, George, 140
Williams, Samuel, 24–25
Winthrop, James, 25, 146, 197–198
    n. 28
Winthrop, John, 22
witch trials, 11, 88
Wollaston, William, 97
Wollstonecraft, Mary, 126–127
women
    Bentley's views on, 49–50,
        129–130
    and church membership, 39–40
    and evangelicalism, 50, 166–167
Worcester, Samuel, 165